THE NEW DIET BUILDING WITH MOUNT FUJI IN THE BACKGROUND

The New Japan

GOVERNMENT AND POLITICS

Harold S. Quigley

AND

John E. Turner

UNIVERSITY OF MINNESOTA PRESS, Minneapolis

TO THE JAPANESE PEOPLE

Preface

THE Japan of 1956 is a new Japan. Not by revolution but by quickened evolution it became a different political entity during the decade that followed World War II. A new constitution and new laws replaced the major elements in the *corpus juris* of the Meiji era. The central pillar of the national polity survived the reformist earthquake, but other institutions of power or prestige went down. How new the new Japan is cannot now be determined, since some of the newness may turn out to be veneer. Yet, if what is veneer wears off, the fact remains that we are observing a transition, that feudal-militarist Japan is passing, and that a new and interesting era has begun.

The authors wish to acknowledge a debt not only to the scholars, statesmen, and journalists of Japan who have contributed to the source materials of the book, but to the thousands of humble translators employed during the postwar Occupation to make available in English a large number of essential documents. Without this help the book could not have been written.

Acknowledgment is due also to members of the Occupation staff, particularly to Dr. Justin Williams of Government Section, and to Dr. Harry E. Wildes, Mr. Kenneth Colton, Lt. Col. David Tait, and Miss Naomi Fukuda of Civil Intelligence Section, for assistance in obtaining source materials as well as for their generous sharing of exceptional knowledge and insight. So far as humanly possible — and that is not far enough — reference has been made to the many workers in the Far Eastern vineyard who have, through their writing, provided additional aid.

Gratitude is due to our colleagues Professor George A. Warp and Professor Lloyd M. Short; to Dr. Hattie K. Colton; to a goodly number of seminar students with whom our subject has been discussed; to Mr. Fumihiko Suzuki, of the Embassy of Japan; to Mr. John Rue; to Miss Huldah Ledin, secretary of the Department of Political Science, University of Minnesota; and to the very able staff of the University of Minnesota Press. For aid as translators special credit is due to Mr. Yo Nagai, Mr. Roy Yamaguchi, and Mr. Yasuo Okamura.

Finally, the authors acknowledge with appreciation the importance of grants and research funds from the Graduate School of the University of Minnesota and from the Cephas D. Allin Research Fund, which is administered by the faculty of the Department of Political Science of the University of Minnesota.

Table of Contents

APPENDIXES

The New Japan

GOVERNMENT AND POLITICS

1

Residual Forces in Japanese Politics

THE late Ozaki Yukio, Japan's grand old liberal, member, until his death in 1954 of every House of Representatives but one since the origin of the imperial legislature, the Diet, and at eighty-nine a vigorous champion of democracy, spoke frankly to one of the authors of this book in a conversation on January 26, 1947.* He said that the Japanese people were unable to understand the meaning of the word "democracy." "To them," he declared, "it means license, anarchy. A bloody civil war may be needed to teach them the worth of the individual." It would be miraculous if the contrary were true. Japanese political thought and experience have not been teachers of democracy. Ozaki and others of his kind have been studying and preaching it for three-quarters of a century. But that is a brief period in comparison with the seven centuries of struggle that have given firm rootage to democracy in the West. Ozaki's prediction suggests that imported democracy, unlike motorcars, is not automatically operative, though its tenets and agencies may, if freely taken as models by another people, affect the evolution of its political order.

Even so, the likelihood of misunderstanding, of mistaken emphasis, is great. Japanese listeners to WVTR, the Armed Forces radio station in Tokyo, during the Occupation might have concluded that democracy was a potpourri of jazz relieved at long intervals by selections from the classics, sports, an interest in the news so deep that any amount

* This conversation took place during a visit by the author to Ozaki's home in Zushi. He and Ozaki talked before a grate fire which the aged statesman built expertly. Ozaki spoke English well but was quite deaf. His daughter and confidante, Shinaye Ozaki, interpreted when necessary.

3

of repetition and incorrect pronunciation was tolerable, an equal devotion to banal comedy and mystery stories, and a dash of piety on Sunday. *Stars and Stripes,* Pacific edition, printed a sensitive cartoon by Berry, one of an admirable series entitled "Too Far East." It depicts a Japanese husband and his wife and child at a frugal meal. A radio is playing this song:

> Ah'm jest a lonesome hillbilly
> Who's got a sorry tale
> Mah sweet-heart's daid —
> Shot through the haid
> She lies thar cold an' pale
> Oh, Ah'm going to hate to chuck her out.
> But Ah think she's gittin' stale.

The husband appears to understand English, judging from his worried face and his remark: "We should learn to appreciate American culture."

Peoples that have worked out their own salvation on the principles of individual liberty and private enterprise are prone to assume that no other politico-economic ideology is comparably mature and that the development of a peaceful international order is dependent upon worldwide acceptance and establishment of democracy. They have difficulty also in believing that democracy can mean different things and take different forms in different countries. These prejudgments are natural, but they have not been proved to be sociologically sound. They underlay much of the support which Americans gave to the program for military occupation of Japan, a program whose results will not be known for many years. But Japanese civilization, in view of its great age and corresponding stability, will continue, one may safely predict, to give distinctive character to politics and government.

Caution is advisable in the interpretation of Western words when applied to Japanese agencies and their functioning. Such words as "right," "constitutional," "parliamentary," and "democratic" are likely to mean one thing in the West, another in the Orient. Their use cannot be avoided, but they are to be regarded as approximations rather than precise descriptive terms. Ambiguity can sometimes be lessened by the use of Japanese terms, for example, *Jiyuto* instead of "Liberal party" and *Tenno* instead of "emperor."

The residual forces that have underlain and to some degree continue

4

to underlie Japanese political life are elements of Japanese culture. They are difficult for Westerners to understand. But it is important to understand them sufficiently to appreciate the obstacles they raise to the rapid acceptance of democracy. Even more important is the obligation to recognize that the democratic principle of self-determination applies universally. That principle is not merely an expression of what ought to be. It is the product of historical experience. Peoples with long histories *are* self-determining. They develop national personalities just as individuals grow up to be different from one another. National cultures are not static but they change slowly. Whether a particular culture is good or bad is wholly a question of point of view. To the people who possess it it is good. To be permanent, any change in it must come about because those people want the change. The people of Japan are notably alert to aspects of other cultures which may be adaptable to theirs. But they are stubbornly, though politely, inert to forced feeding. In this regard they differ from some other peoples less in their stubbornness than in their disarming and often confusing politeness.

Dynasticism

Strongest of residual forces in contemporary Japanese politics is the devotion of the people to the imperial dynasty. Its strength was proved beyond argument by the obedience given to Emperor Hirohito's command to the troops — millions of whom had not been in combat — to lay down their arms, thus bringing World War II to an end.[1] It was exhibited also in the effort made by the last wartime cabinet to set retention of the emperor's prerogatives as the single condition of surrender.[2] The hysterical demonstration of popular feeling which greeted the emperor and empress on the occasion of the promulgation of the new constitution seemed to mean that the dynasty had lost nothing by the defeat. Appreciation of the profound significance of the imperial house in Japanese political life led the Allies to permit its survival as a political institution.

The people of Japan have not regarded the emperor as an absolute monarch, though the Meiji constitution recognized that all power resided in him.[3] Their conception of him as a combination of religious leader and affectionate father derives from legend which describes the founding of the Japanese race by the gods. The Yamato, or im-

5

perial house, descends from the Sun Goddess, Amaterasu, and is the family of highest rank; the people are related to it through their descent from other gods related to Amaterasu. This legend is the core of Shinto, Japan's native religion. It is doubly unifying, since it makes of the Japanese one great family, of which the emperor is the head, and infuses into this blood relationship a religious sanction. The resulting national polity is called *kokutai*, the oneness of the reigning dynasty with the state.

Buddhism and Confucianism, received from Korea and China, have added richness to the Shinto conception. These importations were patronized in the beginning by emperors and subsequently repaid their patrons by adding ethical obligations to the Shinto foundation of faith and loyalty. All three religions, which merge rather than conflict in Japanese culture, instill the worship of ancestors, culminating in emperor worship. Thus it is logical that the term *matsuri goto*, affairs of worship, should be used for "government." [4] The state is not the patron and protector of religion; rather, religion is the matrix of the state.

The impact of Christianity, democratic principles, and natural science upon Japanese youth shook the foundations of the political edifice, leading the Restoration governments of the later nineteenth century to re-enunciate the dogmas of imperial divinity and racial superiority and to require acceptance of the cult of Shinto by all Japanese. Ultranationalism, chauvinism, and irrational superpatriotism were evil fruits of this harking back to mythology. But it may be anticipated that the core of the traditional concept of the unity between religion and government, symbolized by the position of the imperial household, will not be destroyed as the Japanese turn away from these artificial stimulants and resume their march toward liberalism and internationalism.

This opinion is based upon the fact that liberal and learned Japanese hold as profound a belief in the imperial institution as the simplest citizen. They hold it on rational bases rather than superstition, but their reasoning is difficult for Western peoples to understand. It finds no bar to the evolution of democracy in tennoism (imperial headship). To quote Dr. Takagi Yasaka, formerly professor of American history at the Imperial University of Tokyo:

Our form of government is characterized by the reign of *Tenno* —

Emperors of a line of an unbroken dynasty — with the assistance and support of the people. Its characteristic is the "sharing of government by the *Tenno* (Emperor) and the people." It may perhaps be described as the government of the *Tenno*, by the people (or with the people), for the people. It is based on popular national sentiments or beliefs, resulting from the historical facts of centuries of our national life, in which the sense of unity and cooperation has come to prevail in the unique relationship between a long line of beneficent rulers on the one hand and an essentially docile people consisting of agricultural communities on the other. That the *Tenno* has always "made the mind (will) of the people his own" is the universally accepted concept of the Emperor of Japan.[5]

The same point of view is expressed by Ozaki Yukio:

The sovereign has no mind of his own: the mind of the people is his mind, and on this principle our successive emperors have acted. It implies the guiding of, as well as acting upon, the sentiments of the people. The two are indeed different in their conception but they are identical in effect — that is, to procure an agreement between the will of the sovereign and the sentiments of the people, and to assure the prosperity of the Imperial House. It does not matter one iota whether public opinion is guided or acted upon, so long as the prosperity of the Imperial House and the safety of the state are guaranteed. The one thing essential is to follow whatever is most advantageous in view of the tendencies of the age and the sentiments of the people.[6]

Clearly, the Japanese did not develop a parallel to the Western theory of sovereignty in which political authority is opposed to private rights. Nor is their conception of sovereignty one of monarchical absolutism. It is paternalistic, contemplating the ruler as the benign father of the national family. Its members are not entitled to rebel, but neither is he to oppress them. While far from the democratic doctrine of popular sovereignty, it allows for the development of democracy through the conviction of the emperor that democracy is desired by his people, or that he should take the initiative in guiding them to appreciate and practice it.

That the Japanese conception of sovereignty is not the product of popular acceptance of the doctrine above defined but the "result of feudalism and despotism — a deformed condition, no less, caused by the prevention of the Japanese people's natural development by militarism and nationalism," is ably argued by Professor Yokota Kisaburo. Taking issue with Professor Takagi, he writes:

7

The New Japan

The national character of Japan is not, in the final analysis, an exception to the "universal principle" of mankind. Although it is said that the tradition of confrontation between monarch and people is western while that of Japan is oneness of the two elements, and even if this were so up to now, it was because the Japanese people, held as they were under the despotic rule of monarchism and feudalism, had no consciousness of their individuality, no understanding of the value of freedom nor of the concept of equality.

As a result of the war, the Japanese people have discarded feudalism and despotism. Once liberated from these ancient bonds, they began to clamor for popular sovereignty, their voice growing daily in their demand for the establishment of democratic government founded upon the sovereign will of the people. What better proof can there be of the Japanese people's desire to submit to the "universal principle" of mankind? [7]

Dualism

The unique conception of sovereignty in Japan developed concurrently with a system of government bearing little resemblance to that conception. Kingly or imperial rule, which emerged early in the Christian era, was weak because of the tribal and clan separatism which flourished among the many hills and mountains. As early as the sixth century the struggle for power among the clan chiefs had begun to affect the position of the Yamato dynasty. In the seventh century occurred the Great Reform (*Taikwa*), an attempt to import Chinese principles and practices, including the mature T'ang system of government, into Japan. The attempt was but temporarily and partially successful and did not stop the trend toward dualism. With the rise of the Fujiwara clan to superior strength in the ninth century, its heads became the actual rulers and remained such for three centuries. The system continued and was not abolished until 1868.

It is impossible to reconcile the tactics of the usurping clan leaders with the Japanese claim to fame for unswerving loyalty. The military might of the Fujiwara enabled them to attain the office of chief adviser (*kwampaku*), which they magnified into that of chief administrator and conducted as a dictatorship. The Yamato house was dependent upon the prestige attached to its legendary origin for recognition of its authority. To the Fujiwara the descent of emperors from the Sun Goddess justified the treatment of them as priests rather than administrators and was taken as a convenient excuse for relieving them of the mundane cares of political office. The office itself was not

8

assailed, but successive emperors became the puppets of their chief ministers. While maintaining the Shinto doctrine of imperial divinity, which the usurpers found useful in obtaining obedience to rescripts inspired by themselves, they manipulated the legal rulers at will. Thus Japan's ship of state had two captains, the emperor, who was in political matters a figurehead, and the chief minister, who actually held command.

In the twelfth century feudalism replaced the civilian administrative system of the Fujiwara, owing to the rise of vigorous provincial clans organized upon a military basis. A new officer, theoretically but not always actually generalissimo over all military forces, entitled the *shogun*, took over the position of *kwampaku*, but again without challenge to the imperial throne. The emperors remained "behind the curtain," surrounded by a group of nobles who formed a court in which dignity and ceremonial deference were accepted as the face-saving substitutes for power. In 1603 the Tokugawa clan fought its way to the shogunate, which it held until the dual system itself was discarded in 1868.

Dualism did not disappear from the Japanese government with its legal abolition, as later chapters will reveal more fully. It remains today, a heritage of extraordinarily long and unbroken practice. Apparently it responds to qualities in the Japanese character as well as to Japanese beliefs and sentiments. Japanese are ambitious. They seek and enjoy the exercise of power. But they shrink from responsibility. They surround executive officers with elders, advisers, and councils, thereby distributing responsibility and shielding themselves from criticism. Extraordinary efforts are made to maintain secrecy on relatively unimportant matters. Products of long experience in a police state, these characteristics are not likely to be rapidly outgrown.

Bureaucracy

The word "bureaucracy" applied to aspects of Japanese political development carries the full meaning of the Greek *kratia* (power), from which its final syllables are derived. Administration by appointive officers, combined with control of policy determination by a self-constituted oligarchy, has prevailed in Japan since the state was founded. An official class was free to develop without interference

9

from political parties or a representative legislature, neither of which appeared until late in the nineteenth century.

Oligarchy at the top and bureaucracy at the national, provincial, and local levels of administration instilled in the people an acceptance and fear of officialdom. They expected to be spied upon and regimented in every activity. The dualistic system of government strengthened the bureaucracy by enabling it to disguise its orders as expressions of the imperial will. Conformity with that will identified a subject as a moral person. Only the most intolerable economic distress would induce a Japanese to rebel against this key principle in the cultural decalogue. The people did not enjoy regimentation and they enjoyed joking about stupid officials.[8] But they were obedient because they were helpless against official displeasure.

Too easily overlooked is the fact that democratic principles in the West are the product of the nineteenth century. A comparison of earlier Western practices of government, and the laws supporting them, with their Oriental counterparts would be at once fairer and more scholarly than a comparison based on contemporary practices, though the Orient would still be revealed as a century or more behind the Occident in legislation for popular rights. The early law codes and customary law afforded limited protection against purely personal judgments, but they did not recognize an individual's right to bring a legal action. At best, judicial administration allowed wide latitude in interpretation, and wise men settled their disputes privately. Penalties were very severe, a fact to which Sansom ascribes much of the incentive for suicide.[9] Thus the official attained a status above that of the layman, and the principle of inequality which is found in Shinto was mirrored in public administration.

Since the individual could not assert a right to legal protection and knew the laws only through the judgments of officials, law as such was secondary in his mind to the bureaucracy. He accepted the principle implicit in the system that government was the prerogative of a superior class of men. He had no conception of government by law. Bureaucracy was not merely a method of government, it was an accepted way of life, complementary to dynasticism. One might coin the word "bureaucratism" to express the attitude of the people toward bureaucratic administration. The rise of a strong merchant class in the Tokugawa period broadened the base of the system but did not challenge it in principle. After the Restoration it was renovated, westernized in form, and solidly established with the blessing of the leaders of the new military organization.

Militarism

Feudalism made its contribution to the legacies already described; that contribution was more influential than others in determining the nature of dualism and bureaucracy in Japan. But the most characteristic bequest of *bushido*, Japan's feudal code, was militarism, i.e., the exaltation of military ideals. *Bushido* was the code of the *samurai*, the knightly retainers of the *daimyo* who headed the feudal fiefs into which Japan was divided for seven centuries (1185–1871). The samurai not only captained the armies of the shogun and the daimyo. They were also civil magistrates, a new bureaucracy which wore armor and two swords.

Chivalry placed loyalty to one's feudal lord above every other obligation, even that of obedience to the emperor. It emphasized duty and self-sacrifice, but like its European counterpart did not apply outside the aristocracy. The warriors topped the social scale and might maltreat or kill *heimin* (commoners) with impunity. Because they were nonproducers, socially above manual labor, they were a heavy burden upon the peasantry as their numbers increased. Civil wars between clans made them indispensable to the daimyo. But in their conduct, culture, or exemplification of the ideals they professed, there was little to arouse admiration.

Foreign wars and efforts to create a colonial empire are singularly infrequent in the history of feudal Japan. There were piratical expeditions of freebooters — the Japanese equivalents of Sir Francis Drake — who roved the South Pacific, but no expeditions seeking territorial gains. Korea was invaded, but no serious effort was made to conquer it. Japanese settled in the Ryukyu (Liu-ch'iu) Islands, but raised no claims of sovereignty until the nineteenth century was well advanced. Since the Japanese were aware of Western exploration and colonizing ventures, they might have been expected to stake out claims of their own. Instead they remained at home and even closed their doors to Western traders and missionaries. Their policy aimed at self-preservation, not expansion. Militarism in the sense of aggressiveness toward other peoples is a recent, not a residual, force in Japanese politics.

11

Feudalism did, however, leave the tradition of rule by military men, and a correspondingly conditioned mass mentality, to plague the liberal reformers of the Restoration.[10] It left also a number of extremely able ex-samurai to seek office in the Restoration government. Some of these men were the architects of the new military structure and the inspirers of constitutional and other legal bases for the authority of the Yamagatas, Tanakas, and Tojos who led the nation to disaster. But Dr. E. H. Norman very properly points out that Japan owes a great debt to the Restoration leaders:

The machinery for the epochal changes accompanying the Restoration was a government formed from the ablest, most self-sacrificing of clan military bureaucrats who utilized to the full and with remarkable dexterity those autocratic powers which they steadily strengthened. In looking back to the stormy years of that period, whatever one may think of the words "military" and "bureaucrat," it seems an incontrovertible fact that these military bureaucrats were the spearpoint of advance, the vanguard of modernization, in the establishment of a modern state in Japan.

He quotes with approval Iwasaki's estimate: "It is not fair to the bureaucrats to condemn them as destructive reactionaries. They did much good. In a period of transition someone must take the helm, and they were expert pilots. But the period of transition is now over." [11] Unfortunately, however, Iwasaki was overoptimistic. The new Japan is inclined to believe that the "period of transition" has been unduly prolonged.

Dynasticism, dualism, bureaucracy, and militarism together constitute a heavy residual inertia against the rapid development of democracy in Japan. In view of their long reign as characteristic features of Japanese politics it might be conjectured that the people had made its choice and would prefer not to supplant them. But when it is recognized that democracy has been known to the most literate Japanese for less than a century and that to the mass of the people it is still little more than a foreign word, such a conjecture will be dismissed as premature. Moreover, as the following chapter evidences, the Japanese have been experimenting with democracy for three-quarters of a century with some success. Consideration of the forces that have handicapped their efforts counsels, not that they cannot overcome them, but that time is needed, as it has been needed in the

West, both for understanding democracy and for adjusting older cultural forces to it.

Group Consciousness

Although the Japanese did not evolve the principles of individual liberty and representative government, they have had many centuries of experience with forms of group discussion and action. Agreement among the members of the group rather than mute acceptance of the leader's authority has been traditional procedure. Originating in the family council, this procedure was followed in the administration of family and neighborhood groups and of village affairs. While authority was recognized to lie in the heads of the groups, they were expected to discuss matters of importance with group members. The heads were elected by group elders and were responsible to the appointive officials, who could overrule them. Local authority was limited but real because the bureaucracy found it convenient and inexpensive. It was paternalistic rather than democratic, but it preserved some degree of respect for and in the local group.[12] The fact that the neighborhood associations, particularly the federations of such associations, known as *tonarigumi*, were used by the feudal officials as agencies of control seems not to justify their treatment as mere nerve ends of the bureaucratic ganglia.

Japanese may reasonably point to the cooperative spirit supported by group life, particularly in rural communities, as an inheritance conducive to the development of democracy. The recent trend in the West toward greater emphasis upon the economic and social aspects of democracy suggests that the Japanese may have a contribution to make toward a well-rounded democratic order. They, on the other hand, have failed so far to enliven their social solidarity with the individualism needed to give it moral fiber. The Japanese overstress duty, Western peoples rights. What is needed for the good society is a synthesis in which the individual accepts his responsibility to the community, but retains his freedom of conscience and moral integrity.

Notes

[1] Imperial Rescript on Surrender, September 1–2, 1945, in *The Axis in Defeat*, pp. 33–34, U.S. Department of State, Publication 2423.

[2] First Japanese Offer of Surrender, August 10, 1945, in *Occupation of Japan, Policy and Progress*, pp. 56–57, Department of State, Publication 2671, Far Eastern Series 17.

[3] Article 4 (see below, Appendix II).

[4] N. Hozumi, *Ancestor Worship and Japanese Law* (Tokyo, 1912), pp. 71–72.

[5] Y. Takagi, unpublished essay in the authors' possession. Similar views are expressed by Professor Takagi in *Chuo Koron*, July 1946.

[6] Y. Ozaki, *The Voice of Japanese Democracy* (Yokohama, 1918), p. 11.

[7] K. Yokota, "Sovereignty under the War Constitution," *Contemporary Japan*, XVI (April–June 1946), 140–144.

[8] For Chaucerian humor at the expense of officialdom, see the delightful work *Hizakurigé* (Tokaido Circuit), by Ikku Jippensha (Kobe, 1929), *passim*.

[9] G. B. Sansom, *Japan, A Short Cultural History*, rev. ed. (New York, 1943), p. 428.

[10] "Restoration" is the term applied to the period beginning November 3, 1867, during which the shogunate and feudal system were abolished and the imperial house restored to undivided headship of the state. Although the legal change had been completed in August 1871, it is customary to consider the Restoration period as inclusive of the subsequent years of reform. For indications of the possible appearance of a similar plague today see H. Kinoshita, "Echoes of Militarism in Japan," in *Pacific Affairs*, XXVI (1953), 244–251.

[11] E. H. Norman, *Japan's Emergence as a Modern State* (New York, 1940), pp. 102–103; U. Iwasaki, *The Working Forces in Japanese Politics* (New York, 1921), p. 52.

[12] S. Shimizu, in S. Okuma, *Fifty Years of New Japan* (London, 1909), I, 320–327.

2

The Prewar Government

As THE nineteenth century passed into its last quarter, there was agitation in Japan for a people's parliament. Scarcely ten years had elapsed since the last of the Tokugawa shoguns, Keiki, had surrendered his office to the youthful Emperor Meiji, and with it the actual headship of the government which his family had monopolized for three and a half centuries, in order that administrative authority might be centralized and the empire enabled to "maintain its rank and dignity among the nations." During that decade political societies had appeared, led by no lesser persons than Okuma Shigenobu of the Hizen clan and Itagaki Taisuke of Tosa, provoked by the apparent intention of the leaders of the greater western clans, Choshu and Satsuma, to constitute themselves sole heirs of the governmental power which the Tokugawa daimyo had monopolized since the sixteenth century. Okuma and Itagaki, together with other disgruntled lesser clansmen, purposed to call into political life a new force, public opinion, to assist them in a struggle for a division of the Tokugawa legacy.

On a winter's day in 1889 the agitation of the "politicians," as the leaders of the popular movement came to be called, in distinction from their opponents, the Satsuma and Choshu oligarchs, bore fruit. Before a distinguished company in the palace at Tokyo, the constitution was

NOTE. For a comprehensive treatment see H. S. Quigley, *Japanese Government and Politics* (New York, 1932), *passim*. See also K. Colegrove's articles on the Japanese emperor, the cabinet, and the constitution in the *American Political Science Review*, XXVI (1932), 642–659 and 828–845; XXX (1936), 903–921; and XXXI (1937), 1027–1049, respectively.

read on February 11, a day already consecrated as Kigensetsu, the legendary date of the founding, in 660 B.C., of the imperial Yamato dynasty, which continues to the present moment. Shorter even than the constitution of the United States, the Japanese instrument was modeled upon the constitutions of prerevolutionary Prussia and other German states. Its drafters had made a study of the American constitution but found in it only warnings, signposts of dangers to be avoided.

Were the demands of the newly fledged political parties for a share in governmental power satisfied? Hardly. The constitution was less a concession to them than to those great Occidental states with which Japan had entered into treaties that she regarded as shameful. The Western states were insistent that the surrender of consular jurisdiction must be preceded by a modernization, that is, a westernization, of law and administration. Hence Japan conformed, publishing in succession codes of criminal law and procedure modeled upon those of France, of civil law and procedure mingling French and German with native principles, and a constitution of essentially German pattern. But she took care to inscribe in the first article of the constitution the basic idea known as *kokutai*, the eternal oneness of the reigning dynasty with the state. This idea was fully supported by the centralization of all power in the emperor.

Centralization, however, in name only: the relation of the emperor to the government was altered only in form. The constitution codified the Restoration of 1868, a restoration of the emperor to dignity, not to power. Throughout the seven centuries of feudalism the imperial office had in theory been the location of authority, but so completely had the fact of shogunal domination obscured this theory that the theory itself was forgotten and was only resurrected by scholars in the late eighteenth century. The Restoration had restored the theory but continued the fact of vicarious rule, simply transferring the reality of power from one group of oligarchs to another. The constitution drafted by the new oligarchy set up but feeble checks upon its program of usurpation.

From the point of view of the liberals, the effect of this variance between the letter and the spirit was of no immediate importance. Their efforts to breathe life into the infant Diet were maintained for a few years, but it proved a puny thing for lack of exercise, albeit not lacking in lung power. All too soon they gave up the struggle and entered into alliances with the oligarchs, salvaging their pride with such appearances of influence as appointments to ministerial posts and association with such mighty clansmen as Ito Hirobumi, Katsura Taro, and Tanaka Giichi (who accepted the presidency of one or another party), and often content to forget their pride at the price of a fat concession or a retainer sufficient to win a parliamentary seat. Ultimately, the weapon of the latter-day usurpers was to turn in their hands, as it had in the grasp of the Tokugawa.

Briefly we may set down the component agencies of the prewar Japanese government. At the apex was the emperor, at once the head of the extraconstitutional imperial court and of the constitutional government. Emperor Hirohito's house is the oldest reigning dynasty and, thanks to concubinage and adoption, it has reigned longer than any other in the history of the world. In the Middle Ages the imperial scepter was transformed into a priest's baton, the emperor taking on divine attributes as head of the Shinto religion and being forced into seclusion by ambitious officials. Though the curtain that screened divinity from secular eyes had been withdrawn, the belief of the masses of the people in the imperial godhead still continued. Educated Japanese no longer accepted as history the mythology of the divine origin of the state or the emperor, yet the old dogmas were given lip service in deference to popular belief. Furthermore, all acts of state were referred to as though performed by the emperor, in strict observance of the terms of the constitution.

What may be called the "crown," that is, the executive department of the government, was a composite of the emperor; two extraconstitutional agencies, the *genro*, or elder statesmen, and the Imperial Household Ministry; and three constitutional organs, the Privy Council, the "Supreme Command," and the cabinet. The genro had originally included five highly influential clan leaders, Yamagata Aritomo, Ito Hirobumi, and Inouye Tsuyoshiaki, of Choshu, and Oyama Iwao and Matsukata Masayoshi, of Satsuma. Later two others were designated, Katsura Taro, of Choshu, and Saionji Kimmochi, a member of the older civilian nobility, the *kugé*, which antedates feudalism. All but Saionji, who was eighty-one years old in 1930, were dead. Saionji was understood to desire that the institution should die with him. There were, however, certain so-called Senior Statesmen (quasi-genro) who were consulted on crucial issues, so that the future of the genro was somewhat doubtful. The genro was called by the emperor and the cabinet to advise them in every serious difficulty, and it enjoyed a reputation for well-nigh infallible wisdom.

The Imperial Household Ministry was an organ of the court. Most influential of the dignitaries that composed it was the Lord Keeper of the Privy Seal, while only slightly less important were the minister himself and the Lord Chamberlain. The emperor took no action without the advice of this agency, relying particularly upon the Lord Keeper. The latter, therefore, was second only to Prince Saionji in his influence upon imperial decisions.

The Privy Council was a body of twenty-five advisers, chosen for their proved loyalty and conservatism. All important laws, treaties, and ordinances were submitted for the Council's approval, and so influential were its members that the custom had developed of asking their approval even of comparatively unimportant proposals. The Privy Council was the interpreter of the constitution, and conceived its duty in that field to be strict rather than liberal construction.

The "Supreme Command," sometimes termed the "Camp," included the ministers of war and the navy, the chiefs of the army and naval staffs, the board of marshals and admirals, and the supreme military council. Separately and collectively, these organs enjoyed the privilege of advising the emperor directly — that is, without the collaboration of the premier or the cabinet as a whole — on matters of national defense, strategy, and tactics. Since the ministers of war and the navy were, by ordinance, required to be high-ranking officers (active or retired), of the army and navy respectively, they formed with their colleagues in the staffs and the advisory councils a closed corporation of a wholly military character. This is not, of course, to say that they might not have been men of wide knowledge and statesmanlike outlook, but rather that their affiliations with the defense services surrounded them with men of a certain *esprit de corps* that operated, on occasion, as a severe handicap to independent thought or action.

Anomalous as it may seem, the cabinet was the least important of the elements of the crown in the determination of policy. The harsh term "usurpation," above applied to the activities of the various agencies already defined, was justified by the constitution itself, which provided in Article 55 that "the respective ministers of state shall give their advice to the Emperor and be responsible for it." It is, of course, a common and essential feature of cabinet or parliamentary government that the ministers rather than the titular head of the state determine policy and accept responsibility for it. But in Japan the ministers took responsibility for policies which they did not and could not determine. Determination of policy still rested with the traditional agencies above described. These agencies could not be held responsible, since the emperor, while theoretically all-powerful, was in fact powerless. Thus, the cabinet must be said in general to have been limited to suggestion rather than to decision, to administration rather than to discretionary action.

The explanation of this situation lies in the nature of the Japanese social order. To understand it, we must recognize that the older people of prewar Japan were brought up under the feudal system, which was abolished only eighty-odd years ago (1871). Moreover, its abolition was not the product of a popular revolt, but the voluntary proposal of the more powerful clan leaders. Democratic ideas had percolated to the masses slowly, interpreted by newspapers and teachers under strict government control. The bulk of the population was composed of very poor peasants to whom the emperor, as father and chief priest, and the landowner — a scion of the feudal house which their ancestors had served since time out of mind — as ruler of their economic destiny, constituted what they knew of the state lying beyond the village limits.

The constitution did not, however, leave the "people" entirely unrepresented. It provided for a Diet, a two-chamber assembly composed of a highly aristocratic and plutocratic House of Peers and of a House of Representatives chosen by direct manhood suffrage in which women did not share. It met annually and in special sessions for very brief periods. In 1936 a magnificent new Diet building, the finest structure in Japan, was dedicated — an earnest, it may be hoped, of a future more worthy of that body than the past has been.

The extreme conservatism of the Japanese people was revealed in the percentage of elderly men elected to the House of Representatives. Whereas in the first election, when voters were required to pay fifteen yen (normally $7.50) in direct national taxes, only 13.7 per cent of the members elected were over fifty years old, only 3.7 per cent over sixty, and none over seventy, in the 1930 election, under manhood suffrage, 60.3 per cent were over fifty, 22.3 per cent over sixty, and 1.7 per cent over seventy. Meanwhile the balance of political power shifted from the country to the town. Forty-eight per cent of the members of the House in 1890 came from the farms, in 1928 only 9.5 per cent; in 1890 27.9 per cent were businessmen, industrialists, journalists, lawyers, and doctors; in 1928 57 per cent were. More than half of the representatives elected in 1930 were college or university graduates. A member's salary (3,000 yen), if viewed as an annual rather than a quarterly stipend (the regular annual session lasted a maximum of three months but members had to attend frequent extraordinary sessions), was comparable to the salary of an official in the third (*sonin*) grade of the civil service, not a complimentary status for members, nor one that was tempting to men of considerable ability.

The Diet was something more than a debating society. Its approval was required for the passage of laws and for amendment of the constitution. The budget was laid before it, and it might, unless an emergency or a deficiency could be alleged by the government, prevent appropriations (saving certain excepted categories) or taxes additional to those embodied in the preceding budget. Its consent to loans was necessary, and it shared in the power of audit. It might discuss any topic freely, its members being protected from prosecution for voicing their sentiments. It had several means of showing concern over or disapproval of cabinet acts or programs, though it could not compel the government to resign and there existed no process of impeachment beyond a vote in either house.

These were meager legislative powers compared to those of the executive, which, acting through the cabinet, controlled the convoking and adjourning of the houses, dissolved the lower house at pleasure, introduced all important bills, and possessed the power of veto — which was never needed. It dominated finance through control over various categories of appropriations which were excepted from the scope of Diet participation and through its capacity for using emergency and deficiency appropriations and reserve funds and even for re-executing the budget of the previous year if the Diet proved altogether recalcitrant. The executive power to issue ordinances was exercisable over the whole field of legislation, though ordinances which amended or repealed a statute required ex post facto approval of the

Diet, a process for saving the Diet's face without interfering with executive government.

The House of Peers was an abler body than the House of Representatives, conducting its debates with decorum and intelligence. But it was so largely representative of wealth and the nobility that it was little more than an enlarged edition of the Privy Council, and its handling of policy was sympathetic toward the oligarchy. The House of Representatives was packed with professional politicians, men of small intellect and strong vocal chords, who followed their party leaders like vassals following their feudal chiefs. Debate there was almost unknown. Instead there was badgering of the government's supporters, often accompanied by fisticuffs in which, on occasion, hired ruffians participated. Yet the galleries of the lower house were often packed with excited citizens of both sexes, while those of the House of Peers were likely to be deserted.

Why was the public interested in the House of Representatives? Because, inferior as were its members and few and feeble as were its powers, the people, or the part of the people that was politically conscious, recognized in it that organ of government over which they had some control and in which they saw their own views to some degree reflected. The interest of the people in elections was keen, attendance at campaign meetings was large, the franchise was exercised by 80 per cent of the qualified voters. Some allowance must be made for official and employer persuasion, some for bribery and other corrupt practices, but personal observations made during the general election of 1930 convinced one of the writers that to a praiseworthy degree the popular interest was spontaneous.

Party life had become firmly interwoven with the bureaucracy in the texture of the political order. The two large parties, the Seiyukai (Party of Friends of Constitutional Government) and the Minseito (Democratic party) each claimed over three million registered members and each of them usually polled about four million votes. These parties were not easily distinguishable from one another, but it may be ventured that the Minseito was somewhat more inclined to liberalism and internationalism than the Seiyukai, while the Seiyukai had prospered by its consistent subservience to the Choshu clan and the great business house of Mitsui. The Seiyukai was stronger in the rural districts, the Minseito in the cities. There were several other groups, among them the Kokumin Doshikai (Nationalist Fellow-Thinkers Society), a businessmen's party with a platform of getting the government out of business, but all these were so small as to be significant only when able to swing the balance of power to one or other of the major parties. A so-called Liberal party, the Meiseikai, elected a half-dozen members in 1928 but failed to seat any candidate in 1930 or 1932.

Until 1896 no party men had been appointed heads of ministries. Until 1918, when Hara Takashi was designated, no commoner had reached the premiership. After 1900, when Count Ito, by accepting the presidency of the newly organized Seiyukai, affiliated the oligarchy with the politicians, it became usual for the genro to recommend the appointment of a party leader to the premiership, though there are gaps in the record, such as that which began with the appointment of Viscount Saito in May 1932. Party premiers had appointed party cabinets, but party cabinets had not meant party government, in view of the retention of power in the traditional agencies of the crown. They had, however, meant closer contact between the government and the people.

Labor had organized a number of parties since the passage of the manhood suffrage act in 1925, but they had not polled more than a half-million votes in a national election and they had but five members in the Diet. Their platforms were vague manifestoes of the rights of workers and peasants, necessarily so if they would exist, since the government had dissolved without a hearing parties that had exhibited radical tendencies. In 1928 Premier Tanaka obtained the imperial signature to an ordinance that made joining a society opposed to the existing political or economic order punishable by death. Nevertheless, communism was constantly increasing in strength through underground tactics in the late twenties.

All parties, including those of labor, were under a cloud of popular criticism because of the frequent cases of graft in which their members had been involved. The level of literacy in Japan was high enough for the people to read the newspapers and to get from them accounts of actions in the courts against members of the Diet and local assemblies. The reaction had been damaging to the democratic cause and helpful to that of the permanent bureaucracy, the small fry who swam with the bigger fish in the oligarchical sea; helpful also, and especially so, to the army and navy, which stood out as paragons of purity against the gray background of political jobbery, though they too had their scandals and their secret-service funds.

It should be said on behalf of the politicians that the cost of elections was so far beyond the means of most of them that to be successful, they had to beg funds from the great trusts. Although the manhood suffrage act limited a candidate's outlay to an average sum of 10,000 to 12,000 yen, the amount actually spent was reckoned at an average of 50,000 yen ($25,000 at par). The nobility were poor and could not subsidize the parties directly, but their relations with men of wealth were close, so that matters could be arranged without interference with the dominant position of the nobility in state affairs. However, the alliance between traditionalism and business was weakening in proportion as the latter attained experience and self-esteem. This tendency held out the largest hope for those who would break the stranglehold of the military services upon governmental policy.

To the laborites and their unregistered but by no means negligible liberal supporters an exchange of militaristic government for unadulterated capitalism had unfavorable aspects. War on the field of glory was an occasional event; the war of capital and labor was continuous. On the other hand, industrialists and bankers relied upon the army and navy to counterbalance the direct actionists among the timid wage earners. Thus, there was no clean-cut basis for labor and capital to act on, either separately or in alliance, against the military services. Still, the general attitude of both great economic groups was hostile to military domination of the state.

To turn now from analysis to illustration, in order that we may observe the effects of a usurpation of power upon which concurrent events in China cast revealing, if fantastic, light. Incidents might be drawn from the domestic field showing interference with the normal course of justice in cases involving military officers, but space permits only a reference to some outstanding instances in which the control of foreign affairs was hindered or entirely usurped by the "Supreme Command."

The dispatch of 70,000 troops to Siberia in 1918, following the invitation of the United States to send but 7,000, was contrary to the judgment of the Japanese Foreign Office, as was the continued occupation of Saghalien after joint intervention had ceased. During the period of intervention the War Office strongly insisted upon independent action in both Manchuria and Siberia. It gave up the idea only when convinced by the Foreign Office, speaking for the commercial interests, that it would mean war with the United States. At that time two treaties were negotiated with China by Japanese army and navy officers.

During the premiership of General Baron Tanaka, head of the Choshu clan, who acted also as minister of foreign affairs (1927–1929), a program of "positivism" was worked out and partially put into effect. Intervention in Shantung delayed the taking of Peking by the allied opponents of Marshal Chang Tso-lin, Japan's Manchurian protégé. A year later Chang was driven out of Peking, only to meet death by assassination when his train was bombed while passing under the viaduct that carries the South Manchuria Railway over the Peking-Mukden line. He had lost favor with Japan on various counts. Responsibility for his death was not made public, but certain high Japanese army officers were mildly disciplined in connection with it.*

The intervention in Manchuria that began on September 18, 1931, might be viewed as a defensive move within the purview of the Supreme Command were it not for the failure of the military departments to turn over to the Foreign Office the handling of the issue after the first defensive moves. Baron Shidehara, the foreign minister, had the negotiations with Mukden over the assassination of Captain Nakamura well in hand when the destruction of a few feet of the right of way of the South Manchuria Railway occurred. The army command has not yet demonstrated to foreign satisfaction that the destruction was wrought without Japanese connivance, but granting for argument's sake that it was, the failure of the Chinese forces in Manchuria to resist the first attacks of the Japanese left the way open to diplomatic treatment of the whole issue. Instead, as is well known, the Japanese forces were augmented without reference to civilian cabinet opinion, and the intervention went on until the army's objectives were attained. Subsequently the Foreign Office entered the case, but only as the spokesman of the army. The creation of the puppet state Manchukuo was a feature of the Tanaka plan, as was the amalgamation of the several Japanese civilian governmental

---

* Subsequently the guilt of army officers was authenticated by Harada Kumao, private secretary to Prince Saionji.

services in Manchuria with the Manchurian command under a military viceroy.

This *coup d'armée* came with special force after the defeat of the naval staff in 1930 over the London naval treaty. Admiral Kato Kanji, chief of the naval staff, fought strenuously during the London Conference for the tonnage and categories recommended by the staff and proposed to the Conference by the Japanese delegation. When Premier Hamaguchi overruled him and ordered acceptance of a compromise, Kato went to the emperor and later issued a statement declaring that the treaty was unsatisfactory. Popular sentiment, however, supported the compromise, and the government won a general election by a landslide while the Conference was in session. Upon the return of the delegation it was greeted with enthusiastic *banzai* by welcoming crowds. Brought before the Privy Council, the treaty was approved. The Supreme Military Council heard the treaty denounced by Admiral Kato but did not advise the emperor against ratification. The treaty was ratified. Kato resigned, but his place was filled while still warm. (It had got thoroughly warmed during Kato's last weeks in office.)

The defeat of the naval staff is explainable when we recall that Premier Hamaguchi's order to sign the treaty could only be sent upon the command of the emperor, advised by the genro and the Imperial Household Ministry. Signature thus was tantamount to ratification, unless the traditional advisers "behind the curtain" should change their minds. They preferred to maintain their original position. Thus the oligarchy was split — to the advantage of cabinet policy. In the Manchurian case there was no such split, so far as we know, and the civilian ministers had to retreat in disorder.

The army and navy had always been the spearhead of the oligarchy in the processes of usurpation. While the greatest of the genro, Prince Yamagata Aritomo, was alive — that is, until 1922 — there was no cleavage possible between the various elements of the oligarchy. He was head of the Choshu clan and he dominated the genro, the Privy Council, the Imperial Household Ministry, and the Supreme Command. After his death the military services replaced the genro as initiators of policy, and the genro, reduced in numbers and in vigor, had to be content with an advisory status. The Privy Council sought to replace the genro and it gained in influence in some degree, but it was still secondary to the older agencies.

Democratic ideas also had to combat a highly chauvinistic spirit in the populace, both high and low, which aided and abetted the oligarchy. This showed itself in the organization of so-called patriotic societies, such as the *Kokusuikai,* or National Essence Society, for the cherishing of militant nationalism. It showed itself also in the creation of a young men's association, with a huge membership, in which athletic and patriotic interests were combined. Into the patriotic societies entered thousands of men whom the Japanese called *soshi,* or "ruffians," who stopped at nothing in the execution of a patriotic mission and who conceived patriotism frequently in the sense of destroying individuals who were opposed to the purposes of the military clique. Unfortunately, civilian ministers stooped to use such men at times, even while seeking legislative means to prevent their activities. It was these gang tactics that were responsible for the death of two premiers, Hamaguchi and Inukai; a minister of finance, Inouye; and the executive head of the Mitsui trust, Baron Dan; and for unsuccessful attacks upon the emperor, Count Makino, and former Foreign Minister Shidehara, within two years. Gangdom had penetrated the army, as the assassination of Premier Inukai proved.

It was the fashion in 1930 to speak of fascism as a recent phenomenon in Japanese political life. But in fact only the name was new, and that was borrowed. However, the use of the word appeared to reflect an intensification and extension of the nationalistic fervor that had previously distinguished Japan. There were astounding plots among military officers, reaching close, if not quite, to the sacred throne. Even the labor parties were riven by the mania. Japan was in a psychopathic condition, and life was unsafe there for liberals, even for those of neutral tint if they spoke from positions of influence in criticism of military policy, which was another term for national policy.

To be in the prevailing mode, one spoke of the Japan of 1930 as "at the crossroads," one way leading to further exaltation of militaristic oligarchy, the other to parliamentary government; the former to war, the latter to peace. This bit of rhetoric was not true to the facts. Actually there was no choice for Japan then. She had to continue on the only road she knew for some time to come.

It must not be overlooked that genro government had been highly successful government, that Japan had advanced under it economically at a marvelous pace. In the field of foreign relations it had brought Japan recognition as a great power, large influence, and a considerable amount of territory. Its leading figures had been men of ability and honesty. Most important of all, it epitomized the inward spirit of Dai Nippon, the national character that, as in all countries of any history, is the product of the experience of the society it incorporates.

Parliamentarism in Japan, as in the West, had labored during the previous two decades under the handicap of the strenuous conditions of war and the aftermath of war. It would be ungenerous to expect a newborn parliament to have shown progress in a period when old parliaments were offering unparalleled criticism and immature ones, for purposes of policy determination, were succumbing to executive agencies. The future of popular government in Japan was wrapped up with that of older constitutional systems.

It was clear also that democracy would not flourish in Japan so long as the existing unhappy combination of "complexes" — inferiority toward certain other great powers and superiority toward China (the latter further complicated by the fear of the growth of China to military strength) — persisted. One of the influences most tending to provoke and preserve this mental condition was the American attitude toward immigration. Another irritant was the American program of plucking the Manchurian beam from Japan's eye while feeling no apparent discomfort from the several Caribbean motes in its own. Another was the international combination against Japan in the determination of relative naval strength. There were answers to all Japan's remonstrances in these matters, but the answers did not satisfy Japan.

Rumors were heard in 1930 of a communist revolution in Japan, one that would have as devastating effects as that in Russia. The intensification of chauvinism, of "fascism," revealed apprehensions based in part upon the growth of communism. The Japanese army was a peasant army; revolt therein would spell the downfall of the oligarchy. The Japanese peasantry was in distress; it was difficult to conceive how it could, even if it would, support a long war. The development of communism in Germany, where the people, like the Japanese, seemed to desire drillmaster government, had its counterpart in Japan. But the close-knit fabric of Japanese society and the efficiency and honesty of the bureaucracy, taken together with the strength of the cult of devotion to the emperor and the progress of literacy, argued powerfully against any thesis of a communist revolution.

To one who predicated the persistence of parliamentarism (or better, perhaps, the revival of parliamentarism) in some form in the West, it seemed wise to project the unrevolutionary history of Japanese politics into the future and to anticipate a gradual evolution of cabinet government. By conventional, rather than formal, constitutional processes the emperor would assume the status of the king of England, the genro would disappear, the Imperial Household Ministry would sink to mere ceremonial significance, the Privy Council would cease to advise on political issues, the military services would confine themselves to technical functions, and the House of Peers would be reconstituted or deprived of a veto. Fortunately for Japan, this development might occur without amendment of the constitution. Formal amendment seemed to be impossible, but there had unquestionably already taken place an adjustment of political influence in favor of the people's chamber in the Diet. The next obvious step was woman suffrage, which had been voted for local elections in the House of Representatives but had been blocked by the Peers.

The emergence of the emperor and the imperial family from seclusion was an index of the growth of democracy. The people saw their Tenno frequently, his brothers and their consorts attended public gatherings and traveled abroad, and the newspapers freely printed photographs and personal items recording happenings in the lives of their beloved sovereign. No people were more keenly sensitive than the Japanese to the attitude of other nations toward their institutions, or more desirous of a respected place in the van of progress. No country possessed more alert newspapers, a wider reading public, more conscientious and able judges, or more penetrating and enlightened juristic minds in the ranks of scholarship. Japan might yet make her contribution to the annals of true constitutional government.

3

The Parties versus the Army

THE period 1930–1937 began with political parties at the peak of their influence and ended with them bloody but unbowed.[1] Men as violent as the natural forces of earthquake, typhoon, and volcano which rock and tear and sear the land ruthlessly disrupted the parties by murdering experienced leaders and sympathetic senior statesmen. So long, however, as the parties remained in existence they won the elections and maintained a barrage of questions in the House of Representatives. By proving themselves undefeatable they invited a suggestion of *hara-kiri* (suicide) from that most perfect, gentle knight, Prince Konoye.

Murder of Inukai

Inukai Tsuyoshi, president of the Seiyukai, was the last party leader to hold the premiership in wartime Japan. His age and continuous membership in the House of Representatives did not save him from assassination when, on May 15, 1932, a militarist outbreak expressed with violence the impatience of young officers in the armed services toward civilian administration. Inukai had succeeded Wakatsuki Reijiro, president of the Minseito, in December 1931 after the latter's minister of finance, Inouye Junnosuke, a strong and capable opponent of the army's budget demands, had also antagonized *zaibatsu* speculators in dollars by refusing to embargo gold. The Seiyukai, which monopolized the party ministries in the new cabinet, conducted a general election on February 20, 1932, and won a sizable majority in the House of Representatives. Emperor Hirohito took occasion to warn

Inukai that he was in personal danger from the army. The premier kept out of the public eye, making use of his son Ken as his mouth-piece and go-between. Finance Minister Takahashi Korekiyo bore the brunt of resistance to army demands, courageously opposing the expedition to Shanghai and arguing that Japan lacked resources for a major war. But the army already had one foot in the stirrups and refused to be thwarted even by the surviving genro, Prince Saionji. The murder of Inouye in February and of Baron Dan Takuma, man-aging director of Mitsui, greatest of the zaibatsu, in March 1932 cast the shadow of death upon other representatives of the liberal regime so recently of seemingly great promise.

Premier Inukai was assassinated in his official residence, No. 1, Nagata-cho, Tokyo, by young army and navy officers. The earlier political murders had been committed by civilian "patriots" who had not been severely punished. Although the trial of the officers proved that the defendants were not only assassins but plotters against the constitution, seeking to establish emperor rule under army di-rection, none of them received a heavier sentence than fifteen years' imprisonment.[2] The judges in the courts-martial knew, of course, that many high-ranking officers, including the minister of war, General Araki Sadao, sympathized with the young men and had stimulated them to action by contemptuous criticism of political parties and profiteering businessmen. They were deterred from greater severity also by numerous appeals for clemency, among them one from the Osaka Bar Association.

Takahashi versus Araki

Since the army refused to approve acceptance by a military officer of the war ministry in the succeeding cabinet if it were to have a civilian premier, Prince Saionji recommended Admiral Viscount Saito Makoto to head a compromise "national cabinet" of politicians, peers, and military men. Three Seiyukai and two Minseito leaders accepted portfolios. General Araki, a fire-breathing fanatic, continued as min-ister of war. Admiral Okada Keisuke, like Saito a moderate, was navy minister. He was replaced after eight months by Admiral Osumi Mineo. Mr. Takahashi stayed on as finance minister, much against his will. Araki and Takahashi were consistently at odds, the former demanding more money for the army, the latter arguing that a great military establishment would mean disaster, not security, since its cost would undermine the country's financial structure. Takahashi enjoyed his quarrels with Araki, whom he easily outargued, though he foresaw that his stand against reckless outlay for armaments would endanger his life. Seiyukai members were divided in their attitudes toward Takahashi. They criticized him for casual treatment of the party's interest in gubernatorial changes and for disregard of its views on financial policy.[3] The party was, however, appreciative of having so able and liberal a public financier as its nominal representative in an important ministry.

The Parties under Fire

The Seiyukai, with three hundred seats in the House of Representatives, did not view the appointment of Admiral Saito as a stop sign to party cabinets. It elected its candidates to all five chairmanships of the standing committees in the sixty-third session of the Diet, which opened on August 23, 1932.[4] But the party was so faction-ridden that it was constrained to select a representative committee of seven for preliminary consideration of policy. Paradoxically, the Seiyukai was more critical of the government than the Minseito, which had been weakened by the defection of the thug-patron Adachi Kenzo and some thirty of his followers, who had formed the Kokumin Domei (Nationalist League) on a platform of nationalism. This group announced that it would oppose the government, which was, though professedly nationalist, less nationalistic than Adachi. But Premier Saito had little difficulty during the special session, which was called to pass bills for a variety of relief projects wanted by everyone.

It is clear that the parties and the newspapers anticipated that Saito would be followed by a party leader. Apparently this expectation reflected their acceptance of party cabinets as a feature of Japanese constitutionalism. Unfortunately for the parties, they stood between the army and the "patriots," who were determined to expand in Asia at any cost, and the voters, who would not respond to a program of increased taxation such as expansionism would entail if the yen were to be protected. The militarists could substitute loans for taxes with equanimity, since their power did not depend upon a solvent electorate. Not so the party leaders, whose popularity would fall with the buying power of the yen.

31

Party cabinets did not mean parliamentary government in Japan. The oligarchy still held the reins, and in 1933 the army dominated the oligarchy. Hence it was incumbent upon the parties, if they were to tie up the broken thread of cabinet leadership, to find their way into the army's confidence. Elections might confirm Prince Saionji's nod. They could not prompt it, however willing the great Genro might be to advance the representative principle. This bitter fact explains the growing chauvinism of party platforms.

Premier Saito showed an admirable understanding of the uncomfortable position of the parties and kept consistently in touch with them. He sought to assure himself of party support through personal conferences and in other ways. For this attitude he was criticized vigorously by the exponents of oligarchical rule in the guise of imperial benevolence. One may instance the advice of General Tanaka Kunishige, president of the reactionist Meirinkai: "Ignore the parties," he urged; "dissolve the Diet if it supports them against you." [5] Even the liberal Saionji failed to speak out clearly for the parties, which vied in corruption and selfishness, to his mind, with the militarists' reckless readiness to rule or ruin the state.

Matsuoka Yosuke, a seceder from the Seiyukai and one of Japan's ablest Western-educated bureaucrats, head of the Japanese delegation at Geneva when his government rejected the League of Nations' recommendations on the Manchurian issue, gave distinguished leadership to civilian antagonists of the parties when he demanded publicly that there be an end to party politics. Nearly seven years before the parties were dissolved he called for their dissolution, arguing that party government had proved to be unsuited to Japan. He maintained that parliamentary government should be continued — thereby he evaded charges of *lèse majesté* — but that each member of the Diet should be free to speak his mind, untrammeled by obligations to any party.[6] Matsuoka was highly qualified for leadership in a movement to reform the parties. His choice of the opposite course was a disheartening commentary upon an idealistic belief in the internationalizing effects of intercultural relations.

There were various possible alternatives to the sweeping demand of Matsuoka and many army antagonists of the parties. One was that the parties should cleanse themselves. It had theoretical but not practical support. Another was that there be a merger of the Seiyukai and the Minseito. This would do away — so it was argued — with greedy factionalism and would prevent the government from playing one party against another. Voices were raised in favor of this alternative in the last months of 1933. There were joint meetings of Seiyukai and Minseito leaders who exchanged generalities and civilities. But no steps were taken toward the actual formation of a single powerful party. A third alternative was the replacement of all the parties with a national nonpartisan association, after the fashion of the Fascisti in Italy and the National Socialists in Germany. This might have existing parties as its core, or it might be entirely new. Ultimately the last-named alternative was adopted, but not until it had been bitterly contested by the parties for several years.

Army Propaganda

General Araki resigned as minister of war early in 1934 and was succeeded by his own nominee, General Hayashi Senjuro. Araki was angered by the cabinet's failure to find the funds for farm relief without cutting military estimates below the safety line. Since Araki was the most alarmist of the highly placed prophets of an early crisis in Japan's foreign relations, he was also the person most responsible for the lack of money to avert a domestic crisis. With a national debt of 10 billion yen, increasing annually by nearly 1 billion yen, Takahashi was compelled to hold the line of government expenditures for relief, greatly as he would have preferred to enlarge them. Army propaganda, widely diffused, took credit for sympathy with the farmers and attacked the politicians for willfully ignoring them. Against these crocodile tears the parties were powerless since they drew their own support from the zaibatsu and the secret funds of the armed services. They were handicapped also by the fear of being charged with lack of patriotism if they opposed additional outlays for armaments.

Admiral Saito and his cabinet resigned on July 11, 1934, ostensibly to show responsibility for acts of bribery involving members of the cabinet. Genro Saionji's choice of a new premier, Admiral Okada Keisuke, which came as a surprise, was designed to maintain the moderate nationalism of Admiral Saito. The new cabinet included two Minseito and three Seiyukai veterans, but the latter were expelled from their party for accepting office in a second nonparty cabinet. Although the scandal in the Finance Ministry did not touch Mr.

Takahashi, he declined to succeed himself. But he was persuaded to return after his successor failed to satisfy the army. Except for him the members of the cabinet were not men of distinction.

While the issuance of propaganda by the army was not new, a pamphlet calling for the restriction of economic individualism in the interest of the people's livelihood brought consternation to the cabinet, the business world, and the politicians. The aggressive tone of this pamphlet, issued without prior notice to the cabinet, presented the country with the shocking reality of the army's confidence in its predominant position in the state. The argument centered in the contention that unrestrained free enterprise was incompatible with the general welfare, therefore with national safety.[7]

The major parties rallied bravely against this blow. The Seiyukai denied that state control of economic life was essential to security. It upbraided the army for meddling in matters outside its proper sphere and for "blitzing" the cabinet. The Minseito took the same attitude and reminded the army that General Araki had declared in the Diet that soldiers should refrain from political maneuvering. New moves were made by factional leaders to unite the two parties for the preservation of their hard-earned but waning influence. On the other hand the Kokumin Domei defended the pamphlet. And the resignation of the able Wakatsuki Reijiro from the presidency of the Minseito deprived the liberal elements of an influential mouthpiece. Machida Chuji was chosen to succeed him. He was a veteran of the party, past seventy, a competent businessman, but without courage or distinction.

Okada's cabinet faced stronger and stronger pressure from the army for larger appropriations, to be financed by bond issues. The Finance Ministry opposed new loans but consented to an increase in taxes. Takahashi found himself again the target of military criticism and still faced with the urgent issue of relief for the farmers. Members of his party, the Seiyukai, which had disowned him for taking office, attacked his budgets for their inadequacy in relief funds. A lengthy diatribe against "modern civilization based upon individualism" was added to the army's shelf of propaganda. Japan was held up as the nation peculiarly fitted to dispel not only its own borrowed "darkness" but that of the peoples who had never known the light.[8]

Remarkably, foreign affairs — the departure from the League of Nations, the issue of abrogation of naval ratios, and the growing tension in Japanese-American relations especially — were not important subjects of party discussion. The cabinet was left free to deal with them, the only restraint being the interpellations in the Diet directed toward obtaining information and assurances that the national interests were being furthered. With rare exceptions such comments as were made by politicians were inflammatory rather than dampening of the government's expansionism. Such an exception came from Ozaki Yukio, who told his countrymen in plain terms that Japan and not America or Britain was forcing an international crisis and that the army and navy were leading the country to war. Quite unintentionally the navy gave support to Ozaki in an opportune pamphlet condemning naval ratios and demanding freedom to establish superiority of power in eastern Asiatic waters.[9]

Omens of Fascism

The years between the murder of Inukai and the *putsch* of February 2, 1936, were filled with the multiplication of patriotic groups, conspiracies, and other evidences of readiness to use intimidation and violence against anyone seeking to maintain the parliamentary system. Members of the Jimmukai (Emperor Jimmu Society) were tried and convicted of a plot to kill Premier Saito. Threats were published against the great liberal statesman Ozaki Yukio, who was guarded by police, though he wrote in wistful fashion of the common fate of Japan's greatest politicians and included a poem:

> Praise be to men who may attempt my life.
> If their motive is to die for their country.[10]

The "patriots" rounded up by police usually were civilians, but their activities went on as a counterpoint to a continuous military harping upon the theme of Japan's mission to save Asia from liberalism, capitalism, internationalism, and communism. The Kodokai (Imperial Way Society), inaugurated in April 1933 by retired army and navy officers, was typical of so-called national defense organizations being spawned in all parts of Japan with the windy blessing of General Araki or some other representative of the Supreme Command. In a country of "joiners" already bowed under the weight of uncounted Ku Kluxist breast-beaters, the expressed goal of ten million youth members of defense societies was not unattainable.[11]

In the face of burgeoning militarism, labor parties continued their efforts toward unity.[12] Aso Hisashi and Abe Isoo, veteran leaders of the Zenkoku Rono Taishuto (All Japan Labor, Farmer and Masses party) and the Shakai Minshuto (Social Democratic party) respectively, managed to reach a working agreement to merge in July 1932 under the name Shakai Taishuto (Social Mass party). Their new platform included among its planks four that were distasteful to the Metropolitan Police Board of Tokyo, which ordered their removal without apparent concern lest the party fall through the gaping hole thereby created. The banned planks were establishment of socialism, labor control of industry, organization of a labor-farmer army, and world-wide emancipation of colonies.[13] Speeches endorsing the new party were interrupted by police, who were present in force at its inauguration. The new party was more aggressively socialist than the old Shakai Minshuto, more representative of Oyama Ikuo than of Abe Isoo, but it was definitely anticommunist.

Labor's ranks had been shaken by the expansionist fever, a section of the old Shakai Minshuto, under Akamatsu Katsumaro, having seceded from the party in 1931 because it refused to adopt a national socialist program. Similarly the Zenkoku Rono Taishuto had been weakened by the defection of members to the nationalist cause. The dissenting laborites had formed the Kokumin Nihonto (Japan People's party), which described itself in negatives: antiparliamentarist, antiinternationalist, and anticapitalist. The Nihonto appealed more strongly to the farm laborers, the Shakai Minshuto to the urban proletariat.[14]

Nationalist infiltration of labor unions paralleled the rise of national socialism in proletarian parties. Two of the vicious Adachi's henchmen, Nakano Seigo and Sugiura Takeo, obtained influential posts in the communications workers' union, the Teiyu Doshikai. Their fascist doctrines were expressed unmistakably in six tenets adopted by the union on October 8, 1933, from which a typical paragraph may be quoted: "Laborers and farmers must take the foremost line in promoting the collective national power (inclusive of the military and economic power of the state, the physical power of the working classes, the intellectual power of the farmers and the spiritual power of the masses), by the display of their respective functions, thereby contributing to the establishment of a controlled economy.[15]

Violence begetting resistance, the reactionary program was challenged by Communist threats of terrorism and agitation among factory workers and students. Professors, judges, younger members of wealthy families, even geisha, were found to be collecting funds and holding secret meetings to organize opposition to the ambitious projects of the superpatriots. These manifestations aroused far greater apprehension among politicians as well as peers and plutocrats than the well-understood tactics of the feudalistic fascists. But the rightists had no copyright on the term "patriot," which the leftists proceeded to misuse, though less violently, for their own protection. They were, however, sternly and effectively suppressed by the police and *gendarmerie*.

Samurai Ethics

As in other lands, Japan's military services were not lacking in divisive internal jealousies and rival ambitions. In part these were the natural result of competition among many able men for a limited number of positions. In part they reflected differences of views on political issues. Not all the officers were ultranationalist or convinced that army rule was best for Japan. A number believed that they would better represent Emperor Hirohito by opposing the drift toward fascism and war.

The murder of Major General Nagata Tetsuzan, director of the Military Affairs Bureau, by Lieutenant Colonel Aizawa Saburo, in August 1935 was an act of vengeance and mistaken patriotism. Aizawa plunged his sword into Nagata's back because Nagata had been involved in the transfer of General Masaki Jinsaburo from the coveted office of Inspector-General of Military Education to the comparative quietude of the Supreme War Council. But he also believed that Nagata was opposing the officers who were hounding Professor Minobe Tatsukichi for his theory that the emperor was an organ of the state. Aizawa tried but failed to obtain an interview with General Ugaki Kazushige, a moderate among extremists but with blemishes on his record for liberal politics, hoping to kill him.[16] Aizawa's trial was legally a farce but politically of great consequence, since it revealed fully the explosive ideas of the younger army officers, ideas rooted in emperor worship and seeking to flower in fascism. And underlying these ideas, as the trial also revealed, was the principle of dualism which the liberals in all political strata had been working to eradicate — the theory that within its self-interpreted sphere the Supreme

Command was independent of the government. Aizawa was condemned and executed. But while his trial was proceeding, his fanatical colleagues brought the fascist movement to a climax in the bloody insurrection of February 26, 1936.

Militarist intransigence toward parliamentarism reached its most daring height in this *coup de force*. The insurrection was not unpremeditated, indeed it might well have occurred earlier: in November 1933 a small group of unknowns belonging to a reactionary society, the Kokoku Seinen Horyukai, had been arrested and charged with plotting to murder Dr. Suzuki Kisaburo, president of the Seiyukai. They admitted the plot and confessed also to having planned to kill the premier, Prince Saionji, the Lord Keeper of the Privy Seal, the presidents of other leading parties, prominent industrialists, and liberally-inclined military officers.[17] Their list of prospective victims contained the names of many men attacked in 1936. Since Dr. Suzuki, Admiral Saito, and others on the blacklist were themselves members of nationalistic societies, it is evident that no clear line distinguished the antagonists from the proponents of fascism.[18]

Fourteen hundred officers and men took part, in 1936, in the brutal challenge to the imperial authority which they pretended to revere. Their motive was to destroy civilian government and force the establishment of a samurai state. They murdered Finance Minister Takahashi, Lord Keeper of the Privy Seal (Admiral) Saito, Inspector General of Military Training (General) Watanabe, and Colonel Matsuo Denzo, who was mistaken for his brother-in-law, Premier Okada. They wounded Grand Chamberlain (Admiral) Suzuki Kantaro, and failed to kill Prince Saionji and Count Makino Nobuaki, who had resigned as Lord Keeper of the Privy Seal shortly before, only because these two were aided to escape.

But the constitution stood. No strong man or group admitted a share in the plot or took the lead in the creation of a new shogunate. Seventeen of the conspirators were executed while their mentors in high places kept silent. A civilian, Hirota Koki, who had satisfied the army as foreign minister, was made premier after Prince Konoye had declined appointment. The seventeen young men had died in vain. Their elders were too jealous of one another to single out one of themselves for the mantle of a Japanese Mussolini. None of them stood out like a Yamagata above the others. But it would be forgetful of Japanese history and tradition to look for a Japanese Mussolini.

Japanese government seldom has been openly centered in one man. The shogun were not autocrats. They ruled as directed by a council of the clan. Distributed responsibility has been the screen behind which individuals have exercised great influence without risk to themselves, wherefore the assassination of a group of men rather than a single dictator in the February uprising. So, after the restoration of order, the armed services clinched their grip but maintained the fiction of distribution. Their tactics were shrewd. They confused the foreigner but did not deceive the Japanese. They afforded the army a disguise and a set of puppets, enabling it to appear to be observing the constitution while prostituting its civilian supporters.

Thus the net result of the abortive coup was the strengthening of the military hand over the government. General Terauchi Hisaichi, minister of war, was the most influential figure, Admiral Nagano Osami, navy minister, second only to him. Although a new House of Representatives had been elected in February 1936, the Genro, in nominating the premier, ignored the Minseito, which had been successful in winning a plurality over the Seiyukai. Finance Minister Baba Eiichi deserted Takahashi's cautious policy in order to obtain greatly increased funds for the armed services. Army pamphlets more openly denounced party government, and new laws were passed to curb critics of totalitarian trends.

Resistance of the Parties

That liberalism had real, if shallow, rootage in Japan was proved by the refusal of the Seiyukai, the Minseito, and the Shakai Taishuto to be intimidated by the army's demand for unquestioning support in "advancing the national destiny." The Hirota cabinet resigned within a year of taking office because the House of Representatives showed itself to be violently hostile to it immediately after the customary addresses of the premier, foreign minister, and finance minister had been made. Leading the attack, Hamada Kunimatsu, Seiyukai, declared that the military leaders had brought pressure upon the cabinet, had disregarded the Diet, were attempting to establish a veiled dictatorship, and had forced the government to accept a budget far beyond the people's capacity to pay. He defended political parties, terming them public organs for the exercise of constitutional government. If they were corrupt, he said, militarist bribery had helped to corrupt them. When General Terauchi replied that Hamada's charges might be construed as implying contempt for the army, Hamada's indignation led him to say: "The Japanese samurai used to prize honor. It would be beneath a gentleman to make accusations without facts to substantiate them. If, upon examining the stenographic record, I discover that I have used language insulting to the army, I will apologize to you by committing *harakiri*. If, on the other hand, the stenographic record is not found to contain any such language, you should commit *harakari*." [19]

Terauchi's insistence upon dissolution of the Diet was further proof that the army had no regard for constitutional processes. Unable or unwilling to meet the combined opposition of the three major parties to its foreign and financial policies, the army sought to force dissolution, but had to be content with an adjournment. Navy Minister Nagano, who opposed dissolution, played an important part in this compromise. Since Terauchi insisted upon resigning, Hirota and his cabinet also resigned, believing it unlikely that a new minister of war could be obtained without a change of premiers.

General Ugaki Kazushige tried, at the emperor's command, to form a cabinet. He was a military man *sui generis* in that he was on openly cordial terms with the Minseito. Without offering an explanation, and without the support of the navy, the army refused to tolerate acceptance of the Ministry of War by any of its officers. Thereby the new shogunate without a shogun showed its contempt for the imperial prerogative of appointment. Ugaki withdrew to lick his wounds. General Hayashi, recently minister of war, became premier, meekly accepting war and navy ministers recommended by their respective services. The Diet, apparently dazed by the rapid course of events, failed to protest. But when Hayashi offered ministries to Nagai Ryutaro, Minseito, and Nakajima Chikuhei, Seiyukai, on condition that they resign from their parties, both declined. Yamazaki Tatsunosuke, Showakai — the seceders from the Seiyukai originally led by Tokonami Takejiro — accepted the condition and a ministry. Thus the Hayashi cabinet contained no ministers representative of the parties. The Diet was on the brink of a return to its early status — that of a mere advisory body. The Shakai Taishuto's denunciation of the cabinet as a mere robot in the hands of the army, bureaucrats, and financial magnates came close to describing the Diet.[20]

Ozaki Yukio did not permit Hamada Kunimatsu to eclipse him as the champion of parliamentary government. On February 17, 1937, he "interpellated" with his usual skill and verve for an hour and forty-five minutes! He asked Premier Hayashi to explain how the anticommunist pact would aid Japan, why a nation of such spirit as the Japanese should call for another's help, where the crisis was located, against whom defense was required, etc. Ozaki's devotion to the emperor made him impregnable and permitted him to say:

The Army or Navy cannot lift a finger except by exercise of the supreme command prerogative of the Emperor but in these days we find that in many cases army men are moving about of their own volition. . . . According to the reply made by the Premier yesterday, the war or navy minister has the right as a member of the cabinet to express his political views, but as his function is to assist the premier he is absolutely not authorized to publish his personal views and force them on the government. In the papers such statements frequently appear as "The army is watching the attitude of the political parties." If these reports are mistaken, the army should quickly make the papers correct them. As it has never done so, it would seem that such reports are not at all erroneous. . . .

It appears that there are extremely authoritative persons somewhere in the army. Not only the War Minister but even public opinion is guided by some of these illustrious personages. In my sixty years of political life, never have I seen such great personages as they appear to be. Never have I heard of any group of people directing the whole trend of public opinion with a word or gesture.[21]

That Ozaki's speech mirrored the thought of the House of Representatives may be assumed from the sustained and vigorous applause that followed it. Other members followed his example and the session was a stormy one. Dissolution on March 31, 1937, was a disciplinary gesture which cannot be reconciled with constitutionalism. General Hayashi, moreover, was incredibly ill-informed to suppose that he could win a favorable majority in an open challenge to both major parties. His only allies were the discredited Kokumin Domei and the lukewarm Showakai, both small. The growing movement for a new mass party was still in embryo. The Japanese aphorism "the government always wins" would hardly apply to a nonparty government. The surprise of the election was not that the Minseito won 179 seats, the Seiyukai 175, and the Kokumin Domei and Showakai only 29 between them, but that the Shakai Taishuto elected 36 members, exactly twice its previous representation.[22] There was no other course open to the cabinet but to resign, which it did on May 31, 1937. The parties appeared to be unbeatable on their own ground.

The New Japan

Notes

[1] For development of party politics before 1932 see H. S. Quigley, *Japanese Government and Politics* (New York, 1932), Chapter 12. See also K. Colegrove, "Labor Parties in Japan," *American Political Science Review*, XXIII (1929), 329–363.

[2] Hugh Byas, *Government by Assassination* (New York, 1942), Chapter 3. One of the participants, Tachibana Kozaburo, declared belligerently that the coup's principal objective was the establishment of General Araki as a military dictator ruling under martial law. Tachibana called himself a utopian, a disciple of Robert Owen, seeking a decent existence for farmers (*Japan Weekly Chronicle*, October 5, 1933, p. 426; October 19, 1933, p. 497).

[3] *Japan Weekly Chronicle*, July 7, 1932, p. 22.

[4] *Ibid.*, September 1, 1932, p. 277.

[5] *Ibid.*, August 31, 1933, p. 265.

[6] Y. Matsuoka, "Dissolve the Political Parties," *Contemporary Japan*, II (March 1934), 661–667. Matsuoka and Shiratori Toshio were the most outspoken of many Western-educated officials.

[7] *Japan Weekly Chronicle*, October 11, 1934, pp. 490–491. The pamphlet dwelt strongly upon the failure of the existing system to provide for farmers and laborers. In 1934 the number of girls sold to brothels and factories by farmers in Tohoku reached 14,000.

[8] *Ibid.*, March 7, 1935, p. 308.

[9] *Ibid.*, May 9, 1935, pp. 597–598.

[10] *Ibid.*, December 22, 1932, p. 871.

[11] *Ibid.*, April 13, 1933, p. 516.

[12] For the earlier successes of these efforts see Quigley, *op. cit.*, pp. 241–244.

[13] *Japan Weekly Chronicle*, July 28, 1932, p. 114; August 4, p. 146.

[14] E. H. Anstice, "Japan's Labor Parties," *ibid.*, November 24, 1932, pp. 712–713.

[15] *Japan Weekly Chronicle*, October 19, 1933, p. 487.

[16] *Ibid.*, November 7, 1935, p. 573; Byas, *op. cit.*, Chapter 8; see also brief statement by General Masaki in *Nippon Times*, November 19, 1945.

[17] *Japan Weekly Chronicle*, April 5, 1934, p. 463.

[18] *Ibid.*, April 12, 1934, pp. 494–495, a review of R. Iwai, *Zaikai Shin Tosho Den*, a book on the growth of fascism in Japan.

[19] *Ibid.*, January 28, 1937, pp. 100–101.

[20] *Ibid.*, February 18, 1937, p. 198.

[21] *Ibid.*, February 25, 1937, pp. 232–233.

[22] *Ibid.*, May 6, 1937, p. 554.

4

The Wartime Government

JAPAN's constitutional system was not altered in fundamentals under the prolonged strain of war. The older institutions weathered the storm. Prince Saionji's death in 1940 brought an end to the genro but not to their function. New ministries, councils, and boards were established in a characteristically Japanese effort to share responsibility while seeking to unify and invigorate administration. The premiership increased in authority within the cabinet. The same may be said of the Ministry of War within the Supreme Command. The Diet met annually and in special sessions, interpellating cabinet ministers to the end but becoming continuously more subservient to the executive. While reflecting the retreat of liberalism and the Pyrrhic triumph of militarist-capitalist politics, the constitutional history of the war period is interesting and worthy of record.

The Emperor

The constitutional status and political prestige of the emperor were not, apparently, affected by the war. Although Hirohito exhibited great interest in political affairs and expressed opinions to his advisers, his influence upon the general course of events cannot be identified. In so far as his personal views are known — for example, his opposition to the growth of military control of the government — it is apparent that they did not prevail. The dispatch of troops from Korea to Manchuria in 1931 was carried out without imperial sanction. The emperor stood by the cabinet in 1934, refusing to give attention to a navy proposal presented by Admiral Prince Fushimi, chief of the Naval Staff Board, until it had gone to the cabinet under

Admiral Okada. Hirohito's interpretation of the imperial office was revealed in his comment upon the theory of Professor Minobe Tatsu-kichi that the emperor was not the state but an organ of the state. Said he, "Of course the Emperor is an organ but the issue is negligible because the Emperor and the State are identical." He sympathized with Minobe, who was forced to resign from the House of Peers because of military denunciation of his teachings; but his sympathy failed to protect the scholar from persecution.[1]

That an imperial offer of the premiership was not a command was demonstrated in 1936 when Prince Konoye, nominated by the Genro, declined the position. The emperor was nettled by Konoye's refusal and declined to appoint him Lord Keeper of the Privy Seal. Hiro-hito's dignity suffered a more severe jolt, however, when in 1937 General Ugaki, after accepting the premiership, had to report failure to form a cabinet. The army leaders were responsible for his failure since they had prevented any high-ranking officer from taking the War Ministry. It is impossible to reconcile this contemptuous action with the constitutional prerogatives of the emperor. The incident throws a revealing light upon the realities of the imperial status, which customarily were kept hidden in a fog of sentimental rhetoric.[2]

No precedent is known to justify the assumptions that the em-peror would or could have taken it upon himself to declare war upon the United States or other countries, to acquiesce in the request of President Roosevelt that peace be maintained, or to accept the Allies' terms of surrender. All available evidence points to the con-clusion that wartime decisions except the acceptance of the terms of surrender were made by the emperor's advisers, the oligarchy that ruled in his name. Apparently Hirohito insisted upon acceptance. Moreover, the continuing prestige of the imperial sign manual was manifested in the obedience of military commanders to the humiliat-ing order to lay down their arms. This amazing reaction does not attest that the troops believed their emperor to have done more than put the seal of his approval upon the decision to surrender. But that seal was essential.

The Genro and the Other High Advisers

Prince Saionji, last of the genro, died in 1940 at the age of ninety-one. He was the only living genro at the beginning of the Manchurian

"Incident." With his death the institution of the genro passed out of existence, but during the previous decade one somewhat similar had evolved. Saionji kept in touch with political developments through visits of his private secretary, Baron Harada Kumao, with Imperial Household officials, with the prime minister and other members of the cabinet, with high military and naval officers, political party leaders, influential businessmen, and with others. He also held interviews with the most important of these men from time to time. Frequently he expressed his views upon an impending issue to Harada, who conveyed them to persons in the government. But Saionji's antagonism to militarism and to the foreign policy of Japan during his last years made him *persona non grata* to the army chauvinists, who paid little attention to his opinions. Except for a timely warning he would have been attacked and probably killed in the attempted *coup d'état* of February 26, 1936.

The great Genro, however, continued almost until his death to advise the emperor upon the selection of prime ministers. Requests for such advice came to him at his villa in Okitsu or his summer residence at Gotemba from the Lord Keeper of the Privy Seal, to whom the imperial request was addressed. Saionji on occasion journeyed to Tokyo to confer with the Lord Keeper, the Imperial Household Minister, the Lord Chamberlain — the principal palace officials — and with a somewhat variable group known as the Senior Statesmen (quasi-genro). This group included the retiring premier, all living ex-premiers and the president of the Privy Council. Irregularly the most influential army and navy officers also were consulted. Frailty in his last years kept Saionji at home, but after consultation had been conducted through Harada or otherwise the Genro had the final word. After his death the procedure above described continued, minus the role of the Genro. The Lord Privy Seal thus became the key figure in the recommendation process. An ex officio group of Senior Statesmen, based upon custom rather than law, replaced the smaller genro group. This group not only advised upon the premiership but was called upon during the last years of the war to exchange views in meetings with cabinet ministers.[3]

An interesting by-product of the genro function was the extraordinary part played by Baron Harada outside his secretarial duties. He knew everyone of any importance, including the judges and police

45

chiefs. As he moved from office to office he picked up information and opinions which he exchanged for more of both. Often he was asked to inform a minister of developments which, one would suppose, should have been revealed to him through regular administrative channels. He became an oracle who never hesitated to give advice, not even to an imperial prince. Following his movements, one becomes aware of the extraordinary degree to which Japanese government was a matter of secret and personal arrangement. The greatest care was taken to prevent the newspapers from following the devious course of this political maneuvering. Restaurants, clubs, and teahouses were rendezvous for confidential conferences. Harada was a Japanese Pepys, whose diary has greatly enriched our understanding of Japanese politics.

The Privy Council, constitutional advisorate of the emperor and the cabinet, maintained its position throughout the war period. No new functions were imposed upon it, but it continued to advise upon laws, ordinances, and appointments.

The Supreme Command

Wartime exigencies prompted the establishment of an Imperial Headquarters on November 20, 1937. The ordinance creating it termed the agency the "highest body of the Supreme Command," placed it under imperial supervision, and required the chiefs of the army and navy General Staffs to assist the emperor. Their functions in this capacity were to formulate strategic plans and to coordinate the operations of the army and navy.[4] Members of the Headquarters in addition to the chiefs of staff were the ministers of war and the navy and specially appointed officers — thus it was a smaller edition of the Supreme Military Council. In the same year the ministers of war and the navy and the two chiefs of staff were grouped as a Liaison Committee between the cabinet and Imperial Headquarters. In September 1941 a supplementary General Defense Headquarters was added to plan the defense of the home islands and adjacent areas: Korea, Formosa, and Karafuto.[5]

Growing apprehension resulting from defeats in the Pacific and the first B-29 raids caused Premier Koiso to drop the Liaison Committee and to erect the Supreme Council for the Direction of the War in August 1944. This body was termed at origin the highest political authority under the emperor, with the final word upon important domestic issues as well as upon military policy. In practice it was rather a continuance of the Liaison Committee, with a larger membership of military officers and cabinet members. That it did not displace the Imperial Headquarters in policy decisions was demonstrated in March 1945 by the inclusion of Premier Koiso in the Headquarters. Apparently this arrangement was designed to increase the Supreme Command's control over the cabinet.* Precedents for it were found in procedures followed during the Sino-Japanese (1894–1895) and Russo-Japanese (1904–1905) wars.

The dualism which characterized the Japanese system of government in consequence of the constitutional division of delegated powers between the cabinet and the Supreme Command disappeared with the establishment of military control of the cabinet. Division of opinion within the Supreme Command, particularly troublesome within the army, hampered but did not prevent the usurpation of power. The expression of individual views upon national policy was curbed after the abortive but bloody coup of February 26, 1936. The minister of war was authorized to be the sole spokesman for the army in political affairs.[6] In 1937 the army set the seal upon its dominance by rejecting the appointment the emperor had made to the premiership, General Ugaki.

Cabinet Ministries and Advisory Agencies

Comparing the central government of 1945 with that of 1931 one finds that wartime developments altered the list of cabinet ministries and caused the addition of new agencies.[7] The number of ministries, exclusive of the Prime Ministry, was twelve in both years. But only seven of the ministries of 1931 remained as then constituted: those of Foreign Affairs, Home Affairs, Finance, War, the Navy, Justice, and Education. The Ministries of Agriculture and Forestry and of Commerce and Industry had been combined in 1943 in a new Ministry of Agriculture and Commerce; those of Communications and of Railways, in the same year, in a Ministry of Transportation and Communications. The Ministry of Overseas Affairs, dealing with colonies, had been absorbed in 1943 by the Ministry of Greater East Asia, established in November 1942. There were two other new ministries

* See chart on p. 48.

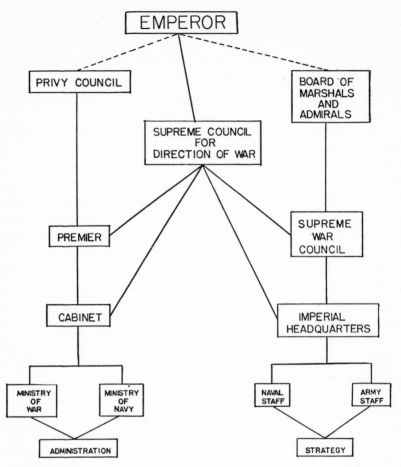

Koiso's System for Direction of the War (The dotted line indicates an advisory relation.)

in 1945, that of Welfare, which had begun to function in 1938, and the Ministry of Munitions, inaugurated in October 1943.

Alarm over the poor health of peasant conscripts and the high death rate, coupled with concern that social conditions were correspondingly unfavorable to the success of the ambitious program of leadership which Japan had enunciated, accounts for the establishment of the Ministry of Welfare. It was admitted that a "deplorable condition in national health" existed and that Japan stood "far inferior to other civilized countries in respect to mortality, conditions of contracting disease, and the average length of life."[8] In 1935, the mortality rate per thousand people was, in Japan, 16.8. In Italy the rate was 15.8, in France 15.1, in England 12, and in the United States 10.7 per thousand.[9] Ten per cent of the two million babies born annually in Japan died before they were a year old, 20 per cent before they were five years old.[10]

The Ministry of Welfare was organized with five bureaus — physical strength, public health, disease prevention, social affairs, and labor — and a board of insurance. The functions and personnel of the bureaus of public health and of social welfare were transferred to it from the Ministry of Home Affairs. Jurisdiction over labor hygiene in mines was transferred from the Ministry of Commerce and Industry; that over physical education and sports outside of schools from the Ministry of Education; and that over life insurance, in part, from the post office bureau of the Ministry of Communications.[11] The new ministry was soon burdened with heavy responsibilities. It was required to study improvement of the health insurance system, which covered 3,700,000 industrial workers in 1938, and to administer new laws bringing farm workers, city people on low incomes, and salaried employees under the compulsory health insurance system.[12] Other tasks imposed upon the Ministry were a survey of the physiques of selected age groups,[13] a study for more effective utilization of labor in industry,[14] supervision and expansion of the Institute of Public Health opened in 1938,[15] application of a law of 1931 guaranteeing employment to discharged military service men,[16] the taking of a labor census,[17] supervision of more than 16,000 seasonal day nurseries,[18] and the provision of medical examinations and care for infants.[19] While all these measures were undertaken to assure a larger and sturdier supply of cannon fodder, their peacetime value is not to be overlooked.

The Ministry of Greater East Asia was an expansion of the China Affairs Board, created in 1938 to aid the cabinet in plans to exploit areas overrun by Japanese forces in China. Headed by a civilian, Aoki Kazuo, the Ministry wore the guise of a puppeteer but was actually an enlarged colonial department. After a tussle with the Ministry of Foreign Affairs, which resented the consequent restriction of its field of activity, "purely diplomatic relationships" in the "co-prosperity sphere" were left to it, a rather dry sop. The new Ministry was provided with three geographically constituted bureaus, a general affairs bureau, and four advisers.[20] When Tojo resigned in July 1944, Foreign Office control was brought belatedly into the Ministry through the appointment of Shigemitsu Mamoru, minister of foreign affairs, to the concurrent post of minister for Greater East Asia.

The Ministry of Munitions was the answer to the necessity recognized by Premier Tojo of coordinating production for war and particularly of expanding and hastening the output of aircraft. Tojo himself headed the ministry, which had eight bureaus. It took over certain of the functions of several ministries, obtaining jurisdiction over a wide range of related matters: general mobilization of resources, reorganization and strengthening of control over production, distribution, consumption, and prices of mineral and industrial products, electricity, and water power, and regulation of capital and labor in key enterprises. It absorbed the functions of the Planning Board, set up in 1937 within the Cabinet Office to advise the cabinet upon important aspects of policy.[21]

Centralization

Centralization of policy making and administration was the prime objective of wartime government in Japan as it was in other states at war. Japanese ministers were greatly hampered in their efforts to deal broadly with large matters of policy by the influence of their respective departmental associates. The self-interest of the several ministries is not peculiar to Japan, but it is doubtful whether the strength of bureaucracy in that country can be matched elsewhere. Ministers drawn from political parties felt the drag upon their initiative in much the same degree as career heads. Unless the premier was extraordinarily gifted and highly respected he was unable to overcome ministerial separatism. Constitutionally he was merely first among equals and without authority to remove a minister or otherwise to compel his acquiescence in a common policy. Not until January 1943 did any premier request legal provision for directive authority over other ministers. At that time Premier Tojo brought a bill into the Diet for that purpose. After rather severe criticism the Diet passed the measure.

Unity and accelerated action were sought in two types of procedure, one type including different devices within the cabinet, the other embracing advisory bodies outside it. The former type is observable in the Five Ministers' Council created in 1937 to discuss national defense and foreign policy, composed of the prime minister and the ministers of foreign affairs, finance, war, and the navy. Similar in nature was the Four Ministers' Council established in 1938, including the prime minister and the ministers of home affairs, finance, and education, to deal with important domestic issues. On occasion other ministers were invited into the latter group. Another device of this nature was the use of several ministers without portfolio to relieve the heads of departments, in some degree, of the obligation to attend conferences on policy. A fourth expedient, similar in purpose to the last-mentioned, was the formation in 1944 of an Emergency Cabinet Council composed of the cabinet ministers, their usual administrative functions being assigned to the vice-ministers who formed what might be termed a junior or deputy cabinet.

The cabinet employed two devices of the second type: planning boards and advisory councils, to bring pressure for centralization. The Planning Board appointed in 1937 was an influential aid to the premiers in overcoming ministerial prejudices against transfers of powers and personnel. However, as its members, while not technicians, were experienced laymen rather than important political figures, Premier Konoye found it expedient to add a Cabinet Advisory Council (1937), composed of military, party, and business leaders, to offset tendencies to disunity and to buttress cabinet decisions.[22] To assure liaison and cooperation the president of the Planning Board was given the concurrent office of vice-president of the Advisory Council.[23] The latter body to a considerable degree replaced the ministers as a policy-discussion group, meeting twice a week with the premier. Cabinet meetings thus tended to become confined to administrative matters although the ministers remained responsible for policy.[24] No true parliamentary system could operate in this fashion. But it was quite in accord with the pseudo-parliamentarism of Japan.

Premier Tojo dispensed with the Council in 1941 and transferred the functions of the Board to the Ministry of Munitions in 1943. He found it advisable, under criticism of his conduct of the war, to install a new Advisory Council in March 1943. However, in October 1944 Premier Koiso returned to the original idea of a General Planning Board. Whereas the Council advised principally upon economic problems, the Board embraced all policy fields except military and foreign affairs. Its principal members were a general director, three sectional directors, three councillors, and twelve advisers, all of whom held ministerial rank and were entitled to report within the cabinet, meeting as a Council of State. The advisers were men of distinction and experience: a university president, a newspaper publisher, a financier, an agricultural expert, three specialists in industrial management, a general, two admirals, a diplomat, and a political party leader.

In addition to the general planning and advisory agencies successive governments appointed numerous commissions of investigation and advice in special fields: mobilization, unemployment, prices, transportation, electric power, health, aeroplane production, etc. These were, as a rule, headed by a cabinet member and included both officials and laymen.

The Diet

An impressive new building to house the national legislature (Diet) was dedicated in November 1936. It occupied a commanding site and was the finest modern building in Japan. If the speeches of dedication rang somewhat hollowly at the end of that year of political assassinations, it can be said at least that the Diet met regularly throughout the war. In but one instance was the term of a House of Representatives prolonged beyond its legal expiration date — April 30, 1941 — and that for one year only. However annoying the antics of the party leaders or the interpellations of their disciples, they could not be brushed off by closing the doors of the Diet. Only the emperor could have done that, by initiating an amendment to the constitution, a line of action which neither his advisers in brass nor those in silk ventured to suggest. So the annual sessions sanctioned by the constitution, and special sessions as well, continued to the end of the war.

It is worth noting that the members of both Houses made extensive use of interpellations even after bombs began to fall on Tokyo. Possibly they were influenced by the comparative security of the Diet, which was not bombed, though everything near it was destroyed. But one may doubt that they were conducting a disguised filibuster against adjournment. Rather they were exhibiting the Japanese proclivity for obtaining, in one way or another, explanations of proposals or decisions made by authorities whom they cannot control. It is fully apparent that interpellations were employed regularly as a process for the appraisal of the Tojo, Koiso, and Suzuki cabinets as well as of their predecessors. This evidence of maintained morale in the presence of disaster and defeat deserves attention. The indication is that Japan's brand of parliamentary control — such as it was — did not collapse in the crisis.

Interest in extending representation in the Diet to colonies had been academic until the course of the war prompted a gesture of good will. In March 1945 the Diet passed two laws, one authorizing appointment of seven Koreans, three Formosans, and one resident of Karafuto[25] to the House of Peers, the other providing for the election of twenty-three Koreans, five Formosans, and three Karafutans to the House of Representatives. In April 1945 the emperor appointed seven Koreans and three Formosans — the latter were Japanese resident in Formosa — upon Premier Koiso's recommendation, to seven-year terms in the House of Peers. The effectuation of the other provisions of the two laws awaited elections scheduled for September 1945, which did not take place. The end of the war was the end also of Japan's colonial rule, for a foreseeable period; consequently the amiable gesture came too late.

Prefectural and Local Government

Prefectural and local institutions were modified but not fundamentally altered in the pursuit of more expeditious administration and increased production. The outstanding innovation was the grouping of prefectures into nine, subsequently into eight, regions or regional administrative districts. Hokkaido and Karafuto composed the most northerly region; Okinawa was included in the most southerly. The nine regions were delimited in 1943, the eight in 1945. The following table of composition indicates also the coordination of army administration areas with the eight regions:

Army Districts	Regional Administrative Districts	Prefectures Included
Northern	Hokkaido	Hokkaido and Karafuto
Tohoku	Tohoku	Aomori, Iwate, Miyagi, Akita, Yamagata, Fukushima

Eastern	Kanto-Shinetsu	Ibaragi, Tochigi, Gumma, Saitama, Chiba, Tokyo, Kanagawa, Yamanashi, Niigata, Nagano
Tokai	Tokai-Hokuriku	Gifu, Shizuoka, Aichi, Mie, Ishikawa, Toyama
Central	Kinki	Shiga, Kyoto, Osaka, Hyogo, Nara, Wadayama, Fukui
Central	Chugoku	Tottori, Shimane, Okayama, Hiroshima, Yamaguchi
Central	Shikoku	Tokushima, Kagawa, Ehime, Kochi
Western	Kyushu	Fukuoka, Saga, Nagasaki, Kumamoto, Oita, Miyazaki, Kagoshima, Okinawa

Each region or district was administered by a chairman, a person of *shinnin* rank. Such authority as the central government delegated to the region reposed in the chairman, who was advised by a Regional Council composed of the governors of the included prefectures and the chiefs of bureaus established at the regional capitals to supervise prefectural bureaus hitherto supervised from Tokyo. The chairman was granted authority to direct the governors in the performance of functions of special national concern. He was aided in this work by an executive councillor selected by the home minister and responsible for getting action from prefectural authorities upon orders which the central government had sent to the regional councils. The chairman and the executive councillor might be concurrently a prefectural governor or an official of the central government. Monthly conferences were held by the premier with the regional chairmen and by the home minister with the executive councillors. Close collaboration was maintained with the army's regional superintendent of munitions production, who sat on the regional council.

This supplementary regionalism was recognized as an emergency program. Obviously it reflected Premier Tojo's desire to bring every phase of administration under his personal direction. It enabled a premier to have frequent contacts with representative prefectural governors and to use such contacts as occasions for urging more strenuous efforts to step up production. It did not diminish national authority or prefectural functions. There appeared to be no theoretical advantage in it as a peacetime system. As might have been anticipated, the Regional Councils were found to be a drag on the wheel and were abolished in June 1945. Thereafter the chairmen of the councils were entitled general superintendents and carried on as before. The office of munitions production became a bureau under the general superintendent. It is a testimony to Japanese reliance upon bureaucracy that no popular assembly was provided in the regional experiment and that no serious attention was paid to the ex officio Regional Councils. This was true although the fear of invasion was prevalent and regionalism was regarded as a last resort in preparation for the anticipated breakdown of centralized administration.

Centralized administration of the capital city and adjacent territory was the objective sought in combining the former prefecture (*fu*) and city (*shi*) of Tokyo into a special prefecture (*to*) in January 1943. Policing of the metropolis was not altered by the merger but continued to be administered by the Metropolitan Police Board, which was directly responsible to the Home Ministry. Tokyo-to was governed like a *fu* (urban prefecture), but with more bureaus — eight rather than three or four. The home rule position of the former city of Tokyo was surrendered, the powers of the elective assembly being the same as those of other prefectures. Although prefectural elections were suspended in June 1943, the assembly of the new *to* was elected on September 13, 1943. Sitting members of *ken*, *fu*, and *to* assemblies were given extensions of their terms by the Diet in March 1944 and 1945.

Other wartime prefectural and local developments were the delegation of additional powers to the governors — subject to central control — in order to relieve the overburdened ministries; dilution of the power of municipal assemblies to elect mayors by requiring the assemblies to accept nominees of the governors, decreed in 1943; establishment of Karafuto as a special prefecture (*cho*) in April 1943;[26] and extension in 1943 to Osaka, the commercial capital, of the police pattern of Tokyo — a Metropolitan Police Board directly responsible to the Ministry of Home Affairs. In terms of effective contribution to the war effort, the most significant development was the reestablishment of the "neighborhood associations." These groups, the *tonarigumi*, existed during the feudal age and appear to have been modeled upon Chinese prototypes. They were composed of five or ten families (*goningumi* or *juningumi*). Originally privately organized for mutual aid, they were used by the Tokugawa administrators as aids in the collection of taxes, the apprehension of criminals, and the control of personal conduct. Although deprived of official status after feudalism fell, they continued as private associations varying in vigor from one locality to another.

In 1940 the *tonarigumi* were revived as public bodies. They were constituted of groups averaging ten households living contiguous to one another. These groups were organized in larger units, called *chonaikai*, or block associations in cities and towns, and *burakukai*, or hamlet associations in villages. The government stated quite clearly that community activities must be so organized as to conform to national purposes. "By and large," ran the Home Ministry's explanation, "the community and district councils are an institution for training the people to do away with individualistic thinking and living and for developing true national character by stressing public service rather than private profit." [27] This was a bit of rhetoric to justify the imposing of official duties without paying salaries to the local neighborhood heads. The latter might be elected by the people composing the *gumi* or the *kai*, but in every instance the approval of or direct appointment by the mayor or headman of the locality was required. All inhabitants of a neighborhood were entitled to attend council meetings, which were expected to occur at least once a month. For practical operation the *kai* councils were composed of representatives of the *tonarigumi*. Rotational service was employed in the conduct of functions, which became more numerous and burdensome as the national resources flagged. The element of local autonomy in the associational network was small and was likely to be monopolized by headmen who were sometimes corrupt and frequently tyrannical. In 1942 the associations were integrated with the Imperial Rule Assistance Association.

Among such functions the most important was the distribution of rationed commodities; in rural districts aid was given in the assessment and collection of rice and other quotas for rationing. The associations maintained a registry of the population and issued certificates of residence and of unemployment. They conducted drives for the collection of scrap metal, the sale of war bonds, and the observance of public health regulations. They collaborated in air raid defense,

The Wartime Government

shouted *banzai* to departing and returning troops — in short, they were an omnibus into which public responsibilities were loaded when other vehicles were unavailable.

Notes

[1] The data were obtained from the Saionji-Harada memoirs, the most revealing source book available for the study of genro government. The Japanese version is a six volume work, K. Harada, *Saionji Ko to Seikyoku* (Prince Saionji and the Political Situation), Tokyo, 1950. The memoirs were issued in English in a limited mimeographed edition by SCAP.

[2] It is difficult to appraise the remark of Count Makino, quoted by Mr. Grew, in the face of the army's repudiation of Ugaki less than three years later. Makino, with tears in his eyes, said, "There will never be 'danger' from military fascism or communism or from any other kind of 'ism' simply because the Emperor is supreme and will *always* have the last word" (Joseph C. Grew, *Ten Years in Japan*, New York, 1944, p. 156). Mr. Grew also cites a "reliable Japanese informant" as having said that just prior to the fall of the Konoye cabinet in October 1941, the emperor ordered the army and navy not to make war upon the United States (*ibid.*, p. 462). If so, the emperor's action was without precedent — and without effect.

[3] Cf. C. N. Spinks, "Japan's New Genro," *Contemporary Japan*, IX (July 1940), 840–847.

[4] Hugh Borton, *Japan since 1931* (New York, 1940), p. 60.

[5] *New York Times*, September 12, 13, 1941.

[6] C. B. Fahs, *Government in Japan* (New York, 1940), p. 79.

[7] For the functions of the ministries in 1931 see H. S. Quigley, *Japanese Government and Politics* (New York, 1932), Chapter 8.

[8] *Tokyo Gazette*, February 1938, p. 13.

[9] *Ibid.*, May 1939, p. 20.

[10] *Ibid.*, June 1940, p. 459.

[11] *Ibid.*, February 1938, pp. 10–12.

[12] *Ibid.*, August 1938, p. 14; May 1939, pp. 20–24.

[13] *Ibid.*, November 1938, pp. 22–23.

[14] *Ibid.*, August 1939, pp. 16–22.

[15] *Ibid.*, September 1939, pp. 94–99.

[16] *Ibid.*, November 1939, pp. 181–186.

[17] *Ibid.*, January 1940, pp. 247–251.

[18] *Ibid.*, April 1940, pp. 375–378.

[19] *Ibid.*, June 1940, pp. 459–463.

[20] A. J. Grajdanzev, "Japan's Co-Prosperity Sphere," *Pacific Affairs*, XVI (September 1943), p. 314.

[21] Borton, *op. cit.*, pp. 57, 128.

[22] *Ibid.*, pp. 58–59. This body recalls the Diplomatic Advisory Council of 1917–1922 (Quigley, *op. cit.*, pp. 99–100).

[23] *Tokyo Gazette*, May 1938, p. 48.

[24] Y. Sekiguchi, "The Changing Status of the Cabinet in Japan," *Pacific Affairs*, XI (March 1938), p. 5.

[25] Karafuto (Japan's half of Saghalien for forty years) was a colony until September 1942; from that time until April 1943 it was administered under the Home Ministry; thereafter it was made a *cho*, similar to Hokkaido.

[26] *Cho* differ from *ken*, *fu*, and *to* in that they are divided into branch administrations (*shicho*).

[27] *Tokyo Gazette*, January 1941, pp. 258–265.

5

Political Parties and the IRAA

The Konoye Era

IF THE political parties could not be beaten in a fair or even in an unfair election, they could be required to beat themselves by committing suicide. Far more satisfactory to the militarists would have been the indefinite suspension of the Diet. But that was a constitutional agency, touched by the scepter of Emperor Meiji. Plenty of hotheads were willing to revise the constitution, but the oligarchy preferred to win another way. Once question Meiji and where would questioning stop? The parties, on the other hand, were contrivances of ordinary men. Arguments that they were essential to constitutional government could be brushed aside; parties were not mentioned in the sacred document.

Quite in character with Japanese precedents, the velvet glove on the iron hand that gave the *coup de grâce* to the parties in 1940 was Prince Konoye. When the Genro prevailed upon Konoye Fumimaro to take the premiership in June 1937, he selected the only person in Japan who was capable of playing Pied Piper to the politicians. The Prince was the apple of Saionji's eye and the idol of the whole nation, second only to Hirohito in public esteem. He had the magnetism of Franklin Roosevelt. Although of ancient lineage, he dealt with "patriots" and racketeers as easily as with peers and professors. But he lacked force and originality. He was not a leader but was torn hither and yon in his desire to please everyone. He was opposed to war but he could not control the forces that were demanding it. Less violently critical of Western policies in Asia than Matsuoka and Shiratori, he was *persona grata* to the army because he was strongly though quietly nationalist and imperialist.

The four years between June 1937 and October 1941 might be termed the Konoye era. The peerless Prince held the premiership from June 1, 1937, to January 4, 1939. Failing to satisfy the army, he then resigned, but was again appointed on July 22, 1940, and re-appointed on July 17, 1941, after resigning in order to rid the cabinet of the luckless Foreign Minister Matsuoka. Between his first and second terms Japan had three short-lived cabinets, headed, in order, by Baron Hiranuma Kiichiro, a gentleman-intriguer unfailingly ultra-militarist but too wily to commit himself publicly, General Abe Nobuyuki, a political weakling, and Admiral Yonai Mitsumasa, a moderate militarist. Konoye resigned on October 16, 1941, to be suc-ceeded by General Tojo Hideki, who took Japan into war with the United States.

The Prince Premier brought Nagai Ryutaro, Minseito, and Naka-jima Chikuhei, Seiyukai, into his first cabinet as influential politi-cians, not as representatives of their respective parties. Hiranuma, Abe, and Yonai also included in their cabinets from two to four party leaders. The outbreak of the China "Incident" on July 7, 1937, stimu-lated the movement for a national political society replacing all parties. Although Konoye disclaimed interest in heading such a society he was a prime mover for its establishment. Nakajima Chiku-hei, leader of a large faction of the Seiyukai, supported the move-ment in its early stages on the ground that existing parties were not representative of men of talent. For that reason, also, he held that a mere amalgamation of the parties would be unsatisfactory. He did not, apparently, consider the alternative of broadening the member-ship of his own and other parties.

"Patriots" played a characteristic part in the movement to over-throw the parties. In January 1938 the *Bokyo Gokoku Dan* (Anti-Comintern and National Defense Unit) was organized, one of numer-ous similar societies. Its members wore uniforms and spent their time attempting to convince politicians and businessmen, by intimidation if necessary, that the parties were a menace to national security. Not a few party members joined the Unit. On February 17, 1938, the headquarters of the Seiyukai and Minseito were occupied forcibly by the Unit. Although the police ousted the usurpers and arrested many of them, Home Minister Admiral Suetsugu Nobumasa was severely criticized in the Diet for allowing the Unit to operate.[1]

While renegades within their ranks were going over to the enemy, the parties fought on against submergence or dissolution. They attacked certain provisions of the National Mobilization Bill as fascistic, comparing it with Hitlerian ordinances. However, the precariousness of their position was reflected in their argument that the bill sought to restrict the imperial prerogative of legislation by authorizing extensive resort to imperial ordinances. Obviously this was the "patriotic" way to assert the constitutional power of the Diet but it was far from a bold challenge to the executive. Nor was it logical, since the imperial prerogative was not being restricted but merely relocated by extension of the sphere of action by ordinance. But in the only way open to it, the House of Representatives was struggling to hold its constitutional position.[2]

Discord in the Seiyukai

Factionalism within the Seiyukai had prevented election of a successor to the ailing president, Dr. Suzuki Kisaburo. Hatoyama Ichiro, Suzuki's brother-in-law and an extremely suave and clever lawyer, led one faction. Nakajima Chikuhei, a wealthy industrialist, ardent advocate of a national political society, led another. Both men were candidates for the presidency. Election lay with the members of the party in the Diet and two members from each prefecture. Pending an election, the four senior directors, among them Hatoyama and Nakajima, performed the duties of a president. Neither faction being disposed to endanger the party's existence by insisting upon an election, maneuvers toward reconciliation were dragged out for many months. Eventually a third candidate emerged, Kuhara Fusanosuke, a chauvinistic copper magnate who was one of the party elders and who had been an intimate friend of that jovial swashbuckler, Premier General Baron Tanaka Giichi. Among the three candidates no major differences in principle or policy existed; their supporters were divided mainly on personal grounds.

The retiring President, Dr. Suzuki, finally nominated Kuhara, who was accepted without enthusiasm. He was better qualified to associate with militarists than to champion parliamentarism. His speech of acceptance offered the following tenets of party faith, all of them in line with army propaganda: (1) Development of culture traits embodied in the concept of *Nippon shugi* (the Japanese principle). (2) Reform of political organization. (3) Strengthening of national power and productivity. (4) Stabilization of national life. (5) Creation of a new order in East Asia. (6) Advocacy of *kodo* (the way of the emperor) as the basis of foreign relations.[3]

Until the dissolution of the parties the Nakajima faction, which previously had elected Nakajima president of the party without benefit of legality, attempted to maintain pseudoindependence and to upset the election of Kuhara. Party headquarters became the scene of interfactional brawls. Nakajima and Kuhara resorted to meeting their respective factions separately. The former had ninety-eight member followers, the latter seventy, when the breach occurred, but each faction lost and gained members from time to time. Twelve Seiyukai members — among them Inukai Ken, a pale but clever reflection of his murdered father — belonged to no faction. Neither Nakajima nor Kuhara was representative of the principles of party government. They agreed upon a secondary position for the Diet. To quote Kuhara: "The duty of the Diet is to supervise the administration of the Government, criticize it and guide it."[4]

Labor Pains

As tension increased in Japan's relations with the United States, an amazing shift of sentiment occurred in the hitherto moderately socialist Shakai Taishuto. That party authorized its officers to arrange a merger with the small but vociferous Tohokai, led by Nakano Seigo, explaining its action as an initial step toward the formation of a people's party dedicated to domestic reform and invigoration of the national spirit. This capitulation to fascism undoubtedly was motivated by fear and exhibited a readiness to sacrifice cherished ideals in order to preserve party members from persecution. But the merger also exposed the mental confusion engendered by military propaganda for social welfare. This appeared to provide a platform upon which nationalists and socialists could stand together. Fortunately, the refusal of President Abe Isoo of the Shakai Taishuto to support the merger, and controversy over offices in the proposed new party, caused the project to be abandoned.[5] Whereupon the Tohokai joined with Adachi's clique, the Kokumin Domei, to form the short-lived

Jikyoku Doshikai (Comrades in Crisis), comprising thirty-two members in the House of Representatives.

Saito Speaks Out

Hiranuma held office for less than eight months, resigning with his cabinet on August 28, 1939. He and General Abe, who followed him, attempted to further the Konoye program of national unification and government control of the economic order. Both premiers were in continual conflict with the parties and with business interests opposed to the establishment of controls over prices and materials. However, the principal cause of Hiranuma's resignation was the humiliation suffered when Japan's only powerful friend, the German Reich, signed a nonaggression treaty with the Soviet Union without reference to Tokyo. The Abe cabinet endured for less than five months, retiring on January 14, 1940, without waiting for a vote on a resolution of nonconfidence. Admiral Yonai sought to appease the parties and found himself at odds with his war minister, General Hata Shunroku, whose resignation brought down the cabinet on July 16, 1940.[6]

A final flicker of liberalism lit up the gloom enshrouding the disorganized and discredited parties on February 2, 1940, when a Minseito veteran, Saito Takao, an eighty-pound fighter for parliamentarism, interpellated the ministry regarding the government's policy toward China. In a historic statement, which won him ultimate honor but also immediate expulsion from the House of Representatives, Saito deprecated the term "holy" as applied to the war, pointed to the enormous cost in lives and money, and demanded assurances that the end was in sight. The Minseito failed, however, to support him and even the Shakai Taishuto condemned his utterance of divisive sentiments.[7] Since no legal action was brought against him, it is probable that his repudiation by fellow members saved him from a prison sentence. His defense of his remarks before the Disciplinary Committee of the House, in which he denied having questioned the righteousness of Japan's cause, dimmed the luster of his protest.

The Saito case had important consequences for the Shakai Taishuto. Nine of its members who opposed the banning of Saito were expelled from the party. A month later President Abe withdrew from it with the approval of the Tokyo branch of the General Federation of Labor. A new party, affiliated with the Federation, was projected by

Abe and the nine dissenters. But on the eve of its organization the Home Ministry issued an order of prohibition on the ground that its proposed tenets were socialistic and detrimental to national unity.[8] Home Minister Kodama Hideo was opposed to any connection between labor unions and a political party and was urging the unions to move in the opposite direction, i.e., to transform themselves into industrial patriotic societies (*sangyo hokokukai*).

"Spiritual Mobilization"

Like his patron, Saionji, Konoye lacked confidence in political parties. But unlike Saionji, who was realistic to the bone, Konoye had an emotional temperament which inclined him toward acceptance of leadership of a "reformist" movement, i.e., a spiritual movement to eradicate institutions and ideas borrowed from the West that might be regarded as hindrances to the realization of Japan's "mission." Shortly after his first appointment as premier he addressed a meeting at which the Movement for National Spiritual Mobilization was initiated. This address pledged Konoye to the nationalist ideal and foreshadowed his attack upon political parties and representative government. Among other things he said:

The conception that the state is not a promiscuous association for purposes of profit, but a community having a definite cultural mission, while the subject is not a profit-seeking, materialistic entity but a spiritual entity whose purpose is to make certain contributions to humanity through the structure of a nation-state, is attracting serious attention today among thinking people who are not satisfied with the materialistic aspects of Western culture. We in Japan are certainly witnessing a rising tide of such a conception and a strong desire for its realization. This conception is inherently materialized in the national structure of Japan which orientates itself around the throne occupied by a single dynasty from time immemorial. . . .

In this fateful moment of human history, Japan is called upon to perform the significant mission of bringing together the moral principles of the East and the civilization of the West in perfect synthesis and harmony.[9]

With this call to a fascistic order, Konoye, like Matsuoka before him,[10] repudiated the materialistic mores of the West, based upon individualism, and sought to rally the people around the emperor in selfless devotion. For a man who had made some study of democracy, this was a paradoxical move, carrying him and those who could easily be propagandized into the camp of the army and away from an intelligent consideration of national interests through the agency of representative institutions. In making it, Konoye displayed the same weakness of character that permitted him to remain premier after the war in China had been resumed a few months earlier. His action was characteristic also of the emotionalism which underlies Japanese taciturnity, leading that great people at times to reckless decisions. In thus prostituting himself, Konoye became a responsible party to the ultimate trial by battle. With an opportunity to offer the people leadership toward peace and unparalleled prosperity, he accepted the militarists' slogans and the role of a reactionary nationalist and imperialist. He lowered himself so far as to draw the emperor into the coterie of expansionists by quoting the imperial message to the Diet of September 4, 1937: "It is our wish, in view of the present extraordinary situation, that our subjects, united in their faithful service to the state and in their devotion to the throne, will seek to achieve the purpose of the Empire." [11]

Prince Konoye was termed a "reformist"; he was one of a number of political and other figures who wanted to improve administration. The reformists were reactionary — they were critical of the parties, the Diet, and the civil service. They were opposed by supporters of the governmental *status quo*, who were in general progressives. The reformists besought Konoye to organize a national political society, but he bided his time. Premier Hiranuma was not a reformist. He saw no need to gild the lily of Japanese loyalty to the throne. Apparently he feared that a popular movement might develop out of reformist ideas which would not strengthen the imperial house but, like the French Revolution, destroy it.[12] Such an outcome was, of course, the opposite of what the reformists had in mind.

The flag of "spiritual mobilization" was raised to the masthead officially a second time on April 11, 1939, when the Hiranuma government declared that "with the development of a new phase of the [China] Affair in which long-term activities for spiritual as well as material construction have to be carried out in the midst of the most complicated, strained international relations, further enlightenment on the essential nature of the current emergency and new emphasis in the policies and program of this important movement have been felt [to be required] by its leaders and the government." [13] The statement explained: "The China Affair has now developed into the great task of constructing a New Order in East Asia." Consequently, "the necessity facing the Japanese nation today is to augment the entire national strength by combining all its traditional spiritual forces for the purpose of achieving the task of constructing a new East Asia in accordance with the spirit and ideal on which the Empire was founded, and for that of overcoming the world crisis in international relations." The people were to be fully informed upon actual conditions and underlying issues. They were to work harder and more unitedly in order that production of essential materials might be increased. They were to realize that they were engaged in a "free national movement."

In a statement published in June 1940 the Yonai government admitted "failures in the past caused by over-comprehensiveness and too great a variety of objectives" and announced that henceforth the program would be more practical and less theoretical. While reminding the people that the year 1940 was the 2600th anniversary of the founding of the empire, the government said that emphasis upon effective execution of the program would be sought by combining the two agencies which had been engaged in mobilizing the national spirit. These were the National Spiritual Mobilization Commission under the prime minister, a general planning body, and the Central Council of the National Spiritual Mobilization League, privately conducted but affiliated with the Commission. The new agency, not named in this statement, was to have the prime minister as president and the minister of home affairs and the president of the board of directors of the movement — the board was privately elected — as vice-presidents. Prefectural and local organs were to carry the movement to the grass roots; private institutions were to be "mobilized and given necessary assistance for local activities, thus ensuring and making the best of the popular character of the movement." [14] This humorless sentence reveals the government's consciousness of popular indifference and its own responsibility for pumping up enthusiasm in an impoverished nation.

Dissolution of the Parties

The Shakai Taishuto became the first party to prepare the way for the Imperial Rule Assistance Association (Taisei Yokusan Kai) by dissolving itself on July 3, 1940. That the least illiberal of the parties should be the first to disappear was logical since it was the most open to suspicion and most subject to nationalist pressure. Within a few days of this action the Federation of Labor, under threat of suppression, followed the party's example.[15] The Kuhara faction of the Seiyukai went out of existence on July 16, 1940,[16] the Kokumin Domei on July 27,[17] the Nakajima faction of the Seiyukai on July 30,[18] and the Minseito on August 15.[19] Organizations of a political character, whether or not they participated in elections, were expected to dissolve.[20] Accordingly the Tohokai and the Seinenkai (Young Men's Association) committed quasi-hara-kiri in October, i.e., they declared themselves converted into "cultural societies."[21] The patriotic societies were not required to disband, but were encouraged to participate in the Association. The parties in the House of Peers were not dissolved, though their contention that they were not political associations was not borne out in their activities.

The Imperial Rule Assistance Association

Prince Konoye resigned as president of the Privy Council on June 24, 1940, informing the public that he had decided to exert himself toward the formation of a new political organization. He declared emphatically that this must not be a mere regrouping of the old political parties, but rather a wholly new and idealistic national society.[22] Thus he checkmated the Seisen Kantetsu Giin Renmei (League of Diet Members for the Holy War), composed of approximately one hundred members, and other party leaders who had expressed themselves as favoring a great merger of the parties. Konoye was shrewd in this line of strategy, since the parties had never been popular organizations and were regarded by the people as greedy and conscienceless seekers for power. On the other hand the parties were opposed to militarist domination, and in choosing to oppose them, Konoye became an ally of the militarists.

Count Arima Yoriyasu, Konoye's first minister of agriculture and forestry, was a student of agriculture and of village life. He was president of the Central Bank for Cooperative Societies and of the Central Association of Cooperative Societies; he had founded an institute of research on agrarian conditions, and had fostered the patriotic Seinenkai. Arima, an intimate friend of Konoye, was a simon-pure bureaucrat who had not become embroiled with the politicians. He had been an early advocate of what was generally called the "new party movement." In his mind the proper models for it were the Fascist and National Socialist movements in Europe.[23] Like Konoye he desired an inchoate, malleable membership unaccustomed to working together against the army and the bureaucracy. Like him, also, he was capable of associating with men of every shade of opinion. By some he was even stigmatized as a leftist. The choice of Count Arima as the first director-general of the new society was an index of its true nature.

Prince Konoye interpreted his second call to the premiership in July 1940 as one "to realize first a new structure within the government itself." [24] He regretted that the critical position of the country did not permit the government to wait for a spontaneous people's movement, but he sought to inspire the belief that it was a "common undertaking of government and people." Again he rejected proposals for a political party, while acknowledging that "in Japan the parties stood up against the clannish and bureaucratic influences to make heard the voice of the people." Parties were, he said, instrumentalities of liberalism, with individual and sectional interests as their principal concern. They were, however, "often not in keeping with the essential function of the Diet, which is to assist the throne." [25] Obviously, a movement which repudiated liberalism was logical in repudiating political parties.

Konoye, however, refused to sanction a single all-embracing national party. His explanation for this attitude was convincing: "Such a political system takes a 'part' and makes of it a 'whole'; it considers the State and the Party as one and the same thing, and views any opposition to the Party as a revolt against the State; it renders permanent the ruling position of one Party, with the head of that Party as a permanent wielder of the power to govern. No matter what brilliant results such a system may have reaped in other lands, it is not acceptable in Japan as it is contrary to the basic principle of our national polity of 'One Sovereign over All.' In Japan, it is the privilege of every one of His Imperial Majesty's subjects to assist the Throne, and that privilege cannot be monopolized by the power of either a single person or a single party." [26]

Premier Konoye appointed a Preparatory Committee for the National Structure, which held its first meeting on August 28, 1940.

With the premier as chairman the Committee was composed of all members of the cabinet and twenty-six others drawn from the houses of the Diet, business, diplomacy, the patriotic societies, education, the press, and local public bodies.[27] A half-dozen influential members of the defunct major parties were included, sharing the doubtful honor of representation with the Tohokai and the Black Dragon Society. Officers of the *Asahi, Mainichi,* and *Yomiuri,* Tokyo's principal newspapers, accepted membership. The Committee was a body of able and successful men, well-selected to impress the people with the importance of the enterprise. On the other hand such sinister figures as Nakano Seigo and Colonel Hashimoto and the ebullient Shiratori Toshio were warning enough that moderate counsels would be unlikely to prevail.

After six meetings the Preparatory Committee agreed upon the organization of the Imperial Rule Assistance Association (Taisei Yokusan Kai).* On October 12, 1940, the IRAA began to function with Premier Konoye as president ex officio.[28] Count Arima was appointed director-general and as such was the administrative head. He headed the General Affairs Bureau and supervised other bureaus and departments. Within a few months the title of vice-president was substituted for that of director-general. The working units were enshrouded in a host of advisers, counselors, and directors, among them a number of party politicians. Many members of the Preparatory Committee reappeared as directors. These men were largely window dressing, yes-men who attended occasional meetings and lent dignity and weight to the Association. Prince Konoye admitted with regret that he had been unable to appoint many "new" men because of insufficient evidence upon the capacities of "unknowns." [29] Konoye's enormous prestige was revealed in his personal exercise of the appointive power throughout the organization.

Alongside the executive structure of the IRAA was established the Central People's Cooperation Congress (sometimes termed Council). A body of several hundred members, nominated by subordinate councils and appointed by the president, the Congress was not to decide upon national policy. Like the executive branch it was to promote the more united and effective working of the government. It had no direct contact with government agencies, including the Diet, but fed ideas to the executive branch. It was not a representative body,

* For organization chart see below, p. 71.

despite its name, but an additional advisory organ composed of bureaucrats, landowners, and businessmen, another anchor to windward.

The organization of the IRAA extended into the prefectures and the localities. Its general lines were the same, exhibiting executive departments and people's congresses. At the base of the pyramid the neighborhood associations (tonarigumi) were reinvigorated to "promote the spirit of neighborly solidarity, sharing mutually joys and sorrows." [30] All prefectural and local officers were appointed by the president. Many of the officers were governors, mayors, and village headmen. No popular elections were held at any level.

The hollowness of any pretense that the IRAA was an expression of a people's movement, spontaneous or otherwise, was revealed in the provisions for membership. Cynical indifference to personal dignity and suspicions of the loyalty of a people to whom loyalty is a religion stand out strikingly in these provisions, which are to be kept in mind when appraising the lamentable failure of the Association to hold the people's support:

The Association for Assisting the Throne, being a movement that concerns the entire nation, every individual of the Japanese race is by birthright qualified for membership in it in the widest sense of the term. Inasmuch, however, as the Association is a practical organization to play the role of prime mover in the National Movement, *the President of the Association designates for membership such persons from among the people as are ready to devote themselves to the cause, truly appreciating the fundamental principles of the Movement.* In consequence, mere payment of membership fees would never make a faithful member. The function of members of this Association is analogous to that of officers in other organizations. Since all the members cannot become officers in any organization, in the new Movement, which comprises the entire nation, all the people cannot become members of the Association. Such being the peculiar nature of its membership, and in view of the fact that the Association so organized plays the principal part in the Movement, it might lead some to imagine that the movement, despite its professedly nation-wide undertaking, is run by a small group of people and that the rest, therefore, have nothing to do with the affair. Of course this is not the case. The fact that one is not a member of the Association should by no means hinder one from working actively for the Movement.[31]

In essence, the members were the elite, the masses were "the majority of humankind, which is inert and cowardly." [32] However, one large segment of the population which might have been expected to join the Association in a body did not do so. That segment was composed of the armed services. While offering "positive and unreserved cooperation," War Minister Tojo, in a masterpiece of casuistry, explained that "since the central organ of this movement is essentially of a highly political character and is engaged in energetic political activities, the Army cannot consider it proper to allow men in active service to participate directly in the organization of this Movement, in the light of the principles upon which the Army was founded." [33] But high-ranking officers holding posts in the government might become advisers or counselors.

Apparently the army and navy preferred to keep clear of the Association and to continue their political activities from the lofty plane to which no civilian could aspire. But the early collapse of the public enthusiasm which greeted the new Association forced them to come to its aid. Their influence was exerted to obtain funds for it from the Diet and young reservists were ordered to accept membership. Premier Tojo Hideki, successor to Konoye as president of the IRAA, brought about the organization of the adjunct Imperial Rule Assistance Political Society (see p. 73), formed a supporting Youth Corps, and made use of local branches to stimulate production and other wartime efforts.

The Diet and the IRAA

Prince Konoye and his fellow reformists were able to demobilize the political parties with an ease that was deceiving. Since they could not get rid of the Diet it was their purpose to "reform" it. "It is characteristic," they urged, "of our constitutionalism that it [the Diet] is an institution for assisting the Throne. . . . In view of the grave situation confronting the nation today, especial stress must be placed on the cooperation between the Government and the Diet. . . . for this reason it is imperative that the very organization of the institution should be reformed." [34] Crudely paraphrased this meant that the Diet was to cease criticizing the cabinet and settle into the harness as a good team should, straining unitedly under the whip of the oligarchy. But the Diet declined this role. It continued to meet regularly throughout the war and to interpellate the government frequently and searchingly to the end. The dissolved parties found new means of asserting their views.

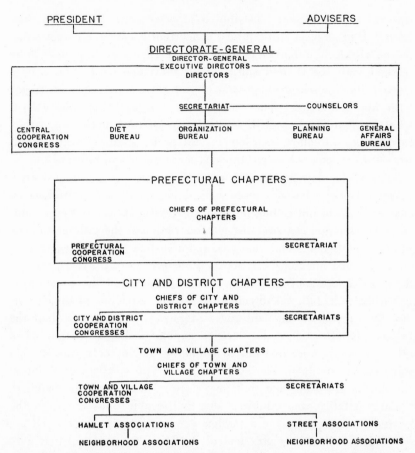

PRESIDENT   ADVISERS

DIRECTORATE-GENERAL
DIRECTOR-GENERAL
EXECUTIVE DIRECTORS
DIRECTORS

SECRETARIAT ———————— COUNSELORS

CENTRAL   DIET   ORGANIZATION   PLANNING   GENERAL
COOPERATION   BUREAU   BUREAU   BUREAU   AFFAIRS
CONGRESS   BUREAU

PREFECTURAL CHAPTERS

CHIEFS OF PREFECTURAL
CHAPTERS

PREFECTURAL   SECRETARIAT
COOPERATION
CONGRESS

CITY AND DISTRICT CHAPTERS

CHIEFS OF CITY AND
DISTRICT CHAPTERS

CITY AND DISTRICT   SECRETARIATS
COOPERATION
CONGRESSES

TOWN AND VILLAGE CHAPTERS

CHIEFS OF TOWN AND
VILLAGE CHAPTERS

TOWN AND VILLAGE   SECRETARIATS
COOPERATION
CONGRESSES

HAMLET ASSOCIATIONS   STREET ASSOCIATIONS

NEIGHBORHOOD ASSOCIATIONS   NEIGHBORHOOD ASSOCIATIONS

*Organization of the Imperial Rule Assistance Association**

To calm the fears of the House of Representatives that the IRAA Cooperation Congress would usurp the Diet's functions, a Diet bureau of one hundred members of the House of Representatives was established as an IRAA organ. Members of that House who belonged to the Association also were permitted to organize a Diet (Giin) Club and to divide the club members into groups for liaison with the cabinet ministries.[35] The club was designed to provide a forum of discussion replacing the caucuses of the submerged parties. Within it, however, the old party divisions could be discerned, and in meetings held to decide upon interpellations in the House, assignments to make

* From K. Takasugi, "The Diet under the New Political Structure," *Contemporary Japan*, IX (November 1940), 1410.

the interpellations were distributed in accordance with those divisions.[36] Had an election been held concurrently with the inauguration of the IRAA it is barely possible that a House of Representatives imbued with the desired spirit of self-effacement might have been elected. But the seasoned veterans of yesteryear were not to be caught with honeyed words. They understood full well that the IRAA, whatever it might be called, was in fact a political machine and they saw no reason to allow themselves — the professional political machinists — to be demoted to positions as mere oilers and wipers.

That the shadow parties still were effective was soon demonstrated. Premier Konoye found himself balked in attempts to introduce an electoral reform bill calling for a much smaller House of Representatives, much larger electoral districts, restriction of the suffrage to male heads of households and veterans, and a system by which candidates would be "recommended" by local *ad hoc* groups of thirty voters.[37] A noteworthy antagonism, which eventually prompted the government to withhold the bill, was directed against the restriction of the electorate. Diet members and editorial writers saw more clearly than the cabinet that the bill would dampen popular feeling at a time when other measures were in train to stimulate it. Not only was the old electoral law retained. The Diet received a year's extension of life on the mistaken assumption that new electoral lists would be required.

Party vitality was exhibited also in the objections raised to the government's request for 8 million yen to help finance the IRAA. Machida Chuji, former president of the Minseito, proposed that only 3 million yen be appropriated. After heated debate the amount requested was allowed, but the Association was subjected to criticism on such grounds as its political activities, its personnel, its mechanism, and its secrecy regarding financial operations. In short, this "reformist" enterprise was itself the target of reformers. The danger of a stalemate was real. Konoye was a Machiavelli, not a Bismarck, and his program called for blood-and-iron leadership. Yet it may be doubted that a Japanese Bismarck could have conjured a unified mass organization out of Japan's intricate and irregular pattern of parties, patriotic societies, clubs, religious sects, oyabun-kobun (chief-follower) gangs, and other well-established social units. Certainly the little Bismarcks who tried it after him were no more successful than Konoye.

Political Parties and the IRAA

The Imperial Rule Assistance Political Society (Taisei Yokusan Seiji Kai), created in May 1942 to complement the IRAA, must be evaluated as a concession by the reformists to the old-line political party leaders and their supporters. At its inception this was simply the Diet Bureau of the IRAA expanded to include all members of the Diet who desired to join. Outsiders were eligible to membership, but very few of them joined. It was designed to thwart efforts to revive the old parties or to create new ones in their image, and to provide a means, in the absence of parties, of nominating candidates for election to the House of Representatives. In the election of April 30, 1942, 381 of the successful 466 candidates were nominated by the IRAA. This election, since it was conducted under Premier General Tojo Hideki, produced what is called the "Tojo Diet." But the membership of this Diet contained the same subsurface parties and the same intraparty factions as its predecessor. As in any country conducting successful war, the national legislature was easily controlled by the executive. But as the fortunes of war changed, Tojo found his dispositions challenged. As early as April 1943 he felt it expedient to appoint two veteran party leaders to his cabinet. His successor, Premier Koiso, appointed two former Seiyukai stalwarts and one former Minseito partisan to ministries. The IRAPS may best be described as a compromise by which, in return for the recognition the society was given as the central political organ of the IRAA, the House of Representatives, operating through the shadow parties, was transformed from a zoo filled with snarling, biting malcontents into a beehive of cooperative workers.

General Abe Nobuyuki was the first president of the IRAPS. Under him were a varying number of departments headed by directors. Attached to each department were committees made up of Diet members. The Peers stood aloof, as they had from the IRAA, distrusting the whole enterprise as a danger to the throne. But without them the organization became the political instrument of the nationalist movement. Its committees propelled bills through the House, assigned interpellations to members, and made investigations of economic and social problems in preparation for legislation. It found no opportunity for electoral activities since no national, prefectural, or local elections were held after its creation. This monopoly of political functions reduced the IRAA to propaganda and public service activities. Efforts to prevent serious friction between the IRAA, the IRAPS, and the cabinet were in the hands of a Central Liaison Headquarters composed of representatives of the three bodies.

Dai Nippon Seiji Kai

Failure of the Association and its Political Society to maintain public morale in the face of military disaster led Tojo's successor, Premier General Koiso Kuniaki, to urge return to Konoye's plan of a single, streamlined organization, incorporating the Association, the Society, and the Youth Corps. He declared that the IRAPS had been unable to "move the people," that it appealed to them even less than the old parties had done. Koiso insisted that this outcome was the natural result of governmental failure to allow the people to organize the movement. But Admiral Kobayashi Seizo, the new president of IRAPS, opposed the merger and Koiso yielded. The result was unfavorable to the IRAA, which became less active as IRAPS assumed a heavier role. Members of the prefectural and of the six largest municipal assemblies, as well as prefectural officials, were invited to join the latter. None the less, both bodies were severely criticized for failure to "rouse the people to action," though what more the people could have added to the war effort was never demonstrated.[38] Increasing support was expressed for Koiso's proposal, the profound belief apparently being that all would be well if only the magic formula of organization could be discovered.

Out of confusion and desperation appeared a new society, the Dai Nippon Seiji Kai (Political Association of Great Japan) at the instance of the IRAPS. This did not occur without influential voices inside and outside the House of Representatives being raised in favor of restoring the old party system. Their arguments were that the single party had failed in its mission of exciting the popular imagination and that party rivalry would contribute to winning the war. Recrimination between the IRAPS, the IRAA, and the Young Men's Corps also hampered and delayed the birth of the new body.

Endorsed by Kobayashi, who resigned from the cabinet to devote himself to organizing the new body, the Dai Nippon Seiji Kai was inaugurated on March 30, 1945. That the deadening hand of militarist bureaucracy was guiding the sponsors of the Political Association was glaringly revealed in the nomination of seventy-year-old General

Minami Jiro for the presidency by a committee of six leaders of IRAA and IRAPS. Minami was a lesser Araki, differentiated from him principally by a less forthright nature and a wispy beard. He was a symbol of feudalism, his selection an omen of defeat. Other more capable men declined the office.

Dissolution of the IRAPS occurred with the advent of the Seiji Kai. The IRAA lived on until June 13, 1945. Suzuki's replacement of Koiso as premier on April 6, 1945, signified that Japan was preparing to admit defeat, but no indication of defeatism appeared in Seiji Kai propaganda. However, a group of thirty members of the House of Representatives, calling itself the Defense of the Fatherland Movement, which had been vigorous in demanding a more active agency, declined to join the Seiji Kai. This group was insignificant beside the 355 members of the House who joined the Association, thereby largely determining its character. Its scope of operations was nationwide, comprehending localities as well as the House of Representatives.

In structure the Seiji Kai resembled the IRAA. A president, a director-general, a secretary-general, and a number of advisers, counselors, and auditors composed the directorate. Under it, at Tokyo, were a political investigation committee, an organization department, a Diet committee, a House of Representatives department, and a practical enforcement department. Within the last-named office were sections in charge of activities related to propaganda, defense, civilian life, production, and youth. Special committees were added as need arose. Branch offices of the association were located in all prefectures. Thus the Seiji Kai resembled the IRAA rather than the IRAPS in functions as well as in organization.[39] It is best described as an attempt to combine the two and thereby obviate jealousy and controversy. Koiso's proposal was therefore implemented with Diet support. Such credit as may be due them for their rise to prominence in the frustrated spiritual mobilization movement is owing the members of the dissolved but animate political parties. At least, they had proved that they were an integral element of the Japanese political mélange. As in the past, unfortunately, they had compromised with principle in so doing.

Affiliates of the IRAA were dissolved with the parent body, among them the Men's Corps, Youth Corps, the Women's Association, the Young Men and Boys' Association, the Commercial Patriotic Service

The New Japan

Association, and the Home Front Patriotic Service Association. Other affiliates of a specialized nature, such as the patriotic associations of labor, agriculture, industry, and maritime workers, were retained. Members of the dissolved bodies were enrolled in the Civilian Volunteer Corps, which was described by Premier Suzuki as "an expansion of the Imperial Rule Assistance movement." But the propensities of the Japanese were not satisfied with one mass organization; they flowered in numerous new leagues and societies to declaim the spirit of last-man resistance, unaware of the government's moves to obtain a tolerable peace.

After the imperial broadcast of surrender on August 15, the Seiji Kai issued a statement urging the people to obey the emperor and to exert themselves in reconstruction measures. One month later, on September 14, 1945, the association was dissolved formally at a meeting in the chamber of the House of Representatives.[40] Within the early months of the Occupation all ultranationalist bodies were outlawed in accordance with directives of the Supreme Commander for the Allied Powers. The way was opened for the re-emergence of political parties. That party spirit and party cadres had remained lively while in eclipse was evidenced immediately by the revival of the old parties under new names and by the spate of new parties.[41]

Notes

[1] *Japan Weekly Chronicle*, February 24, 1938, pp. 234–235.

[2] *Ibid.*, March 3, 1938, pp. 266–270. However, the major parties discredited themselves by voting to expel Nishio Suehiro, prominent in the Shakai Taishuto, from the House of Representatives (*ibid.*, March 31, 1938, p. 395). Nishio had referred to Stalin indiscreetly.

[3] *Ibid.*, May 25, 1939, p. 624.

[4] *Ibid.*, December 28, 1939, p. 713. Kuhara outlined his totalitarian views in his article, "The Basis for a Single Party," *Contemporary Japan*, IX (July 1940), 811–817.

[5] *Japan Weekly Chronicle*, February 16, 1939, p. 188; March 2, p. 254. Abe had been attacked and injured by ruffians.

[6] *Japan Year Book*, 1940–1941, pp. 159–164.

[7] *Japan Weekly Chronicle*, February 8, 1940, pp. 154–155; February 29, p. 254; March 14, p. 301; S. Kashiwagi, "The Seventy-fifth Session of the Diet," *Jitsugyo no Nippon*, April 1940, excerpted in *Contemporary Japan*, IX (May 1940), 620–624.

[8] *Japan Weekly Chronicle*, March 28, 1940, p. 372; May 16, p. 576.

[9] *Tokyo Gazette*, October 1937, pp. 4–5.

[10] See above, p. 32.

[11] *Tokyo Gazette*, October 1937, p. 5. For a character sketch of Konoye see S. Takaishi, "Prince Konoye, a Portrait," *Contemporary Japan*, IX (August 1940), 984–993.

[12] T. Baba, "War and Parliamentary Politics," *Contemporary Japan*, VIII (April 1939), 183–193.

[12] *Tokyo Gazette*, June 1939, pp. 27–29.

[14] *Ibid.*, June 1940, pp. 465–467.

[15] *Japan Weekly Chronicle*, July 4, 1940, p. 13; July 18, p. 72.

[16] *Ibid.*, July 18, p. 76.

[17] *Ibid.*, August 1, p. 137.

[18] *Contemporary Japan*, IX (September 1940), 1218.

[19] *Japan Weekly Chronicle*, August 22, 1940, p. 229.

[20] *Tokyo Gazette*, November 1940, p. 191.

[21] *Japan Weekly Chronicle*, October 31, 1940, p. 540.

[22] *Ibid.*, June 27, 1940, p. 737.

[23] *Ibid.*, June 20, 1940, p. 700.

[24] *Tokyo Gazette*, August 1940, p. 46.

[25] *Ibid.*, October 1940, pp. 134–135.

[26] *Ibid.*, pp. 135–136. In effect, however, the Imperial Rule Assistance Association (IRAA) was manipulated as a political party.

[27] *Japan Weekly Chronicle*, August 29, 1940, p. 254.

[28] After much debate the decision was taken that the premier should hold his position in order to avoid the danger that a magnetic personality outside the government might, as head of the IRAA, become a rival in power to the premier. This decision was in accordance with Konoye's views.

[29] *Japan Weekly Chronicle*, November 28, 1940, p. 669.

[30] *Tokyo Gazette*, November 1940, p. 187.

[31] *Ibid.*, p. 188. The italics are not in the original.

[32] A. Hitler, *Mein Kampf*, English ed. (New York, 1939), p. 850.

[33] *Tokyo Gazette*, November 1940, p. 186.

[34] *Ibid.*, p. 190.

[35] *Contemporary Japan*, X (January 1941), 7.

[36] *Japan Weekly Chronicle*, January 16, 1941, p. 34.

[37] *Ibid.*, November 28, 1940, p. 668; December 12, 1940, p. 746; S. Fuki, "The Cabinet, the Diet, and the Taisei Yokusan Kai," *Contemporary Japan*, X (April 1941), 490.

[38] *New York Times*, January 19, 1945.

[39] Foreign Broadcast Intelligence Service, Federal Communications Commission, *Radio Report on the Far East*, No. 70, April 20, 1945, pp. BA1–BA3.

[40] SCAP, *Monthly Summation of Non-Military Activities in Japan and Korea*, No. 1, September–October 1945, Part 2, p. 2.

[41] See below, Chapters 6 and 19.

6

The Aftermath of Surrender

THE selection of Emperor Hirohito's cousin, General and Prince Higashi-kuni Naruhiko, as prime minister in Japan's hour of defeat was an interesting move. He was well known in political party circles as well as among his military colleagues and his associates at the imperial court. He enjoyed mixing with politicians, was somewhat indiscreet in his observations upon the proper functions of the emperor, and on one occasion, after pleading illness in order to escape from an official meeting, had turned up at a horse race. Although Higashi-kuni had studied military and political science in France and was regarded as antimilitarist, the selection of a career general and a symbol of the army's leadership to the debacle was a fitting choice; and the unprecedented appointment of a prince of the blood to the premiership relieved some less elevated but more responsible general from great embarrassment. The Prince also may have strengthened the imperial hand in obtaining obedience to rescripts calling for orderly acceptance of whatever hardships the surrender might entail. It is not to be supposed that the Supreme Command opposed the appointment of Higashi-kuni, although individual militarists sought to prevent the surrender.

Higashi-kuni was appointed premier on August 16, 1945. On the following day his cabinet was announced. It included the wartime list of ministries, but among the ministers there were but two generals and one admiral, the latter Admiral Yonai, navy minister in several cabinets and premier for six months of 1940. Shigemitsu returned to the Foreign Ministry and to the Ministry of Greater East Asia. Prince

The Aftermath of Surrender

Konoye appeared without portfolio, as did Ogata Taketora, vice-president of the *Asahi Shimbun* (Tokyo), who held the concurrent post of president of the Board of Information. The remaining members also were able and experienced men. The old parties were hardly represented by Nakajima Chikuhei, minister of munitions, at one time president of the Seiyukai. What was sought for the cabinet was expertness in fields that would require immediate constructive attention: agriculture, Sengoku Kotaro; transportation, Kohiyama Naoto; and finance, Tsushima Juichi.[1]

The Diet was convened in extra session for two days, September 4–5, 1945. In preparation for the revival of political party life, the premier and other ministers publicly encouraged "wholesome association" and "energetic and open discussion." General Minami Jiro resigned from the presidency of the Dai Nippon Seiji Kai, which, as previously noted, was dissolved shortly thereafter.[2] It had counted 377 members in the House of Representatives, the IRAPS 21; there were 26 Independents and 42 vacant seats.[3] No business was transacted during the brief session, but the emperor and the premier reported upon the surrender and its consequences.

The Japanese View of Surrender

Approximately a month elapsed between August 15, 1945, when the emperor's rescript announcing the acceptance by Japan of the Potsdam terms of surrender was broadcast to the Japanese people,* and September 10, when General MacArthur revealed salient aspects of the United States statement of initial postsurrender policy for Japan. During that period, it is apparent from various evidences, Japanese officials and others were either whistling to keep up their courage or testing the temper of the American government and Occupation authorities. It is clear they hoped for a very liberal interpretation of the terms of surrender, one amounting to little or no interference with or direction of the Japanese government's postwar program in any field, including the punishment of "war criminals." Indications of the attitude of highly placed Japanese toward the victor nations during the period are of greater reliability than those observable subsequently under Occupation controls.

* The rescript was broadcast from a recorded transcription. This procedure was designed to ensure against imperial mike-fright and the possibility of a military coup.

The imperial rescript of August 17, 1945, calling upon the troops to conform with the decision to make peace, contains no hint of a sense of error or of guilt. On the contrary the emperor exalts the military effort with these words: "At the same time we believe that the loyalty and achievements of you officers and men of the imperial forces will for all time be the quintessence of our nation." The premier's message to the troops on the same day congratulates them upon this imperial commendation. In his speech to the people the premier also voiced no regret other than to the emperor for having lost the war. He went so far as to suggest that the "mutual situations" in which the war left Japan, China, and East Asia generally would enable them to "encourage each other in the development of East Asia." He called on every citizen to endure the unendurable in order that the future of Japan might not be in enemy hands but that the "tradition of the Yamato race, which will surely rise, [may] be preserved and the wishes of His Imperial Majesty be fulfilled."[4]

Higashi-kuni's address to the Diet on September 5, 1945, began with the ambiguous statement that "the termination of the war has been brought about solely through the benevolence of our sovereign." He meant, no doubt, to explain Japan's decision to surrender, not the factors that called for a decision. His purpose was to interpret the surrender as a benevolent act, in contrast to the brutalities of war, characteristic of the emperor's mind, which was "as deep and broad as the ocean." Thereby he would deflect the people's wrath from the real authors of their misery and ignominy — the traditional mode of deceiving the people by associating Jacob's voice with Esau's hand. The premier had the effrontery, though he must have known better, to say that the Potsdam terms had been accepted with the understanding that they carried no prejudice to "the prerogatives of His Majesty as the sovereign ruler."[5]

Incidental indications of attitude were numerous. Among them were requests from the Foreign Ministry for "fair" treatment, declared to be the condition of future friendship; General Tojo's statement that history might repudiate affirmations upon the responsibility for the war; Higashi-kuni's suggestion that Americans forget Pearl Harbor in return for the forgetting by the Japanese of the atom bomb; the use of the egregious General Doihara to carry the army's offer to "cooperate" with the Occupation forces; and newspaper criticism of Occupation performance and personnel. Reports of these expressions provoked unjustifiable criticism in the United States of General MacArthur's leniency. Not until Japan was occupied militarily could Occupation policy begin to reveal a specific program. In view of these evidences and others that might be cited, however, it was illogical of the Public Relations Office of SCAP to appear to place confidence in the Japanese protestations of love, good will, and desire for a prolonged occupation that could be quoted after the nature of the regime came to be understood. Quite obviously such protestations were one means of obeying the imperial command to tolerate the intolerable in order to bring it more quickly to an end. To interpret them otherwise and to play them up while minimizing reports of less amiable sentiments were SCAP publicity tactics tending to deceive the American public.

Governmental Reorganization

A number of changes in the governmental system were made immediately, some upon Japanese initiative, others at the behest of the Occupation authorities.* Early in September 1945 the Imperial General Headquarters, the Ministry of Munitions, and the Ministry of Greater East Asia were abolished. The ministries of Agriculture and Commerce and of Transportation and Communications were divided along prewar lines, constituting four departments. *Pro tempore* the ministries of War and Navy were not included in the ban, but they were displaced on December 1, 1945, by the First (Army) and Second (Navy) Demobilization Boards.[6] Thus by the end of 1945 the ministries numbered eleven and were as follows: Prime Minister, Foreign Affairs, Home Affairs, Finance, Justice, Education, Communications, Transportation, Commerce and Industry, Agriculture and Forestry, and Welfare. Wartime advisory councils, boards, and commissions dropped away. The Board of Information, which had assumed an unnatural importance as a propaganda center, was abolished on December 31, 1945.[7]

Reorganization reached into the Imperial Household, doing away with the office of Lord Keeper of the Privy Seal on November 24, and thereby opening a direct channel between the cabinet and the emperor. The last Lord Keeper, Marquis Kido Koichi, was trans-

* For the program of the Occupation see below, Chapter 7.

ferred to Sugamo Prison as one of the defendants before the International Military Tribunal. Return to the prewar prefectural system also was early. Replacement of the eight regional administrations by regional bureaus was accomplished by ordinance early in November 1945 at Japanese initiative.

Although the Occupation dealt with Japanese administrative units informally through its many staff sections, the formal channel of communication was the Central Liaison Office. This office of the Japanese government was set up in the Foreign Ministry and for practical purposes it *was* the Foreign Ministry since Japan had no direct relations with foreign states during the Occupation.

The foreign minister was ex officio president of the Central Liaison Office and there were two vice-presidents. The office was composed of seven divisions: General Affairs, Political Affairs, Economic Affairs, Transportation and Communications, Accommodation, Repatriation, and Reparations.[8] A table of organization will indicate the functions of the several divisions:

1. Division of General Affairs
   a. General Affairs Section
   b. Liaison Section
2. Division of Political Affairs
   a. Political Section
   b. Military Section
   c. Home Affairs Section
   d. Education Section
   e. Judicial Section
3. Division of Economic Affairs
   a. Finance Section
   b. Economic Section
   c. Commerce and Industry Section
   d. Agriculture and Forestry Section
4. Division of Transportation and Communications
   a. Land Transportation Section
   b. Marine Transportation Section
   c. Communications Section
5. Division of Accommodation
   a. Procurement and General Affairs Section
   b. Accommodation and Labor Section
   c. Account Section
6. Division of Repatriation
   a. Overseas Japanese Section
   b. Home Affairs Section
   c. Special Property Section
7. Division of Reparations
   a. General Affairs Section
   b. Execution of Reparations Section
   c. Transport Section

Divisional and sectional titles are self-explanatory except for that of the "Division of Accommodation." That division was the connecting link between General Headquarters and Japanese housing and construction agencies, performing an extremely important function. Supplementing the Central Liaison Office were local offices in the principal cities, dealing directly with the military government units of the Occupation.

Shidehara Replaces Higashi-kuni

Prince Higashi-kuni resigned as prime minister on October 5, 1945, and his cabinet with him. The retirement was unexpected, although the cabinet had been regarded as transitional. General MacArthur's order of October 4, "Removal of Restrictions on Political, Civil and Religious Liberties," was given as the provocation for resignation. The order was not only a sweeping denunciation of existing laws and ordinances. It called also for the removal of Home Minister Yamazaki Iwao, the freeing of political prisoners, and the dissolution of all secret police organs. Apparently it offended the premier's princely sense of dignity, which had led him to assume an air of authority that the situation did not warrant.

Baron Shidehara accepted the emperor's invitation to become prime minister on October 9. At the age of seventy-three, he was remarkably vigorous and enjoyed an almost unrivaled position in the confidence of Western governments. He was known as a liberal bureaucrat and an able diplomat who had opposed war with China and remained out of politics throughout the war. He had been associated with leaders of the pre-1940 Minseito but had not joined the party. As son-in-law of Baron Iwasaki, founder of Mitsubishi, he represented the more internationalist strain in Japanese business.

Shidehara retained Mr. Yoshida as foreign minister, Admiral Yonai as minister of the navy, General Shimomura as minister of war, Iwata Chuzo as minister of justice, and Maeda Tamon as minister of education. Yoshida was a political twin of Shidehara. Maeda was a liberal bureaucrat without vigorous self-confidence. Other ministers were Ashida Hitoshi, welfare, who had served as vice-minister of foreign affairs and as wartime president of the *Japan Times*; Horikiri Zenjiro, home minister, at one time mayor of Tokyo; Tanaka Takeo, minister of transportation; Shibusawa Keizo, minister of finance; Matsumura Kenzo, agriculture and forestry; and Ogasawara Sankuro, commerce and industry. Thus it is apparent that the second postwar cabinet, like the first, was a group of exceptionally able career officials, and that Shidehara had not sought only notable liberal figures of the pre-1940 parties. A bureaucrat himself, he waited for the parties to revive rather than assisted them to revive. It was not long before they were demanding consideration.

Revival of Political Parties*

When the eighty-ninth session (extra) of the Diet convened on November 26, 1945, political party representation along pre-1940 lines had already come into being, adequate evidence that the IRAA and its successor had not wiped out but merely covered up party lines. Party names and members in the House of Representatives were Shimpoto (Progressive party), 277 members; Jiyuto (Liberal party), 44; Shakaito (Socialist party), 15;[9] and Independents (these formed an Unattached Club), 90. Forty seats were vacant.[10] The membership of the House was approximately the same as that of the eighty-eighth session, which means that the great majority of the 398 Seiji Kai and IRAPS members plumped for the Shimpoto, attracted possibly by the thought that the name "Progressive" would have an appeal for Americans. The Diet was the last wartime legislature, elected in 1942 and originally known as the Tojo Diet.

The Shimpoto was launched on November 16, 1945, at a meeting in Tokyo over which Mr. Saito Takao presided.[11] Saito was known to the few Americans who were observers of Japanese day-to-day politics as the member of the Minseito who had dared to criticize the militarists in 1940 for their treatment of China. Supporting him were Machida Chuji, a Minseito veteran of eighty-two who ultimately obtained the presidency of the party, Shimada Toshio, onetime Speaker of the House of Representatives, and others. It is fair to say that the Shimpoto was essentially a revival of the Minseito.

The Jiyuto, after an early indication of wider support, degenerated into a revived Seiyukai.[12] Hatoyama Ichiro, who dominated the new party until the purge removed him from politics, had been a Seiyukai wheel horse. Kono Ichiro, Ando Masazumi, and Matsuno Tsuruhei all had worked for many years in the Seiyukai vineyard. Two Minseito leaders originally inclined to join with Ashida Hitoshi and Katayama Tetsu, labor party executive, in organizing the Jiyuto, were Saito Takao and Kawasaki Katsu. Ashida stayed with the ambitious Hato-

* For a full treatment of postwar political parties see below, Chapters 19–21.

yama, but the other three turned to greener pastures. Hatoyama managed, however, to hold the support of an influential group of bureaucrats: Yoshida Shigeru, who became president of the Jiyuto, Okubo Tomejiro, and Arita Hachiro.

The Shakaito was a revival of the pre-1940 Social Mass party (Shakai Taishuto), the Labor party (Rodoto), and the Proletarian party (Musanto).[13] The variance of views among its constituent sources is reflected in the party, which was inaugurated on November 2, 1945. No president was elected. Instead Katayama Tetsu became Chief Secretary and Nishio Suehiro, a steel worker who had risen to be vice-president of the Trade Union Federation, chairman of the Central Executive Committee. Both officers were on the right wing of the Shakaito.

No Kyosanto (Communist party) representation appeared in the eighty-ninth session of the Diet. In December 1945 the party held a convention in Tokyo at which a Central Committee of seven men was elected.[14] Shiga Yoshio and Tokuda Kyuichi, both of whom were released from an imprisonment of seventeen years by Occupational directive, were the ablest and best known members of the Committee. Shiga was a journalist, Tokuda a lawyer. In January 1946 Nozaka Sanzo returned from Yenan, China, to constitute with Shiga and Tokuda a triumvirate of remarkable ability, cooperative spirit, and aggressive attitude toward the opportunities offered to labor by the defeat and Occupation.

No pre-1940 ancestor can be cited for the Kyodoto (Cooperative party), which was organized in December 1945 and became the Kyodo Minshuto (Cooperative Democratic party) in May 1946. Sengoku Toratero (Kotaro), minister of agriculture and forestry in the first postwar cabinet and a prominent dairyman, was instigator of this party. Another dairyman, the Hokkaido "Butter King," Kurasawa Torizo, collaborated at its birth. These men sought successfully to utilize the agricultural associations to influence elections. A third organizer, Funada Naka, and a fourth, Fujiyama Aiichiro, who were Chamber of Commerce officials, exerted their efforts to bring urban industrial and business support to the party.[15]

In addition to the five principal parties, some sixty minor groups emerged in Tokyo and some thirty in the provinces before the end of the year. The names of these groups indicate specific objectives, and their true purpose usually was to make favorable bargains for affiliating or merging with one of the stronger parties.[16] A number of men held memberships in more than one party. Between two and three hundred of the miniature parties, some with but one member, were fleetingly observable in the transition period.

Little doctrinal difference separated the Shimpoto and Jiyuto, both of whom were conservative at the outset. Both parties favored retention of the imperial headship of the state, increased power for the Diet, free enterprise in economic relations, and advancement of individual morality and respect for human rights. Both were supported by big business, landowners, tenant farmers, the majority of the bureaucracy, and a portion of the intelligentsia. The men who reorganized them were experienced politicians, and their association with one group rather than another was determined by personal, not doctrinal, considerations. None of the leaders was new, none was recognizable as representative of the new day of democracy which supposedly was dawning. Rather, the situation was comparable to a reawakening of the Republican party in the United States after a long sleep under the Democrats, or vice versa. The Kyodoto at origin may be classed with the Shimpoto and the Jiyuto as essentially representative of the *status quo* or pre-1940 parliamentarism rather than reformist in spirit and leadership.

The Socialists, gauged by two-thirds of their representation in the Diet sessions of 1946, were moderates to whom retention of the dynasty was acceptable. They were antibureaucratic and strongly democratic, favoring a broadened suffrage and the election of prefectural governors, mayors, and headmen by popular vote. They applied democracy to industrial, agricultural, and cultural fields, but went beyond it in advocating public ownership of essential industries and financial institutions. Thus the Shakaito was well suited to cooperation with the Occupation administration in its readiness to discard traditional controls, but tended to arouse fears because of its socialistic ideals.

Communism's few but experienced and extremely able leaders stood alone for eradication of the imperial figurehead from the government. The Kyosanto sought a united front against reactionary forces and advocated parliamentary rather than revolutionary procedures to attain a socialistic order. Full-fledged communism was not preached.

The Aftermath of Surrender

The Kyosanto differed from the Shakaito less in avowed doctrine than in inner spirit. To themselves, at least, they were the only sincere fighters for democracy, the only party that understood the necessity of destroying feudal and bureaucratic controls in government, industry, and agriculture. Upon this basis they sought to infiltrate labor unions and agricultural societies, claiming to offer them the leadership best qualified to obtain success for their programs. The ultimate goal was a national democratic-socialist front led by the Kyosanto. Not at all strangely, the other parties failed to appreciate or to take advantage of the Kyosanto's hypocritically self-sacrificing attitude.

The Eighty-ninth Diet Session

Occupation prime ministers were in an unenviable position before the Diet. It was their duty to pretend that they were heads of government, that the policies they were proposing were Japanese policies. At the same time they were required not to depreciate the ideas and ideals of the occupying administrators. They might refer to the "difficult conditions" that prevailed, and that phrase or an equivalent came to carry meanings hitherto unsuspected. The members knew that it was the government's way of explaining that the Occupation was insistent upon the matter in hand, yet they could not always be sure that the government was not using this device for purposes of its own.

Emperor Hirohito received the traditional homage as he opened the eighty-ninth (extra) session. The House of Representatives replied to his brief address as follows:

We, the subjects, are deeply moved when we reverently reflect that a ceremony opening the 89th session of the Imperial Diet was conducted in the presence of His Majesty and a gracious Imperial message was granted.

We, the subjects, are determined to comply humbly with His Majesty's wishes and to fulfill for the people, in return for their trust, the duty of helping to conduct state affairs with careful deliberation.[17]

The national deference to dynasticism and Shinto was shared by Shidehara in his address to the House of Representatives at the same session. He expressed his thanks for appointment as premier and then said: "His Imperial Majesty on November 13 and 14 paid

87

homage at the Grand Shrines of Ise, at Umeji and Momoyama Mausoleums, and at Tama Mausoleum. We are informed that His Majesty reported the termination of the war to our ancestors. We are informed that the sight of the people paying their deep respect to His Majesty deeply moved the Emperor."

On the other hand it was evident that the parties welcomed their renewed opportunity to heckle the members of the cabinet. Shidehara evoked derisive laughter when he evaded the question put by Saito Takao regarding the government's attitude toward the responsibility of Prince Konoye and others for the war. A member shouted, "That's the bureaucrat for you!" when the premier admitted that the cabinet had as yet no concrete proposals for democratizing the government. General Shimomura, minister of war, received loud applause when he replied to another interpellation of Mr. Saito on responsibility for the war. Shimomura's reply seemed to be frank: "Militarism arose because the military men, especially those who were in leading positions, misunderstood many things. The worst thing was that military men got involved in politics. Today we face defeat, and I do not know just how to apologize to the people. All I can say is that I sincerely apologize to the people of the nation."[18] The minister apologized for defeat. By inference he also apologized for the war. Kyodo News Agency, in reporting his courageous utterance, did not explain its remark that "his words transcended the ordinary Diet debates and carried historic significance." Was the samurai singing the swan song of his order or pledging it to redeem itself?

Foreign Minister Yoshida rasped the sensitive skin of representatives when he gave an evasive reply to a member's question and stated that members wishing fuller data might call at his office. He did not deserve the tumultuous reaction, since the question involved confidential foreign relations, but the members chose to regard themselves as insulted, some of them denouncing Yoshida as undemocratic and bureaucratic — a healthy if theatrical gesture. Yoshida apologized.[19]

Important statutes passed during the session were the revised election law for the House of Representatives, an Agricultural Lands Adjustment Law, and a Labor Union Law, all prompted by MacArthur or his aids. The emperor issued a rescript of dissolution on December 18, 1945, bringing to an end the life of the last wartime Diet.

The Aftermath of Surrender

Notes

[1] Foreign Broadcast Intelligence Service (FBIS), Federal Communications Commission, *Radio Report on the Far East*, No. 80, August 25, 1945, p. B25.

[2] SCAP, *Monthly Summation of Non-Military Activities in Japan and Korea*, No. 1, September–October 1945, Part 2, p. 2.

[3] *New York Times*, September 4, 1945.

[4] *Ibid.*, August 18, 1945.

[5] *Ibid.*, September 6, 1945.

[6] SCAP, *Monthly Summation*, No. 2, November 1945, Part 2, p. 4. These bureaus were known originally as ministries.

[7] *Ibid.*, No. 3, December 1945, p. 28.

[8] S. Hasegawa, "How Japan's Government Functions," *Nippon Times Magazine*, December 7, 1946, p. 1; also GHQ, SCAP, Government Section, "Report on the Organization of the Japanese Government" (as of November 1, 1946), pp. 8–11.

[9] The English translation which the Socialists preferred for *Shakaito* was "Social Democratic party." This is inaccurate, as they knew, but was used in order not to prejudice the party in American minds. *Shakaito* — literally Social party — was used rather than *Shakai Minshuto* — Social Democratic party — in order to dissociate the party from the prewar *Shakai Minshuto*.

[10] SCAP, *Monthly Summation*, No. 2, November 1945, Part 2, p. 1.

[11] H. E. Wildes, "Japanese Political Parties," Report of Government Section, SCAP, June 22, 1946 (mimeographed).

[12] *Ibid.*, June 20, 1946.

[13] *Ibid.*, June 29, 1946.

[14] *Ibid.*, July 24, 1946.

[15] *Ibid.*, July 15, 1946.

[16] SCAP, *Monthly Summation*, No. 3, December 1945, p. 25.

[17] FBIS, *Radio Report on the Far East*, November 28, 1945, p. BA2.

[18] *Ibid.*, November 29, 1945, p. BA1.

[19] *Ibid.*, November 30, 1945, pp. BA4–BA5.

7

Occupation Policy and Administration

APPRAISALS of the accomplishment of the Occupation in Japan remind one of the fable of the blind men and the elephant: each appraiser is prone to judge the whole of an extensive, many-sided enterprise by a part.[1] Whether he judges the Occupation from the outside or as a participant, he forms his judgment on the basis of his own criteria and background of knowledge. The resulting estimates — this one among them — may be unduly favorable or may fail to do justice to an undertaking which, whatever its faults, had high motives and was conscientiously administered. Official releases were invariably incomplete and self-satisfied. Personal observation and study, however, have led one of the authors to conclude, regretfully, that the Occupation's basic objective — the advancement of democratic ideals and institutions — was realized to only a minor degree.

Occupation administration was conducted by General Douglas MacArthur and an almost wholly American staff. Advisory to him in Tokyo, the Allied Council of four, one each from Britain, Russia, China, and the United States, was not an important body. It was for a time a critic and to some degree a check, but not a continuous and confident consultant. Subsequently most of its meetings were adjourned without any discussion. General MacArthur was not, however, solely an administrator. In a major sense he determined policy. In some instances he did so in the absence of policy directives from

NOTE. This chapter, in slightly different form, was published in the *Political Quarterly* (London), XXI (1950), 29–39.

The abbreviation "SCAP" was used to denote both the "Supreme Commander for the Allied Powers" and the "Supreme Command." In this chapter it denotes the latter.

Washington. In others he interpreted such directives as he saw fit. The Far Eastern Commission in Washington was unable to exert its full authority in relations with the Supreme Commander, who was, in many matters, a law unto himself. Why the FEC and the American government acquiesced in this self-enlargement they have not explained. The American people, having little information upon the conduct and cost of the Occupation, have not yet asked for an explanation.

American policy was in process of formulation in the Departments of State, War, and Navy, and in other U.S. agencies before the end of the war. It embodied the views of men who knew Japan well. At the end of the war the most influential of these men were no longer in office, but their successors revised their draft of policy and radioed it to Japan on August 29, 1945.[2] In the Occupation program as it evolved, it would be impossible to read the comparatively general and flexible lines of the "U.S. Initial Post-Surrender Policy for Japan." It is impossible also to find the program in subsequent directives from Washington. On the contrary, Washington is found to be asking SCAP for information, sometimes in a plaintive tone. It is apparent, therefore, that the original policy was expanded and modified in the process of interpretation and implementation in Tokyo.

In this process the representative of the Department of State in Tokyo had little or no share. General MacArthur resided in the American Embassy, while the chief of the Diplomatic Section — one of many subdivisions of General Headquarters — lived in an unpretentious house near by. Their offices were in different buildings located several blocks apart. In practice the diplomatic representative was merely MacArthur's mouthpiece in the Allied Council, not his confrère in the consideration of policy. This relation reflects the anomalous position of the State Department in Occupation policy and administration. It was not a desirable one, nor one in proper accord with the responsibilities of our foreign office.

Occupation administration in Japan was military administration. It follows that decisions upon nonmilitary questions — and these were the important ones — were made by military officers. Although there were many able civilians in General Headquarters, and some sections in which their ideas were influential, in other sections their knowledge, ability, and enthusiastic interest often were well recompensed but poorly utilized. Conflicting views on fundamental issues and anxiety for recognition of accomplishment among the heads of sections complicated SCAP's tremendous problem of indirect rule. An officer's fear of being criticized for inadvertently stepping across sectional lines was paralleled by an alertness to challenge a brother officer or one of his subordinates for such a step. This attitude at times was carried to the point where exchange of information between and within sections was impeded. The staff members of different sections did not mingle freely with one another in the discussion of common problems. There was no sense of being members of a community engaged in a great enterprise, though a man of MacArthur's magnetism and rhetorical powers might easily have stimulated a strong consciousness of individual importance and collective responsibility in so loyal and competent a body. That he did not seek to do so is the more strange in view of his evident concern for the well-being and comfort of occupying personnel.

The most devoted of bilateral — i.e., military-civilian — bureaucracies, however, could not have overcome the ignorance of Japanese culture and the lack of experience in civilian administration inherent in a military control of decisions. What was needed, if the Occupation was to be a tutorial as well as a military mission, was the separation of the two functions and the restriction of military men to the latter. Once it was demonstrated — as it was within six months — that the Japanese people had accepted defeat and were prepared, if treated fairly, to endure its consequences, this separation became feasible. With a civil administrator and staff equal in status to the military staff, advisory tutelage in political, economic, social, and scientific reorganization might have proceeded more sensitively and with a greater assurance of permanent results.

Students of Japanese history have noted the ironical resemblance between the feudal shogunate and the regime of the Occupation. The parallel is not perfect, since the shogunate administered as well as ruled, but the central feature in both systems was military control. Fear rather than confidence was the sanction of the military police. The Japanese understood this system, an understanding that may have contributed to their acceptance of it. But it can hardly have been what they expected of democratic occupiers. Nor could it represent effectively what it did not itself express. Not the spirit of its operation, which was lenient and humane and generous to an extraordinary degree, but the system itself was the handicap to accomplishment of the Occupation's principal aim.

Occupation policy touched many sectors of Japanese culture: the family, religion, government, business and industry, education, science, journalism, public health, and others. It did not alter the direction of traffic nor prescribe aesthetic standards. It released Communist party leaders who had spent seventeen years in prison, legalized freedom of speech, press, and assembly, and encouraged the reorganization of the war-strangled political parties and labor organizations. It enfranchised women, bringing a much needed sense of humor into Japanese politics. It divorced religion from the state and dislodged the imperial house from the family tree of Amaterasu-O-Mikami. It revised or replaced textbooks and instructed reporters in the ethics of their craft. It wrote a new constitution, new laws of government, new civil and criminal codes. It embarked upon the dissolution of the family cartels — *zaibatsu* — and compelled the government to redistribute a great part of the agricultural land. It swept some 200,000 men out of offices in the state, the schools, business, and political parties. These and many other actions were taken in furtherance of the objectives declared by President Truman: (1) "to insure that Japan will not again become a menace to the United States or to the peace and security of the world"; (2) "to bring about the eventual establishment of a peaceful and responsible government" conforming "as closely as may be to principles of democratic self-government."

Let it be admitted that the reformist or tutorial phase of Occupation policy was at least a labor for Hercules, at most a utopian dream. Only Americans would have undertaken it. That we did so is at once a tribute to our physical vigor, to our zeal as missionaries of democracy, and a demonstration of our self-confidence, rooted in good intentions, inexperience, and inadequate study. Startling is the nonchalance with which a so recently isolationist America set out to be the mentor of older civilizations. Having fought two wars to save the world *for* democracy, she now attempted to save it *with* democracy. No greater conception is possible to the minds of men, and Americans are responsive to exponents of bigger and better ideas when they are to be carried out by Americans. We refuse to acknowledge that power can corrupt our leaders, while being highly sensitive to that danger in the leaders of even friendly nations. We are impatient for results and receptive to optimistic evaluations of accomplishment. We are willing to place enormous responsibility upon individuals who represent, we believe, our way of life. Thus we assume immeasurable burdens without public debate, and we are indisposed to question the wisdom of our original action or the measures taken to implement it.

In the political realm, the Occupation program confused the Japanese by its aggressive liberalism in legislation and its tolerance of conservatism in politics and administration. At Potsdam we engaged to withdraw our forces "as soon as there has been established *in accordance with the freely expressed will of the Japanese people* a peacefully inclined and responsible government" (italics added). Reference to this statement occurred a number of times in the course of the Diet's discussion of the draft constitution, each time in a critical vein.[3] Americans should not have expected the Japanese to accept the sophistry that they were free to reject a document prepared in the main in Government Section and enthusiastically endorsed by SCAP. One must ask, Why the hurry? The Meiji constitution was not found to be a bar to the issuance of directives on civil rights or to the enfranchisement of women. With the emperor at its beck and call SCAP had no need to worry over the choice of cabinet ministers or the direction of their responsibility. For a paper accomplishment to signalize the rapid progress of Japanese democracy SCAP risked the reputation of American democracy and the good will of Japanese intellectuals, to whom the imposition of a constitution by foreign authors was well-nigh intolerable. It is a remarkable fact that the most fundamental legal change brought about by the Occupation was the least seriously studied despite the great concern of the Far Eastern Commission that the Potsdam promise should be honored.

The new constitution and accompanying laws for the reform of the Imperial House, the Diet, the cabinet, the civil service, the courts, and local government all are revolutionary in varying degrees. Have they affected the conduct of government? What is their prospect of survival? To the second question there is no confident answer now. All that can be suggested is that survival will depend upon (a) the inertia in their favor that existed when the war ended, and (b) the strength of the opposition, now that the Occupation has ended. It was possible during the Occupation to adduce some evidence helpful toward answering the first question. But one would be foolhardy to believe that he could go beyond very tentative conclusions. The Japanese were not saying what they thought. In their actions they were exhibiting the restraint of a mature culture, capable of enduring and waiting. But it can hardly be doubted that for them the Occupation was an interlude, not the play.

American policy as it was worked out left the administration of their government to the Japanese, subject to supervision and occasional intervention. Save for the purge of high-level officials, politicians, and businessmen — the effect of which probably was not significant in politics — SCAP observed consistently the principle that distinguished the occupation of Japan from that of Germany. It follows that a wide gulf developed between legislation and administration. And since laws are static whereas politics are dynamic, SCAP was operating through Japanese officials who were openly or secretly inhospitable to the new laws and ever alert to delay their implementation. The failure to find a satisfactory modus vivendi with the labor movement threw SCAP into an apparent reliance upon political elements fearful of change. This unenviable position between the two stools of radical legislation and conservative administration grew less comfortable with time.

Liberalism proved a heady wine to the labor leaders of Japan. Their hopes were high. Unionization progressed rapidly. The Socialist party attracted support beyond its dreams. But the party was not unified, was inexperienced, and was opposing revived party machines with more know-how and wider rootage in the electorate. The party sought to represent labor but proved to be too slow a vehicle for it, dependent as the parties are upon the deliberate procedures of a parliament accustomed to executive control. Labor did not find the reform legislation directly and immediately helpful to it. It resorted to more dramatic methods — huge parades, mass meetings, demonstrations before the premier's residence, strikes, and the unique device of "production control," i.e., the usurping of industrial management until its demands were met. A general strike of government workers was called for February 1, 1947. At this point a provision of the American statement of policy previously cited met its first test: "Changes in the form of government initiated by the Japanese people or government in the direction of modifying the feudal and authoritarian tendencies are to be permitted and favored. In the event that the effectuation of such changes involves the use of force by the Japanese people or government against persons opposed thereto, the Supreme Commander should intervene only where necessary to ensure the security of his forces and the attainment of all other objectives of the occupation." General MacArthur forbade the strike and his order was obeyed.

SCAP eased the blow by directing Premier Yoshida, the bête noire of labor, to hold an election. The Socialists were returned with the largest representation. Their chairman, Mr. Katayama, was elected premier but was obliged — in order to obtain a majority in the House of Representatives — to form a coalition cabinet with the Democrats, whose leader, Baron Shidehara, a near-replica of Mr. Yoshida, was so disturbed by the unpleasant contact that he left his party. Katayama went to the length of denying cabinet posts to his own left wing. In such a bargain, socialist principles were sacrificed to the appearance of power. Katayama's legislative program failed dismally, and he resigned within eight months. In the third election the Socialists lost two-thirds of their seats, Katayama himself being defeated by a Communist. Thus the party of labor, the party most sympathetic to SCAP's reform program, was overwhelmed by Yoshida's Minshu-Jiyuto (Democratic-Liberal party). The opponents of reform — the leftist direct actionists and the rightest traditionalists — triumphed over the moderate socialists. Undoubtedly a factor in the setback was Katayama's sincere effort to accommodate his party's ideas to those of the Occupation.

Could this *détente* have been prevented by SCAP? Undoubtedly MacArthur in all sincerity complimented Japan upon obtaining in Katayama a "Christian" prime minister, but did not this gesture indicate to the ultrasensitive Japanese that Katayama's religion — professed by a very small number of them — was more acceptable to SCAP than his party? How were they to reconcile an insistence upon laws to dissolve big business and to break up big estates with a hands-off, if not a deprecatory, attitude toward the one major Japanese party that favored these laws? A more wholehearted expression of satisfaction — comparable, for example, to the support of the draft constitution — and subsequent friendly counsel might have furthered the evolution of a genuinely liberal party. It may well be that General MacArthur was strongly influenced on this crucial issue by American conservatism; but it may well be also that, if he had wished, he could have presented the issue to the American public so effectively that he would have won for himself the freedom of action that the situation demanded.

General MacArthur, in approving Prime Minister Yoshida's victory in the January election of 1949, did not deplore the fact that Yoshida was not of the Christian faith. His approbation reflected instead his own conservatism: "The people of the free world everywhere can take satisfaction in this enthusiastic and orderly Japanese election, which, at this critical moment in Asiatic history, has given a clear and decisive mandate for the conservative philosophy of government." [4] This pat on the back for Yoshida was given after its recipient had returned, in effect, to the prewar system by inducing the House of Representatives to vote nonconfidence in him in order that he might dissolve it, hold a new election, and strengthen his position by increasing his plurality. When MacArthur's comments upon Katayama and Yoshida are compared, they assist in explaining Yoshida's retention of the premiership from 1948 to 1954.

SCAP is entitled to credit for the release of political prisoners and for permitting free speech and a free press within the limits of a censorship which, if sometimes applied arbitrarily and stupidly, was unavoidable. It is not surprising that MacArthur should have resented the advantage taken of their freedom by the Communists. On the other hand, neither is it surprising that they should have taken it. Nor that Russia, denounced by him as "an inciter of disorder and violence in an otherwise orderly Japanese society," [5] should have seized every opportunity to win devotees by criticisms of his program. Communism gives no quarter and has found a devastated industrial economy fertile ground for direct action. It cannot be answered with words or with guns. The workers of Japan must believe that their legitimate grievances are to be remedied or they will turn in greater numbers to violent leadership and action. A reservoir of discharged soldiers, if unemployed and desperate, provides a good supply of shock troops for revolt.

The Japanese scene at the end of the Occupation was not wholly dark, nor was optimism lacking. Land reform had found favor in the countryside, and the business community had taken our unilateral decision to cancel additional reparations as a vote of confidence. There was evidence that the Diet was enjoying its powers and was finding ways to thwart officialism. Labor had by no means cast its lot with the Communists.

The tactics of red leaders — threats, strikes, sabotage, and violence toward persons and property — had not been approved by labor, despite the discharge of some 400,000 government workers and an unrevealed number of others in private industries under the "austerity program" then being insisted upon. Apparently, however, Premier Yoshida anticipated a renewed leftist offensive. The Communists in the national service were the first to be discharged. These men were, as a result of the discharge, forced out of offices in the labor organizations. Mr. Yoshida demanded also that national control of the entire police system be reestablished and that the police force be enlarged and authorized to revive prewar agencies and methods.

Evidence regarding instances of police treatment of individual nonconformists, and of supporting action by Occupation military police and courts, is not available. But the trend of politics and administration unmistakably was away from announced Occupation principles and toward the older system of bureaucratic government buttressed by the police and *gendarmerie*. After nearly six years of Occupation enlightenment it was baffling to find Japanese editors bowing and scraping in praise of the government for ordering the dissolution of Korean "terroristic" organizations in Japan. Without examination of cases the editorial tendency was to accept the program of repression, in the belief that it had SCAP's approval. "The vast majority of the Japanese people and Korean residents are law-abiding citizens eager *to protect the democratic ideals granted the new Japan*" (italics added), wrote the *Nippon Times* on September 10, 1949. Shades of Meiji! Unless the editor was pulling someone's leg, this solemn gratitude for the "grant" of democratic ideals called for tears. There was a plethora of lip service to democracy, but the old monotonous, smothering readiness to conform when bureaucracy snapped its fingers was still dominant. Until this readiness is replaced by the resistant spirit of free inquiry, criticism, and refusal to be frightened into submission, organized in political parties for effective action, let us not congratulate ourselves upon the "smoothness" of the Occupation. MacArthur and his colleagues will live in history to the extent that they have stimulated rather than stultified that spirit.

Notes

[1] A selected list of books on the Occupation of Japan: W. M. Ball, *Japan: Enemy or Ally?* (New York, 1949); R. Brines, *MacArthur's Japan* (Philadelphia, 1948); William Costello, *Democracy vs Feudalism in Post-War Japan* (Tokyo, 1948); R. A. Fearey, *Occupation of Japan, Second Phase* (New York, 1950); Mark Gayn, *Japan Diary* (New York, 1948); E. M. Martin, *The Allied Occupation of Japan* (Stanford, 1948); SCAP, *Political Reorientation of Japan, I, II* (Washington, 1949); R. B. Textor, *Failure in Japan* (New York, 1951); and H. E. Wildes, *Typhoon in Tokyo* (New York, 1954).

[2] *Department of State Bulletin*, September 23, 1945, pp. 423–427.

[3] See below, Chapters 10 and 11.

[4] *New York Times*, January 25, 1949.

[5] *Nippon Times*, June 14, 1949.

8

The Great Purge

THE purge of ultranationalist elements from the political and social system of Japan has its legal bases in the Japanese government ordinances issued in compliance with SCAPIN 550 (AG 091.1, January 4, 1946),[1] subject: "Removal and Exclusion of Undesirable Personnel from Public Office." An earlier memorandum, SCAPIN 93 (October 4, 1945), had directed the removal from office of high officials in the police administration. Subsequent expansion of the scope of the purge was accomplished by the application of SCAPIN 550 to additional categories of offices. SCAPIN 550 was issued in order to carry out the provision of the Potsdam Proclamation that "There must be eliminated for all time the authority and influence of those who have deceived and misled the people of Japan into embarking on world conquest, for we insist that a new order of peace, security and justice will be impossible until irresponsible militarism is driven from the world."[2] The joint statement of the State, War, and Navy Departments, "U.S. Initial Post-Surrender Policy for Japan," contained the explicit provision that "Persons who have been active exponents of militarism and militant nationalism will be removed from public office and from any other position of public or substantial private responsibility."[3]

Appendix A of SCAPIN 550 listed seven "Removal and Exclusion Categories":

A. War criminals.

NOTE. This chapter, in slightly different form, was published in *Pacific Affairs*, XX (1947), 299–308.

B. Career military and naval personnel, special police, and officials of the war ministries.

C. Influential members of ultranationalistic, terroristic, or secret patriotic societies.

D. Persons influential in the activities of the Imperial Rule Assistance Association (*Taisei Yokusan Kai*), the Imperial Rule Assistance Political Society (*Yokusan Seiji Kai*), and the Political Association of Great Japan (*Dai Nippon Seiji Kai*).

E. Officers of financial and development organizations involved in Japanese expansion.

F. Governors of occupied territories.

G. Additional militarists and ultranationalists.

Under each category were listed offices, or descriptions of persons, that fell within it. Except under Category E, which affected only persons in office between July 7, 1937, and September 2, 1945, the directive was made operative without limitations of time.

The First Phase

The application of the resulting ordinances to national officials and other persons of national prominence constituted the first phase of the purge. Ouster from national office or prohibition from appointment or election to it was the lot of anyone whom the relevant screening agency deemed to fall within one of the seven categories. He was also deprived of pension rights and similar emoluments or benefits. Except for elective members of the Diet, all officials involved were appointive. The objects (popularly termed "purgees") of this first phase of the purge were, in the main, professional politicians and bureaucrats — legislators, administrators, and judges. Screening was made the responsibility of Japanese government ministries or other agencies and was subject to review and reversal by SCAP. All persons who were incumbents of, and all future applicants for, public office or government service were required to fill out questionnaires to assist the screening committees. While it is apparent that the use of officials of long standing on screening committees opened the way to self-protection and discrimination, as members of out-of-office political parties contended, there seemed to be no other practicable procedure, and it was anticipated that the penalties provided for evasion of the directive and implementing ordinances would ensure honest action.

The New Japan

On September 15, 1946, the Japanese government furnished the following report of action taken:

Report on the Purge as of September 15, 1946

Number of persons screened	7,769
Number of persons passed	6,875
Number of persons barred	894

Number of Persons Screened, Passed, and Barred for Each Ministry or Other Organization

Name of Organization	Screened	Passed	Barred
Privy Council	28	19	9
House of Peers	518	346	172
House of Representatives	465	455	10
Cabinet Office	91	82	9
Foreign Affairs Ministry	110	88	22
Home Affairs Ministry	514	170	344
Finance Ministry	52	46	6
Justice Ministry	232	195	37
Education Ministry	1,712	1,660	52 [4]
Welfare Ministry	85	62	23
Agriculture and Forestry Ministry	75	57	18
Commerce and Industry Ministry	53	39	14
Transportation Ministry	125	117	8
Communications Ministry	4	4	0
Other Organizations	2,151	2,019	132
Electors of "High Tax Paying" Members of House of Peers	1,554	1,516	38
Total	7,769	6,875	894

Expanding the Purge

The purge entered its second phase with the issuance of four imperial ordinances and a supplementary cabinet ordinance on January 4, 1947.[5] The scope of these ordinances was extremely wide, embracing specified offices of numerous private corporations and companies as well as political party offices and a large number of national, prefectural, and local public offices. The sweep of the second dragnet can best be appreciated through a survey of the offices to which it applied. All these offices became, by virtue of the ordinances, "public" offices. To name them would require unavailable space, but they may be grouped as follows:

1. National offices of first-grade civil service rank.

2. Membership in the Diet.

3. Membership in national or prefectural commissions or committees established by law or ordinances; in the case of the Land Committees municipal and other local memberships were included in the purge.

4. Offices in prefectures, from the governorship to poll superintendency, including membership in the assemblies.

5. Offices in cities, towns, and villages, from the mayoralty to poll superintendency, including membership in the assemblies.

6. Offices of chiefs of community groups (*chonaikai* and *burakukai*). (The intolerable burden involved in screening prompted the government to abolish these associations as of March 31, 1947.)

7. Offices in special companies, banks, or corporations in which the national government or a governmental unit is the chief stockholder.

8. Offices in 78 organizations established under special legislation, including the Lawyers Society (*Bengoshi Kai*), the Central Horse Affairs Society (*Chuo Baji Kai*), and the Fishing Association (*Gyogyo Kai*); many of these were governmentally subsidized.

9. Offices in 21 political parties, from the chairmanship to membership on the executive board.

10. Offices in 278 named and other unnamed industrial, commercial, and financial institutions, from the chairmanship to auditorship.

11. Offices in 62 named and other unnamed newspapers, publishing houses, theaters, broadcasting companies, etc.

Extent of the Purge

The application of the ordinances of January 4, 1947, meant that to hold, receive, or be a candidate for election to any of these offices, a person must pass through the very fine screen set up by the seven categories of SCAPIN 550, as amended. Under Category C (III) were listed 123 societies, "influential" membership in which, down to their village branches, was legal warrant for purge. Under Category D (IV) between 150 and 200 offices in IRAA and its affiliates were named as constituting "influential membership." This number must be multiplied by the number of branches of these organizations to arrive at the purge potentiality of even ex officio membership in one or another of them. For the purposes of the purge, to have been "influential" in a village branch of IRAA was of equal importance with having been president of the national body. And the screen was woven still finer with the strands of Category E (V), which barred former occupants of any one of seven offices in thirty named and additional unnamed financial and development organizations, such as the South Manchuria Railway Company or the Bank of Chosen.

The ordinances of January 4, 1947, also applied to relatives of purged officials. Relatives within the third degree were prohibited for a period of ten years from occupying an office held by an official who had been removed, unless that office was elective. This provision was designed to prevent the frustration of the cleansing process by the appointment of a new officer who would be readily amenable to the control of the purged officer. The estimated grand total of potential ineligibles thus reached the staggering figure of 1,000,000 persons.[6] Though only an esimate, the figure is as likely to have been too low as too high. However, the abolition on March 31, 1947, of the federations of neighborhood associations — the *chonaikai* and the *burakukai* — as official bodies greatly reduced the number of persons subject to the purge.

Penalties

Penal servitude or imprisonment for up to three years or fines up to 15,000 yen were prescribed for persons convicted of falsifying their answers on the questionnaires or violating the requirements relating to the cessation of activities of purged officials. Convicted persons would also forfeit their rights to office whether or not they were found ineligible under the basic provisions of the ordinances.

The scope of the purge was expanded further by a cabinet decision, January 14, 1947, upon an ordinance barring from office in labor organizations persons who were leaders in any wartime ultranationalist labor organization. This ordinance supplemented that of December 14, 1946, under which 11,295 persons had been removed from office, a figure in striking contrast to the 894 purgees reported by the government on September 15, 1946. Striking also was the apparent absence of any suggestion from SCAP that this action be taken, since no reference to labor organizations appeared in the ordinances of January 4, 1947. *Mainichi Shimbun* (Tokyo) reported that an estimated 3,670 additional labor leaders would be disqualified under the supplementary ordinance.[7]

No Purge of Religion

The directives and implementing ordinances did not include offices in any religious organization. This may be evidence of SCAP's sensitiveness to criticism from the clergy and from lay churchmen. Beyond doubt there were many ultranationalist priests of Shinto and a lesser proportion of like-minded men in other religious bodies. Since the end of the war a considerable number of ex-officers of the army and navy have entered the priesthood.

Screening

The expansion of the purge involved the establishment of a more elaborate screening process. Examination of prospective purgees, like the drafting and legalization of the questionnaires, was administrative. The power to designate officials to be removed was vested in the premier for the principal offices and in the prefectural governors for other offices, the positions in each of the two classes being defined by ordinance. These officials received the questionnaires and were required to submit them to the competent screening committees — legally described as Public Office Qualifications Examination Committees. The Central Committee sat in Tokyo, a prefectural committee sat in each prefecture, and a municipal committee sat in each city that had a population of 50,000 or was designated by the premier. The Central Committee might review the decisions of the others, and the prefectural committees might review those of relevant municipal committees.

Committee members — called commissioners — were appointed, respectively, by the cabinet, the prefectural governors, and the mayors. The Central Committee consisted of nine members, the others of five. They selected one of their members as chairman, and he had a second vote in the event of a tie. Seven members formed a quorum in the Central Committee, three members in the prefectural and municipal committees. The municipal committees reported to the prefectural committees, which reported to the governors, who reported to the premier. The ordinance was not explicit upon whether or not the premier might decide contrary to the recommendations of the committees. Presumably he might do so, but would be deterred from discriminatory action by the ultimate authority of SCAP to overrule him. He was also controlled by the requirement to publish his decisions.

The New Japan

Public Sentiment on the Purge

Japanese reactions to these searching measures designed to break the crust of traditional control cannot be accurately gauged. Available evidence indicates that early enthusiasm for the expanded purge cooled rather rapidly. Those who favored the purge called it a chance for young people to advance, a boon to socialists, a needed house-cleaning before reconstruction; those critical of it feared that it would cause confusion and profit leftism, that younger businessmen would be less capable than their predecessors of meeting current difficulties, and that many innocent leaders would be caught with the guilty. It may properly be assumed that both censorship and timidity caused the expression of Japanese views to be weighted on the side favorable to the purge, though SCAP itself was divided in its attitude toward so radical a housecleaning. The following newspaper comments offer further interesting evidence of opinion.

Asahi Shimbun (Tokyo) called the purge a "revolution" involving a "tremendous number of people," but was cordial toward it "as a means of promoting democratization," which it regarded as dependent upon impartiality in carrying out the program.[8] *Tokyo Shimbun* preferred quick and drastic execution to the government's "lukewarm attitude," and called for the appointment of "men of talent" rather than "inexperienced opportunists" for the new era.[9] *Hokkai Times* (Sapporo) charged the government with discrimination in applying the ordinances and called for fair play.[10] *Shin Hochi* (Tokyo) asked further extension to include men who were members of the Diet during the third Konoye and the Tojo regimes. It urged the authorities "not to catch the flies and let the hornets go free."[11] *Godo Shimbun* (Okayama) believed that the ban on relatives "will prove a strong factor for the thoroughgoing democratization of the financial world."[12] *Mainichi Shimbun* (Tokyo) recognized that persons of a democratic turn of mind might be engulfed, but argued that this was not too great a sacrifice for the needed change of leadership.[13] *Akahata* (Tokyo Communist daily) declared that certain companies were omitted from the purge list in order not to embarrass the five cabinet ministers concerned with economic affairs.[14] *Mimpo* (Tokyo) pointed to the danger resulting from the continued freedom of purged ultranationalists to join cultural societies and to talk and write for the public.[15] *Shin Hochi* (Tokyo) was extremely doubtful that the purge would be conducted fairly, averring that only "those who, from the time of the outbreak of the Sino-Japanese Incident to Japan's surrender, had done their best to prevent or to suspend war through their pacifistic ideals will be qualified to act as commissioners." [16] *Tokai Yukan* (Gifu) pointed to loopholes in the ordinances which permitted dyed-in-the-wool bureaucrats and younger ultranationalists who "pretend to be apostles of democracy" to replace their elder counterparts.[17] *Yukan Miyako* (Tokyo) criticized purging by administrative action, urging that since the deprivation of constitutional rights was involved, the courts were the proper forum for an analysis of qualifications.[18] This view also appeared in the *Sanyo Choho* of Okayama.[19] *Minami Nippon Shimbun* (Kagoshima) noted the technical difficulty of distinguishing between aggressive militarists and the "honest people who were led to believe that the war was for the defense of their country and contributed their utmost efforts." [20]

Operation of the Purge

The figures given above on the first phase of the purge indicate that the screening committees were extremely lenient, barring only 894 persons of 7,769 screened, or 11½ per cent. A similar inclination toward leniency marked the later phases of the purge. This attitude led SCAP to order the dissolution of the Central Teachers Screening Committee, a subsidiary of the Central Public Office Qualifications Examination Committee, on January 31, 1947.[21] A rescreening of teachers who had appealed from the decisions of local or university committees was necessitated by this order. Numerous officials did not wait to be examined, but resigned in anticipation of removal, in some instances with a sizable bonus voted to them by a local assembly.[22]

Criticism of the deep surgery required by the ordinances of 1947 seemed to work against their full application. Although Osaka financial circles were reported unperturbed because the purgees anticipated that their successors would seek their assistance even at the risk of the penalties prescribed, influential voices were raised in SCAP against the indiscriminate guillotining of experienced managers of firms which were supplying goods and services for the Occupation. The basic objection to the procedure employed was that it was aimed at the positions held rather than at the individuals who held them. In numerous instances it worked to disqualify men who held such positions ex officio and willy-nilly. It amounted to a general indictment of the Japanese people applied to selected categories. Its application to great grandsons, cousins, nephews, *et al.* was an especially dissonant note in the democratic concord.

The plight of the hundred thousand ex-officers of the Japanese army and navy who were automatically brought under the ordinances was serious, not only because the government service and business firms were thereby deprived of the services of many able doctors, lawyers, engineers, and accountants, but because the loss of employment, combined with loss of pensions, was embittering and provocative of antagonism toward the Occupation. Some ten thousand of these officers were youths unable to complete their educations and trained only in violence. Many of these immature men joined labor unions and were largely responsible for the movement toward the general strike. The older labor leaders deplored this movement, but were intimidated by the young firebrands who did not relish such vocations as shoe-shining, black-marketing, and patent-medicine vending.[23] Their precarious economic position made them highly vulnerable to revolutionary leadership from the right or left.[24]

A serious aspect of the operation of the purge was its control by a highly conservative cabinet which could, by judicious timing, affect the political prospects of opposing political leaders. That the Yoshida administration used this power is strongly suggested by events that followed the organization of the Minshuto (Democratic party) to replace the Shimpoto on March 31, 1947. This reorganization was the culmination of a year's effort led by Inukai Ken of the Progressive party and Ashida Hitoshi of the Liberal party (Jiyuto) to establish a genuinely liberal party and to prevent the merger of the Liberals and Progressives under the dominance of the Yoshida-Shidehara tradition of bureaucratic rule. For contemporary Japan it was a promising move toward democracy such as SCAP would be expected to favor. But within eight days after the birth of the new party Inukai had been purged, along with his principal lieutenants, Ishiguro Takeshige and Narahashi Wataru, and a number of other members. With the election of April 25, 1947, only a few days away, the elimination of Inukai was a body blow which undoubtedly aided the Liberals and assured them of a cordial attitude toward a coalition, if not a union, that would continue to exhibit a synthetic majority in the House of Representatives. It seems highly unlikely that this opportune emasculation of the Democratic party was purely coincidental.

Conclusion

General MacArthur revealed on January 31, 1947, that he was directed early in the Occupation to assume, "in the absence of evidence to the contrary," that "any persons who have held key positions of high responsibility since 1937 in industry, finance, commerce and agriculture have been active exponents of militant nationalism and aggression." [25] By so doing he placed responsibility for general principles upon the Far Eastern Commission in Washington. But he acknowledged that he used "the normal discretion of a field commander in the matter of both details and timing." It may be questioned whether sufficient attention was paid to the clause "in the absence of evidence to the contrary" in the FEC directive. Actually no mitigating evidence was considered in the great majority of cases, which were decided solely upon the fact of occupancy of a designated office. Some careful students of Japanese opinion have concluded that the moral effect of the purge declined when it engulfed the ex officio little men in the Imperial Rule Assistance Association and departed from its earlier attack upon top-flight militarists to include great numbers of people whom the Japanese regarded as catspaws or nonentities. Japan's greatest liberal, Ozaki Yukio, expressed the same view. Frank observers also averred that political bias had affected the work of the screening committees, slowing the progress of democracy and damaging the prestige of the Occupation.

Notes

[1] The abbreviation "SCAPIN" was used to denote directives of the Supreme Command for the Allied Powers.
[2] *Department of State Bulletin*, Vol. XIII, No. 318, July 29, 1945, p. 137.
[3] *Ibid.*, No. 326, September 23, 1945, p. 424.
[4] Teachers and professors were included.
[5] *Official Gazette*, Extra, January 4, 1947, *passim*.
[6] *Stars and Stripes*, Tokyo, January 5, 1947.
[7] January 15, 1947.
[8] January 6, 1947.
[9] January 7, 1947.
[10] January 4, 1947.
[11] January 10, 1947.
[12] January 6, 1947.

[13] January 7, 1947.
[14] January 8, 1947.
[15] January 15, 1947.
[16] January 7, 1947.
[17] January 7, 1947.
[18] January 18, 1947.
[19] January 19, 1947.
[20] January 11, 1947.
[21] *Jiji Shimpo*, February 10, 1947. (For all the newspaper comments listed in notes 7 through 21 credit for the English translation is due to the Allied Translation and Interpreter Service — ATIS — a highly useful agency maintained during the Occupation.)
[22] A Tokyo rumor that a club of purgees had invited the chief of Government Section, SCAP, to join as an honorary member seems too flattering to the sense of humor of the Japanese male.
[23] Y. Matsushita, "The Problem of Purged Career Soldiers," *Japan Review*, January 31, 1947, pp. 25–30.
[24] The Potsdam Proclamation, cited above, promised the disarmed forces of Japan "the opportunity to lead peaceful and productive lives."
[25] Release of Public Relations Office, Tokyo, January 31, 1947.

9

Drafting the New Constitution

JAPANESE statesmen at the end of the war were not considering the revision or replacement of the Meiji constitution. Its place in their political thinking was second only to that of the imperial dynasty, from which, in legal theory, it had been received. The conservatives preferred to have it interpreted in practice as the embodiment of enlightened and benevolent monarchy. The liberals, led by a courageous scholar, Minobe Tatsukichi, believed that it would permit the development of democracy if interpreted by advocates rather than by antagonists of democracy.[1] Above all other considerations in the minds of educated Japanese was the desire to avoid an imposed revision in the guise of one contrived by themselves. This very natural attitude was expressed with force and feeling by Dr. Takagi Yasaka, professor of American history, Imperial University of Tokyo:

It would be a mistake to adopt any constitution other than one based on the strong conviction of its [a country's] people themselves. Our constitution should be the expression of the Japanese mind and the embodiment of our own genius, with historical continuity with our past national life. It would be a disgrace for our people if, consciously or unconsciously, they made their decision in submissive obedience, under difficult circumstances. For history abounds in instances of the breakdown and setback of too "idealistic" constitutions. It would be below the dignity of humanity itself if we allowed recurrence, after the second World War, of any such unfortunate eventuality.[2]

No reliable public opinion poll existed in Japan at the end of the war, but various agencies were employed by the Japanese to sound

111

opinion, among them the Public Opinion Survey Center in Tokyo. Of 2,400 persons — distributed among a variety of activities: politics, business, education, agriculture, and labor — questioned in December 1945 and January 1946, 53 per cent voted to entrust the drafting of a constitution to a committee elected by the people, 24 per cent to one elected by the Diet, and 20 per cent to one appointed by the emperor.[3]

Knowledge of developments in this field was lacking among American political scientists. No approach was made to them as a specially qualified group by the Department of State. The several sections of SCAP were recruited confidentially, among them one known as the Government Section. This section was headed by Brigadier General Courtney Whitney, who was not a specialist in government or in Japanese history and culture. None of the colonels and lieutenant colonels who composed the chain of authority in the Section was a specialist in government or in Japanese history and culture. Among the officers of lesser rank and among civilian members of the Section were a number of well-qualified men. What influence these latter had upon the policy of the Section must be left to their telling.

In early October 1945 General MacArthur informed Premier Shidehara that it would be necessary to liberalize the constitution. No demand was made that a new procedure be adopted; the assumption was not that Japan would have a new constitution written by the people or their elected representatives but that the existing constitution would be revised in accordance with its own Article 73, which had never been applied. This reads as follows:

When it has become necessary in future to amend the provisions of the present constitution, a project to that effect shall be submitted to the Imperial Diet by Imperial order.

In the above case neither House can open the debate unless not less than two-thirds of the whole number of members are present, and no amendment can be passed unless a majority of not less than two-thirds of the members present is obtained.

There was an air of unreality about the application of the quoted article. The emperor was to lose his sovereignty, yet his power to initiate the deprivation was formally respected. The people were to be recognized as the repository of sovereignty, yet the constitution was to be drafted by bureaucrats appointed by bureaucrats. The Diet was to receive full legislative power, yet it was to share in the drafting process only secondarily, through the procedure of interpellation. And the whole process was to be conducted under the supervision and guidance of an occupying military commander and his staff.

Yet there was deep and widespread interest among the leaders of Japanese political parties and in private study groups, many of which drafted proposals for complete or partial revision. All the larger parties did so, and among the private groups may be mentioned the Federation of Bar Associations, the Constitution Discussion Group led by Ozaki Yukio, and the Constitution Investigation Association, most active member of which was Dr. Takano Iwasaburo, an adviser of the Socialist party. He was the only prominent non-Communist to propose that Japan become a republic.[4]

Konoye and the Constitution

Characteristic of the uncertainty of the Japanese regarding the status under the Occupation of their wartime statesmen was the appointment of Prince Konoye by the Privy Council to prepare a report on the subject.[5] He had been appointed previously to membership in the Higashi-kuni cabinet. His name was not on the first list (September 11, 1945) of forty-seven men accused of war crimes or on the list of fifty-nine made public on December 2, 1945. His appointment to revise the constitution was announced on October 11, 1945. On December 6, 1945, he was listed for arrest as a suspected war criminal. Ten days were allowed him to prepare for Sugamo Prison. Early on December 16 he was found dead, a suicide by poison.

The prince's brief memoirs contain no reference to the Occupation.[6] Between August 30 and December 6, 1945, apparently some influences were at work that sought to save him and other influences that were determined he should stand trial. On October 19 Foreign Minister Yoshida called Konoye "more or less the central figure in state affairs," and stated that he was heading a group of political reformers close to the throne.[7] Konoye himself asserted that MacArthur had suggested this action.[8] He was required by the emperor to report upon two questions: (1) Should the constitution be revised? (2) If it should be revised, how extensive should revision be?[9] This bit of imperial byplay could, of course, have emanated only from the imperial advisers since the emperor's relationship to the government had not changed. Not until November 1, two weeks after Konoye's claim to SCAP sponsorship was published, did SCAP, through the Public Relations Office in Tokyo, deny such sponsorship. Curiously, the denial admitted, by inference, some contact between SCAP and the Imperial House regarding the problem, since it declared that "Konoye's connection with the matter arises entirely from his relationship with the Imperial Household." [10] The fact that Konoye was extremely conservative in his remarks to the press upon the nature of feasible constitutional changes may be relevant to the subsequent disclaimer of SCAP sponsorship.

SCAP's disclaimer did not terminate Konoye's activities looking toward revision of the constitution. The prince or his colleague Dr. Sasaki reported from time to time to the emperor.[11] But no comprehensive or formal report was made public. Undoubtedly the bitter attack upon Konoye by Saito Takao in the Diet on November 26, 1945, brought home to Occupation authorities the inconsistency of Konoye's confidential position with his war record. Saito blamed Konoye for refusing to deal with Chiang Kai-shek, for supporting Wang Ching-wei, and for leading Japan into alliance with Germany and Italy. The fiery Progressive concluded his attack with these words: "If Prince Konoye has any sense of honor, I do not see how he can feel at ease today." [12] Denunciation in such severe terms is seldom voiced in the Diet. The newspaper *Yomiuri-Hochi* (Tokyo) classed Konoye with Tojo as a "top-ranking war criminal" and urged that it was "the Japanese people's job to keep ambitious and guilty politicians like Konoye from ruling Japan again." [13]

The Matsumoto Committee

Paralleling the work of the Konoye-Sasaki committee a second investigation was being conducted by Dr. Matsumoto Joji, minister without portfolio in Baron Shidehara's cabinet. He was appointed on October 13, 1945, to report to the cabinet on the same general questions submitted to Konoye. He was seventy years old and by career a professor-bureaucrat, one of that hard core of dyed-in-the-wool civil servants, graduates of Tokyo Imperial University's law school, that has been formed in the administrative organism of Japan like a pearl in an oyster. His preferences, like those of Premier Shidehara, were for as little revision as possible, and he particularly desired to avoid any public discussion of the tennoate.[14] Shidehara indicated his own views to the House of Peers on November 28, saying that the government intended to revise only those sections of the constitution which had been abused.[15] The unwillingness of a man noted as a liberal to speak clearly and forcefully for democracy was impressive evidence of the inertia to be overcome if Japan were ever to be counted among the democracies.

In the Diet on November 29, 1945, Shidehara revealed his devotion to tradition while using the terms of liberalism: "Democracy is based on the will of the people, who make it the basis of political thought. Regarding this point, it is needless to mention that the Emperor has a strong and definite conviction. I have a strong conviction that we could build a true and unique Japanese democracy with the Emperor as the center and with the fullest cooperation and unification of the Sovereign and the subjects, and thereby contribute to the progress of the world."[16]

Shidehara also expressed his approval of a statement made in the Diet on the same day by Hatoyama Ichiro, leader of the Liberal party at that time. Hatoyama's view, like Shidehara's, was vaguely put, seemingly seeking to find a formula satisfactory to everyone rather than to voice a conviction: "The United States, England and Russia have their own forms of democracy, and the democracy that the Japanese people are trying to establish must naturally be suited to Japan. A democracy suited to Japan means one in which the Emperor shall hold supreme power, with the Diet and the Government carrying the entire responsibility of government under an administration suited to the people."[17]

Foreign Minister Yoshida had expressed identical sentiments a month earlier. He declared that Japan's existing constitution was democratic, i.e., that it provided for a government of, by, and for the people. Like Shidehara he regarded revision as necessary only to prevent misuse of certain provisions by militarists and other recalcitrant elements.[18] Obviously, Dr. Matsumoto could not expect great latitude in his investigation from a cabinet representing so conservative a political philosophy. Obviously Shidehara and Yoshida were disinclined toward any revision whatever and were taking action only under the spur of Occupation prompting.

Dr. Matsumoto's Constitutional Problem Investigation Committee held a number of meetings. It compiled the opinions of legal scholars and the findings of surveys of public and group opinion regarding revision.[19] The committee also drafted a "revision bill," which was accepted as satisfactory by the cabinet early in February 1946.[20] But the bill failed to satisfy SCAP. The directives of October 4, 1945, and January 4, 1946, inaugurating a purge of officialdom and requiring the repeal of laws restrictive of personal liberty and the dissolution of militaristic organizations, should have been jolting blows to smug assumptions that, except for the punishment of war criminals, the Japanese civilian oligarchs would be allowed to contrive a new Japan in the old image. These directives seemed to be reflected in Matsumoto's remark early in January, "It is necessary, for drastic constitutional reform, to achieve substantial democratization of the existing constitution, and I do not believe that the revision of a single principle or theory will serve the real intention of constitutional reform."[21] His committee's proposals, however, were disappointingly stale and unrepresentative of the burgeoning popular interest in democracy. Such limited indications of their content as were made public suggested that no serious effort had been made to meet the Potsdam terms but that the old constitution had been copied almost verbatim.[22]

The MacArthur Draft

On March 4, 1946, it became known that the Matsumoto draft of the constitution had been rejected by the cabinet.[23] On March 6 came the unexpected announcement that a constitution of democratic and pacifistic principles had been accepted by that body.[24] Appearing so soon after Dr. Matsumoto's efforts had been repudiated, the new document obviously was not the work of his committee. No official indication was given regarding primacy of authorship, but readers familiar with General MacArthur's sonorous rhetoric immediately noted its resemblance to that of the new draft. MacArthur himself announced its appearance in the following highly complimentary statement:

It is with a sense of deep satisfaction that I am today able to announce a decision of the Emperor and Government of Japan to submit to the Japanese people a new and enlightened constitution which has my full approval. This instrument has been drafted after painstaking investigation and frequent conference between members of the Japanese Government and this Headquarters following my initial direction to the Cabinet five months ago.

Declared by its terms to be the supreme law for Japan, it places sovereignty squarely in the hands of the people. It establishes governmental authority with the predominant power vested in an elected legislature, as representative of the people, but with adequate check upon that power, as well as upon the power of the executive and judiciary, to insure that no branch of government may become autocratic or arbitrary in the administration of affairs of state. It leaves the throne without governmental authority or state property, subject to the people's will, a symbol of the people's unity. It provides for and guarantees to the people fundamental human liberties which satisfy the most exacting standards of enlightened thought. It severs for all time the shackles of feudalism and in its place raises the dignity of man under protection of the people's sovereignty. It is throughout responsive to the most advanced concept of human relations — is an eclectic instrument, realistically blending the several divergent political philosophies which intellectually honest men advocate.

Foremost of its provisions is that which, abolishing war as a sovereign right of the nation, forever renounces the threat or use of force as a means of settling disputes with any other nation and forbids in future the authorization of any army, navy, air force or other war potential or assumption of rights of belligerency by the state. By this undertaking and commitment Japan surrenders rights inherent in her own sovereignty and renders her future security and very survival subject to the good faith and justice of the peace-loving peoples of the world. By it does a nation, recognizing the futility of war as an arbiter of international issues, chart a new course oriented to faith in the justice, tolerance and understanding of mankind.

The Japanese people thus turn their backs firmly upon the mysticism and unreality of the past and face instead a future of realism with a new faith and a new hope.[25]

The imperial rescript and the statement of Premier Shidehara issued on the same day are also of historical importance, less for what they contain than for the fact that they contain it. The emperor said:

Consequent upon our acceptance of the Potsdam Declaration [properly "Proclamation"], the ultimate form of Japanese government is to be determined by the freely expressed will of the Japanese people. I am fully aware of our nation's strong consciousness of justice, its aspirations to live a peaceful life and promote cultural enlightenment and its firm resolve to renounce war and to foster friendship with all the countries of the world. It is, therefore, my desire that the constitution of our empire be revised drastically upon the basis of the general will of the people and the principle of respect for the fundamental human rights. I command hereby the competent authorities of my government to put forth in conformity with my wish their best efforts toward the accomplishment of this end.²⁶

Shidehara left to the final line of his admirable statement any indication of Japanese authorship of the new instrument. He said:

His Majesty the Emperor was pleased to grant to the Cabinet an imperial message yesterday. In order that our nation may fall in line with other nations on the march toward the attainment of the universal ideal of mankind, His Majesty with a great decision has commanded that the existing constitution be fundamentally revised so as to establish the foundation upon which a democratic and peaceful Japan is to be built.

From war that has afflicted mankind for centuries past the world is moving slowly but steadily toward peace; from cruelty to mercy, from slavery to liberty, and from tyranny and confusion to order. If our people are to occupy a place of honor in the family of nations we must see to it that our constitution internally establishes firmly the foundation for a democratic government, and externally leads the rest of the world for the abolition of war. Namely, we must renounce for all time war as a sovereign right of the state and declare to all the world our determination to settle by peaceful means all disputes with other nations.

I believe that all our people, in response to the most affable and benevolent wish of our Sovereign and for the sake of the tranquility and well-being of the country, will join their forces toward the creation of this momentous document. It is in that hope that the Government has made public an outline of its draft constitution.²⁷

Actual Drafting Process

While SCAP's eulogy of the draft referred to the participation by Occupation officials in the drafting process, it placed emphasis upon the Japanese effort to write a liberal constitution. At the time of publication and throughout the Diet's discussion of the draft, secrecy was maintained regarding the contribution of the Occupation. The draft was consistently described as a Japanese product, and mention of Occupation authorship was not made in the Japanese press. Not until 1950, with the publication of two volumes of text and documents, prepared by the Government Section of SCAP under the title *The Political Reorientation of Japan*, was the veil of secrecy lifted officially.²⁸ The record shows that the draft was an American, not a Japanese, product. With a frankness in striking contrast to the earlier ambiguity, the writer — apparently in extenuation of SCAP's decision to prepare a model instrument — points to the disparity between the conservatism of the Matsumoto draft and the liberalism of drafts written by political party committees and private persons and organizations. He recounts the actual procedure of SCAP substantially as follows.

On February 3, 1946, General MacArthur instructed Brigadier General Courtney Whitney, Chief of Government Section, to prepare a draft constitution. He required that on five subjects — the status of the emperor, military and war powers, feudal survivals, the peerage, and the budget — his own ideas be incorporated. General Whitney, after conference with three members of Government Section — Colonel C. L. Kades, Lieutenant Colonel M. E. Rowell, and Commander A. R. Hussey — appointed a steering committee and a number of special committees. The latter drafted sections of the document which were revised by the steering committee. No indication is given that any Japanese were members of these committees. On February 12 the draft received MacArthur's approval, and on February 13 it was presented to Foreign Minister Yoshida. The cabinet received it "with a distinct sense of shock." General Whitney stated in presenting it that "there was no compulsion upon them to take further action," but he said also that the "Supreme Commander" deemed its principles to be "basic," required that they be given "the fullest consideration," and intended, if the cabinet disappointed him, "to lay the issue before the people himself." [29]

Dr. Matsumoto tried in vain to persuade SCAP that his committee's draft was better suited to Japan's existing stage of political development. In this view he was supported by Yoshida, while Prime Minister Shidehara suggested compromise. MacArthur declined to discuss the issue, and Emperor Hirohito supported the American draft. The cabinet then surrendered, prepared a Japanese translation of the draft, and brought it to SCAP. Upon retranslation into English it was found to be acceptable except for minor changes. It was then retranslated into Japanese "that would fairly and satisfactorily convey the intent of the English translation." On April 15, 1946, a revised version, in terminology more acceptable to the Japanese, was prepared, and this draft was the one submitted to the Diet.

In the presence of the demonstrated unwillingness of Japan's post-surrender officials to prepare a revised constitution conceived in liberty, the problem of SCAP was a difficult one. The political wisdom of imposing a constitution upon a people of another culture, and the wise timing of the revision, were not the only things involved. The authority of the occupying powers under the Potsdam Proclamation, and the authority of SCAP in relation to that of the occupying powers represented in the Far Eastern Commission, were two major aspects of the problem. General MacArthur solved the problem *pro tempore* in militant fashion. But some consideration is called for here of the relation between these aspects of the problem and his solution of it.

The Issue of Authority

Article 12 of the Potsdam Proclamation states: "The occupying forces of the Allies shall be withdrawn from Japan as soon as these objectives have been accomplished and there has been established *in accordance with the freely expressed will of the Japanese people* a peacefully inclined and responsible government."[30] The condition indicated by italics is repeated in the form of a separate, positive statement in Secretary of State Byrnes's reply of August 11, 1945, to the first Japanese offer of surrender: "The ultimate form of government of Japan shall, in accordance with the Potsdam Declaration [i.e., Proclamation], be established *by the freely expressed will of the Japanese people*."[31]

It may be doubted whether the "freely expressed will of the Japanese people" was ascertainable in 1946–1947, even if the Supreme Commander of the occupying forces had intervened to help bring it to the surface. The aftermath of war was much too confusing, and the necessities of living were much too pressing, to leave minds free for autonomous political expression. A military occupation is not encouraging to free expression, however sincerely its commander may desire that it should be. Moreover, a people unaccustomed to free expression of its will requires time to adjust itself to a climate of political freedom.

An assumption underlies the Potsdam Proclamation which may be unwarranted, *viz.*, that the freely expressed will of the Japanese people would favor establishment of a democratic government. It is found also in the statement of "United States Initial Post-Surrender

Policy for Japan."[32] SCAP undoubtedly made this assumption and drew from it justification for accelerating the natural historical process. This was to be done by writing a constitution for the Japanese and by insisting that it be accepted with relatively minor changes within a short period of time. Konoye, Shidehara, Matsumoto, and company were to be regarded as having failed to rise to the historic opportunity. Unfortunately for Shidehara, however, he was required to sponsor a document for which he had no enthusiasm, thereby bringing down upon himself the undeserved censure of Dr. Nambara Shigeru, president of Tokyo Imperial University and member of the House of Peers, for his spineless failure to make public the findings of the Matsumoto committee.[33] Actually it was Shidehara's independence of mind, coupled with his dependence of position, that created a dilemma from which there was no dignified exit. He, like Hirohito, was but a symbol of power. He had to do what SCAP directed.

The Supreme Commander could not regard himself as under orders to impose a constitution upon the Japanese. The objective set by the statement of United States Initial Post-Surrender Policy for Japan was that the "Japanese people shall be encouraged to develop a desire for individual liberties," etc. It declared specifically that "it is not the responsibility of the Allied Powers to impose upon Japan any form of government not supported by the freely expressed will of the people." The men who wrote the statement were so thoroughly democratic that they were willing to contemplate the use of force by the Japanese people to free themselves from "feudal and authoritarian tendencies." But they were alert to the danger that the imposition of political change by a conqueror would be interpreted as a hypocritical repudiation of democracy. They were alert also to the necessity of the people's understanding the changes if these were to be enduring. They contemplated aiding, not forcing, Japan toward an "eventual" regime of "peaceful and responsible government."

MacArthur versus the Far Eastern Commission

The Far Eastern Commission, seated in Washington, was highly concerned to ensure respect on the part of SCAP for the Potsdam Proclamation and the United States' policy statement. It was, furthermore, entitled to be consulted. The Moscow Agreement of December 27, 1945, signed by the foreign ministers of the United States, the

United Kingdom, and Soviet Russia, and adhered to by China, provides that "any directives dealing with fundamental changes in the Japanese constitutional structure or in the regime of control, or dealing with a change in the Japanese government as a whole, will be issued only following consultation and following the attainment of agreement in the Far Eastern Commission." The Commission was not fully operative before the issuance of the MacArthur draft. But on March 21, 1946, it sent an inquiry to MacArthur which exhibits apprehension concerning the effects of too early an election upon the progress of constitutional revision.

The emphasis of the Commission's excellent analysis is on the measures best calculated to arrive at the freely expressed will of the people:

The Far Eastern Commission has given some short preliminary and tentative consideration to the position that may arise after the forthcoming Japanese elections. Having regard to the established position throughout the country of the more reactionary political parties, and to the very short period available to the parties of a more liberal tendency to circulate their views and organize support, the members of the Commission are not without the apprehension that the holding of the election at such an early date may well give a decisive advantage to the reactionary parties and thus create the embarrassment of a Japanese Government elected in terms of the Potsdam Declaration [i.e., Proclamation] "in accordance with the freely expressed will of the Japanese people," which might not, in fact, truly represent their wishes, and with which it might prove impossible for the Supreme Commander to cooperate. From another point of view, the Commission feels the difficulty of expecting a fully instructed, intelligent and authoritative expression of the views of the Japanese people on their political future during this uncertain period when the whole of the future economic structure of Japan is still in doubt, and when a proportion of the electorate must necessarily be disfranchised owing to absence. Finally, the issue of the draft Constitution, of which you have approved, makes the Constitution at this late stage an election issue, upon which there can be little time for consideration by the Japanese people, and at the same time may give an undue political advantage to the political party preferring this Constitution.[34]

MacArthur was on safe ground in pointing to the need of a Diet for routine legislative functions. But other statements in his sharply impatient response were not in accordance with known facts, he took no heed of the danger of haste in the passage of constitutional laws, and he revealed his inverted conception of democracy as administered by himself. "There is no ground," he said, "for supposition that the reactionary party will secure a greater advantage as a result of the election at this time than at a later date." A comparison of the election results in 1947 with those of 1946 is an adequate contradiction of that statement. To quote him again: "All parties in Japan, except the Communistic [*sic*] Party, overwhelmingly favor the proposed constitution, which represents the work of men from many different groups and many different affiliations." And finally: "Should the results of the election prove disadvantageous to the purposes of the occupation, the remedy is always in my power to require the dissolution of the Diet and the holding of a new election under such provisions as are deemed necessary."[35] Surely the implications of a democratic Occupation could hardly have been more completely misstated than they were in that sentence.

The concern of the Far Eastern Commission that the Proclamation should be respected was much greater than that for its own dignity. It desired to carry out its international obligation whether or not the Supreme Commander chose to recognize its authority. Undaunted by its earlier experience, the Commission wrote a valuable statement of its views upon methods of revision to General MacArthur on April 12, 1946:

1. The Far Eastern Commission has a responsibility to ensure that any new Japanese Constitution conforms to the principles of the Potsdam Declaration. The Commission has under consideration a draft of a set of principles by which any proposed Constitution should be judged in the light of the Potsdam Declaration. To discharge appropriately its duties in this respect, the Far Eastern Commission is concerned, however, not only with the actual content of a Constitution, finally adopted by the Japanese people, but also with the method and machinery by which the Constitution is adopted in order to ensure that the Constitution embodies the "freely expressed will of the Japanese people." The Commission is also of the opinion that sufficient time should be allowed for the mature consideration of all these constitutional problems by as wide a section of the Japanese people as possible.

2. In the meantime, the Commission believes that as regards the method, machinery and procedure for the adoption of a new Constitution, there are many different paths by which the basic objective of a democratic Constitution embodying the will of the Japanese people could be reached. Accordingly, the Commission considers that it is

most important that it should be kept informed of the plans of the Japanese Government in this respect, and of the hopes and ideas of the Japanese people as voiced by individuals or associations, in the press, or in public discussion.

3. It is not an easy matter for the Commission to formulate exactly the specific information which it requires, because the Commission lacks much of the necessary knowledge of current developments and plans of the Japanese Government. In order to assist the Supreme Commander for the Allied Powers to appreciate the scope of the information desired, the following are some instances of matters upon which the Commission would like to be informed:

a. To what extent and in what manner have other drafts of constitutions been brought to the knowledge of the Japanese people and how have they been discussed?

b. What evidence have the Japanese people shown of applying democratic principles in considering a new proposed Constitution?

c. In what manner have the Japanese people been encouraged to abolish the Imperial institution or to reform it along more democratic lines?

d. Are the various methods for adoption of a new Constitution being discussed irrespective of the limitations imposed by Article 73 of the Constitution of 1889? In particular, and only by way of example, are the following possible methods of adoption being considered: (1) By the Diet, (2) By constitutional convention, (3) By plebiscite?

4. For these reasons the Far Eastern Commission requests its chairman to ask the Supreme Commander to send a member of his staff to Washington to inform the Commission on the plans of the Japanese Government for the adoption of a Constitution, and also to discuss with the Commission broad questions relating to a new Constitution for Japan. The Commission would also profit greatly if the deputed officer were also in a position to communicate to it the Supreme Commander's own views on these matters.[36]

To this carefully worded, thoughtful, and wholly relevant communication the Far Eastern Commission received the following response via the Department of State on May 29, nearly seven weeks later:

The request of the Far Eastern Commission that General MacArthur send to Washington a staff officer to confer with the Commission on the matter of Japanese constitutional reform contained in your letter of April 12, 1946, has been referred to the Supreme Commander and a reply has now been received from General MacArthur in which he states that he is in full agreement with the need for a closer working arrangement and understanding between SCAP and the Commission *and stands ready to do everything in his power to further this end.* He states, however, that it is impossible for him to send an officer to act as his deputy in the broad matters involving constitutional reform, as he has given his personal attention to this question and there is no officer in a position to express in detail his views. Furthermore, due to the rapid demobilization of officer personnel, the release of a key officer for this purpose could not be effected without impairment to the Command. He also adds that the situation in Japan is a fluid one, necessitating constant on-the-ground observation to permit a comprehensive understanding of it from day to day.[37]

Disregard of the Allied Council

The intention of the Moscow Agreement was that the Allied Council for Japan would be utilized by the Supreme Commander as a consultant and adviser, and to the Council, in part, the exercise of control authority was entrusted. Specifically, with respect to so fundamental a matter as constitutional revision, the Agreement states: "If, regarding the implementation of policy decisions of the Far Eastern Commission on questions concerning a change in the regime of control, fundamental changes in the Japanese constitutional structure, and a change in the Japanese Government as a whole, a member of the Council disagrees with the Supreme Commander (or his Deputy), the Supreme Commander will withhold the issuance of orders on these questions pending agreement thereon in the Far Eastern Commission."

Nothing could be more obvious than that General MacArthur had elected himself Solon in order to be a lawgiver to the Japanese. In doing so, he appears to the authors to have been unwise and to have placed in jeopardy whatever contribution the able and sincere scholars of Government Section had made toward a liberalized system of government. Given more time and with the friendly collaboration of foreign political scientists, the Japanese were likely to have drafted an acceptable constitution. There was no compelling reason for great haste; there were many good reasons for making haste slowly. The authors also would question whether the Supreme Commander acted in accordance with the spirit of the Potsdam Proclamation, of the Moscow Agreement, and of the statement of United States' initial policy, whatever may be thought of the formal legality of his action.

Notes

[1] SCAP, *Monthly Summation of Non-Military Activities in Japan and Korea,* November 1945, p. 3.

[2] Manuscript article given to Professor Quigley by Professor Takagi in Tokyo, July 1946.

[3] Foreign Broadcast Intelligence Service, Federal Communications Commission, *Radio Report on the Far East*, February 5, 1946, p. BB1.

[4] *Ibid.*, January 28, 1946, p. BB9.

[5] *New York Times*, October 12, 1945. Konoye's appointment was that of an adviser to Marquis Kido, at that date still Lord Keeper of the Privy Seal; but Konoye and Professor Sasaki Soichi were appointed as co-advisers to Kido for the purpose of revising the constitution. SCAP's *Monthly Summation*, No. 1, the Occupation's official report of its current activities, states (Part II, Section 1, p. 4) that "Prince Konoye, under Lord Keeper of the Privy Seal Marquis Kido, is in charge of a group conducting similar [constitutional] investigations on behalf of the Privy Council."

[6] Konoye's *Memoirs* were translated into English from the *Asahi Shimbun* (Tokyo) and issued in mimeographed form by Okuyama Service (Tokyo) in 1946.

[7] *New York Times*, October 20, 1945.

[8] *Ibid.*, October 22, 1945.

[9] *Ibid.*, October 23, 1945.

[10] *Ibid.*, November 2, 1945.

[11] FBIS, *Radio Report on the Far East*, November 26, 1945, p. BA5.

[12] *Ibid.*, November 28, 1945, p. BA7.

[13] *Ibid.*, December 1, 1945, pp. BA4–5.

[14] *Ibid.*, November 26, 1945, p. BA5.

[15] *Ibid.*, November 29, 1945, p. BA7.

[16] *Ibid.*, November 30, 1945, p. BA2.

[17] *Ibid.*, p. BA4.

[18] *New York Times*, October 20, 1945.

[19] FBIS, *Radio Report on the Far East*, January 3, 1946, p. BA1.

[20] *Ibid.*, February 6, 1946, pp. BB1–2.

[21] *Ibid.*, January 11, 1946, p. BB3.

[22] Ibid., January 11, 1946, p. BB2.

[23] *Ibid.*, March 5, 1946, p. BB10.

[24] *Ibid.*, March 7, 1946, pp. BB1–2.

[25] SCAP, *Monthly Summation*, No. 6, March 1946, pp. 17–18.

[26] *Ibid.*, p. 18.

[27] *Ibid.*, pp. 18–19.

[28] *The Political Reorientation of Japan*, I, 82–118. See also, T. McNelly, "American Influence and Japan's No-War Constitution," *Political Science Quarterly*, LXVII (1952) 589–598.

[29] Mark Gayn, in *Japan Diary* (New York, 1948), pp. 125–131, gives a dramatized version of the procedure which, on the whole, corresponds with the SCAP account. He notes that, by coincidence, an American bomber buzzed the meeting place of Whitney and Yoshida. See also Harry E. Wildes, *Typhoon in Tokyo* (New York, 1954), pp. 38–50.

[30] Department of State, *Occupation of Japan, Policy and Progress*, Far Eastern Series, 17, Publication 267, p. 55. Italics are not in the original.

[31] *Ibid.*, p. 58. Italics are not in the original.

[32] *Department of State Bulletin*, September 23, 1945, p. 423.

[33] *Nippon Times*, August 28, 1946.

[34] Department of State, *Occupation of Japan, Policy and Progress*, pp. 136–137.

[35] *Ibid.*, pp. 138–140.

[36] *Department of State Bulletin*, June 9, 1946, pp. 991–992.

[37] *Ibid.*, p. 991. Italics are not in the original.

10

The Draft Constitution in the House
of Representatives

On June 20, 1946, the newly appointed Yoshida cabinet presented
the "constitution bill" to the House of Representatives in the ninetieth session of the Diet. In April a colloquial Japanese edition of the
draft had been issued, and this was employed in the bill. The bill
received its first reading during the period June 25 to June 28. It was
referred to a special committee, which reported approval on August
21, 1946. It passed its second and third readings on August 24 and was
sent to the House of Peers. During the six weeks taken to discuss the
bill by the House of Representatives four days only were devoted to
plenary sessions. The special committee held twenty-two meetings,
a subcommittee thirteen meetings. Fifty-nine members presented 183
interpellations in the course of the committee hearings.

Dr. Kanamori Tokujiro, minister of state designated by Premier
Yoshida to explain the document in both Houses, spoke 1,300 times,
his longest speech taking an hour and a half.[1] His burden was increased by his having to reply *ex tempore* without benefit of an opportunity to peruse the questions and consider his response outside the
chambers. His assignment was unenviable, in view of limitations upon
his interpretative statements implied in the authorship and endorsement of the draft and in the supervision of SCAP over Diet proceedings. He could hardly be blamed for explanations that were at times
triumphs of vague, confusing, and irresponsible treatment of the
issues raised. It was unfortunate that circumstances worked against

forthright scholarly utterances on certain points. On the whole the "minister for the constitution" fulfilled his mission ably if not always sincerely.

Action of the Privy Council

Before its entrance into the Diet, the bill embodying the draft constitution was sent to the Privy Council, which discussed it during May and early June 1946. Eleven meetings upon the bill were held by a Privy Council Deliberation Committee. On June 8 the Council approved the bill in plenary session without amendment. Chairman Ushio Keinosuke of the Deliberation Committee made a noncommittal report to the Council: "The extent of revision of the constitution is appropriate in view of Japan's acceptance of the Potsdam Declaration. There are portions in the minor regulations which cannot be called ideal, but because there is need, in view of the present situation at home and abroad, to speed the revision of the constitution, this matter is being ignored. However, in relation to the administration of the revision, it is desired that the Government take all necessary measures in order that no mistakes be made."[2]

Composition of the Diet

The ninetieth session of the Diet met after an election in which 377 of a total membership of 466 in the House of Representatives were elected for the first time. This uncharacteristic result was due to the effects of the purge of political figures.* The House of Representatives contained a sprinkling of able lawyers and politicians, but was less well qualified than the House of Peers for the great responsibility it was expected to shoulder. Nevertheless, serious students who read the constitutional debate will be impressed by the evidence of substantial legal learning and knowledge of Western governments which it reveals in both Houses and by the scarcity of the windy oratory that is sometimes substituted for knowledge in the Congress of the United States. He will be distressed, however, by the emphasis placed by members, even the most liberal, upon the views of one or another of the cabinet ministers. The private member seemed bound to the tradition of executive superiority, unable to throw off the apologetic tone.

* See above, Chapter 8.

The Draft Constitution in the House of Representatives

One may ask why the members of the Diet spent approximately three months in deliberation upon a document which had been drafted substantially by the Occupation command. Why did they not say, "We accept the constitution, as we accepted the Prussian-born constitution from the Emperor Meiji; there is no help for it," and pass to other matters? Before attempting to answer this question, one does well to analyze the interpellatory speeches and the replies of the government.

Matters of Major Interest

Interpellations in the plenary sessions of the House of Representatives, after the first reading of the bill and before its reference to committee, were not so arranged as to cover its provisions in sequence, but touched upon articles of special interest to a political party or a private member. Their principal purpose was, of course, to express party views, and all were of considerable length. The issues of primary concern were:

1. The reasons for revision.
2. The right of Diet members to propose amendments to the imperially tendered draft.
3. The nature of the drafting process.
4. The location of sovereignty.
5. The implications of unilateral disarmament and renunciation of war or force.
6. The scope and substance of the human rights clauses.
7. The possibility of conflict between the Diet and the Supreme Court.

Why a Revision?

Kita Reikichi, Jiyuto, at the outset of the discussion in the House of Representatives, asked why the constitution was being revised.[3] He regarded the Meiji constitution as democratic, though not democratically enforced. Premier Yoshida, who shared the responsibility for replies with Mr. Kanamori and others, explained the necessity of revision: (1) the old constitution was liable to distorted interpretation, as the war had proved; (2) the Potsdam Proclamation called for its revision. Yoshida characterized the Matsumoto draft as "provisional" and as having failed to satisfy the Allied powers. He did not suggest that it was unsatisfactory per se. On the contrary, he expatiated upon the point that the new constitution was not introducing democracy to Japan; he thought that the Charter Oath of Emperor Meiji fully represented the spirit of Japanese democracy and that the spirit of democracy, long existent in Japan, would now be represented in new terms. Mr. Yoshida, like Baron Shidehara, was expressing a conception of democracy remote from that of the framers of the document he was now championing.[4]

Morito Tatsuo, Shakaito, while appreciative of the government's incapacity to postpone revision until men's minds were less confused and their bodies stronger, very aptly argued that a constitution adopted in the turmoil of postwar conditions must take as its paramount functions the setting of political and social ideals and the indication of methods for their ultimate attainment rather than the definition of existing principles. He asked why the social ideal had been omitted. Kanamori pointed out that the draft contained articles protective of economic and social well-being and that these could be supplemented by law as additional protections were demanded by society.[5]

Apparently no representative directly charged that the draft was written by Americans, although several members noted resemblances to American phraseology as well as to the constitution of the United States. Nuno Toshiaki, of the Japan Democratic Party Preparatory Committee, likened Japan's "democracy" to that of the Angora and the Weimar republics. "So it's better to refrain from war as best we can," said Nuno, his subsequent remarks suggesting that the applause had gone to his head.[6]

Nozaka Sanzo, Kyosanto, was easily the most effective interpellator, revealing a brilliant mind, but much of his argument was special pleading. His challenge to the House was striking: "Today, the Japanese people are demanding and crying for, the construction of a new and democratic Japan. . . . The people of Japan, especially we, members of the Diet, are as if we were sitting for the entrance examination of a new school . . . If we fail to make a democratic constitution, we shall be failed in the examination." [7]

Nozaka then attacked Premier Yoshida's characterization of the Emperor Meiji's Oath above cited. His plausible but unsubstantiated criticism deserves quotation:

From our [i.e., the Communist party's] point of view, the written Oath of Five Articles was the Meiji Government's declaration of bureaucratism against the feudalistic influence of the Tokugawa. . . . It was the declaration by which the new bureaucratic government of Meiji defended itself against the influence of the feudal system of the Tokugawas. . . . One of the five articles in the written Oath reads: "Men shall be summoned from all parts of the country and publicly discuss and decide upon all affairs of state." This, however, has nothing to do with the democratic Diet as of today . . . This refers to the conference of the local governors of those days which was reactionary in nature.[8]

It was Nozaka's purpose, pursued with the skill of a seasoned debater, to pillory Yoshida primarily and Kanamori secondarily for their apologetics upon the "democracy" of Meiji legislation, including the constitution, and to demonstrate the necessity of an entirely new departure in Japan's fundamental law. He contended, however, that the time was not ripe for a new constitution. He challenged the theory of Morito Tatsuo that a constitution was a program for action in the future, arguing instead that "The object of the constitution is to secure the fruits of a social reform by means of laws following the completion of such a social reform."[9] He deplored haste in the presence of conditions far from symbolic of democracy, charging that "militarists and other reactionary elements in the country are continuing their activities either openly or secretly."[10] He did not believe that the Japanese could regain their national credit or reputation "through the simple act of making a new constitution." To which Kanamori's response was dry humor: "In our judgment from the practical point of view the time is already here which is suitable for the enactment of a new constitution."[11]

Could the Diet Amend?

Morito Tatsuo, Shakaito, raised the issue of the Diet's right, under Article 73 of the Meiji constitution, to propose amendments to the constitution bill. He very cogently remarked that the Potsdam Proclamation called not for a revised but for a new constitution. "Must we examine the present bill," he asked, "with a limitation imposed upon our deliberations by Article 73 of the old constitution?" Kanamori proceeded to settle a moot point of law very concisely by assuring the members that "the presentation of the draft under the provisions of Article 73 . . . does not in the least restrict the freedom of amendment by the Diet."[12] Morito seemed to doubt Kanamori's authority for deciding against the weight of scholarly opinion, which had been that the Diet might approve or disapprove but might not amend an imperial bill for amendment of the constitution.*

Nozaka of the Kyosanto repeated Morito's question and raised the bogey of post-Occupation repudiation, which, he feared, would be advocated by resurrected ultranationalists on the score of unconstitutional procedure. Kanamori rather bluntly responded that there was no need for anyone to worry about the constitutionality of amendments made by agreement of the responsible executive and legislative authorities.[13]

How Was the Draft Produced?

Morito Tatsuo put an embarrassing question when he asked the government "what positive steps" had been taken "to ascertain the free will of the people in drafting the present bill." Unquestionably Morito was expressing the attitude of many members in saying:

In framing the present bill the Government must surely have sought the views of various bodies and organizations. The constitution to be enacted is an instrument of the greatest importance as the supreme law of Japan. The popular will freely expressed must, I believe, be the determining factor also in the preparation of the draft. Did the Government make every effort to have the popular will elicited in this regard? Did the Government consult important political organizations, academic societies, etc.? Did the Government hold public hearings and inquiries, or did the Government take any other step than the publication of the draft in the newspapers, in order to ascertain the popular aspirations? To what extent is the free will of the people reflected in the bill produced by the Government?[14]

Premier Yoshida replied rather lamely to this interpellation, admitting that "due to international reasons" the government had been constrained to publish the revision "it had just drafted" without first obtaining the public comment it would have desired. He informed the House that the government's drafting committee had worked for three months and had submitted "two or three draft revisions." But he did not offer an explanation of the government's failure to publish all the drafts but one. Apparently he thought that to be self-evident. Yoshida expressed the opinion, without elaboration, that "from the results

* No bill for amendment had been submitted prior to 1946.

of the election we are led to believe that the rights and wrongs of the draft were subjected to thorough criticism by the people." [15]

Sovereignty

By far the most absorbing questions were those of the meaning and future locus of sovereignty, which were closely entwined with others relating to the national structure and the position of the dynasty. Hara Fujiro, Shimpoto, invited Mr. Kanamori to disentangle from one another the conceptions that sovereignty resided in the state, that it belonged to the people, and that the emperor was a participant in sovereignty as one of the people. Kanamori responded that "if the word 'sovereignty' is to be taken as the source from which the will of the state is actually derived . . . I think it is right to answer that in Japan 'sovereignty', without any doubt, resides in the whole people, including the Emperor." He continued: "Mr. Hara wanted to know in what part of the draft constitution, then, that connotation was provided for. That is not written in so many words in the draft constitution. That is because in Japan the Emperor and the people are one, the whole people being bound together through the spiritual ties with the Emperor which are deep-rooted in the bottom of their hearts, and this union constitutes the foundation of the existence of the state. This fact requires no explanation." [16]

The government spokesmen used this line of persuasion in their efforts to convince the members that Japan's national structure and character would remain unaltered. Yoshida maintained that emperor and people were one, that they did not stand opposed to each other. He admitted at one point that the Allies at Potsdam had not contracted with Japan that the national structure should be preserved, but he relied upon the principle of the Potsdam Proclamation — that the government should accord with the freely expressed will of the people — to preserve the national structure.[17] To Yoshida's thinking, the will of the people was to preserve the sovereignty of the emperor, i.e., the national structure.* Yoshida inconsistently stated one day later that the Allies and the Japanese government were of two minds upon the question of the obligations upon the Allies, Japan holding that sur-

---

* Yoshida spoke as though verbal reference had been made to the "national structure" in Japan's offer of surrender of August 10, 1945. Actually those words did not appear. Instead the request was for the preservation of "the prerogatives of His Majesty as a Sovereign Ruler."

render had taken place upon condition that the emperor's prerogatives should be respected, the Allies denying that any condition had been accepted.[18]

The ministers were, however, very hard-pressed to demonstrate that the status of the emperor had not been altered in the draft submitted to the Diet. Kanamori sought to reconcile the new dominant position of the Diet with that of the continuance of imperial participation in sovereignty on the ground that the emperor was the "symbol" of the state, the Diet its highest "organ." He acknowledged that the term "attestation" (Article 7) had been employed, rather than "sanction," with reference to certain imperial functions in order not to overstep the emperor's proper sphere of action.[19] Kitaura Keitaro, Jiyuto, denied with regret that any sphere of action had been left to the emperor. His remarks were interesting:

Firstly, concerning the constitutional prerogative of the Emperor, that is his independent authority to make a decision, the existing constitution . . . contains as many as . . . 13 articles providing for the Emperor's prerogative. But times have changed, and those articles have been altogether eliminated from the present draft. Doubting my understanding, I read Article 1 of the draft over and over again. No allusion whatever is made therein to legislative, judicial or administrative authority. I continued my perusal and found the Emperor defined as an emblem of the country of Japan and a symbol of the unity of the Japanese nation, his position being established on their supreme total will.
The language used is beautiful, gorgeous, like golden-colored flowers. It makes a fine work of literature or, in a sense, a great philosophy. Nevertheless, when viewed from a juridical angle, what is implied therein? Nothing. . . . As Mr. Kanamori knows very well the constitution should be the fundamental law for the administration of the state. . . . I do not want to listen to any philosophical or literary explanation, but I must ask for a juridical explanation.[20]

Kanamori refused to be drawn into the juridical field but contented himself with reiterating the dogma of the spiritual relation between the emperor and the people which, he averred, "is by no means based on mythology or anything irrational but is derived from the sovereign will of the Japanese people as is clearly and manifestly provided in Article 1 of the draft constitution . . ."[21]

The demand for clarity was renewed by Suzuki Yoshio, Shakaito, and Nozaka Sanzo, Kyosanto. Suzuki contended that by accepting the Potsdam terms the emperor had established that sovereignty was to rest with the people, since the new government was to be determined upon in accordance with the freely expressed will of the people.[22] He asked why the draft was not clear on this fundamental point. Suzuki himself was remarkably clear in asserting: "The notion of the Japanese people toward the Imperial House transcends all laws and their respect has nothing to do with power but is purely moralistic and emotional. Their respect and affection toward the Emperor is not affected in the least by whether he has administrative power or not." He insisted that the emperor no longer would be the repository of sovereignty, that the government should cease to be vague and nebulous on the subject, and that the wording of the draft should be modified in order that complete clarity upon its embodiment of popular sovereignty should prevail.

Suzuki's comprehension of democracy was eloquently exhibited in the following sentences: "We cherish the aspiration to make the proposed constitution the canons of national education in the future. If only from this point of view, it would make a great contribution to the enhancement of the self-awakening of the people to make them, every one of them, conscious that they have the right to participate in the enactment or amendment of the highest law of the State, in other words, to cause the whole people to have the pride of being the possessors of sovereignty." [23]

Again Kanamori reaffirmed his vague generalizations, while denying any intention to sound ambiguous. Disappointingly, Saito Takao, Shimpoto, merely endorsed Kanamori's statement, possibly out of pique that Suzuki had challenged him to exhibit his democracy.[24] Premier Yoshida also underscored Kanamori's refusal to recognize that democracy and absolute monarchy were incompatible within a single constitution. The Socialist Morito Tatsuo struck a more consistent note when he advocated the thorough realization of democracy, but held that this was possible without loss of the "time-honored national character" if the emperor were regarded not as sovereign but as symbol, as the draft provided.[25]

The pendulum again was swung hard in the opposite direction by Sakai Toshio, Independent, who demanded that Kanamori stipulate whether the emperor was the head or merely a finger of the body politic comprising emperor and people.[26] Sakai declined to accept the subterfuge that the emperor was one of the people, pointing out that the constitution itself distinguished one from the other. He reminded the representatives of their election speeches, which, he thought, pledged them to support the imperial sovereignty. He even suggested that the emperor be empowered to submit acts of the Diet to popular referendum.[27] But Kanamori held fast to his doctrine, on the theory perhaps that frequent affirmation of an illogical position would make it sound logical.

Hososako Kanemitsu, Shinko Club member but speaking on his own behalf, argued that the so-called ceremonial functions were in fact powers of government, emphasizing especially the implications of the imperial function of promulgation of laws.[28] He held that the emperor should be held responsible for his conduct of the allotted functions, refusing to accept the "trick" phrase "ministerial responsibility." He cogently urged: "This dilemma cannot be solved except by placing the Emperor completely out of the sphere of government or by removing the veto power [i.e., the power of promulgation] of the Emperor."

The Communist party spokesman, Nozaka Sanzo, demanded the abolition of the "Emperor System" and argued like Hososako that the so-called ceremonial functions allotted to the emperor in Chapter I of the draft constitution might be employed to veto laws, obstruct appointments, and prevent the operation of the Diet. Nozaka apparently feared that ministers constitutionally responsible to the Diet would fail to honor that responsibility, hiding behind the throne as their feudal and militarist-bureaucratic predecessors had done. In reply to Morito's suggestion that an emperor was compatible with democracy, he said: "The circumstances of the present or the near future are very favorable to the retention of the power of the militarists and reactionaries in substantial measure. Under such circumstances it is undesirable to leave such rights in the hands of the Emperor, because these reactionary elements, by taking advantage of such rights, may start a second war in the Pacific or other wars of invasion. We foresee such dangers. That is why we want to have such rights abolished. That is why we want Article 7 struck out and replaced by provisions making it clear that sovereignty is in the hands of the people."[29]

The Draft Constitution in the House of Representatives
Renunciation of War

Hara Fujiro, Shimpoto, was deeply concerned as to whether or not Japan was renouncing the right of self-defense. "I can understand," he said, "that the provisions had to be inserted in view of the international situation." But he pointed out that if a country was unable to defend itself, other countries should bind themselves to defend it.[30] Premier Yoshida sagely replied that while the right of self-defense was not "directly" denied, it was not to be manifested by means of war or the use of military forces. He thought that the Japanese should "renounce voluntarily the right of belligerency" and "march forward in the vanguard of the world's peace-loving nations," confident that if an aggressor attacked the country, Japan and other peace-loving peoples would "get together and assist each other." [31] The inference was that Japan would become a member of an international organization and as such be free to exercise the right of self-defense. Obviously that freedom would require an amendment of the constitution — to which the premier did not allude.

Kita Reikichi, Jiyuto, suggested the alternative of treaties of neutrality, but Suzuki Yoshio, Shakaito, chided him for his anachronistic proposal and offered instead that of early entrance into the United Nations and into treaties of security.[32]

Strongest critic of the clauses renouncing resort to force and war was Nozaka, representing the Communist position. He insisted that "war for self-defense may be said to be a right war" and that Japan should retain the right to engage in such a war. He was prepared to renounce "wars of invasion" and advocated Japanese cooperation with other peoples in "the international structure to maintain the universal peace based on democracy." Nozaka realistically argued that war was not to be abolished by provisions in constitutions; conditional to its abolition was the rooting out of all the fundamental causes of war. He presented the government with an imposing list of measures that would contribute toward getting rid of war:

1. An admission by Premier Yoshida that the recent war was a war of invasion made by Japan.

2. The proper disposition of reactionary bodies and their leaders, still existing openly or secretly.

3. Destruction of bureaucratism.

4. Dissolution of plutocracy.

5. Abolition of feudal principles of land ownership.

6. Education upon Japan's criminal imperialism and military aggression.[33]

Human Rights

Suzuki Yoshio, for the Socialists, advanced the doctrine of expanding the scope of the human rights clauses in Chapter III, contending that the provisions for the protection of economic and social welfare were meager in comparison with those relating to political and civil liberties.[34] He advocated the inclusion of an obligation upon able-bodied persons to work, standards for working conditions, wages and hours of work, the right to paid holidays, social insurance, limitations upon land ownership, and other tenets of the Shakaito. His interpellation degenerated into a tiresome catalogue of idealistic principles, arousing efforts to shout him down, but another Socialist, Morito Tatsuo, ably seconded him on the following day.[35] Morito called needed attention to the importance of clearly defining the line between the fields of legislation by ordinance and legislation by statute, instancing education as a victim of bureaucratic policy making.

Abe Shungo, on the other hand, speaking as an individual, expressed gratitude for guarantees of human dignity and freedom, but asked for express embodiment of the "spirit and theory of the American Habeas Corpus Act" in an article of the constitution.[36] Kanamori responded that Article 31 was a fundamental protection and that it would be supported by new laws.[37] Abe also asked for a guarantee of the right to trial by jury. The Communist interpellator, Nozaka, wanted it stated clearly in the constitution that "fundamental human rights are guaranteed against infringement in the name of law." He recalled Kanamori's assurance that the courts would protect civil rights "within the limits of the public welfare," but reminded the representatives: "The Peace Maintenance Law and other bad laws that were intended for the oppression of the people were enacted under such fine pretences as the maintenance of law and order, the promotion of public welfare, etc." [38]

Nozaka went beyond the Shakaito in demands for adequate provision for human rights. Without funds to pay for meeting halls and printing establishments, he said, freedom of speech and of the press are more nominal than real to the poor. He asked for "concrete"

provisions implementing the general protections given by the proposed charter of freedom: "For instance . . . laborers' right of participation in industries, right to take rest, relief for the aged workers,
protection of the disabled, the jobless, and women; supply of houses
to live in, extension of compulsory education to middle school [high
school] students, etc."[39]

Judicial Powers

Yoshida Yasushi, Shimpoto, called for assurance that the Supreme
Court, through the power to declare laws unconstitutional, would not
frustrate the Diet, the "highest organ of state power." Kanamori's
reply was thoughtful. He said that the probability of conflicts between
the two organs was high, but that out of such conflicts between the
Diet — a progressive, forward-looking body — and the Court — a more
conservative agency which "preserves as far as possible one flow of
ideas" — would be derived the utmost in public welfare.[40] He explained how the protection of civil rights would thereafter rest with
the courts:

I may now point out that in Chapter III of the draft constitution,
various rights under the constitution are definitely laid down — freedoms are ensured and such and such things are said to be inviolate —
but that all these things are within the limits of the public welfare.
Under the current constitution, with regard to rights corresponding
to those under Chapter III of the draft constitution, it is provided
that the liberty of residence and removal, the liberty of speech, writing and publication are possessed in accordance with the provisions
of law.

Thus, all the rights of the people, with a very few exceptions, are
put within the limits of law. Therefore, those rights can by law be
curtailed or restricted to any extent. This is not the case, however,
with the greater portion of rights under the draft constitution. Under
it freedoms cannot even by law be encroached upon, though they can
be restrained by a certain principle of public welfare which is to be
conceived of in the abstract. They are within the limits of the public
welfare, but they are not within the limits of law.

Then, what limits are there to the public welfare, to the public welfare conceived of from the standpoint of the state? This is a question
which is to be judged principally by the Supreme Court. The Supreme
Court, then, has the very onerous function of fully considering a given
act of the Diet and definitely ascertaining whether its provisions are
within the restrictions permissible under the constitution.

Kanamori acknowledged the difficulty of reconciling the progressive inclinations of an elected, short-term legislature with the conservative attitude of a judiciary appointed for long terms. The draft contained no "clear means of adjustment" between them, he further acknowledged. The provision for a decennial popular review of Supreme Court appointees, embodied in Chapter VI of the draft, was termed by Kanamori a "lukewarm" device that would aid toward adjustment. He suggested that means should be found to publicize the views and contributions of individual judges so that the people might act intelligently when called upon to review the appointments.

The Family System

A topic which might well have aroused more prolonged inquiry was that of the future of the family system. The sharp-tongued Kitaura Keitaro, Jiyuto, expressed fear that it would be destroyed. With the head of the family deprived of traditional rights, filial piety, the foundation of morals, would be weakened. Hara Fujiro, Shimpoto, took the same view, pointing to the interdependence of the family system and the imperial order. They were assured by Kanamori that such changes as might be legalized in the family system would not destroy the rights of the family head or of parents.[41]

Representatives were not always more conservative than the draft or their interpretation of it. Demands were put forward for provisions against cruel and unusual punishments, for protection of the rights of authors and inventors, and for systems of social insurance. A Socialist suggested that capitalists become, like their emperor, mere symbols: he of political power, they of economic power. Another Socialist, Suzuki Yoshio, introduced a bit of humor into his request for a dignified, heart-straining preamble. He thought the government's form of preamble "too tedious and loose. One feels as if he [were] reading the story of the Genji* rewritten in legal terms."[42] Members of the Socialist and Communist parties strongly urged that the new Diet be composed of the House of Representatives only.

Report of Special Committee

The Constitutional Amendments Committee of seventy-two members, to which the draft was referred at the end of the plenary hear-

*The *Genji Monogatari* is a masterpiece of romantic literature written in the eleventh century by Lady Murasaki Shikibu.

ings, reported on August 24, 1946, through its chairman, Ashida Hitoshi, Jiyuto, a man of exceptional prestige for character and ability but not by career a politician. Ashida's report showed that the committee hearings had been concerned principally with the issues raised in the plenary sessions. Stated briefly, the following are the contributions of the report to the clarification and definition of principles laid down in the draft:

1. National character remained unaltered although sovereignty had passed from emperor to people.

2. The powers of the emperor were symbolic, not governmental.

3. The emperor was one with and of the people, the center of their life and the source of their spiritual guidance.

4. To eradicate war Japan should lead the world to effectuate its renunciation by all states, operating through a universal United Nations.

5. The human rights clauses were democratic but left to the future play of politics the decisions upon the addition of socialistic principles.

6. The Supreme Court's power of judicial review "was . . . [a] negative and restrictive function," exercise of which did not affect the position of the Diet.

7. The House of Councillors would combine special knowledge with public election.

8. The cabinet's responsibility would be exercised collectively through the prime minister.[43]

With respect to the terminology of the draft, marked by "not a few terms of crudeness," Ashida regretted that changes had been held to a minimum "in view of the circumstance that the domestic and foreign situation required a speedy completion of constitutional revision."

Amendments

The committee brought in one highly important amendment in the substance of the draft. This amendment was demanded by the Far Eastern Commission, to which Ashida made no reference. The clause in the preamble which read "do proclaim the sovereignty of the people's will" was amended to read "do proclaim that sovereignty resides with the people." To match this change the clause "with whom resides sovereign power" was added to Article 1, which previously had recognized "the sovereign will of the people," the word "sovereign" before "will" now being omitted as redundant.

A second amendment was offered to authorize the emperor to appoint the chief judge of the Supreme Court in accordance with cabinet designation (Article 6). This procedure was believed to add dignity to the judicial post and to symbolize the principle of the equality of the three departments of government: legislative, executive, and judicial.

A third substantive amendment brought in a new article, Article 10: "The conditions necessary for being a Japanese national shall be determined by law." A fourth became Article 30: "The people are liable to taxation as provided by law." Articles 17 and 40 were also added, to assure the right of action for redress against officials in prescribed circumstances. Articles 23–25, which became Articles 25–27, were considerably liberalized in consequence of the Socialist and Communist insistence on socializing the chapter on human rights. Article 64 (68), covering appointment and removal of cabinet ministers, was modified in significant measure. An important change in the legal status of treaties in Japan was provided for by the deletion from Article 94 (98) of the clause equating them with the constitution as the supreme law of the land. Finally, Article 97, which maintained existing peerages for the lifetime of their holders, was dropped. Thus, in addition to amended articles, the draft constitution had 103 articles instead of the 100 originally presented to the House.[44]

Ashida reported that additional amendments proposed by the Socialists were defeated in the special committee. He then led the members in an almost tearful farewell tribute to the Meiji constitution, declared that the renunciation of war was the "greatest characteristic" of the new constitution, and asked for the endorsement of the House. The veteran member, Ozaki Yukio, made an inspiring address, filled with urgent, challenging advice upon the difficulty and the necessity of rising to hitherto undreamed-of standards of public service if the Diet were to seize the forelock of opportunity.[45] Regrettably, applause was lacking.

Thereupon the second reading of the bill was opened. Hara Shonosuke, Shakaito, proposed additional amendments, but was opposed by Jiyuto and Shimpoto speakers. When the amendments were voted down Katayama Tetsu, head of the Shakaito, joined spokesmen for all parties save the Kyosanto in approving the report of Ashida. Nozaka for the Kyosanto summed up his party's views by remarking that the draft "reminds us of the saying: 'to cry up wine and sell vinegar'."[46] The tremendous ideological gap between Westernists and Easternists in the House was evidenced by the contrast between Nozaka's speech and that of Hayashi Heima, of the Kyodo Minshuto, who won cheers for an esoteric view: "The Emperor Jimmu was bold to declare plainly the basic principle of democracy to the effect that anything should be allowed to be carried out if it be serviceable for the benefit of the people . . . I am convinced that in this thought and practice of democratic service, the imperial throne has been succeeded to during these twenty-six centuries."[47]

The amendment bill passed its second reading, in the form reported by Ashida, by a standing vote. Only seven votes were opposed to it. The third reading was opened immediately and there was no further discussion. Voting by ballot upon third reading, 420 members supported, 8 opposed the bill.[48] The six Communist members all were among the eight opponents. The two others in opposition were Hososako Kanemitsu, Shinko Club, and Hozumi Shichiro, Shinseikai.

Why the Deliberation?

Perhaps an answer may now be ventured to the question posed at the beginning of this chapter. Allowing for absences and other evidences of indifference, the fact remains that throughout two hot and humid months a working majority of representatives raised and re-stated issues of major significance to them, refusing to be put off with ambiguities in ministerial replies. It may be assumed that face-saving was one motive and that another was the desire not to provoke a dissolution of the House. Fear should not be ruled out as a factor in the attitude of some members.

It would appear, however, that there were two principal interests served by the interpellations, one representative of conservatism, the other of radicalism of a socialistic tinge. The former interest was to preserve as much as possible of the dignity and influence of the dynasty. The latter was to lessen the prestige of the dynasty and to advance the cause of popular sovereignty. The Jiyuto and the Shimpoto exhibited the former interest, the Shakaito and the Kyosanto the latter.

Second only to these major incentives to debate was the need of assurance that disarmed Japan would be allowed some means of self-defense. On this issue all parties were agreed, though they differed as to methods. The interpellations brought out official interpretations which would remain on the record.

That "appearances sometimes are deceiving" applies to certain of the amendments made by the House of Representatives and to the acceptance by the House of the provisions affecting the position of the emperor. Nothing is clearer from a perusal of the interpellations than that the majority would gladly have supported Premier Yoshida in repudiating that portion of the draft if not the whole of it. On the other hand the sizable Socialist and Communist support of the draft's liberalism was given in spite of the natural dislike of the members to having their nation's fundamental law written by outsiders and imposed upon them. The net result of the discussion was the passage of the revision bill without fundamental changes.

The Final Phase

The House of Representatives took final action upon the constitution revision bill on October 7, 1946. On that day 347 members (out of a total membership of 466) were present and voted upon the bill as returned with amendments by the House of Peers. No discussion was held upon the amendments. The vote for final passage was 342 in favor, 5 (the Communist members) opposed. Premier Yoshida thanked the House for its labors and said:

I deeply congratulate the people and all concerned that the revision of the constitution as the basis for the construction of new Japan has been settled.

I need hardly say that the great task of building up New Japan and realizing the ideals of this constitution requires stupendous efforts of the whole nation. The Government is determined to go forward toward the attainment of this great object, in close cooperation with the people.[49]

Notes

[1] *Nippon Times*, October 11, 1946.

[2] Foreign Broadcast Intelligence Service, Federal Communications Commission, *Radio Report on the Far East*, June 10, 1946, p. BB1.

[3] *Nippon Times*, June 27, 1946.

[4] Yoshida's conception of the spirit of Japanese democracy was that embodied in the modern form of Emperor Meiji's Charter Oath of 1868:

I. An assembly widely convoked shall be established, and thus great stress shall be laid upon public opinion.

The Draft Constitution in the House of Representatives

II. The welfare of the whole nation shall be promoted by the everlasting efforts of both the governing and the governed classes.

III. All subjects, civil and military officers, as well as other people shall do their best, and never grow weary in accomplishing their legitimate purposes.

IV. All absurd usages shall be abandoned; justice and righteousness shall regulate all actions.

V. Knowledge shall be sought for all over the world, and thus shall be strengthened the foundations of the Imperial Polity. (W. W. McLaren, "Japanese Government Documents," *Transactions of the Asiatic Society of Japan* (Tokyo), XLII (1914), Pt. I, p. 8.

[5] House of Representatives, 90th Session of Diet, Minutes of June 28, 1946, English ed., *Official Gazette*, Extra, pp. 8-9, 12. (Hereafter cited as H.R., 90th Session.)

[6] *Ibid.*, June 29, 1946, p. 7.

[7] *Ibid.*, p. 9.

[8] *Ibid.*

[9] *Ibid.*, p. 10.

[10] *Ibid.*, p. 11.

[11] *Ibid.*, p. 15.

[12] *Ibid.*, June 28, 1946, pp. 7, 11.

[13] *Ibid.*, June 29, 1946, p. 15.

[14] *Ibid.*, June 28, 1946, pp. 7-8.

[15] *Ibid.*, p. 11.

[16] *Ibid.*, June 27, 1946, p. 4.

[17] *Ibid.*, p. 3.

[18] *Ibid.*, June 28, p. 5.

[19] *Nippon Times*, June 27, 1946.

[20] H.R. 90th Session, June 27, p. 5.

[21] *Ibid.*, p. 10.

[22] *Ibid.*, p. 13.

[23] *Ibid.*, p. 15.

[24] *Ibid.*, p. 19.

[25] *Ibid.*, June 28, 1946, p. 10.

[26] *Ibid.*, p. 14.

[27] *Ibid.*, pp. 15-16.

[28] *Ibid.*, June 29, 1946, p. 5.

[29] *Ibid.*, p. 13.

[30] *Ibid.*, June 27, 1946, p. 2.

[31] *Ibid.*, p. 4.

[32] *Ibid.*, p. 15.

[33] *Ibid.*, June 29, 1946, p. 14.

[34] *Ibid.*, June 27, 1946, pp. 16-17.

[35] *Ibid.*, June 28, 1946, p. 9.

[36] *Ibid.*, June 29, 1946, p. 1.

[37] *Ibid.*, p. 4.

[38] *Ibid.*, p. 13.

[39] *Ibid.*, p. 14.

[40] *Ibid.*, June 28, 1946, p. 6.

[41] *Ibid.*, June 27, 1946, pp. 8, 10-11.

[42] *Ibid.*, p. 12.

[43] *Ibid.*, August 26, 1946, pp. 2-6.

[44] *Ibid.*, pp. 6-8.

[45] *Ibid.*, pp. 9-11.

[46] *Ibid.*, p. 20.

[47] *Ibid.*, p. 28.

[48] *Ibid.*, p. 31.

[49] *Ibid.*, October 8, 1946, p. 2.

11

The Draft Constitution in the House of Peers

THE House of Peers which deliberated upon the draft constitution was the wartime House, but it contained an appreciable number of replacements of members who had resigned in anticipation of ouster by the political purge called for by SCAP directives.* Several of Japan's most authoritative scholars in the fields of constitutional and administrative law were members. Dr. Kanamori Tokujiro, so-called "minister of the constitution," pled guilty to justifiable insomnia induced by nightly fears of being talked down by the savants. The hard-pressed government spokesman was diffuse and confusing in his replies to the interpellations of the Peers, no doubt because of those fears. His rationalizations upon imperial sovereignty and the national polity were severely shaken, and he was compelled to revise them though they were expressive of the government's position.

Although the Peers had access to the minutes of the Representatives, they were not thereby inhibited from interpellating the government upon issues the Representatives had raised. Their interpellations were fewer and more lengthy than those of their less learned colleagues in the other House. They were also expressive of the personal authority and political views of the individual questioners as well as representative of the Peers' parties. The Peers were conservatives, in general, since they included no Socialists or Communists. They were also bolder in their criticisms, less awed by the endorsement given the draft by the Occupation authorities.

The House of Peers had appointed in June 1946 a Constitution

* See above, Chapter 8.

146

Revision Draft Study Committee of some thirty members.[1] Its purpose was to provide the House of Representatives with the opinions of a group of recognized authorities on constitutional law and history to aid it in its deliberations and also to shorten the subsequent deliberations of the House of Peers.* Formal consideration of the draft began in the second chamber after the revision bill had been passed by the House of Representatives. Five days, August 26 to 30 inclusive, were spent in plenary sessions. While allowance must be made, in evaluating the interpellations, for the effect of the Occupation upon self-expression, there is no more informative source for one who would understand the Japanese point of view and gauge Japanese standards of law and government than the Diet discussion.

The Peers' interpellators in both plenary sessions and committee hearings were chiefly concerned with the same problems as those broached by the Representatives (discussed in the preceding chapter). Other issues of greater or less interest were the importance and difficulty of building a moral foundation for democracy; changes in the nature of the family system; relations between the Houses of the Diet; the premier's power over other ministers; and the effect of the new constitution upon the legal system of the country. Members were permitted to wander far afield, and a very vague relevance was sufficient to justify a member in indulging his specialty of knowledge or interest before his colleagues.

The Issue of Revision

It is noteworthy that the Peers' interpellators were not unwilling to revise the Meiji constitution, although they preferred that it be retained as the core of the organic law, not replaced by a new document grounded in Anglo-American law and political theory. Takayanagi Kenzo, professor of law at the Imperial University of Tokyo, a liberal scholar of international reputation, reminded the Peers that the call for revision came not only from the victor powers but from Japanese who had suffered from the war or who resented the "political and economic oppression of the militarists and bureaucrats."[2]

Sawada Ushimaro voiced a vehement protest at the hasty and careless drafting of the "makeshift draft constitution," quite in contrast

* No reference to the views of this committee was made in the plenary sessions of either House.

to the "impressive style" and "extremely grand and lofty scale" of the Meiji document.[3] He made an impassioned argument to the effect that it was the man who advised the emperor badly and not the constitutional system itself that needed to be replaced. Oblivious to the reality of the emperor's position, Sawada exclaimed: "The Emperor, by combining in himself the rights of sovereignty, holds the rivet for coordination of the three powers. I think that this [Meiji] is the most ideal and splendid constitution."

The cat came out of the bag in Sawada's speech. Said he: "Of course I have not compiled statistics on this point, but I have met and talked with so many people who said that this [draft] constitution was terrible. Some say this is no sort of Japanese constitution. I think that this is a true and frank expression of the people's minds. Some people in the influential positions or others aiming at some advantages for the future may keep silence, saying nothing but to urge the people that now is the time to endure. But such an attitude cannot be considered proper, because now is the time for the Japanese people to discuss a constitution that should last forever."[4]

Professor Itakura Takuzo might have been suspected of dealing in irony in his fulsome praise of the draft. He called it "excellent," likely to become the best constitution in the world.[5] Miyazawa Toshiyoshi, one of the ablest commentators, did not oppose revision, but he argued effectively that a revision which would establish popular sovereignty could not be carried out under Article 73 of the Meiji constitution. Legal authorities were agreed that that document could not be interpreted as providing a means of repealing the central principle upon which it was written. In Miyazawa's view, therefore, revision was "super-constitutional . . . necessitated by the termination of the war."[6]

The Diet and the Amendment Process

Professor Miyazawa doubted that revision under Article 73 of the old constitution could be regarded as satisfying the requirement of establishment by the will of the people. Was it proper to regard Diet approval and imperial sanction as expressions of the people's will? The Peers and the emperor could thwart the Representatives. He argued that the Preamble's statement that the Japanese people ordained and established the new constitution was inaccurate.

The Draft Constitution in the House of Peers

President Nambara Shigeru of the Imperial University of Tokyo, a leading political scientist and the most trenchant of the Peers' interpellators, held a somewhat contrary view. He thought that a logical inference from the Potsdam Proclamation was that "the revision bill [should] be drawn up by the Diet, which is the elected representative of the people," a democratic challenge which might well have been voiced earlier.[7] He argued that the necessity of proceeding under Article 73 should not have prevented the association of Diet committees with the drafting process. And the House of Peers, representing only certain elements of the population, should not, Nambara believed, consider itself entitled to amend the draft which had been accepted by the more representative House. On the contrary, he urged, acceptance of the Potsdam Proclamation obligated the government to submit the draft to a referendum of the people.

Who Wrote the Draft?

Sawada Ushimaro, least inhibited of all the interpellators, was unable to comprehend why the Japanese government, with a "considerable number of legal experts," had presented "such an incoherent and queer draft" to the Diet. He referred to a rumor that the draft was not to be touched, that it was "taboo." General MacArthur's published encouragement of free discussion and amendment should have assured the government of its freedom to produce an acceptable document, he thought. Instead of doing so, however, it had written "rules for a society of self-culture," or "directions for drafting a constitution."[8] Kanamori twisted Sawada's words, in replying, into a statement that the draft was "drawn up like a textbook of our policy of legislation." His reply was an admission that in part the draft was an expression of ideals, not of immediately practicable rules. But he carefully avoided any indication that an alien hand had done any actual drafting.[9]

President Nambara probed uncomfortably into the relation of former Premier Shidehara's cabinet to SCAP. His position was that the Matsumoto committee was not alert to the necessities imposed by the Occupation and was consequently caught with an unacceptable draft and obliged to substitute one which was written "outside." Nambara showed exceptional courage in criticizing SCAP also on the ground that its part in preparing the draft was not in accord with the Potsdam Proclamation. The importance of this issue justifies a quotation from Nambara's remarkable address:

> It may be beyond the imagination of General MacArthur what great effects and consequences the draft drawn up in this manner and announced under the full support and approval of the Supreme Commander for the Allied Powers [would have]. This is endorsed by the fact that from the day following the announcement . . . the drafts prepared and announced up to that time by the various political parties have disappeared and these political parties have come to approve the draft in question unanimously.

> Such may not have been the case in a state where democracy has developed to such an extent as in the United States, but this is the present state of affairs in Japan.[10]

Shidehara's reply was couched in the language of a master of diplomacy, but its meaning was apparent: "Dr. Nambara has questioned why we have suddenly changed our policy relative to the amendment of the constitution. My reply to his question, therefore, will be as follows: our policy in this respect has been suddenly altered and changed because the international situation has led us to the conclusion that the old constitution must be practically replaced, that we must strictly follow the demand of the times. I should think that Dr. Nambara's reproaches against us that we lost considerable time due to our delay in deciding our policy are not correctly directed."[11]

On the following day Premier Yoshida stated without qualification that "the original draft of the revised constitution was drawn up by the Government . . . submitted to the Diet. . . ." Dr. Nambara thus had obtained two answers, and at the same time no answer, on this point.

Nambara found the phraseology of the draft another indication of foreign authorship. He recalled that the Meiji constitution was of Prussian origin; but "what great pains," he exclaimed, "were taken by our seniors to remodel it into one thoroughly Japanese."[12] The new draft lacked "a style worthy of being handed down to our posterity."

Another high-ranking scholar, Dr. Sasaki Soichi, pressed the government upon the issue of authorship. He sought to meet previous explanations by reciting again the provisions of the Potsdam Proclamation which assured the Japanese people of their freedom to decide their form of government. Then he directly asked Kanamori what part he and what part the Matsumoto committee had played in writing the draft which was before the House. The minister replied that "it was some time in March that I was first connected with the mature stage of constitution-drafting."[13] From this reply it seems logical to infer that Kanamori acted as liaison man for the Shidehara cabinet in the eleventh-hour negotiations with SCAP after the Matsumoto draft had been rejected by the latter. That brief contact would constitute a briefing by SCAP rather than serious participation in drafting. Kanamori's reply does not bear out Yoshida's statement above quoted. And it failed to include any reference to the part played by Matsumoto and his colleagues.

Sasaki's resentment at alien authorship may also be read between the lines of his interpellation upon Chapter X of the draft, entitled, "Supreme Law." He proposed that this chapter be deleted. His argument was that it had no relevance to Japanese history or to the unitary system of government. The forthright professor spoke sharply: "Principles expounded therein will be taken for granted without express provisions. Because they are written, suggestion is likely to be made that some special necessity exists for those express provisions. If so, they are improper." Which was Sasaki's way of saying that SCAP should not be accepted as lawgiver for Japan.

But Sasaki went further.[14] In concluding his lengthy critique he asked: "Could not the Government withdraw the present bill . . . investigate the matter with the utmost care, publish the results of such investigation especially with a view to subjecting them to the scrutiny of the people, and after the lapse of a certain period of time submit it to the deliberations of the Diet convened for that purpose? . . . if the present draft passed as it is, I fear that we shall become a butt for the ridicule of the world."*

Sovereignty: What and Where

Professor Itakura praised the draft highly but asserted that it meant revolution through the transfer of sovereign power from the emperor to the people.[15] He likened this revolution to Britain's Glorious Revolution of 1688. To Itakura, although 1946 was Japan's 1688,

---

* Dr. Sasaki quoted the American magazine *Time*. The article was captioned, "We the Mimics" and appeared in the issue of March 18, 1946, written with that degree of sensitiveness and attention to accuracy one expects of *Time* correspondents.

the traditional national character (*kokutai*) had "undergone a complete change," Mr. Kanamori to the contrary notwithstanding. Itakura thought Kanamori a sentimentalist. Moreover, he pointed out, the British king is the unifying center of the "yearning adoration" of the British people, so why regard this sentiment as definitive of Japan's national character? He reminded Kanamori that Queen Victoria's footprint in the sand at Kirkcaldy was preserved in plaster by the loyal citizens of the place. And he denied also that the symbolic position of the imperial house was peculiar to Japan, citing in evidence the Preamble of the Statute of Westminster: "Inasmuch as the Crown is the symbol of the free association of the members of the British Commonwealth of Nations. . . ." He even cited a letter in *Newsweek* portraying President Truman as a symbol.

Itakura considered that the draft would reduce the powers of the emperor below those of the British king. He pointed also to the British peerage—far larger than the Japanese. One can hardly doubt that his conclusion was ironical: "Why is the Government hesitating . . . to state frankly, straightforwardly and with pride that Japan's national character has become new and splendid . . . ?"

Professor Miyazawa Toshiyoshi, a proponent of the draft, considered that the acceptance of the Potsdam Proclamation constituted an adoption of the principle of popular sovereignty. He declined to accept Kanamori's farfetched proposition that the emperor always had ruled as directed by the people, though granting that he had had a paternal attitude to which the people were responsive. Miyazawa deserves a citation on this point:

Nevertheless, the form of state ruling was always attributed to a divine will; at least it was not considered to be fundamentally due to the people's will. Despite that, the Government seems to maintain that popular sovereignty has been the basic principle of our country from before the termination of the war. Theoretically speaking, such an assertion of the Government, I am afraid, can by no means be called reasonable. Where could the principle of popular sovereignty be found in the Meiji constitution, which is said to have been established for the purpose of clarifying the instructions of the imperial ancestors and setting forth the standard precedents of ruling left by them for their succeeding rulers to follow?

If such constitution were to be called one based on the principle of popular sovereignty, what country would there be whose ruling should not be regarded as being based on popular sovereignty as long as it has any continuity of existence at all? In such case, there would be no theoretical distinction between monarchical sovereignty and popular sovereignty, and as a result, the assertion of popular sovereignty in the draft new constitution would lose all significance. Perhaps it is thought useful in some way or other from the actual viewpoint of politics to affirm the recognition of popular sovereignty prior to the termination of the war, though it is, in my opinion, theoretically wrong. In these days, however, when Japan is going to effect its political rebirth as never before since its foundation, the assertion of no change in fundamental principles cannot fail, I should think, to obstruct a correct understanding of the drastic reform that Japan is now undertaking and does not fit the practical purpose of attaining the democratization of politics in its true sense.[16]

Miyazawa disposed with equally clear logic of Kanamori's argument that the emperor shared in the sovereignty as one of the people:

When it is asserted on one hand that the position of the Emperor depends upon the total will of the sovereign people, what ground or what sense can there possibly be for explaining the term "people," on the other hand, as including the Emperor? It is a matter of course that the Emperor, who is an individual in such a position and a member of the Japanese nation as an individual, should be included among the people of Japan as a Japanese individual, and there is, I think, no need of making a special mention of such a matter. The question is as to the existence of the Emperor as a constitutional institution, and the existence of the Emperor as such an institution is clearly based on the total will of the sovereign people.[17]

This very able interpellator warned the government against raising unjustified suspicions that it was "declaring openly the principle of popular sovereignty and secretly insinuating the traditional principle of imperial sovereignty." He then completed his devastating attack upon Kanamori's structure of interpretation by pointing to the first official use of the term "national character" in the Public Peace Maintenance Law (Peace Preservation or "Dangerous Thoughts" Act) of 1925. In explaining the term, the Supreme Court had said, "It is the national character of this Empire that the Emperor of one family line unbroken for all ages rules over it and holds the reins of its government . . ." Miyazawa was able to recall that Kanamori had admitted that the emperor would not, under the proposed constitution, "hold the reins of government." His conclusion was that the minister must concede error in maintaining that the national structure would not be affected by the change of constitutions. But he made light of the legal issue by concluding sensibly that juridical revolution would not change the nature of the people, their unity, or the state itself. Kanamori gave reluctant consent to this line of reasoning.[18]

Dr. Nambara was another realist upon the issues centering in sovereignty. To his mind the draft emperor was not even an organ of the state but a ceremonial and ornamental figure only. Consequently the political character of the state would undergo a fundamental change. He would have none of Kanamori's quibbling about the emperor's being one of the people. He called it self-deception which was the more to be avoided because the success of the new principle of popular sovereignty depended upon "whether the people are conscious of the reform and are desirous of it." He feared that "if affairs are allowed to go on as they do now, it will only serve to give an excuse or ground for causing reaction among the people at a later date, say ten or twenty years from now."

Nambara denied that "the moment the Potsdam Proclamation was accepted sovereignty of the people was established in Japan," agreeing with Kanamori on that point. He argued that the Proclamation offered the people the opportunity to decide their future, and his conception of a desirable choice was a "national community" (*kokumin kyodotai*), headed by the emperor as a constitutional monarch, stripped of "the ancient idea of divine power or the feudalistic idea of the mediaeval age or a new romantic mysticism such as [Kanamori's dogma of] the 'center of adoration'." Nambara's proposal was British-inspired, but placed greater emphasis upon race as the significant element in nationality. He expressed a very reasonable doubt that the three departments of government could be held together by a "mere symbol."[19]

Outdoing in conservatism previous interpellators upon this central theme of the constitutional debate, Professor Sasaki Soichi affirmed that "the Tenno system in the correct sense of the term . . . stands abolished in the present bill." That system, he maintained, had two distinctive features: that the emperor held the right to govern (*tochiken-wo-soran*), and that he held it solely by virtue of his lineage. *Tenno*, therefore, was not merely the Japanese word for "monarch." By limiting the emperor to ceremonial functions, and by substituting for lineage the sovereign will of the people as the basis of the right to hold the title of Tenno, the draft would abolish the Tenno system. Sasaki delivered himself of a highly conservative if not naive estimate of the value of the Tenno system as it had existed. His words are quoted here rather for their revelation of the conservative scholar's interpretation than as a realistic description of the figurehead which the emperor was in actuality. Whether Sasaki was clinging to a doctrinaire picture in all sincerity or was seeking to pave the way to the substitution of constitutional monarchy for mere symbolism, his widely shared concept of the value of the Tenno is suggestive of democracy's obstacle race:

The question of whether such an institution as the Tenno is necessary or not may very well be discussed when a new state is to be established; but in a country like Japan where, under the Tenno, the government of the country, historically considered, has been conducted fairly well, is there any reason to deny positive political functions to the Tenno? However unselfish the Japanese may be, and however peaceful they may be in disposition, is it possible to assume that there will be no strife between individuals and classes? Such an assumption is nothing but self-deception of the first magnitude.

For better or for worse, capitalists, workers, politicians, government officials, etc., will think largely if not exclusively, in terms of their own interests. This is a hard fact of human life. If so, it is well to have an institution raised above classes and parties and capable of thinking of the well-being of the nation as a whole and of acting from that point of view. As a matter of fact, the creation of such an institution is extremely difficult. A president, though guardian of the national interests as a whole, has still to think of his party position. In this country, however, the Tenno as an institution has filled such a role. I cannot understand why the political functions of the Emperor should be suppressed.[20]

Professor Sasaki did himself no credit in challenging, on the score that the word had "multifarious" meanings, the use of the term "sovereignty" to define the authority of the Japanese people to rule. Moreover, his logic was hardly sound when he asked, "Can we ever find any special reason to ostracize the Emperor from the field of legislation who has never yet refused to give his assent to any single bill?" The interpellator confused presidential with parliamentary government, to the detriment of clarity and his reputation. And he completely shunned historical evidence upon the abuses of the Tenno system. Much of his very lengthy speech was a tilting at straw men, a rhetorical diatribe against what he considered a Western monstrosity.[21]

Noblesse Oblige the Armed

To renounce war, Professor Takayanagi observed, was reasonable only for the members of a world federation. Japan could not survive except as a member of such an organization.[22] His colleague, Dr. Nambara, agreed, and urged the government to maintain the right of self-defense against external attack and internal disorder. Otherwise independence could not be asserted. Dr. Sasaki affirmed that he doubted the ethics or wisdom of a renunciation of war by a single country. The renunciation of war was properly an international responsibility to be signified by an international act of renunciation.[23]

Human Rights

Takayanagi noted that the human rights clauses "seem to represent certain concessions to socialistic ideas," and he commented acutely, "We . . . find herein the twentieth century version of the American constitution." He believed that a document such as the draft, under which the issue of capitalism versus socialism was left undecided and in which capitalism and socialism can carry on their "political struggles on an equal footing," was well suited to Japan.[24]

Nambara was more critical. He wanted "cooperative democracy," i.e., the "democratization of the people's economic life," along with the political liberties guaranteed by Chapter III of the draft. "Social justice," he believed, was far more important to the Japanese people than eighteenth- or nineteenth-century individualism. At this point Dr. Nambara was an able proxy for the Shakaito. He asked for assurances, for example, that the constitutional guarantee of the right to work would not be frustrated by the public welfare clause. As for the "right to maintain minimum standards of wholesome and cultured living," he inquired, "How do the Government authorities view the present living conditions of the masses?" He justly affirmed that "any right of such a character will prove meaningless without enthusiasm and exertion on the part of the Government, however expressly it is provided for in the constitution."[25]

Dr. Makino Eiichi, a professor of civil and criminal law, went more deeply into the problem of effectuating human rights. He termed Chapter III an obsolete, nineteenth-century form for this purpose. His view of the proper form for a 1946 constitution may be broadly described as one which obligated the government in specific terms to implement civil rights and to apply the criminal law upon the principle of reform rather than revenge.[26]

Supreme Court versus Diet and People

To Takayanagi the power of judicial review was difficult to reconcile with the new Diet's supremacy over other "organs of state power." Quite clearly, Kanamori agreed with him, though he advanced a halfhearted explanation: the usefulness of "check and balance."[27] Sasaki, in line with his traditionalist point of view, approved of giving the Supreme Court the power to declare laws unconstitutional. He did not explain his approval, but qualified it by maintaining that the Court should be enabled to give advisory opinions as well as to decide cases in this field. On the other hand, he condemned the provision for a decennial referendum upon the supreme bench. Applause greeted his contention that the judges might better be bureaucratic than subservient to public opinion.[28]

Conditions of Democracy in Practice

Takayanagi asked how the Japanese people, with an ingrained morality of passive obedience, could be taught to operate a constitution of an advanced democratic type. Only a profound student of social change could have analyzed, as he did, the historical forces that have operated to promote in the Japanese a habit of deductive thinking accommodated to their European legal models. The need of "a more vigorous training in the art of evolving and discussing policies to meet the practical needs of life" was ably presented, the inescapable inference being that educational reform was the key to the problem.[29]

The Fate of the Family System

The family system, bridgehead in the fight to maintain the national character, was denied in substance by the draft, in the view of Sawada Ushimaro. A similar though less positive conclusion was reached by Makino Eiichi. They were reassured by Minister of Justice Kimura Tokutaro that only the feudal features, such as the authority of the family head to decide questions of marriage and residence, would be abolished. Kimura thought that "when it comes to the point of worshipping our ancestors and respecting our family trees . . . this virtue should be carried over to posterity by all means."[30]

The New Diet

Amidst a number of seemingly ill-considered questions raised by Professor Sasaki were others of some importance. Certain of these dealt with the respective functions of the Houses in the Diet and the control of the electors over them. He doubted the wisdom of having two Houses equally representative of all the people and performing the same functions. He asked what theoretical basis existed for the legal superiority of the House of Representatives and why the inferior House was immune from dissolution. He favored a bicameral Diet with a superior House of Representatives and a House of Councillors constituted on distinctive lines and having distinct functions.[31]

Akita Sanichi delivered a panegyric on the role played by the House of Peers. Perhaps one should call it a funeral oration. Like Sasaki he wished to retain the two-chamber system. He doubted whether the Representatives, though capable of expressing the "ideas, feelings and interests of the people," were also capable of originating "far-seeing policies for the state." He spoke of the need of a second chamber to prevent the natural emotionalism of the people from leading them into ill-considered legislation. But the members of the House of Councillors should be chosen upon distinctive bases and by distinctive methods in order that they might rival their predecessors of the House of Peers. They should not, Akita argued, have any relation with political parties in the other House, and they should regard themselves as obligated to supply the supervisory services of the late lamented Privy Council.[32]

Premier and Ministers

Dr. Sasaki dealt ably with the draft provisions relating to the cabinet. He questioned the tenability of the contention that the premier should enjoy the right to "hire and fire" ministers of state. The latter were not to be regarded as "a mere adjunct of the Prime Minister." He advocated imperial appointment of all the ministers, not of the premier only. He called Article 68 "push-button" administration, likely to reduce ministers to the position of clerks.

The Draft Constitution in the House of Peers

Although Sasaki did not relate his fear of the rise of a new type of dictatorship to this aspect of the draft, he might well have done so, since his fear was prompted by the anticipated loss of the unifying and integrating powers of the emperor. He envisaged the possible rise of a dominant political party and the ultimate appearance of a Hitler at its head. A dictator in the name of the people, Sasaki thought, would be more dangerous than an isolated dictator, i.e., a military or civilian oligarch.[33]

Effect upon the Legal System

Sawada Ushimaro, who seemed not to regret that he had "idled away [his] days in a law college," nevertheless brought up the important question — admittedly outside the four corners of the constitution — of the effect of an Anglo-American constitution upon the body of Japan's law, drawn so largely from France and Germany. He himself likened it to that of an atomic bomb, crushing everything in its path. A complete revision of the codes would be required, a tremendous task. Adjustment to the new laws would be difficult for the people. With the executive deprived of its former extensive ordinance power legislation would fall much more heavily upon the Diet. To this interpellation there were two replies, one by Saito Takao, who assured Sawada that there was nothing to worry about, the other by Dr. Uyehara Etsujiro, a thorough student of government, who assured him that there was a great deal to worry about. Dr. Uyehara believed, however, that by adopting the Anglo-American principle of applying the laws with a due consideration for circumstances rather than with a rigid adherence to texts, the courts would be able to accommodate Japanese traditions and the new laws to one another.[34]

Report of the Special Committee

Interpellations ended, the Peers voted to refer the revision bill to a special committee of forty-five members with Professor Abe Yoshishige as chairman.[35] This committee, which included many of the elite among Japan's legal authorities, held twenty-two meetings. Subsequently a small subcommittee held four meetings to draft amendments. The report of the latter to the special committee was accepted by it on October 3, 1946. Professor Abe made his report to the Peers on October 5. He expressed satisfaction with the very earnest labors of his committee and named the following matters as being those most fully considered:

1. The possible effects of the proposed constitution upon the Japanese national character (*kokutai*).

2. The interpretation of "unity" in Article 1 and the emperor's function in relation to it.

3. The preparation of a new statement of educational principles to replace the Imperial Rescript on Education.

4. The clarification and amplification of the articles providing for civil rights and duties.

5. The selection of members and the functions of the House of Councillors.

6. The phraseology of the document.

7. Deletion of all or part of the Preamble.

8. Substitute terms for "symbol."

9. Numerous aspects of the position of the emperor.

10. Japan's leadership toward world organization.

11. Meanings of the term "people."

12. The deletion of Chapter X as redundant.[36]

Professor Abe reported further that the special committee was proposing three amendments in substance as well as a number of verbal changes. No entirely new articles were proposed and no deletions, but new sections of some importance were recommended for Articles 15, 59, and 66. The addition proposed to Article 15 was the present third section: "Universal adult suffrage is guaranteed with regard to the election of public officials." Article 59 was supplemented by the section reading: "The provision of the preceding paragraph does not preclude the House of Representatives from calling for the meeting of a joint committee of both Houses, provided for by law." And Article 66 received the section: "The Prime Minister and other Ministers of State must be civilians." Regarding the last-named amendment, Professor Abe said: "This amendment is intended to contribute to securing the lasting peace of the world along with the renunciation of war provided for in Article 9 of Chapter II." He did not comment upon the inconsistency of the amendment with the second section of Article 9, which prohibits armed forces forever! Apparently the amendment was designed to exclude any former military officers from cabinet positions.[37] But it carries another interesting implication apparently not mentioned in the Diet.

Professor Abe's concluding paragraph revealed the distaste he had for his own report:

I need hardly say that the constitutional revision is only a matter of necessity for the Japanese people in view of what they have done in the past by turning the existing constitution to evil account. . . . When we were deliberating on the draft constitution I was full of deep emotions, looking back on the past. Now I cannot necessarily feel overjoyed at the new draft constitution but I think that the Japanese people must act hereafter on the basis of the new constitution with a view to fully developing its good spirits and deriving therefrom great delight and benefit in the future.[38]

There was no discussion of the committee's report. Professor Sasaki delivered a second lengthy address, his purpose being to explain his continued antagonism to the revision bill, which he did with more sentimentalism than sense or scholarship. His address was countered by two speakers, Matsumura Shinichiro and Okouchi Kiko, whose expressions of support of the draft had the air of afterthoughts rather than logical conclusions.[39] A third supporting member, Mizuchi Chuzo, quite eloquently argued that while an understanding of democracy would be slow to pervade the Japanese consciousness, all agencies and professions capable of influencing public understanding were now called upon to give "proper guidance to the people." [40] Without exception the speeches regretted the passing of the Meiji constitution and viewed the acceptance of the draft as an unhappy but unavoidable decision. All sought, in one way or another, to sugar-coat the bitter pill by assuring themselves and their fellow members that the national character would not be affected, and that the national unity, centering in the emperor, would survive.

Action upon the Report

After less than two days of discussion a standing vote was taken upon opening the second reading. Prince Tokugawa Iyemasa, president of the House, did not announce the number voting favorably, merely saying, "I understand that seconders are more than two thirds." At second reading amendments designed to increase the emperor's functions in the conduct of international relations, and in the granting of amnesty, and to require respect for family life were voted down after a brief but sharp interchange of views. The three amendments, all of them minor, offered in the committee report were adopted by standing vote without a count. The third reading was then voted. Without further debate a standing vote was taken upon the revision bill as amended in both Houses. President Tokugawa announced that more than the required two-thirds of the members had voted for the bill. Again he did not announce the number of favorable votes, but his statement was not challenged. Premier Yoshida thanked the House for its "earnest efforts" and for the contribution the members had made to national and foreign comprehension of "the general will of the intelligent classes of our country." [41] Thereupon the House passed to other business.

Notes

[1] *Nippon Times*, June 29, 1946.
[2] House of Peers, 90th Session of Diet, Minutes of August 27, 1946, English ed., *Official Gazette*, Extra, p. 2. (Hereafter cited as H.P., 90th Session.)
[3] *Ibid.*, pp. 9-10.
[4] *Ibid.*, pp. 11-12.
[5] *Ibid.*, p. 15.
[6] *Ibid.*, p. 21.
[7] *Ibid.*, August 28, 1946, pp. 2, 9.
[8] *Ibid.*, August 27, 1946, p. 12.
[9] *Ibid.*, p. 15.
[10] *Ibid.*, August 28, 1946, p. 3.
[11] *Ibid.*, p. 11.
[12] For a Japanese scholar's evidence to the contrary see T. Nakano, *The Ordinance Power of the Japanese Emperor* (Baltimore, 1923), Chapter 15.
[13] H.P., 90th Session, August 29, 1946, p. 14.
[14] *Ibid.*, August 30, 1946, pp. 11-12.
[15] *Ibid.*, August 27, 1946, pp. 16-18.
[16] *Ibid.*, p. 19.
[17] *Ibid.*, p. 20.
[18] *Ibid.*, pp. 20, 22.
[19] *Ibid.*, August 28, 1946, pp. 4-6.
[20] *Ibid.*, August 29, 1946, p. 17.
[21] *Ibid.*, August 30, 1946, pp. 2-4.
[22] *Ibid.*, August 27, 1946, p. 5.
[23] *Ibid.*, August 30, 1946, p. 10.
[24] *Ibid.*, August 27, 1946, p. 3.
[25] *Ibid.*, August 28, 1946, pp. 7-8.
[26] *Ibid.*, pp. 17-29.
[27] *Ibid.*, August 27, 1946, p. 7.
[28] *Ibid.*, August 29, 1946, pp. 5-6.
[29] *Ibid.*, August 27, 1946, pp. 5-6.
[30] *Ibid.*, August 29, 1946, p. 3.
[31] *Ibid.*, August 30, 1946, pp. 4-5.
[32] *Ibid.*, August 31, 1946, pp. 2-6.
[33] *Ibid.*, August 30, 1946, pp. 7, 9.

[34] *Ibid.*, August 31, 1946, pp. 17–18.
[35] *Ibid.*, p. 26.
[36] *Ibid.*, October 6, 1946, pp. 2–7.
[37] *Nippon Times*, September 27, 1946.
[38] H.P., 90th Session, October 6, 1946, p. 9.
[39] *Ibid.*, pp. 10–24, 27–30.
[40] *Ibid.*, October 7, 1940, pp. 1–4.
[41] *Ibid.*, pp. 11–23.

12

The New Constitution

THE Meiji[1] constitution was in effect from November 29, 1890, until May 3, 1947, a period of approximately fifty-six and a half years. The present constitution, which may be known after the demise of Emperor Hirohito as the Showa[2] constitution, was proclaimed to be in effect by Premier Yoshida Shigeru in the presence of Hirohito on May 3, 1947. The proclamation was read from a platform on the palace plaza in Tokyo. The audience of five thousand people which stood in the rain before the platform was small in comparison with the huge crowd that surged around the imperial carriage on November 3, 1946, following the official ceremony of promulgation, but it was equally enthusiastic in its demonstration of loyalty. On both occasions it was apparent that the embarrassed-looking, bespectacled little emperor, and not the constitution itself, was the center of popular interest.

The imperial message given out on November 3, 1946, read:

I have caused this day the constitution of Japan to be promulgated.

This constitution represents a complete revision of the imperial constitution. It seeks the basis of national reconstruction in the universal principle of mankind. It has been decided upon by the freely expressed will of the people. It explicitly stipulates that the people of Japan renounce war of their own accord, that they desire to see the realization of a permanent peace founded on justice and order throughout the world, and that having constant regard to the fundamental human rights, they will conduct the national affairs on the fixed line of democracy.

NOTE. This chapter, in slightly different form, was published in the *American Political Science Review*, XLI (October 1947), 865–874.

The New Constitution

It is my wish to join with my people in directing all our endeavors toward due enforcement of this constitution and the building of a nation of culture tempered by the sense of moderation and responsibility and dedicated to freedom and peace.[3]

The official promulgation ceremony was held in the chamber of the House of Peers and was attended by the members of both houses. The galleries were open to visitors and were well filled. Klieg lights illuminated the rostrum and the imperial chair behind and above it. Press and camera men were present. A solemnity of funereal depth marked the proceedings. No presiding officer appeared, the chamber was not called to order, and none of the speakers was introduced. Premier Yoshida and his cabinet colleagues ranged themselves before the rostrum shortly before Emperor Hirohito entered. His dark-blue suit, buttoned to the neck, was of military cut and bore a single large decoration. He stood before his red-brocaded chair and read aloud the promulgation rescript handed to him by the Grand Chamberlain. The premier then received the rescript and read a brief reply, after returning to the floor of the chamber and reascending to the rostrum.[4] The president of the House of Peers and the speaker of the House of Representatives also read replies to the rescript. There were no *banzai* from the members, who stood silently throughout the ceremony and bowed when the principal participants bowed. Within fifteen minutes the emperor had left the chamber, and the memorable ceremony had ended without formal adjournment.

Continuity was officially declared between the old and the new documents in the imperial rescript of promulgation: "I rejoice that the foundation for the construction of a new Japan has been laid according to the will of the Japanese people, and hereby sanction and promulgate the amendments of the imperial Japanese constitution effected following the consultation with the Privy Council and the decision of the Imperial Diet made in accordance with Article 73 of the said constitution."[5] The words "revision" and "amendments" are, however, descriptive only of the procedure followed. The new constitution is not, in fact, a revision but an entirely new instrument of government. Japan's fundamental law has been fundamentally changed. Whether or not a corresponding change will occur in Japan's political way of life, thus infusing reality into legality, only time will tell.

The New Japan

Form and Models

The new constitution is entitled simply "The Constitution of Japan," and throughout the document the terms "empire" and "imperial" are used less frequently than in the old instrument.[6] In general the sequence of chapters is the same in both, but the new document has eleven chapters, the old seven, the additional chapters being the second, "Renunciation of War"; the eighth, "Local Self-Government"; the ninth, "Amendments"; and the tenth, "Supreme Law." There are 103 articles in the new, 76 in the old constitution. In phraseology the new instrument is somewhat rhetorical and is less definite and legalistic than that of Ito Hirobumi and his codrafters of Meiji.

Whereas the constitutions of Prussia and other German states of the early 1880s were the models used by Meiji statesmen, American, British, and internationalist principles are dominant in the present constitution. The revolutionary change involved cannot be felt more forcefully than by reading a few sentences of the respective Preambles. In 1889 Emperor Mutsuhito prefaced his gift of liberties with these words:

Having, by virtue of the glories of Our Ancestors, ascended the Throne of a lineal succession unbroken for ages eternal . . . we hereby promulgate . . . a fundamental law of State, to exhibit the principles by which We are to be guided in Our conduct. . . .

The rights of sovereignty of the State We have inherited from Our Ancestors and We shall bequeath them to Our descendants . . .

The Preamble of 1947 reads, in part:

We, the Japanese people, acting through our duly elected representatives in the national Diet . . . do proclaim that sovereign power resides with the people and do firmly establish this constitution. Government is a sacred trust of the people, the authority for which is derived from the people, and the benefits of which are enjoyed by the people. This is a universal principle of mankind upon which this constitution is founded. We reject and revoke all constitutions, laws, ordinances, and rescripts in conflict therewith.

Sovereignty and Sovereign

Obviously no Japanese conceived or wrote the lines quoted from the new Preamble. They were composed while the old constitution was in force and would have been arrant *lèse-majesté* under it. But today they are part of Japan's supreme law, which all Japanese, in or out of public office, are bound "to respect and uphold." It is probable that the majority of the people did not know what they meant and that an influential element accepted them only under duress and hoped to see them diluted by interpretation. Among the latter may have been honest men who feared that a too rapid democratization would produce disorder and civil strife. Others cherished the privileges and power of oligarchy and bureaucracy. Perhaps both aspects of this attitude, which, while antimilitarist and pro-Western, is too deeply attached to tradition to welcome popular sovereignty, were revealed in the position taken by Dr. Kanamori Tokujiro, the minister of state, who bore the brunt of the burden of explaining the provisions of the constitution to the members of the Diet. When pressed by an eminent professor of constitutional law, Dr. Sasaki Soichi, as to whether or not the new constitution provided for a change in the national polity (*kokutai*), Kanamori, as previously noted, replied in the negative.[7] He maintained that the constitution does not alter the "characteristics of the state." Dr. Sasaki responded that the principal characteristic of the Japanese state had been the sovereignty of the emperor by virtue of his lineage. He maintained that with the disappearance of this characteristic feature the polity had been fundamentally altered. Kanamori, however, with the support of Premier Yoshida, argued that Sasaki was pointing to a mere legal change which would not affect the moral position of the dynasty — the true index of the national polity.

Kanamori's interpretation was not in accord with facts. To his people the emperor has been all-powerful — legally and politically as well as morally. The people have not comprehended his true position, and they will find extreme difficulty in understanding what changes have taken place. They will not be helped by pseudoscholarly sophistry. It is unfortunate that this process of undermining the democratic movement should have begun during the gestation period of true constitutionalism. Professor Sasaki's view that sovereignty is a legal, not a moral, concept, that the emperor has been both sovereign and moral leader but that he has surrendered sovereignty while retaining moral leadership, exhibited an understanding of the issue. Unless Japan's statesmen are willing and vigorous exponents of popular sovereignty, there can only result a period of confused thinking, cul-

SOVEREIGNTY IN THE OLD CONSTITUTION

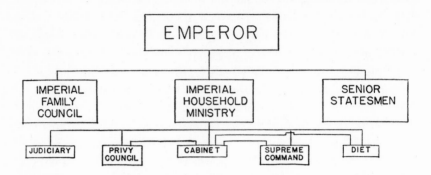

minating in a struggle for power between the forces of liberalism and reaction. ". . . the government's interpretation," wrote Professor Yokota Kisaburo in the article cited above, "was a distortion of the true spirit of the new constitution. It is, therefore, necessary that by fully appreciating the true meaning of the new constitution, we endeavor to guard it from being misinterpreted by conservative concepts or abused to suit reactionary purposes."

A deference to Japanese sentiments underlay the allocating of the emperor's position to Chapter I, as in the old constitution. Article 1

SOVEREIGNTY IN THE NEW CONSTITUTION

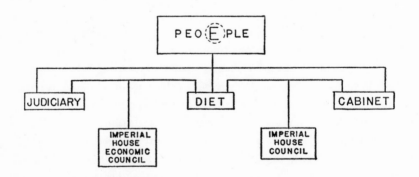

$\left(\widehat{E}\right)$ INDICATES EMPEROR, SYMBOL OF AUTHORITY

of 1947 contrasts with Article 1 of 1889. The former runs: "The Emperor shall be the symbol of the state and of the unity of the people, deriving his position from the will of the people, with whom resides sovereign power." That of 1889: "The Empire of Japan shall be reigned over and governed by a line of Emperors unbroken for ages eternal."

In political terms, the emperor, endowed by the old constitution with supreme executive, legislative, and judicial power, was a symbol of rule, not a ruler.[8] Thus the new constitution embodies in law a political fact many centuries old. By it the emperor is authorized to perform certain "acts of state" but is specifically forbidden to exercise "powers related to government." This prohibition is vague and difficult of enforcement, but its intent is clear. In the light of history, there is small likelihood that a Japanese emperor will seek to govern. The opponent of democracy has been, not autocracy, but bureaucracy.

Renunciation of War

The new constitution is unique in history in its renunciation of war and of the threat or use of force as the means of settling international disputes (Article 9). The right of self-defense has not been renounced, but would be ineffective without military forces, all types of which "will never be maintained." These provisions, as well as the expression of trust "in the justice and faith of the peace-loving peoples of the world," read strangely in the existing world situation. That they will long outlive the re-establishment of Japan's independence is more than doubtful. Not only are political probabilities against their permanence. International law also may be appealed to in justification of repudiation of them unless other states follow the example which Japan, perforce, has set.

Civil Rights

The principle that "subjects" shall enjoy civil rights was recognized and implemented, to a certain extent, in the old constitution. The rights enumerated were, in general, those customarily granted in the constitutions of democratic states. They were not, however, constitutionally guaranteed, since their definition was left to legislation and their standing in the courts was dependent upon it. The control of a bureaucratic, and at times militarist, executive over the Diet, the broad ordinance power, and the weakness of popular agencies of expression contributed to transform the old bill of rights (Articles 18–32) into a declaration of ideals.

A warm sympathy for the common man vitalizes the civil rights chapter of the new constitution. Emphasis, in eloquent rather than precise language, is placed upon "human rights." They are declared to be "eternal and inviolate" and to belong, not to subjects or citizens, but to "the people." They are guaranteed by the constitution itself, all the old references to limiting "provisions of law" having been swept away. In a few articles sentences from the American bill of rights are copied verbatim. But the general character of the provisions is to be traced to the desire to strike at feudal survivals — to assure respect for the individual, to encourage him to struggle to maintain his rights, and to eliminate discrimination between social classes, the sexes, religions, husband and wife, rich and poor. The United Nations Charter may have influenced these articles. But they also have precedents in Oriental legislation, which goes farther than Occidental in mixing high precept with immediately enforceable provisions.

Parliamentary Government

Although Article 55 of the Meiji constitution, "The respective ministers of state shall give their advice to the Emperor and be responsible for it," was indefinite regarding the direction of responsibility, in practice the ministers were responsible primarily to the throne. Since the throne was a symbol rather than a seat of power, the ministers were in practice responsible to themselves or to the oligarchy which ruled from behind the throne. Thus the executive branch actually exercised the legislative power constitutionally vested in the emperor acting with the consent of the Diet. The cabinet was not obliged to resign upon vote of want of confidence. If thwarted in its legislative program, it could resign and seek a new mandate by election. Its ordinance powers were enormous. But its principal asset was the age-old tradition of bureaucratic government that held the people and their elected representatives in thrall.

Today the parliamentary system, on the British pattern, is the central feature of the Japanese government. The Diet is "the highest organ of state power and . . . the sole law-making organ of the state"

(Article 41). The premier is elected by the Diet and the cabinet is responsible to it. Resignation or appeal to the country through election must follow a vote of want of confidence by the House of Representatives. A majority of the cabinet members must be members of the Diet.

Unless the deference to executive rule which has characterized the Diet continues to paralyze the political parties, there can thus be faster progress along the road to democracy. Not only does the new constitution definitely subordinate the cabinet to the Diet, it weakens the executive as a whole by omitting provisions and conventions of the old constitution which prevented a liberal-minded cabinet from exhibiting responsibility to the Diet. Unaided or unhampered by a Privy Council, Imperial Household officials, and a group of powerful military agencies, the cabinet must accept responsibility and need not fear to do so. Stripped of the legislative ordinance power, it must go to the Diet to implement its policies. Its great financial powers no longer exist.

In view of the abolition of the peerage and of the provision (Article 43) that both houses of the Diet shall be elected and "representative of all the people," the subordination of the "upper" to the "lower" house lacks the justification which it has in Great Britain. It is in accord, however, with the expectation that the new upper house, though popularly elected, will tend to carry over the conservatism of its predecessor. As in Great Britain, where the cabinet was and is responsible to the House of Commons, it follows logically that the House of Councillors, like the House of Lords, should be unable to veto cabinet proposals. But a consultative house, combining the valuable attributes of the old Privy Council and House of Peers while deprived of their crippling authority, is an essential feature of successful parliamentarism in Japan.

Repudiation of Dualism

The constitutional position of the composite of agencies known as the Supreme Command had brought about a dualism in the operation of the executive branch which embarrassed and at times paralyzed the cabinet.[9] Manifested most obviously in relation to foreign affairs, dualism affected the whole range of political action. Since the Supreme Command, if it maintained unity, could force acceptance of its views, the net result of dualism was the domination of government by the military.

The new constitution, as noted above, prohibits the maintenance of military forces of any type. One might expect to find a prohibition of ministries of war, navy, or national defense, and of other agencies of military administration. No such provision appears. On the contrary, the implication in Article 66, "The Prime Minister and other ministers of state must be civilians," is that military ministries may be established.[10] However, there is no provision for the exercise of military authority outside the cabinet, in which executive power is vested. Constitutional dualism is abolished. When the efforts of Hara, Hamaguchi, Inukai, Saionji, and Takahashi to confine the military power within its proper limits are recalled, there seems warrant to believe that future conspirators against civilian government will be unable to reinstate the constitutional bases of militarist control.

Judicial Independence and Review

Japan's judges have been men of ability, integrity, and learning. They have been constitutionally protected from executive interference and removal. The courts have been recognized as a separate branch of government, though functioning on behalf of the emperor, the repository of judicial power. Their judgments have not been reversible by the minister of justice. The intent of the framers of the Meiji constitution that the judiciary should be independent of the administrative officers has been realized in considerable measure.

The attainment of complete independence has been delayed, in part by the inclination of judges to defer to the administration — a heritage from feudal times — in part by the authority of the minister of justice to make the rules of judicial procedure, to make appointments and recommend promotions, to direct the work of the procurators, and to initiate prosecution in all criminal cases. The new constitution (Article 6) seeks to strengthen the position of the courts by denying final judicial power to any organ or agency of the executive, by endowing the Supreme Court with extensive rule-making powers, and by authorizing it to nominate the judges of the inferior courts. Presumably other desirable reforms will be made by statute.

The Supreme Court has had the power to declare ordinances unconstitutional. This power is now expanded to cover statutes, a less revolutionary change in law than might be supposed, since the courts have been the implementers of the all-embracing imperial prerogative.[11] In relation to practice, however, the change is revolutionary, enabling the Supreme Court to exercise political power to check the Diet on behalf of the sovereign people.[12] Whether this power will result in strengthening the Diet against an executive as yet new to its responsibility to that body, or will backfire in support of intransigent bureaucracy, will depend upon the rate of growth of the democratic spirit.

Local Self-Government

Local autonomy in prefectures and municipalities is established as a principle in the new constitution, which leaves it to the Diet to implement the principle by law. Except for the election of prefectural governors no specific change in the existing system of local government is prescribed by the constitution.

Amendments

The power of initiating constitutional amendments, formerly residing in the executive, is now shared by the Diet, and ratification by the people is required to complete the process of amendment. Admirable simplicity characterizes the entire process: the concurrence of two-thirds of all members in each house; ratification by majority vote in a special referendum or a specified election.

Conclusion

Professor Minobe Tatsukichi, Japan's foremost liberal commentator on constitutional law, has been quoted as opposed to discarding the Meiji constitution. He believed that democracy could advance under it if it were properly enforced.[13] Professor Minobe devoted his life to interpreting the old constitution upon democratic principles. No one knew as well as he how difficult and dangerous that effort had been. Yet democracy advanced in Japan during his lifetime. Who can say whether new forces released from bondage by the defeat might not have infused new meaning into the old document? Might not the freedoms written into the new constitution have been more clearly understood and more greatly prized if they had come out of struggle and not as a gift? Perhaps the answer is that constitutions are not what is written but what is done, and that the struggle to prevent the misinterpretation or amendment of the new constitution will afford plenty of exercise to such new forces as may emerge.

Assuming that these new liberal forces do emerge, will they feel the handicap, will they themselves resent the implications, of a constitution imposed by alien conquerors? Will the results of arduous and sincere, if overhasty and self-satisfied, effort be swept away by a gust of nationalism? Many factors — Japanese opinion toward Occupation policy, post-treaty trade relations, the attitude of the United Nations, and the position of Russia — may operate to preserve or to destroy this document. Like the Weimar constitution, it represents the political center. Japan today, like Germany in 1920, lacks a strong center party. It may swing wide to the right or to the left. The new constitution is, however, a projection of lines of development that were apparent before the Manchurian crisis occurred. That fact is an augury of its survival.

Notes

[1] Meiji is the title of the period of Emperor Mutsuhito's reign, and means Enlightened Government. The effective date coincided with that of the inauguration of the Diet.

[2] Showa is the title of the period of Emperor Hirohito's reign, and means Radiant Peace.

[3] *Official Gazette*, Extra, November 3, 1946, p. 1.

[4] The descents from the rostrum were difficult as they were required to be made backward, but there were no casualties.

[5] *Official Gazette*, Extra, November 3, 1946, p. 1.

[6] The new and the old constitutions are printed as Appendixes I and II of this book.

[7] See above Chapters 10 and 11. See also K. Yokota, "Sovereignty under the New Constitution," *Contemporary Japan*, XVI (1947), 134–147.

[8] H. S. Quigley, *Japanese Government and Politics* (New York, 1932), Chapter 5.

[9] *Ibid.*, pp. 87–89, 104–117.

[10] Cf. D. N. Rowe, "The New Japanese Constitution — II," *Far Eastern Survey*, February 12, 1947, pp. 32–33.

[11] H. Ito, *Commentaries on the Constitution of the Empire of Japan*, 2nd ed. (Tokyo, 1906), pp. 111–112.

[12] On the nature of judicial review see William Anderson, *American Government*, 3rd ed. (New York, 1946), Chapter 10.

[13] See above, p. 111.

13

The Citizen and His Rights

DEMOCRACY is a political condition in which participants recognize themselves as such and insist upon sharing equally in its benefits while accepting an obligation to maintain it by all means available to them. Liberty, equality, duty — these are the attributes of citizenship; duty alone is the heritage of a subject.

An exceptionally able Japanese editor has intimated that awareness of citizenship is lacking among the people of Japan: "Paradoxically, the very mentality of the people which causes them to welcome democracy so readily without fully understanding its implications is in a sense an evidence of a feudalistic outlook on life which favors truckling to the times and fawning upon the powerful. . . . What difference is there between the present attitude of enthusiasm for democracy on the part of the Japanese people and their previous sycophancy to militarism?"[1]

Another Japanese author has advanced the thought that the Japanese ideas *giri* and *ninjo*, combined as *giri-ninjo* and of ancient usage, are equivalent in meaning to democracy. *Giri* means to love others as one loves himself; *ninjo* means to love oneself.[2] He believes that these ideas were trampled underfoot in Japan's nineteenth-century exaltation of the nation-state. The state replaced society and demanded the undivided devotion of all its people. *Giri-ninjo*, however, was developed under feudalism. True, it embodies ideas essential to democracy, but it is lacking in the aggressive individualism required for effective citizenship in a democracy. Under feudalism the people were regarded as "public treasure" (*o-mitakara*), to be loved and cherished by their rulers, but without rights against them. Moreover "society" under feudalism was a narrower, not a more comprehensive, concept than "state" during the Restoration. It was familistic, not community-wide. Reciprocity of rights and obligations was recognized within the family circle — a comparatively extensive circle, but one within which the motivation was familial, not societal.

Political and civil rights, which are the endowment of a citizen as distinguished from a mere subject, were embodied in the old constitution of Japan.[3] They were subject to definition by statutes passed by a parliament which had not yet put off executive domination; also to restriction by imperial ordinances, administrative interpretation of statutes, and an arbitrary police. It was not, therefore, remarkable that Prince Ito Hirobumi saw no reason to distinguish between the terms "subject" and "citizen." Were he to enjoy resurrection in order to read the new constitution, he would not, it may be ventured, survive the shock of the Preamble.

The Nationality Law

The new constitution, like the old, left the determination of the conditions of nationality to statute.[4] A new nationality law, enacted on May 4, 1950, became effective on July 1, 1950.[5] This law replaced that of 1899, which had been amended twice. It maintains the principle of *jus sanguinis* (law of the blood), under which a child is recognized as Japanese if his father was Japanese at the time of the child's birth or if the mother was Japanese, the father being unknown or stateless. The principle of *jus soli* (law of the soil) applies to a child born in Japan when both parents are unknown or stateless.

Naturalization also is maintained, but with important changes. The Ministry of Justice replaces the Ministry of Home Affairs as the authority competent to grant naturalization. The process involves domicile for five consecutive years in Japan, an age requirement of twenty years, evidence of the applicant's full capacity under his own country's law, of his good character, and of his capacity to support himself. An applicant is required to show either that he has no nationality or that he will lose his nationality upon acquiring that of Japan. An up-to-the-minute touch appears in the final requirement of proof that the applicant is not subversively inclined toward the government.

The minister of justice may, in prescribed instances, grant naturalization upon fewer conditions. He may permit an alien who has rendered especially meritorious service to Japan to receive it if the Diet approves.[6] For an alien husband of a Japanese national only three consecutive years of residence are required. A child of a former Japanese national may be naturalized on the same terms; so may an alien who was born in Japan. A child of a Japanese national adopted while a minor is qualified by a single year's domicile in Japan. An alien born in Japan whose father or mother was born in Japan need not satisfy any specific residence requirement in order to obtain naturalization. A Japanese by birth who has lost his nationality need only be domiciled in Japan and of good conduct to be eligible.

It is to be noted that a husband's naturalization no longer automatically involves the naturalization of his wife and children. Also that marriage to an alien no longer involves loss of her former nationality for a Japanese woman, and that marriage to a Japanese no longer carries with it Japanese nationality for an alien woman. These changes represent an effort to apply the new constitutional principles of the equality of the sexes and of the dignity of the individual. Discriminations against naturalized persons in the old nationality law, making them ineligible for membership in the Diet, the cabinet, and the Supreme Court, were not embodied in the new law.

Loss of nationality occurs when a Japanese national voluntarily acquires the nationality of another state. A Japanese national who has acquired a foreign nationality by birth abroad loses Japanese nationality as from birth unless he or she indicates intent to reserve it in accordance with the family registration law.[7] The renunciation of Japanese nationality by a Japanese who attains foreign nationality is authorized by the new law, as it was by the old. It may be declared by his legal representative for a person under fifteen years of age. No conditions were attached to the right of renunciation but it may be anticipated that the rearming of Japan will have its effect upon this right.[8]

The Bill of Rights

Japanese nationals (*kokumin*) are endowed with the fundamental civil and political rights normally pertaining to citizenship in a democracy by the constitution of 1947.[9] But the new bill of rights goes beyond the provision of the fundamental rights required to protect the individual from arbitrariness of government. It also provides in a number of ways for the participation by government in measures to assure the people's welfare. To quote Professor Wagatsuma Sakae: ". . . whereas the old constitution safeguards the fundamental rights of liberty only by restricting the method of legislation concerning those rights, the new constitution makes those rights tenable against any possible encroachment by the legislature. Secondly, whereas the old constitution safeguards only the fundamental rights of liberty, the new constitution takes a step forward into the sphere of the fundamental rights of existence." [10]

Professor Takayanagi Kenzo may also be quoted to advantage: "The chapter on rights and duties of the people not only provides for most items found in the classical bill of rights, but also elevates social and economic rights of recent origin to the rank of fundamental rights. The exercise of such rights, however, is to be limited by consideration for the public welfare." [11]

Civil as well as political rights pertain to Japanese nationals, not to foreigners. However, the new civil code provides that "aliens enjoy private rights except in cases where it is prohibited by laws, ordinances or treaties." [12] The use of such terms as "the people" and "all persons" in the constitution should not be regarded as in contradiction of the civil code, since it is clear from the fact that these terms appear in relation to rights normally restricted to nationals that they are intended to cover Japanese only. The liberality of the above-quoted provision of the code renders the issue of constitutional protection for the rights of aliens one of no practical significance.

In the new bill of rights, as in that of the constitution of the United States, the rights are granted, not merely listed as to be determined by law as they were in the Meiji constitution. As in any democratic state this does not mean that the national legislature has no power to limit the actual extent of liberty or that public welfare may not be defined by law. It does mean that the granted rights must be implemented by legislation and administration, that they may not be nullified by inaction. It is apparent, however, that the standards of action to be taken lie with the legislative, judicial, and administrative agencies, and with the people.

In view of the probability that the bill of rights written by members of General Douglas MacArthur's staff will undergo revision that will improve its organization, reduce repetition, and eliminate didactic verbiage and irrelevant articles, the present treatment will endeavor to emphasize its more significant and potentially durable elements. To begin with, it is of interest that the major differences between the old and the new bills of rights — aside from that noted in the previous paragraph — are (1) the absence in the latter of any provision for emergency powers for the emperor, (2) the presence in the latter of a considerable number of principles that run counter to the old family system, and of provisions relating to the public welfare, working conditions, indemnification against the state, etc., which are wholly lacking in the Meiji bill, and (3) the far more complete provision in the latter for legal processes to protect personal life and liberty.

On the other hand we find that both bills provide for freedom to select and to change one's place of abode, immunity of residence from entrance and search, inviolability of correspondence, the right to own property, religious freedom, and freedom of speech, publication, and assembly. In the realm of political rights both constitutions grant the right to vote — the old in terms of the election law, the new to all adults — and to hold public office; both also grant the right to petition public authorities. Both impose the duty to pay taxes; only the Meiji bill makes mention of the obligation to do military service. The new bill bans discrimination in political, economic, or social relations because of race, creed, sex, social status, or family origin. It does away with the peerage and forbids the grant of privileges with awards or decorations and the passage of such distinctions by inheritance. It must be kept in mind that the apparent coextensiveness of the two bills of rights in reference to the classical fundamental rights is qualified by the limiting clauses in the Meiji instrument. Yet the apparent similarity is important for the assurance of permanence which it suggests.

New Status for the Individual

While keeping in mind that the Meiji bill of rights reflected a dawning consciousness of the value of the individual as a participant in political action and not merely its object, one is impressed by the extreme earnestness with which the new constitution inculcates this point of view. Article 24 may be termed the heart of the new bill of rights, since it sets up principles incompatible with the feudal type of family system, which was deeply imbedded in the law and customs of Japan. Its provisions may well suffer amendment but they deserve to be quoted here for their historical — and probably for their contemporary — significance:

Marriage shall be based only on the mutual consent of both sexes and it shall be maintained through mutual cooperation with the equal rights of husband and wife as a basis.

With regard to choice of spouse, property rights, inheritance, choice of domicile, divorce and other matters pertaining to marriage and the family, laws shall be enacted from the standpoint of individual dignity and the essential equality of the sexes.[13]

Buttressing this central article in its attack upon the traditional subordination of the individual to the family, particularly to the person recognized as head of the house, are other principles new to Japan's constitution, such as the rights of all people "to maintain minimum standards of wholesome and cultured living" and "to receive an equal education correspondent to their ability, as provided by law." Workers are guaranteed the right to organize and to bargain and act collectively; children are not to be exploited, etc. The whole body of rights related to social welfare may be regarded as upsetting to the old family system. However, these rights are not peculiarly contrived against such a system, but are those familiar to Western law, though not, as a rule, found in Western constitutions. They include a mandate to the state "to use its endeavors for the promotion and extension of social welfare and security, and of public health," to provide compulsory free education for children of both sexes, to set legal standards for wages, hours, and other working conditions. It is apparent that many of these provisions are unattainable in practice at present, but they are not intrinsically utopian.

Position of the *Eta*

Quite apart from the general traditional and financial obstacles that beset the path of social advancement for Japan's unwieldy population, the old problem of the *eta* (outcasts) — sometimes described as Japan's parallel of the Negro problem in the United States — persists.[14] Unlike Negroes, members of the *eta* are not racially distinguishable from other Japanese, although descendants of the aboriginal Ainu are found among them. The prejudice against the *eta* is not racial but religious. As with American Negroes the resultant problem is a social one. Its solution in Japan appears to wait upon the evolution, through education, of a rational attitude toward a considerable portion of the population whose members, through their ancestry or occupations, may have incurred social prejudice despite their legal equality, attained in 1867.

No reliable data exist regarding the numbers and trend of growth of the *eta* — figures given in 1946 ranged from 500,000 to 5,000,000. The increase of the *eta* at that time was stated to be more rapid than that of the population as a whole, but was concealed in part by the escape of many *eta* from segregated villages and their assimilation into the masses. An organization of long standing popularly known as the Suiheisha (Water-Level League) exists to work for the social emancipation of the *eta*. After World War II a new title was devised for this organization: Buraku Kaiho Zenkoku I-Inkai (National Committee for the Emancipation of Oppressed Peoples), but the older name continues to be used. Non-*eta* as well as *eta* compose this organization, its unconventional and melodramatic president during post-World War II years being Matsumoto Jiichiro. He and the majority of Suiheisha officers are members of one or other of the Socialist factions, their preference based upon Shakaito principles: democracy, socialism, and peace. Other less notable bodies exist to plead the *eta* cause.

Due Process of Law

The constitutional systems of Great Britain and the United States have been drawn upon for a comprehensive set of articles designed to support substantive with procedural rights. Articles 31–39 inclusive cover this field, and are supported by Articles 17 and 40, under which a person who has suffered damage through an illegal act of a public official or who has been acquitted after arrest or detention may sue for redress, as provided by law, from the state or a public entity. Articles 31–40 guarantee that no person shall be deprived of life or liberty or be placed under any other criminal penalty except by legal procedure; that no person shall be denied access to the courts or be arrested except upon proper warrant unless taken in the act of committing an offense; that no person shall be arrested or detained without being at once informed of the charges against him or without immediate privilege of counsel, or be detained without adequate cause, which must be shown upon demand. The individual's right to security in his home, papers, and effects against entries, searches, and seizures shall not be impaired except upon warrant issued by a competent judicial officer. Torture and cruel punishments are forbidden. In criminal matters an accused person enjoys the right to a speedy and public trial by an impartial tribunal; he is entitled to examine all witnesses, and to subpoena witnesses and obtain counsel at public expense. He cannot be compelled to testify against himself or be convicted solely upon his own confession of guilt. No person is criminally liable for an act which was lawful when committed, or of which he has been acquitted; no person may be placed in double jeopardy.

Among major statutes passed by the Diet to implement the constitutional protections of civil rights, both substantive and procedural, were the new civil, criminal, and procedural codes, put through conscientiously but under pressure of time and therefore not regarded as fully definitive. The old "house system" was abolished. The family registration system (*koseki*) was reformed correspondingly by separate statute. Women were raised to legal equality with men. *Lèse-majesté* was eliminated from the criminal code.[15] Due process of law was buttressed both by the code of criminal procedure and an entirely new habeas corpus act.[16] A "state redress law" placed the state or the public entity concerned under obligation to compensate any person who might suffer damage from an illegal act of a public official.[17] Freedom of religion was reaffirmed in a "religious juridical persons law." [18] Labor was released from feudal employment practices by a labor standards law.[19] A "Daily Life Protection Law," with the object of promoting "social welfare through the state taking over responsibilities in furnishing protection to persons whose living conditions require assistance, equally and without discrimination or priority," was an early recognition by the Diet of social obligation.[20] In 1948 a Civil Liberties Bureau was created in the Attorney General's office, with branch agencies throughout the country.[21] Civil Liberties Commissioners were appointed in each prefecture to investigate violations of liberties, propagate interest in them, and provide the poor with legal aid.[22]

Popular Attitude toward Rights

On the side of popular action to support constitutional and legal guarantees of civil rights, the organization of a Civil Liberties Union in 1948 was an outstanding action. The Union holds public meetings and endeavors to alert officials to circumstances that endanger or invade individual liberties. Its central office is in Tokyo, branch offices in many localities. More unified and experienced, hence more capable of effective support of civil rights if so inclined, is the Association of Newspaper Publishers and Editors, organized in July 1946.[23] This body declares its purposes to be "to improve and maintain the ethical standards . . . as well as to protect the common interests of newspapers." It is paralleled by the more energetic Union of Newspaper and Radio Workers, whose activities, though more narrowly focused, have a wide influence for the enhancement of liberty. Unquestionably, however, the most courageous and consistent defenders of civil rights are found among the university professors, foremost among them in postwar years being Professor Nambara Shigeru of Tokyo University.[24] University and college students also are stout supporters of freedom. Mention may be made also of the extensive use of letters to the Diet.[25] Both individuals and organizations employ these instruments of complaint and suggestion.

Civil Rights in Practice

Constitutions, laws, and private endeavors fostering individual liberty must be effective in practice if liberty is to be more than an empty shibboleth. Unhappily there is ponderable evidence that the idealism reflected in new institutions, public and private, is not fully operative in practice. While this is due in the main to the persistence of underlying customary controls and habits, it is fair to recall that Occupation regulation of publication, assemblage, labor organizations, and similar groups often was not representative of the principles espoused by the self-elected mentors of the Japanese people.[26] A greater attention to the influence of example and less to that of precept might well have advanced the general Japanese understanding of democracy further than occurred under the Occupation. But to expect democratic action from military rulers is like asking the leopard to change his spots.

Within space limitations one may note a few typical evidences of postwar practice in the field of civil rights. The recruiting of women and girls through contracts for terms of years—the parents and the employers deciding the terms of contract — continued. Large numbers of girls were contracted into prostitution by poverty-stricken parents. The boss system for gangs of male laborers and the strictly regimented dormitory system for women were maintained. A geisha, nineteen years old, was beaten on a Tokyo street in November 1951 by the "Madam" who managed the *demi-mondaine* house in which she was employed. The girl was beaten for going to a movie without permission. Although her earnings were 200,000 yen a month, she received only lodging, food, baths, and hairdressing. Her father was paid 3,000 yen a month.[27] The efforts of labor organizations to obtain political change by demonstrations or strikes were officially denounced as illegal.[28] On the other hand, an order of the Ministry of Welfare which banned use of the Imperial Palace Plaza for May Day labor rallies was annulled by the Tokyo District Court in a suit brought by the General Council of Trade Unions (Sohyo).[29]

Religious freedom remained subject to Shinto cultism. Students were required to offer silent prayers to the spirits of the war dead during the signing of the peace treaty in San Francisco.[30] A minister of education, Amano Teiyu, sought, but failed to issue, a code of ethics which the newspaper *Yomiuri* characterized as a "postwar version of the old Imperial Rescript on Education" and a "challenge to democracy." A subsequent attempt by Minister of Education Ando Masazumi to introduce a compulsory course on ethics into the curriculum of the elementary schools was resisted by some educators who feared the revival of nationalistic education oriented around the emperor system.[31] Imperial reports at ancestral shrines and public ceremonies at military shrines appear to carry their traditional connotation.

Newspaper and book publishers breathe more freely, but the revival of the secret police and military forces is likely to place them under the old restraints. Reputable publishers are required to have their photographs and fingerprints registered at police stations. Book stores protest that the police make frequent inspections in search of "obscene" literature.[32] The Supreme Court ruled that a newspaper reporter may not legally refuse to divulge a news source. The Diet may supply legal protection in such cases, since editors have pointed out that under the above ruling "newspapers will become official gazettes."[33]

The Citizen and His Rights

Two significant issues aroused the academic world to a defense of freedom of teaching. One of these was the question of whether or not to transfer the supervision of university administration from faculties to boards of regents. The other concerned the right of Communist professors to hold their positions. The members of faculties were, in general, opposed to control by regents or trustees and to the discharge of professors on the basis of membership in any political party recognized as legal. They held that such membership, even in the Communist party, was not tantamount to a subversive attitude, and that academic tenure should depend upon attitude and the expression thereof, not upon party membership.[34] Student support of this point of view was vociferous and at times led to clashes with the police.[35]

The police are not effectively restrained from mistreatment of persons under arrest by the new constitutional prohibitions of torture and prolonged detention in police station "pigpens." In 1951 two policemen were sentenced to four months in jail for torturing a suspect to compel him to confess, but they were not required to serve the sentence.[36] Newspaper accounts of shocking brutality in the making of arrests are not difficult to find.[37] In 1952 a new *kempeitai* (military police corps) was established, headed by a "Public Security Investigation Agency" in the office of the attorney general (subsequently minister of justice). Two thousand "public security agents" were stationed throughout Japan.[38]

Both criminal and civil procedure lag behind the principles embodied in the new bill of rights. Arrested persons may be held in jail for long periods without trial while under pressure to confess. Persons arrested on suspicion of one type of offense may be indicted for an entirely different one.[39] The habeas corpus act has been circumvented, at times, by the issuance of a second warrant of arrest, for a different offense, when grounds for indictment have not been found within the allowable ten days.[40] On the other hand, the courts have shown independence in their rulings affecting due process of law. They have refused to adjudge guilt solely upon confession, to accept evidence extorted by police intimidation, or to recognize contracts for prostitution.[41]

Civil rights in Japan require clarification at certain points, in part because some Occupation reforms were inconsistent with constitutional provisions, in part because the fear of communism has prompted legislation and executive orders which run counter to private liberties. The outstanding example of the former type of inconsistency was the land reform program, which has been attacked in the courts as violative of private property rights.[42] Among instances of the latter type are the outlawing of the Korean League, a leftist body in Japan; the arrest of Communist party leaders on warrants but without release of information justifying the arrests; the passage in the Diet of a Subversive Activities Prevention Bill, which was severely criticized for certain of its provisions, particularly by labor organizations; and the revision of the Labor Union Law, the Labor Relations Adjustment Law, and the Public Utilities Labor Union Law.[43]

Notes

[1] *Nippon Times*, April 2, 1946.

[2] "Giri-Ninjo," by A. Kubota, reprinted from *Jiyu* in *Digest Service*, March 25, 1947, pp. 10–12.

[3] H. S. Quigley, *Japanese Government and Politics* (New York, 1932), Chapter 4.

[4] Constitution, Article 10.

[5] Public law No. 147, printed in "Legal Comments" by A. C. Oppler, issued by GHQ, SCAP, May 1950, pp. 3–5.

[6] Permitted under the old law if sanctioned by the emperor.

[7] The family registration law was passed in 1947 and became effective on January 1, 1948; it provides that the family register shall center in the husband and wife, not, as formerly, in the head of the family. The new nationality law does away with the former requirement that states to which this provision applies shall be specially designated.

[8] Dr. Oppler, in his "Legal Comments" (cited above), points out that the new nationality law restricts the right of renunciation of nationality to nationals who have attained foreign nationality, whereas the new constitution, Article 22, provides: "Freedom of all persons to move to a foreign country and to divest themselves of their nationality shall be inviolate." The law rather than the constitution is in accord with the Hague Convention of April 12, 1930, dealing with conflicting nationality laws. According to that convention, which was signed but not ratified by Japan, the issue of an expatriation permit shall not entail the loss of the nationality of the issuing state unless or until the recipient has obtained another nationality.

[9] Chapter III, containing 31 articles, is entitled, "Rights and Duties of the People."

[10] S. Wagatsuma, "Fundamental Human Rights" (in Japanese), *Kokka Gakkai Zassi*, LX (October 1946), 261.

[11] K. Takayanagi, "Foreign Law in Japan," *Nippon Times*, January 21, 1951.

[12] Civil Code, Book I, Chapter 1, Section 1, Article 2.

[13] See the excellent article by Kurt Steiner, "The Revision of the Civil Code of Japan: Provisions Affecting the Family," *Far Eastern Quarterly*, IX (February 1950), 169–184. A. C. Oppler, in "The Reform of Japan's Legal and Judicial System under the Occupation," states that the decision to abolish the house system was not forced by SCAP, but was essentially a Japanese decision in which women played an important role (*Washington Law Review*, XXIV (August 1949), 318).

[14] See *Japan Weekly Chronicle*, May 10, 1923, pp. 655–656, for earlier data respecting the *eta*.

[15] A. C. Oppler questions Professor S. Dando's characterization of the new code of

criminal procedure as "a hybrid of the Continental and Anglo-Saxon systems," preferring to describe it as one in which "the Japanese law has retained its Continental character as codified law," but into which, "in certain fields, where the existing law was irreconcilable with the constitutional safeguards of fundamental human rights, some of the best Anglo-Saxon features were integrated . . . thus aiming at a synthesis of both systems" ("Japan's Courts and Law in Transition," *Contemporary Japan*, XXI (1952), 5). Oppler describes the cooperative process of legal revision in the article cited in note 13 above.

[16] See below, Chapter 22.

[17] State Redress Law, in *Official Gazette*, No. 473, October 27, 1947, p. 1.

[18] Religious Juridical Persons Law, *ibid.*, No. 1504, April 3, 1951, pp. 2–21.

[19] *Nippon Times*, March 6, 1947.

[20] *Official Gazette*, No. 134, September 9, 1946, pp. 1–4.

[21] *Nippon Times*, March 18, 1951.

[22] Cabinet Order, *Official Gazette*, July 17, 1948, pp. 1–2; Attorney General's Ordinance, *ibid.*, August 6, 1949, pp. 1–2. The Civil Liberties Bureau reported 12,880 alleged violations of civil liberties during the year October 1, 1950 to September 30, 1951. Of this number 538 were charged to the police, 757 to public officials, 115 to localities which had expelled local residents (mura-hachi-bu), and 93 to traffickers in human beings (*Nippon Times*, December 6, 1951). An American lawyer in Tokyo, Thomas L. Blakemore, aptly termed the Bureau the government's "hair shirt" in view of its process of channeling and focusing criticism of governmental agencies (*ibid.*, September 11, 1948).

[23] *Nippon Times*, July 24, 27, 1946. The July 27 issue reprints the constitution of the Association.

[24] Primary school teachers sometimes were confused as to the application of democratic principles; a number of them contended that entrance examinations were undemocratic and that students should be admitted by lot (*ibid.*, February 21, 1948).

[25] Prime Minister Yoshida received from citizens in March 1946 702 letters dealing with political, economic, and social problems that touched them; in March 1947 he received 15,584 letters (*ibid.*, April 15, 1946; April 20, 1947). On a single day in 1949 there were 1,837 petitions from citizens in the hands of the Diet (*ibid.*, May 21, 1949).

[26] See above, Chapter 7.

[27] *Nippon Times*, November 13, 1951.

[28] Cf. the declaration of Yoshitake Eiichi, Minister of Labor, noted in *Nippon Times*, May 17, 1952.

[29] *Ibid.*, May 29, 1952.

[30] *Ibid.*, September 14, 1951.

[31] *Ibid.*, November 24, 1951; *Asahi Evening News*, December 23, 1954; February 12, 1955.

[32] *Nippon Times*, July 31, 1951. *Lady Chatterley's Lover*, translated into Japanese. was the issue in the lengthy trial in Tokyo.

[33] *Ibid.*, August 7, 1952.

[34] *Ibid.*, October 18, 1949.

[35] *Ibid.*, May 17, 1950, and numerous subsequent issues during that year; see also the issues for November 22, 1951, and for April 22–24, 1952.

[36] *Ibid.*, November 7, 1951.

[37] *Ibid.*, July 20, 1951.

[38] *Ibid.*, July 23, 1952; *New York Times*, August 12, 1952.

[39] *Nippon Times*, July 27; September 17; October 26, 1948.

[40] *Ibid.*, December 3, 30, 1948.

[41] Oppler, "Japan's Courts and Law in Transition," pp. 25–26.

[42] *Nippon Times*, October 28, 1947.

[43] *Ibid.*, July 9, 1949; September 5, November 11, 1951; April 25, May 1, 2, 6, 16, 25, June 19, 20, July 5, 6, 17, 1952.

14

The Emperor and the Cabinet

SIMPLICITY has replaced complexity in the structure of the executive branch of the Japanese government. The cabinet alone possesses executive authority. The emperor is an instrument of the Diet through the agency of the cabinet. There is no Privy Council, no Lord Keeper of the Privy Seal, no Imperial Household Ministry, no independent Supreme Command, no genro. Serious students of Japanese politics recognize that military and civilian elders are being consulted informally by the prime minister and his colleagues. But such consultation is extraconstitutional and extralegal; its influence is limited to what ministers believe to be expedient or wise to accept. It is founded in tradition and individual capacity, not, as with all these agencies save the genro in prewar Japan, in the fundamental law. In view of the resentment felt by cabinet ministers at the controls exercised over them under the Meiji constitution, it may be anticipated reasonably that future Yamagatas and Saionjis will be to the cabinet what a Colonel House, a Baruch, and a Farley have been to the presidents of the United States — advisers by invitation, not by legal or customary right. Gradual rather than abrupt change is, however, what precedents and prejudices forecast.

The Emperor

Man should be like the pine
That does not change its color
Though bearing the fallen snow.

— Emperor Hirohito, 1946

The emperor as an institution survived the war and the defeat of Japan. Emperor Hirohito and Empress Nagako gained rather than

188

lost in the respect and regard of the people by suffering with them the dangers of war and the humiliation of defeat and the Occupation. The Yamato dynasty, oldest of living royal houses, is the center of equilibrium for the government, of loyalty and confidence for the people. Well-provided with sons, its continuance for the foreseeable future is assured.

The Renunciation of Myths

In an imperial rescript of January 1, 1946, Emperor Hirohito said: "The bonds between us and our countrymen have been tied together from first to last by mutual trust and affection. They do not originate in mere myth and legend. They do not have their basis in the fictitious ideas that the Emperor is manifest god (*akitsu mikami*) and that the Japanese people are a race superior to other races and therefore destined to rule the world." These sentences were embedded in the call to reconstruction which reaffirmed the Charter Oath (1868) and referred to "our countrymen" and "our government" in the patronizing terms of the old regime, concluding, "We expect our countrymen to join us in all exertions looking to accomplishment of this great undertaking with an indomitable spirit." [1]

It may be assumed that an induced "renunciation," drafted by the Religions Division of SCAP, was not accepted by the Japanese government or people as a genuine expression of the imperial will. As recently as 1940 Professor Fujii Shinichi of Waseda University wrote: "The subjects' faith lies in the fact that their *Tenno*, being a descendant of the Sun Goddess, that is, a living god, therefore practices the Way of *Tenno*, or the Way of the Sun Goddess." [2] This conception remains firmly rooted, though unacceptable to persons more scientifically minded. Between complete acceptance and complete rejection of the doctrine of divinity stands the interpretation which retains the doctrine but differentiates the Japanese from the Occidental view of its meaning.

Two recent writers may be cited to illustrate this interpretation. Professor Yanaibara Tadao, Tokyo University, wrote in 1948: "Since the Emperor has never asserted himself as a deity, he simply made public the self-evident fact about his person, but there was no doubt that his declaration had a distinctly negative effect on all thought deifying the Emperor, and consequently the people felt free and enlightened." [3]

The editor of the *Nippon Times* (Tokyo) explained the difference between the Japanese and the Western conception of the emperor's nature:

. . . even in recent years, when the divinity of the Emperor was most strongly stressed, the Japanese never regarded the Emperor as a god in the sense that a Westerner thinks of God. God in the Oriental sense is not a supernatural being possessed of attributes of omnipotence, omniscience and omnipresence, the Creator and Ruler of the Universe. To the Oriental the distinction between the secular and the divine is very slight. All human beings, being a part of the natural phenomena, possess an element of spirituality as well as of the mundane, and in so far as a human being possesses a spiritual nature as well as a physical body he is in that respect divine. Not only the Emperor but all human beings are therefore, in a sense, gods. The Emperor, as head of the Shinto religion, is by reason of his priestly office, endowed with greater sacredness than other people, but his divinity is more a difference in degree than in kind. [4]

Japan was required by an Occupation directive of December 15, 1945, to divorce religion from government. [5] In consequence, all officials, including the emperor, were forbidden, in a "public capacity" to "visit any shrine to report . . . assumption of office, to report on conditions of government or to participate as a representative of government in any ceremony or observance." Shrine attendance for such purposes continued — for example, the emperor reported the promulgation of the new constitution to the three sanctuaries within the palace grounds [6] — but these acts were construed as personal and private, not public functions related to government. Prime Minister Yoshida sent the secretary-general of the Liberal party to report at the Grand Shrine of Ise upon the signing of the peace treaty at San Francisco in 1951. [7] Obviously, the distinction between the old and the new significance of these ceremonial observances lay in the realms of theory and law, not in the understanding of the people, who continued to bow in prayer before the imperial palace.

Imperial Public Relations

More effectively than by rescript the zoologist-Emperor Hirohito aided the people to revise their theology by placing himself in closer contact with them. He began the practice of visiting localities, hospitals, schools, and factories, before World War II but increased such contacts greatly thereafter. His shyness made this difficult, his conversational exchanges were stilted, and on one occasion he was embarrassed by a workman's offer to shake hands. Often the empress accompanied him, smilingly adjusting his necktie and enduring the impertinences of photographers. Since, with the Japanese as with the ancient Greeks, a god may have the qualities of men, their awareness of the fact strengthens their leverage against oligarchical manipulation of deity.

Succession to the Throne

Succession to the throne is limited to legitimate male offspring in the male line of the imperial family, in accordance with the principle of primogeniture. The Imperial House Council may change the order of succession if an imperial heir is incurably diseased "or there is a serious hindrance." Adoption of children is forbidden to an emperor and to other members of the imperial family. An emperor comes of age at eighteen and may not assume the throne earlier. A regent, in the person of a member of the imperial family, acts in the event that an emperor becomes incompetent or dies during the minority of the heir apparent. An heir apparent who has reached his majority is first in line for the regency during the life of an emperor and succeeds to the throne immediately upon the death of the emperor.[8]

Imperial House Organs

In contrast with its predecessor, the Imperial House Council of ten members includes only two members of the imperial family, seven of the councillors being ex officio: the presidents and vice-presidents of the Diet, the prime minister, the head of the Imperial House Office, and the chief judge of the Supreme Court. The tenth councillor is another Supreme Court judge elected by his colleagues. The term of office is four years for the elective judge and for the representatives of the imperial family who are elected by the family.[9] The ex officio members serve on the Council as long as they hold office and until their successors are qualified.

Presiding over the Council's meetings is the prime minister. Six members compose a quorum. Decisions are taken by majority vote except upon stipulated matters for which a two-thirds majority is required. A member may not take part in deliberation upon a matter in which he has a personal interest. Powers of the Council are such as relate to the continuance and dignity of the imperial family — matters of succession, marriages, regency, membership, etc. The Council, on October 13, 1947, deprived of their princely status eleven of the fourteen princely houses related to the dynasty, leaving only the houses of Emperor Hirohito's three brothers — Chichibu, Takamatsu, and Mikasa — within the imperial family.[10]

The replacement of the dynasty's control over palace affairs by that of a body representing the Diet as well as the cabinet and the courts was accompanied by abolition of the powerful office of Lord Keeper of the Privy Seal and the Imperial Household Ministry, both of which operated beyond the authority of the cabinet. A new administrative agency, under cabinet control, entitled the Imperial House Office, was created by statute.[11] Composed of stewards, chamberlains, masters of ceremonies, secretaries, and technicians, it manages the ordinary and ceremonial affairs of the emperor and his family. Custody of the imperial seals rests with the Office. Within it are bureaus in charge respectively of the imperial archives, treasury, and maintenance of buildings. Distinction is lent to the highest officers of the agency — the Grand Steward and the Grand Chamberlain — by the legal requirement that their appointment and dismissal be attested by the emperor. The Grand Chamberlain, through his function of waiting upon the emperor, has opportunities for influence but is, like his colleagues, subject to the orders of the prime minister.

Although the greater part of the imperial family's property and investments was turned over to the state during the Occupation,[12] the Imperial House Economy Council was created by statute to administer relations between the dynasty and the state in regard to property. This body is composed entirely of persons outside the imperial family — the presidents and vice-presidents of the Diet houses, the prime minister, the minister of finance, and the heads of the Imperial House Office and the Board of Audit. It may pass upon assignments or transfers of state property to the use of the imperial house, gifts or sales of property, allocations to members of the house upon leaving it, and similar matters.[13]

The Emperor and the Cabinet

Annual appropriations are made by the Diet in three categories: inner court, imperial court, and imperial family. In the first category fall the daily expenditures of the emperor and his immediate family. They are managed by the family itself. The second category, covering costs of maintenance, social functions, tours, and the like, and the third, providing for the expenses of the three brothers' houses, are administered by the Imperial House Office. Lump sum payments were made in 1947 to the eleven princely families whose members were relegated to the status of commoners at that time. Within limits fixed by law the imperial family may make and accept gifts.

Nature of the Cabinet

No doubt can exist upon the constitutional position of the cabinet: "The Cabinet shall consist of the prime minister, who shall be its head, and other ministers of state, as provided for by law." [14] All members must be civilians.[15] The ministers meet and take action as a cabinet, under the chairmanship of the prime minister. Any minister may propose matters for cabinet consideration and ask that meetings be held. The prime minister is superior to his colleagues both in law and in fact. Like his pre-1947 predecessors, he is politically and actually dominant. He declares the consensus after cabinet discussions, and exercises supervisory control over the ministers, with the right to decide issues of jurisdiction that may arise between them. A prime minister would be exceeding his lawful authority were he to refuse opportunity for discussion of policies mooted by ministers, or fail to carry out the consensus. It is apparent, however, that the opportunity for an autocratically minded prime minister to exalt his position was enhanced by the abolition of the Privy Council and other repositories of traditional forms of control.

Selection of the Cabinet

While bureaucracy, like dynasticism, cannot be frustrated by law alone, it is possible to encourage and legitimatize opposition to it. Among Japan's early postwar premiers, one only, Katayama Tetsu, was not a career official. Since May 3, 1947, however, bureaucrats must turn politicians in order to be eligible for the premiership. The Diet — each House voting separately — elects a prime minister from among its members. Upon the resignation of a cabinet, the speaker of the House of Representatives is entitled to take the initiative in recommending a new prime minister. He attempts to obtain agreement among party leaders upon a nominee. Normally, but not necessarily, the Diet elects as prime minister the head of the political party which holds the largest number of seats in the House of Representatives. There is no prescribed age or other qualification beyond those for Diet membership. Election is by simple majority, and if the two Houses fail to agree, the issue is submitted to a joint committee. If the committee fails to reach agreement the vote of the House of Representatives is decisive.[16] Election of a prime minister occurs after each general election, whether or not the polling returns a majority for the government. Thus a premier is required to resign and to be re-elected as the choice of the Diet. This means — in view of the fact that the cabinet resigns en bloc — that the prime minister is, for a brief period, the sole member of the new cabinet, responsible for all departments. However, the outgoing ministers attend to administrative business until their successors take office. A majority of the ministers must be members of the Diet, but the prime minister selects the ministers and allocates the portfolios without limitation as to the representation of each House. Ministers without portfolio are appointed as well. The prime minister, at his own discretion, may remove a minister. But he may expect to be questioned by the judicial committees of the Diet, not to mention Tom, Dick, and Harry, upon his action, and to be advised *ad nauseam* upon replacement.

Although appointment of fewer than half the ministers from outside the Diet is possible, the extraordinary vigor of political party life exercises compelling pressure upon a prime minister.[17] "Scratch a politician and you wound a bureaucrat" may be aptly applied to many ministers. That former administrative officials who join political parties are elected to the Diet and receive ministerial appointments because of their experience may retard the progress of parliamentary government is obvious. On the other hand, they are supporting higher standards of administration than may be expected from the party leaders until larger nuclei of experienced statesmen have emerged within the parties. They are also checking the natural rise of a spoils system which would disappoint the people's hopes for political integrity to be born out of their travail. Unless reaction destroys the new system the alertness of its chief beneficiaries, the parties, may be relied upon to thwart the forays upon their fold of bureaucratic wolves in political sheep's clothing.

A prime minister often finds the selection of ministers a slow, difficult, and exasperating process. This is true whether or not the cabinet represents a coalition between parties. Factions within each party must be recognized if the cabinet's relations with the Diet are to be tolerable. The selection process is attended by numerous meetings between interested elements. A "cabinet formation headquarters," headed by a confidant of the new prime minister, is established as the center of maneuvers. Near it reporters set up a *tento-mura* (village of tents), equipped with telephones, in order to observe the comings and goings of the politicians. The struggle is worrisome for the secretary-general of any party involved, since a large share of the responsibility for satisfying or propitiating important elements falls to him. Promises relating to policies, ministerial posts, and personal ambitions are needed to attract influential figures into the cabinet. These promises operate subsequently to tie a premier's hands and to frustrate the development of a consistent program of legislation. But failure to respect them leads to defections and weakens the morale of party life.

The prime minister attends at the palace to receive his formal appointment from the emperor. Subsequently he presents the other ministers to the emperor at an attestation ceremony in the palace.

Cabinet Responsibility

The cabinet is responsible "collectively" to the Diet. Its responsibility extends to all official acts of the emperor; this principle, which is stated clearly in the constitution, logically accompanies the requirement of cabinet advice and approval for all such acts.[18] Ministers are protected in the exercise of this responsibility by a constitutional provision barring legal action against them during their tenure of office unless such action has the consent of the prime minister. Joint or collective responsibility for cabinet decisions, individual responsibility for those within the jurisdiction of the ministry involved, constitute the basic rules of cabinet action, modeled upon those of the United Kingdom. Resignation en bloc must follow passage of a non-confidence resolution, or rejection of a resolution of confidence, in the House of Representatives unless the House is dissolved within ten days of either action. Upon resignation, the premier is not required to notify the emperor. When Premier Katayama did so in February 1948, his mistake was pointed to forcefully as an unconstitutional act. The critics viewed the notification as an acknowledgment of responsibility to the throne, a departure from the new principle that the emperor's functions are purely symbolical.[19] It is apparent, however, that such action may be viewed in a different light, i.e., as merely a formal notification to the titular head of the state.

Of greater consequence is the issue of the premier's power to dissolve the House of Representatives in the absence of an expressed want of confidence by its members. Premier Yoshida attempted in 1948 to inaugurate a precedent of action under Article 7 of the constitution, which authorized the emperor, with the advice and approval of the cabinet, to dissolve the House. That practice, while democratically employed in the United Kingdom, was assailed quite logically in Japan as a flouting of Article 69, which was interpreted as requiring, to authorize dissolution, a House of Representatives' vote signifying want of confidence. Unfortunately, Mr. Yoshida got his way by obtaining an agreement among parties in opposition to introduce a resolution of nonconfidence.[20] This device harked back to the prewar system, under which cabinets were appointed without regard to Diet support and were accustomed to dissolving the House of Representatives in order to alter its complexion to suit themselves through an election. Thus the by no means dead spirit of bureaucracy prevailed by one means or another.[21]

Obviously parliamentary government received a setback from this cynical maneuver. It revealed starkly the danger to healthy political party growth that is attendant upon selection of dyed-in-the-wool bureaucrats as party leaders. There was no comfort for liberal observers in the smashing victory of Yoshida's party, the Democratic Liberals, in the ensuing election. On the contrary, his success was testimony that Japan's latent conservatism, i.e., its traditional bureaucratism, was returning to the surface. Like the parties that allowed the premier to make pawns of them, the great majority of the voters appeared to be without concern for the consequences of his stratagem.

Mr. Yoshida previously had identified himself as antiparliamentary by allowing his party's whips to persuade his friend Yamazaki Takeshi, a Democratic Liberal who was favored for the premiership by the Democrats after the resignation of Ashida Hitoshi in 1948, to resign his seat in the House of Representatives. Yamazaki had ambitions for the premiership and was an experienced politician. By resigning, he thwarted the Diet in the exercise of its constitutional right and duty to select a prime minister from its own membership. Yet the Diet swallowed the affront and elected Yoshida, who expressed thanks for Yamazaki's loyalty to his party.[22] One would be entitled to ask, in the face of these developments, whether the Diet was not responsible to the cabinet rather than the cabinet to it.

On the other hand, is it possible for a parliamentary system to operate unless, as in the United Kingdom, a prime minister is empowered, through the instrumentality of the titular head of the state, to dissolve the dominant House and to call for an election? Must it not be assumed that a sense of responsibility will prevent an elective premier from abusing his power of dissolution? As the Diet comes to realize and to employ its high authority, it will exercise greater and greater control over the cabinet. With the reversal of the traditional deference to officialism, the Diet will not submit to the premier's whip. A dissolution then will signify that the majority party believes that a new mandate of the people is opportune. This may, but need not, be demonstrated by a want of confidence vote. Apparently the power to dissolve the House of Representatives may develop by custom, since Article 69 of the constitution does not prohibit such action but does state certain circumstances in which it may be taken, without barring it in other circumstances: "If the House of Representatives passes a non-confidence resolution, or rejects a confidence resolution, the Cabinet shall resign *en bloc* unless the House of Representatives is dissolved within ten days."

Premier Yoshida gave early evidence of his continued belief in this principle and in his power to apply it when he dissolved the House of Representatives in 1952 without benefit of a want of confidence vote. No serious criticism was expressed — the Occupation had ended. However, in 1953 Yoshida, in dissolving the House, acted under both Article 69 and Article 7.

Cabinet Organization

The cabinet, as previously noted, is composed of the prime minister and ministers with or without portfolio. There are eleven portfolios at present: foreign affairs, finance, education, welfare, justice, agri-

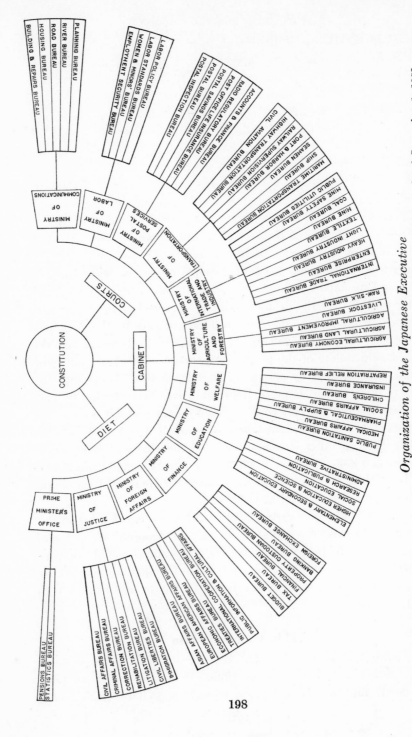

Organization of the Japanese Executive

(This chart originally appeared in a publication of the Administrative Management Agency, dated September 1, 1952. It has been modified slightly to bring it up to date.)

198

culture and forestry, international trade and industry, transportation, postal services, labor, and construction. The prime minister may assume one or more portfolios. Customarily a small number of ministers without portfolio are appointed, to whom important administrative functions may be assigned — for example, those of deputy prime minister or of director-general of a board such as the National Defense Agency. A minister may be designated to act also as deputy prime minister. More than one portfolio may be held by a minister of state. If necessary, the ministries may be supplemented under separate laws, by boards, which normally enjoy the rank of ministries.[23] Commissions or agencies may be similarly constituted as "independent organizations" of the prime ministry or of any ministry.[24] That the executive composes an "organic whole" is attested by the National Government Organization law, which requires its component organs to "maintain liaison with one another so that they may consummate their administrative functions" unitedly.

Each of the ministers except the prime minister is assisted by three vice-ministers, one administrative and two parliamentary. One of the latter is appointed from each House of the Diet and may not serve beyond the term for which he was elected. Administrative vice-ministers resign with the cabinet. The absence of a permanent vice-minister may be ascribed to the unwillingness of members of the permanent civil service to work loyally with a new minister. This attitude, a holdover from the day of bureaucratic administration, entails a serious loss of time and effectiveness. The cabinet, the prime minister, and each organ of ministerial rank are provided with secretariats and with confidential secretaries. Exceptional influence may be wielded by the director of the cabinet secretariat, often referred to as the chief cabinet secretary. This highly regarded position may be held by a minister. Ministries are composed of bureaus, which are in turn composed of sections. Agencies within a ministry are subdivided into secretariats, divisions, and sections. While ministers or their counterparts in the "independent organizations" exercise some authority over the creation and allocation of functions to sections, the general rule of legislative control over administrative organization has replaced the former executive authority in such matters. Ministries may, with legal authorization, create local branch offices and direct their operations, but must not encroach upon the sphere of local autonomy.

The New Japan

Cabinet meetings are held in the official residence of the prime minister, No. 1, Nagata-cho, near the Diet building. Regular meeting days are Tuesday and Friday. All meetings are closed. No minutes are kept. After adjournment a record of decisions taken is circulated among the ministers for their initials (*han*). No votes are taken, the prime minister expressing the consensus after discussion. The cabinet functions without standing committees but employs occasional special committees. Extensive use is made of councils, composed either of ministers whose departments share an overlapping area of administration or of ministers and others — Diet members, judges, businessmen, professors, *et al.*

Notes

[1] Appendix III, below (translation by D. C. Holtom). A popular story of the day represented Emperor Hirohito as saying that the astonishment of Western peoples at the "renunciation" of divinity must have meant that they thought he was divine.

[2] S. Fujii, "Characteristics of the Japanese Constitution," *Contemporary Japan*, IX (March 1940), 262.

[3] T. Yanaibara, *Religion and Democracy in Modern Japan* (Tokyo, 1948), p. 19.

[4] *Nippon Times*, January 5, 1946. See also H. H. Smythe and M. Watanabe, "Japanese Popular Attitudes toward the Emperor," *Pacific Affairs*, XXVI (1953), 335–344.

[5] See below, Appendix III.

[6] *Official Gazette*, No. 178, November 1, 1946, p. 7.

[7] *Nippon Times*, September 16, 1951.

[8] See below, Appendix IV, Articles 1–4. The Japanese observed with humor the appearance of a pretender to the throne, complete with a "grand chamberlain," early in 1946. Hiromichi Kumazawa, a Nagoya grocer, claimed that his line of descent was more direct than Hirohito's (*Nippon Times*, February 2, April 26, 1946).

[9] At the first election, on September 16, 1947, thirty-two of the thirty-three adult members voted, electing Prince Takamatsu and Princess Chichibu to the Council, Prince Makasa and Princess Takamatsu reserve members (*ibid.*, November 14, 1947).

[10] While the Council was engaged in selecting a bride for Crown Prince Akihito, a high imperial court official was quoted as saying that if the Prince should fall in love and insist upon marrying his beloved he should abdicate (*ibid.*, July 30, 1951).

[11] See below, Appendix IV, Articles 28–37. The old Imperial House Law and amendments were repealed on May 1, 1947.

[12] In 1946 the property of the imperial family was valued at 3,715,628,195 yen (*Japan Year Book*, 1946–1948, p. 6); investments at 1,600,000,000 yen in 1945 (*New York Times*, October 31, 1945).

[13] See below, Appendix V.

[14] Constitution, Article 66; Cabinet Law, Article 2.

[15] This provision of the constitution, Article 66, was designed, apparently, to bar civilians who had been but were no longer in military service, since no military organization was in existence at the time the constitution was promulgated.

[16] Katayama polled 420 out of 426 votes in the House of Representatives, 205 out of 207 in the House of Councillors in 1947 (*Nippon Times*, May 25, 1947). In 1954, Hatoyama received 257 votes in the House of Representatives; Jiyuto President Ogata Taketora received 191. In the second chamber the voting was 116 to 85 (*Asahi Evening News*, December 10, 1954). Hatoyama's second election was by a vote of 254 to 160 in the House of Representatives and 99 to 58 in the House of Councillors. At

that time his opponent was Suzuki Mosaburo, a left-wing Socialist (*Mainichi Shimbun*, March 19, 1955).

[17] Katayama's cabinet, but for one Independent, who was a member of the House of Councillors, was composed of Representatives; Ashida's cabinet was similarly composed (1948); Yoshida's second cabinet (1948) contained 2 Councillors, 11 Representatives, and 1 nonparty minister; his third cabinet (1949) 3 Councillors, 12 Representatives, and 1 nonparty. Hatoyama's first cabinet (1954) contained 3 Councillors, 2 non-Diet members, and 12 Representatives. His second (1955) contained 2 Councillors, the remaining members being Representatives.

[18] Constitution, Article 3.

[19] Guy J. Swope, Government Section, SCAP, viewed Katayama's notification to the emperor as an abuse of the attestation function. "If," said he, "the word 'attestation' [Article 7] can be tortured by a bureaucracy steeped in the tradition of monarchic rule so as to permit the reporting to the throne of the resignation of a cabinet . . . then it is possible for such imperialist-minded bureaucrats eventually to usurp the sovereignty of the people, which is the the fountain-head of the constitution" (*Nippon Times*, February 25, 1948).

[20] *Ibid.*, November 28, 1948.

[21] There was no SCAP protest over Yoshida's dereliction such as had greeted that ascribed to Katayama.

[22] *Nippon Times*, October 15, 1948.

[23] National Government Organization Law, Article 24.

[24] National Government Organization Law, Article 3. See also A. W. Burks, "A Note on the Emerging Administrative Structure of the Post-Treaty Japanese National Government," in *Occasional Papers*, No. 3, Center for Japanese Studies, University of Michigan, pp. 47–58.

15

The Powers of the Executive

Constitutional Monarchy

JAPAN's most eminent legal authorities were unable to agree upon the position of the emperor under the new constitution. This was amply attested during the Diet's discussion of the draft, which was but slightly altered before passage.[1] It is apparent, however, that Emperor Hirohito, through his quiet leadership of popular tolerance of the Occupation, as well as through his voicing of his advisers' decision to accept defeat in 1945, placed the dynasty on the road to constitutional monarchy. Paradoxically, the throne became more than the symbol which it had been for many centuries coincidentally with its definition as such in the new constitution. Article 1 thus became obsolescent upon promulgation, as did Article 4, which clumsily states that the emperor "shall not have powers related to government." The latter article is contradicted by others that authorize the emperor to appoint the prime minister and the chief judge of the Supreme Court, to promulgate laws and orders, to convoke the Diet and dissolve the House of Representatives, etc. All such acts are exercises of governmental power, whether or not they are done upon "advice and approval" of the cabinet. They are legitimate powers of a constitutional emperor and are essential to his dignity and consonant with his exercise of the three rights which Bagehot attributed to the English monarchy and of which he maintained that "a King of great sense and sagacity would want no others." They are "the right to be consulted, the right to encourage, the right to warn."[2] Japanese liberals could not do better than to counsel their countrymen to read and digest Bagehot's classic analysis of the values and attributes of monarchy in a constitutional system.

By sweeping away the several powerful legatees of the feudal age — the genro, the Lord Keeper of the Privy Seal, the Imperial Household Ministry, and the Supreme Command in its advisory and thereby deciding capacity — the new constitutional order made it possible for the throne to take its rightful place. So long as the cabinet was but one source of advice, and usually the weakest source, the titular head of the state could not be other than a puppet pulled by a variety of strings and inevitably yielding to the strongest. With advisory power monopolized by the cabinet, the emperor attained the dignity which the Restoration of 1867 purported but failed to accord him. Deprived of the empty autocracy ascribed to himself and his successors by Meiji, the throne became the repository of limited but genuine powers.

It is obvious that a constitutional monarchy cannot exist without a constitutional monarch. Without a head who is more than a symbol the state would be subject to rule by a political party, representative of only part of the citizenry, or by unrepresentative elements such as have dominated the government throughout Japan's history. The head of the state must be above partisanshp, without power to decide, but with a legally defined sphere of action.

The distinction between the old and the new lies in the sources and extent of imperial powers, not in the presence of power in the former and its absence in the latter. From having stood above the law, exercising a timeless, god-given prerogative, the emperor descended to a position subject to the law, exercising such powers and enjoying such rights as are authorized by the constitution and by the Diet.

There is no precedent to warrant apprehension that an emperor of Japan will abuse his powers and rights. On the contrary, there is a basis for anticipating that Hirohito and his successors will welcome an opportunity to support the Diet in a struggle to implement its constitutional position as the "highest organ of state power." Will the Diet make that struggle? Will oligarchy reassert itself? The future of liberalism depends upon the answers to be given to these questions, not upon whether or not the throne will attempt to exalt itself.

The actual functions of the emperor remain substantially what they were before May 3, 1947: the appointment of the prime minister and of the chief judge of the Supreme Court, the attestation, i.e., the certification, of other major appointments and of the accreditation of high diplomatic officers, the reception of foreign ambassadors and ministers, the promulgation of statutes and other legal instruments, the attestation of international agreements, the convocation of the Diet, the dissolution of the House of Representatives, the attestation of amnesties and pardons, the award of honors, and the performance of ceremonies. As hitherto, all imperial acts are performed upon advice, not independently.

New phraseology appears in imperial messages. The emperor merely "promulgates" laws, he no longer gives his "sanction" to them; he "convokes" sessions of the Diet but does not "order" the ministers to introduce bills; his addresses at the opening of Diet sessions are less formal, embodying such phrases as "we, the people," and employing colloquial in place of court language. In referring to himself he uses the pronoun "I," not "we." Members of the Diet, as well as executive officials and common men, continue to bow deferentially in his august presence. In ceremonial matters as well as in political ideas, the throne is leading, not retarding, the trend toward liberalism.[3]

Cabinet Supremacy

"Executive power shall be vested in the Cabinet." So runs the constitution, Article 65. The power is not vested in the crown, to be exercised by the cabinet, but in the cabinet itself. The cabinet is not the equal of the Diet — "the highest organ of state power" (Article 41 of the constitution) — but is supreme within the field of administration. It participates also in the formulation of national policy and in the legislative process. Its rise from its humble position under the old constitution recalls the Biblical prophecy that "the last shall be first." The only administrative agency which is independent of the cabinet is the Board of Audit.[4]

No definition of the expression "executive power" is to be found in the constitution or the cabinet law. In the light of history the probability is high that the power, in operation, will be hard to restrain. It is not, apparently, limited to the specific acts listed in the constitution and the statutes as within its purview. Like the constitution of the United States, which lays it upon the president to "take care that the laws be faithfully executed" (Article II, Section 3), the constitution of Japan requires the cabinet to "administer the law faithfully" (Article 73). Thereby it recognizes the need of an executive not rigidly confined but empowered to meet situations not fully provided for by law through the exercise of its own discretion.[5] Clearly, on the other hand, the cabinet may not act in a manner forbidden by law. The administrative "functions" specifically comprised within the executive power are not listed separately in the constitution but in various articles of its chapters dealing with the emperor, the cabinet, and the judiciary. The most significant function of the cabinet is to advise the emperor, since advice is equivalent to decision on his behalf, subject to such consideration of his views as is consonant with constitutional monarchy.

Appointments and Removals

The power of appointment is exercised upon the principle that positions within organs or agencies directly presided over by the cabinet shall be filled by the cabinet, and that the prime minister, the several ministers holding portfolios, the heads of independent organizations, and the president of the Board of Audit shall appoint personnel to positions within their respective organizational structures.[6] Ambassadors and ministers, members of the National Personnel Authority, and other persons in the "special" — as distinguished from the "regular" or classified — government service are appointed by the cabinet. Members of the Board of Audit are appointed by the prime minister with the consent of the Diet. All judges are appointed by the cabinet, the emperor conferring appointment upon the chief judge of the Supreme Court, as he does upon the prime minister.

Personnel in the special government service, unless especially protected by law as in the case of judges, commissioners of the National Personnel Authority, and members of the Board of Audit, are removable at the discretion of the appointing officer. Regular service officers may be removed only in accordance with the national public service law, which is dealt with in a subsequent chapter. Quite logically, the prime minister is able to play a major part in decisions upon appointment in the special service as in other fields of administrative action. No doctrine of "senatorial courtesy" has been asserted to control patronage by either House of the Diet. It is clear, however, that the necessity of holding a working majority compels a prime minister, be he ever so dictatorial, to allow his cabinet colleagues a share in the making of appointments. In their turn the ministers have to consider the wishes of their allies in the parties and of their election supporters. Changes in high-level personnel are, therefore, frequent and their motivation is primarily political, though affected also by the well-rooted tradition of and respect for competence, as competence is estimated in Japan.

Foreign Affairs

The cabinet is empowered to "manage foreign affairs" and to "conclude treaties." The prime minister reports on foreign relations to the Diet, and must obtain the Diet's approval of treaties. Approval may be sought in advance of conclusion, i.e., of completion of negotiation. In that event the Diet may approve but leave to the cabinet's discretion the settlement of issues which may arise subsequently in negotiation. Or it may be asked to consider a negotiated but unsigned treaty before signature. Disapproval at this juncture will nullify the negotiations but permit of their resumption immediately. Normally the Houses, voting separately and deciding by simple majority, act upon a concluded and signed treaty. Failure to approve nullifies the treaty.

A minister of foreign affairs is under no obligation to report to the Diet upon the course of a particular negotiation. The Diet expects, however, to be informed upon the general content of a treaty before signature. Whether or not such information is given depends upon the attitude of the prime minister. Prime Minister Yoshida, in 1951, was disinclined to inform the Diet upon the terms of the treaty of peace about to be signed at San Francisco, and only consented to meet the Diet in order to assure himself of the delegation he desired. His speech was confined to background matters already well known to Diet members.[7] The circumstances of that period, added to Mr. Yoshida's experience in diplomacy and his possession of a safe majority in the House of Representatives, placed the Diet at a disadvantage. Cabinet ministers who are convinced parliamentarians are likely to desire, as well as to need, continuous liaison with the Diet on foreign affairs. In any case, the Diet's veto power upon treaties is unquestionable. Executive agreements may be concluded independently by the cabinet under its general power to administer foreign relations.

The superiority of treaties to statutes was abolished by the constitutional provision establishing the Diet as the highest organ of state power. Thereby the most recent act of the Diet, whether the approval of a treaty or the passage of a statute, becomes the supreme law of the land, as is true in the United States. Promulgation by the emperor, which involves his signature and seal upon the public notice of promulgation, completes the treaty process.

Amnesties and Pardons

The power of pardon, including general and special (individual) amnesty, commutation of punishment, reprieve, and restoration of rights, lies in the cabinet. When amnesty is granted to groups of persons, cabinet orders are issued specifying the offenses to which it applies. Individuals are notified by writ of the minister of justice, but only upon the recommendation of a procurator or prison director. These officials are required by ordinance to submit petitions of individuals to the minister of justice, together with their opinions upon the proper action to be taken. A deliberative committee, composed of the minister of justice, the procurator general, two other ministers, and four experienced citizens, advises the cabinet upon legal issues involved in execution of the amnesty law and upon modifications of the system of amnesty.[8]

Honors

Honors are awarded by the emperor upon the advice of the cabinet.[9] Titles of nobility are forbidden, and no privileges attend the grant of honors, which are valid only for the life of the recipient.

Military Power and Martial Law

Japan entered into a treaty of security with the United States in September 1951, which was approved by the Diet within two months. Included in the Preamble are the following words:

The treaty of peace recognizes that Japan as a sovereign nation has the right to enter into collective security arrangements and, further, the Charter of the United Nations recognizes that all nations possess an inherent right of individual and collective self-defense.

In the exercise of these rights, Japan desires, as a provisional arrangement for its defense, that the United States of America should maintain armed forces of its own in and about Japan so as to deter armed attack upon Japan.

The United States of America, in the interest of peace and security, is presently willing to maintain certain of its armed forces in and about Japan, in the expectation, however, that Japan will itself assume responsibility for its own defense against direct and indirect aggression, always avoiding any armament which could be an offensive threat or serve other than to promote peace and security in accordance with the purposes and principles of the United Nations Charter.[10]

In identic notes dated September 8, 1951, Prime Minister Yoshida and Secretary of State Acheson took cognizance that "upon the coming into force of the Treaty of Peace signed today, Japan will assume obligations expressed in Article 2 of the Charter of the United Nations which requires the giving to the United Nations of 'every assistance in any action it takes in accordance with the present Charter'." [11]

Prime Minister Yoshida, when presenting the security pact to the Diet, was unimpressed by interpellators who maintained vigorously that the pact contravened Article 9 of the constitution:

Aspiring sincerely to an international peace based on justice and order, the Japanese people forever renounce war as a sovereign right of the nation and the threat or use of force as means of settling international disputes.

In order to accomplish the aim of the preceding paragraph, land, sea, and air forces, as well as other war potential, will never be maintained. The right of belligerency of the state will not be recognized.

Mr. Yoshida contended that the constitution prohibited only the use of armed force in settling international disputes, not in defending the country's independence; he affirmed that the right of self-defense is an attribute of statehood.[12]

It is clear that in prohibiting the establishment of military forces of any kind the constitution rendered impossible the exercise of the right of self-defense. Granted that the right pertains to statehood, it may be forsworn by a state. That the constitution forswore the right can hardly be denied. That the Japanese would have supported the inclusion of Article 9 had they felt free to express themselves against the expressed views of General MacArthur is beyond belief. Article 9 is a quixotic bit of imposed idealism in a world shaking under the misdirected energy of uranium. Until international law, diplomacy, and organization replace national reliance upon national power and alliances, no single state may fairly be expected to stand disarmed.

Japan's new army began life under the title of a national police reserve, the NPR. It was authorized by cabinet order in July 1950, although the Diet was then in session.[13] The original size of the force was 75,100 men. This number was increased to 110,000 in 1952, and has been further enlarged. Command was placed in a director-general, whose appointment was dignified by imperial attestation, and who was responsible directly to the prime minister. The first director-general was a civilian career official. Officers were recruited in part among former army officers ranking up to colonel. Half of the rank and file had been soldiers. They were armed with American carbines, bazookas, mortars, and machine guns, and were organized and trained as troops by American officers. The headquarters of the NPR in Tokyo was independent of the public safety commission, which administers the regular national police system.

Uprisings, strikes, riots, and conspiracies were to be dealt with by the NPR. Japan was divided into four districts, in each of which an NPR unit was centered. Intelligence units were provided. While official statements and documents refrained from recognition of the true nature of the reserve, the Liberals appointed a national defense survey committee, headed by an able and influential elder statesman, Uyehara Etsujiro, which proposed creation of a new "ministry of national safety."[14] In October 1952 the NPR was renamed the National Security Force. Subsequently this body and an embryonic navy were placed under the direction of the Security Board. The navy was composed primarily of war craft leased by the United States. Former professional army and navy officers were appointed to key positions in the new military organization. In 1954 the Security Board was transformed into the Defense Agency, which was authorized to administer three forces: those of land, sea, and air. A civilian minister without portfolio heads the Defense Agency, which is attached to the Office of the Prime Minister. The Agency is in fact a ministry of defense, but remains attached to the Office of the Prime Minister. In 1954 the Diet appropriated nearly 80 billion yen for the three services.[15]

The constitution contains no provision for the imposition of martial law.

The New Japan

Legislative Powers

With the passing of imperial sovereignty the issuance of imperial ordinances ceased. Cabinet orders became the primary method of exercising the executive power to implement and supplement statutes. The prime minister and each minister may issue ordinances as secondary instruments for the execution of laws or cabinet orders relating to matters within their respective spheres of administration. Ministers also may issue rules, orders, and directions of a subsidiary character. This latter power pertains, as well, to the heads of independent organizations. Informational "notifications," "instructions," and "circular notices" are used for public announcements and for conveying directives to subordinate officers.[16]

The enormous ordinance power under the Meiji constitution, which enabled the executive to legislate to a degree that reduced the Diet to an inferior position,[17] now is reduced to the power to "enact Cabinet orders in order to execute the provisions of this constitution and of the law." Even within this limited field the power is constitutionally prohibited from including penal provisions unless authorized by law and still further restricted by law from imposing obligations or restricting rights without specific legal authorization.[18] However, public officials are so accustomed to deference from the members of the Diet that they continue to control legislation to a considerable degree. They do so by drafting the lion's share of the statutes, which are drawn up in general terms and implemented by a network of cabinet and ministerial orders so intricate that only an experienced administrative lawyer can comprehend them. It is extremely doubtful whether the average Diet member is able to detect a departure from the orbit which is prescribed for the ordinance power.[19]

Legislative power is shared by the cabinet through its advisory relation to the emperor's power to convoke the Diet, to dissolve the House of Representatives, to proclaim elections, and to promulgate constitutional amendments, laws, and treaties. Laws require the signatures of the prime minister and appropriate ministers. Preparation of the budget assures the cabinet of major influence upon financial legislation, although the legal limitations upon the Diet's control in this sphere no longer exist. The continued tendency of the Diet to depend upon interpellations rather than debate to evoke information essential to action enables the ministers to retain a po-

The Powers of the Executive

sition of superiority within the legislative process hereafter dealt with. No power of veto is reposed in the executive.

Notes

[1] For this discussion see above, Chapters 10 and 11. For a brief treatment of executive powers under the Meiji constitution see H. S. Quigley, *Japanese Government and Politics* (New York, 1932), pp. 66–72, 101–128.

[2] Walter Bagehot, *The English Constitution* (London, 1944), p. 75.

[3] For a keen observer's estimate of Hirohito's attitude and opposing elements see William Costello, *Democracy v. Feudalism in Postwar Japan* (Tokyo, 1948), pp. 43–72. The new criminal code omits mention of lèse majesté.

[4] Board of Audit Law, Article 1.

[5] A succinct treatment of the U.S. President's discretionary power is given in William Anderson, *American Government* (New York, 1946), pp. 497–505.

[6] National Public Service Law, Article 55.

[7] *Nippon Times*, July 25, 26, August 4, 9, 1951.

[8] Constitution, Articles 7, 73; Amnesty Law, March 28, 1947; Cabinet Order, October 1, 1947; Ordinance of Ministers of Justice, October 1, 1947.

[9] Constitution, Articles 7, 14.

[10] *Department of State Bulletin*, September 17, 1951, p. 464.

[11] *Ibid.*, p. 465.

[12] *Nippon Times*, October 17, 1951.

[13] Such orders were known as "Potsdam" ordinances because issued under authority of SCAP and taking precedence over statutes. The text of the order was printed in the *Nippon Times*, August 10, 1950. Imperial ordinance 542, issued by order of SCAP on September 22, 1945, provided as follows: "In case it is necessary for the enforcement of such matters as are required by the Supreme Commander for the Allied Powers in consequence of our acceptance of the Potsdam Declaration [properly 'Proclamation'], the Government may by order make such provisions as may be required and provide the necessary punishments. This ordinance shall come into operation as from the day of its promulgation."

During the six years between September 22, 1945, and September 22, 1951, approximately 500 orders and ordinances were issued under this authority.

[14] *Nippon Times*, May 28, 1951.

[15] *Information Bulletin*, Japanese Embassy, Washington, D.C., August 9, 1954.

[16] Constitution, Article 73; National Government Organization Law, Articles 12–14.

[17] Quigley, *op. cit.*, pp. 118–123.

[18] Constitution, Article 73; Cabinet Law, Article 11.

[19] Prime Minister Katayama was criticized for using cabinet orders in "emergency" situations (*Nippon Times*, September 6, 1947).

16

The National Public Service

Japan has had a quasiclassified civil service, recruited by examination, since 1887.[1] The prewar service was well organized and attracted capable young men. It had the cordial support of military leaders, to whom it was an ally against parliamentarism. As the instrument of a quasiconstitutional oligarchical system of government it was highly self-conscious and honest. But it attained a degree of power which enabled it to challenge the ministers themselves. The unhealthy respect in which bureaucrats are held was voiced unconsciously by a postwar member of the House of Representatives who opposed a salary scale for Diet members which might draw able persons away from the civil service.[2] To overcome the tradition of deference to rule by an appointive elite is the most difficult task of liberalism in Japan.

Professor Royama Masamichi, one of Japan's foremost political scientists, pointed out early in the postwar era that it is unrealistic to conclude that Japan can attain responsible government by holding the cabinet responsible to the Diet. Government officials, he wrote, must be held responsible to the cabinet. In a vivid phrase he called the official system a "monster which is taking advantage of the great gap" that separates the principles of the new constitution from actual politics. He argued that public officials must be made "public," that the system as it exists must be abolished.[3] Until the nature of "responsibility" is understood and its desirability recognized, the permanent civil servant will maneuver successfully against the political chief, thus aiding to upset the constitutional relationship between Diet and cabinet.

Pent-up resentment against the "almighty government official" found expression in the midst of postwar distress. People blamed officials for shortages of food, utensils, blankets, fuel, etc., and for apathy toward their wretchedness. An editor complained that "there is no country where people are so slighted by the governing class as in Japan." He adjured "all government officials, from top to bottom" to "rectify radically their haughty attitude toward the people." [4] Another editor listed "the evils of Japan's bureaucratic system" as "ludicrous formalism, excessive red tape, inter-departmental jealousies, personal politics, unscrupulous time-serving, inefficiency, incompetence, appalling stupidity and smug arrogance." He pointed to "the bottlenecks in Japan's lumber production resulting from the incompetence of the political careerist monopolizing the responsible administrative positions in the Agriculture and Forestry Ministry." This editor, holder of a doctorate in political science, after noting that the same criticism had been frequently and justly made of the whole official system, affirmed that "it is an irrational system which places inexperienced young law graduates who pass the general civil service examination in high administrative positions, while technical experts of recognized professional competence and long experience are relegated to subordinate posts." He called upon the Diet to employ its power to insist upon a thorough reform but concluded that "the crux of the matter lies in whether the general public is intelligent enough and cares enough to take the action which is in their power to take." [5] *Asahi, Mainichi,* and *Yomiuri,* the most widely read newspapers in Japan, were equally critical of the bureaucratic rank and file.

One may doubt whether lack of intelligence and of care for reform is the major impediment to establishment of a democratic civil service in Japan. The Confucian principle that the ruler shall rule well, i.e., as a benevolent father rules his children, continues to have mass support.[6] Until it becomes clear to the people that their economic well-being will be safer in their own hands than in those of experts, they are not likely to regard "reform" as anything but greater expertness as evidenced by greater attention to their well-being. Until they identify themselves with the political parties — which they will not do until the parties identify the people's interests with their own —

they will not go beyond asking for "good" government. It seems logical to anticipate that the best prospect for "responsible" government lies in the bureaucrats themselves. Educated under a more liberal program, of greater breadth and less bound to legalism, Japan's youth should attain appreciation of the meaning of "public" service long before the people at large can be expected to do so. Thus the key to responsible administration is in the hands of the teachers and of those who determine educational policy.

Obviously, the educational process will require many years. Whether or not educational planners and teachers will desire or be permitted to liberalize, broaden, and humanize the preparation of potential public servants cannot be foretold. The Japanese may prefer to leave a greater share of government in the hands of "management," restricting the elected representatives of the people to a supervisory and approbative role. They know that democracy is the most costly form of government, and they are not rich. They know how difficult it is to keep democratic administration out of the grasp of spoilsmen. If, however, they retain the corporate and reject the parliamentary system, they will not be wise to fail their youth by continuing to train them to regard bureaucracy as a total rather than a participating power in government. To do so would be to ensure the withering away of the political parties, the Diet, and the people's interest in public affairs. That Japan's future constitutional order will be more reliant than our own upon its administrators may be anticipated. That it will include participation by the people cannot be doubted in the light of the past half-century.

It is generally agreed that the bureaucracy is increasing in actual power as well as in size, and that the increase has been continuous since World War II. (The number of civil servants today is more than twice that of 1931.) Several reasons are given for this development. One is the opportunity afforded by the suspension of military activities and the dissolution of the huge composite of military agencies. The disappearance of the military bureaucracy left a vacuum for the civil officials to fill. Another is the necessity that existed for prompt response to SCAP directives and suggestions. Diet processes were too slow. A third is the purge of politicians, which added to the power vacuum. A fourth is the reformist nature of SCAP-inspired legislation, which required planning, planners, and administrators.[7]

The National Public Service

With the Senior Statesmen, the Privy Council, and the higher officers of the Imperial Household off the scene, the way was open to the lesser bureaucrats — the *kanryo*.[8] Faced with the expansion of the elective system, the seasoned officials sought safety in the parties, which received them cordially and presented them, in many instances, with presidencies or other high posts. Inevitably, in a time of crisis experience and training were relied upon, and these qualifications were monopolized by the civil service. It is not surprising that the National Public Service Law, enacted during the Katayama ministry in 1947, was highly unpopular with the bureaucrats and that it was subjected from the outset to overt and covert attacks.

National Public Service Law

The National Public Service law was promulgated on October 21, 1947, and was in force on and after July 1, 1948.* One article, authorizing establishment of a temporary personnel commission to prepare for the enforcement of the law, became operative on November 1, 1947.[9] The law has been amended a number of times, most significantly in 1948 to prohibit collective bargaining and strikes. Supplementary laws and administrative orders and rules compose a considerable body of legislation. The "object of the law" is declared in Article 1 to be "to assure the people democratic and efficient administration of their public affairs by establishing basic standards (including adequate measures to promote the welfare and interest of personnel) which shall be applicable to all personnel who are national public employees, and by providing that personnel shall be so selected and directed by democratic practices as to promote maximum efficiency in the performance of public duties."

Two services, "regular" and "special," are recognized by the new law. The special service comprises high-ranking officers elected or appointed without examination or the application of alternative criteria of ability. Members of the cabinet, the National Personnel Authority and the Board of Audit, the director-general of the cabinet secretariat and his deputy, parliamentary vice-ministers and councillors, confidential secretaries of cabinet ministers, officers elected by one or both Houses of the Diet, Imperial Household chamberlains,

*To avoid encumbering the text with a considerable number of footnote numbers the authors have refrained from citing articles of the basic law. All other laws, orders, and rules referred to have been footnoted.

ambassadors and ministers, and judges and other court officials are members of the special service. They are not subject to the National Public Service law. Within prescribed limits the National Personnel Authority may determine whether positions are properly in either service and to which service they shall be assigned. Legally-recognized positions not included in the special service are *ipso facto* in the regular service.

The new law is administered by a new agency, the National Personnel Authority.[10] This agency is under cabinet jurisdiction. It reports to the prime minister, the cabinet, and, annually, to the Diet. It is not within the Prime Minister's Office nor within any cabinet ministry. It is composed of three full-time commissioners, who rank immediately after cabinet ministers and with members of the Board of Audit. They are appointed by the cabinet — which designates one of them as president — with Diet approval, and are honored by the attestation of appointment by the emperor. Their compensation is the same as that of cabinet ministers.

No two commissioners may be members of the same political party or graduates of the same department of the same university.[11] Somewhat paradoxically, commissioners must be "in known sympathy with the democratic form of government" but must not have been, within five years of appointment, an officer, adviser, or influential member of a political party or a candidate for elective office, national or prefectural. A commissioner's term is four years, his maximum period of service twelve years. He may be removed for incompetence, conviction of crime, or membership in a subversive organization. Removal may be brought about also by impeachment proceedings initiated by the Diet in the Supreme Court.[12]

A director-general, appointed by the Authority and ranking with administrative vice-ministers, is executive assistant to the Authority and attends its weekly meetings. He is also chairman of the National Personnel Council, composed of the personnel directors of the ministries and other appointing organs. The Council is a liaison body between the Authority and the political organs, and may offer recommendations to the Authority. Eight bureaus in Tokyo and eight regional offices composed the staff of the Authority in 1950. Changes subsequently made altered the staff to five bureaus, one office, and twenty sections. They are:

Bureau of Administrative Services
Internal Administration Section
Law Section
National Personnel Authority Library
Personnel Section
Accounts Section
Bureau of Recruitment
Planning and Control Section
First Examination Section
Second Examination Section
Bureau of Compensation
Position Classification Section
First Compensation Section
Second Compensation Section
Third Compensation Section
Retirement Section
Bureau of Equity
Grievances Review Section
Appeals Section
Employee Associations Section
Bureau of Employee Relations
Employee Investigations Section
Efficiency Section
Welfare Section
Health and Safety Section
Public Information Section

Also in the Secretariat are the Board of Equity, the Grievances Review Committee, the Accident Compensation Review Committee, and the Office of Administrative Consultants.[13]

A Civil Service Institute, which began its work in November 1947, gave training to 2,000 members of the service during the first four years of operation. Three advisory councils, one on training, a second on welfare, and a third on employee evaluation and utilization, began to function during this period.

The Authority meets normally once each week in Tokyo. Minutes are kept by the secretary-general. To exercise its important powers, which are listed in the law, the Authority must pass a resolution by majority vote.

Powers of the Authority

The law intended that the Authority, a nonpolitical or neutral organ, should determine and maintain the standards of the "regular" civil service. To quote Blaine Hoover, SCAP's principal adviser in the drafting of the law:

The National Personnel Authority is not designed to be an ordinary agency of government. It is as near a neutral agency having a certain referee character as can be created within the frame-work of government . . . yet it is not above government. . . . The orders of the Authority relating to administrative personnel matters, subject to certain limitations imposed by law, are binding upon all ministries and agencies of government. The administrative decisions of the

Authority are subject to review only under its own procedures but it must fully comply with the law and with respect to its observance of the law is subject to court review.[14]

Article 3 of the National Public Service Law gives a comprehensive statement of the scope and content of the Authority's functions:

Subject to this law the Authority shall develop, co-ordinate, integrate and order policies, standards, procedures, rules and programs, and recommend legislative and other necessary action for personnel with respect to the following matters:

1. Position classification, compensation, dual compensation, pay plan, examination, qualifications, recruitment, employment eligible lists, certification of eligibles, appointment, conditional period, temporary appointment, parttime employment, dual employment, oath of office, promotion, demotion, transfer, reinstatement, re-assignment, retirement, pension, dismissal, reduction in force, evaluation of work performance, the definition of terms of personnel administration and related matters.

2. Hours of work, leave of absence, temporary retirement, health, safety, recreation, education and training, welfare, personal conduct, political activity, exclusion from private enterprise, preservation of secrecy, discipline, separation, equitable treatment, status, guarantee, employee application for administrative action, grievance procedure, compensation for illness and injury while on official duty, and investigation, research, and inspection regarding governmental personnel administration and related matters.

3. Personnel records and statistics, control and audit of payrolls to ascertain whether or not the payment of compensation is made in conformity with this law and rules and directives of the Authority.

4. Administration of the National Personnel Council.

5. Other matters placed under its jurisdiction on the basis of law.

Within the sphere in which the Authority is empowered to act by this law, the decisions and actions of the Authority shall be subject to review only by the Authority under its own procedures.

The provisions of the preceding paragraph shall not in any way affect the right of access to the courts on questions of law.

Specifically, the Authority is empowered:

1. To prepare a budget and present it to the cabinet. An emergency operating fund, under the Authority's control, may be included in its budget. If the cabinet sees fit to revise the budget, it is required to present the original as well as the revised request to the Diet. The budget is all-inclusive of the anticipated costs of the Authority's operations.

2. To make rules and issue directives; these, if within the law, are

binding upon all administrative bodies, including the Prime Minister's Office.

3. To conduct investigations of personnel administration, with the right to subpoena witnesses and to require submission of records.

4. To prescribe the form of personnel records and to require that such records be kept by all offices.

5. To prescribe and administer the reporting of personnel statistics, with authority to require data and the form in which it shall be presented.

6. To control the payment of compensation to personnel.

7. To make recommendations for improvement of personnel administration to appropriate ministries and other agencies; recommendations may concern transfer of personnel within or among agencies.

8. To submit opinions upon the enactment, modification, or repeal of personnel laws and orders to the Diet and the cabinet.

9. To delegate functions to other agencies in accordance with its own regulations.

Operation of the Authority

The Authority was from the outset faced by adverse traditions and unfriendly cabinet ministers. The latter sought to retard the implementation of the National Public Service Law, to restrict drastically the Authority's budget and the number of its personnel, to substitute alternative methods of evaluation for examination, to exclude categories of personnel from the regular service, to hamper cooperation between the Authority and the prefectural and local civil service agencies, and to prevent the Authority from exercising its power to determine salaries and wages. The older departments naturally resented the grant of extensive powers to an independent body, powers which cut across established lines of a tightly-woven hierarchy. The personnel directors in the several ministries and elsewhere were inclined to sympathize with traditional prejudices, to fail to maintain liaison with the Authority, and at times to go to the length of attacking the Authority. The House of Councillors, with its strong contingent of onetime bureaucrats, was less friendly than the House of Representatives. As a result the Authority was forced to move slowly in bringing the law into operation, indeed to be content with functioning as little more than an advisory body on policy.

To a degree the Commissioners were responsible for this situation. They relied heavily upon SCAP and made too little effort to persuade the older departments of the desirability of the new system. Moreover they were content to follow American techniques and to neglect the necessary adaptation to Japanese conditions. Undoubtedly Blaine Hoover's vigorous insistence upon getting an ideal system "on the books" influenced the Commissioners unduly.

As the Occupation came to an end, however, the Authority was able to report that the difficult task of classification was nearly completed, with the identification of 414 occupations, divided into 2,000 classes. By the end of 1954 the number of occupations identified had been reduced to 126, the number of classes of positions to 561. Though unable to avoid the delegation of examinations in many instances to committees in appointing agencies, and though unable to implement its right of approval of appointments to positions below grade ten, it considered that the basic principles of the merit system were being applied to recruitment. Personnel records covering thirty-nine types of personnel actions were being kept systematically. Payroll forms, procedures, and auditing had been established. Pay standards set by the Authority were accepted by the Diet despite the Finance Ministry's opposition. Assistance had been given to the prefectures and localities in the formulation and administration of their civil service systems.

Those among the Authority's responsibilities which had been met less successfully were the development of procedures for equitable treatment of controversies between employing agencies and employees; the conduct of research in the fields of health, welfare, safety, and recreation directed toward the effectuation of ideals of efficiency; the establishment and supervision of uniform standards, and the formulation of personnel policies.

Recruitment

Appointments to offices in the special service are made by the Diet, by the emperor upon designation by the Diet or the cabinet, by attestation of the emperor upon designation by the prime minister, and by officers in the special service. Officers and employees in the regular service, unless their positions have been excepted by law or cabinet order, are appointed upon the bases of written examinations, efficiency, and other tests of abilities. Normally, an initial appointment is made upon the basis of ability demonstrated in a competitive examination. For high level positions experience and other qualifications also are required. Such appointments may be authorized upon evaluation of abilities alone, without competitive tests. Appointing officers receive a list of five eligible candidates for an available position and may select the appointee at discretion from the list. They may not appoint an unlisted person to a nonexcepted position. Promotional appointments are made similarly from lists of five persons eligible for promotion. Promotional lists are compiled normally after competitive examination of incumbents, but may also be based upon other criteria. Initial appointments are probationary for the first six months of employment. Temporary employment up to twelve months may be granted by an appointing officer to unlisted persons. There is no provision for appointments to the regular service without examination or alternative evaluation.

Disqualifications for employment include incompetency, confinement to prison, prior dismissal within two years, or membership in a subversive organization. Forfeiture of position results automatically if an employee disqualifies himself under any of these counts.

Examinations

Examinations are open to all qualified citizens. They are administered by the National Personnel Authority or by other agencies to which the examination function has been delegated. Since 1952 the Ministry for Foreign Affairs has been designated as the examining body for entrance into the Foreign Office and the foreign service, while the administration of all other entrance examinations still remains within the purview of the Authority. The examinations are held on two levels, "higher" and "ordinary." The former are divided into two parts, the first part a test of general administrative ability, the second part varying in accordance with the several classes of occupation included within the positions to be filled, and designed to test technical knowledge.

Tenure and Compensation

An employee may be demoted or dismissed for unsatisfactory performance of duty, incompetence, or lack of fitness for his position;

the position he holds may also be discontinued. He may be retired temporarily in the event of disability or subjection to prosecution for crime. He may be subjected to various forms of disciplinary punishment, from reprimand to dismissal, for illegal or unethical conduct. Normally the appointing officer of the person involved will administer removals, demotions, and disciplinary actions. The Authority, however, may initiate disciplinary proceedings through launching an investigation.

Written notice, setting forth the reasons for any of the actions above listed, is given to the employee concerned. Within thirty days the employee may appeal to the Authority for review of the action. He may also request either a private or a public hearing. The Authority is required to accord the appellant a hearing, at which he may have the aid of counsel, witnesses, and relevant documents. To conduct the hearing the Authority appoints a "board of equity" of three to five members chosen from among the commissioners and secretaries or including "learned and experienced persons" from other government agencies or from private life.[15] The Authority may approve or revise the action taken; or it may disapprove it, restore the employee to his position, correct injustice, and order payment of salary that has been withheld. It may be challenged in the courts only upon the issue of action within the sphere of its legal competence.

No provisions respecting scales of pay, periodic increments in pay, or promotions were included in the basic law. However, it required that supplementary legislation for a system of compensation for employees and, in the event of their death, injury, or illness, for their dependents should be enacted. It provided also that a pension system should be established and that it should be administered by the Authority. Accordingly, in 1948 the Diet enacted a new pay law, amended in 1950; and in 1951 the Authority issued rules embodying standards and procedures for implementing that law in matters of initial salary, promotion, increase of pay within grade, etc.[16] The law established fifteen grades of positions at initial basic salaries of from 2,400 yen per month for the first grade to 18,320 yen per month for grade fifteen. Separate salary schedules and higher salaries were provided for three categories of employees: tax collectors and economic investigators; police, prison employees, and Maritime Safety Board employees; and seamen. Salary levels were fixed, varying in numbers from four to ten in the several grades. A total of seventy-four steps of salary increase, culminating in 23,620 yen per month, were specified. Normal working time was limited to six days, and to a minimum of forty and a maximum of forty-eight hours per week.

To these low salaries increments were added in the form of family allowances varying in amount with the number of dependents, area allowances based upon higher living costs, and special work allowances recognizing difficult conditions in certain occupations. (The family allowance alone, for a family of six persons — 600 yen for wife, 600 yen for one child under eighteen years, and 400 yen each for two other minor children and a grandparent over sixty years — would double the lowest monthly salary.) Year-end allowances and overtime pay also add to the intolerably inadequate incomes of government workers.[17]

The grant of salary increases and promotions is within the province of appointing agencies, subject to approval of the Authority, in cases involving the tenth and higher grades.[18] The Authority is required to make recommendations to the Diet and the cabinet whenever it appraises costs of living as justifying a revision of salary rates. In 1953 the Authority recommended an average increase of 13.9 per cent of the monthly average, which was at that time 13,587 yen.[19]

The government housing law does not recognize responsibility to provide housing for civil service employees.[20] Its purpose is to assist the government in order that it "may perfectly perform its business or work." To that end it authorizes official residences, free of rental, for many officers in the special service and for regular service employees whose duties require them to live in a particular locality. Rentable housing also is made available, funds permitting, in areas of shortage or when administrative efficiency demands emergency action.

Rules for employee evaluation were issued early in 1951, for use "as an effective indicator for necessary guidance and supervision of employees as well as a basis for equitable personnel action, thus giving an impetus to the development and improvement of efficiency of employees." Regular and special evaluations, the former annually, the latter at the request of the Authority, were provided for. An employee's merit was to be appraised by the agency employing him in terms of his performance of assigned duties, fulfillment of responsibilities, character, ability, and aptitude. Measures were to be taken to reward outstanding merit and to encourage and guide employees whose performance was poor. Complete records were to be kept, and inspections were to be made by the Authority's director-general from time to time.[21]

In March 1951 the Authority issued a brief rule to inaugurate partial implementation of the National Public Service Law's requirement that it establish programs to develop efficiency in personnel.[22] Such programs were required by the law in education, health, recreation, safety, and welfare. The employing agencies were requested by the rule to investigate the needs of their employees for training, to plan programs accordingly, and to "make every effort" to administer them. Supervisory employees might be authorized to give training to subordinates through daily contacts. Employees might be permitted to undergo training during work hours, within or outside their agencies.

Limitations

Officers and employees take an oath to perform their duties in the public interest and in obedience to law and to the orders of their superiors. They may belong to political parties and may vote. But they may not be party officers or advisers or participate in political campaigns or other activities of parties. They may not hold positions of authority or influence in a business concern. They may be members of employee organizations, and these organizations may "negotiate" with governmental agencies, but they are expressly denied the right of collective bargaining. Personnel of the police and fire services, of penal institutions, and of the National Defense Agency are prohibited from joining employee organizations. All public service members are denied the right to strike and to engage in actions tending to provoke a strike or to impede the operations of government.

As originally promulgated on October 21, 1947, the National Public Service law did not contain the provisions prohibiting collective bargaining and strikes. The Katayama cabinet, advised by James S. Killen, Chief of the Labor Division of SCAP, was responsible for the omission of these provisions. Its view was that government workers, particularly those in the government-owned railways, communications systems, and other enterprises, should enjoy equality of rights with employees of private business concerns. This view was shared, in part, by the British Commonwealth member of the Allied Council for Japan,

Patrick Shaw of Australia.[23] He did not question the denial of the right to strike to clerical and administrative workers, but urged that "great care should be taken . . . in curtailing any human rights by long term legislation." He pointed out that "in the modern state government employment often embraced what would normally be the sphere of private enterprise" and expressed the view that "in such government enterprises government employees should not necessarily be restricted in the same way as government servants proper." He held that by establishing proper collective negotiation procedure the government could obviate the need to strike, and that "proper" procedure would include the right of appeal to "an external conciliation or arbitration authority recognized by both parties." He said flatly, ". . . the mere right of public servants to carry a petition to a government agency, such as the Japanese Government seems to have in mind, is no substitute for collective bargaining."

The law was amended at the behest of SCAP, although the Central Labor Relations Board was, at the time of the SCAP letter to Prime Minister Ashida, in the process of conciliation of a dispute between employees and the government.[24] Passage of the amendments was opposed by the Socialists as well as by the members of the Shakai Kakushinto (Social Renovation party) and the Ronoto (Labor-Farmer party), and by the Communists. With the passage of the amendments some 2,800,000 employees lost their legal right to join and to utilize labor unions (*rodo kumiai*) and were restricted to entering employee associations (*shokuin kyokai*).[25] Their leverage against continued operation of the tradition of low pay was greatly weakened by this legislation. Influential members of the regular service — those in the higher grades of administrative work — welcomed rather than opposed it, since it interfered with the efforts of the lower grades — the clerks, mechanics, and manual workers in the railways, communications services, and monopoly bureaus — to obtain a more equitable distribution of civil service appropriations.

Restrained from the methods of unionism, employees and their associations are reduced to the right to "make requests of the Authority that appropriate administrative action be accorded by it or by the head of an employing agency relative to salary, wages, or any of the working conditions." Requests must be investigated but need not be acted upon. If the investigation leads the Authority to conclude in favor of action, it may review the prior negotiations between an employing agency and the aggrieved employees or may appoint members of its secretariat and others to hear the arguments as a board of review. The Authority's power to take further action is limited to its own jurisdiction and to recommendations to other government agencies.[26]

Indemnities and Pensions

Principles upon which compensation for injury and illness, retirement allowances, and pensions are to be provided are embodied in the basic law. These comprehend concern for an employee's dependents as well as for the employee. They guarantee "protection . . . against economic distress" during incapacity, damages for loss of earning capacity, and, in the event of an employee's death, payment to his family and other dependents. With regard to retirement they authorize pensions either at the end of a "reasonable period" of service or when an employee is compelled to retire by illness or injury incurred in line of duty. Pensions are to be sufficient "to enable the person concerned and his immediate dependents . . . to maintain . . . a standard of living appropriate to the conditions prevailing at the time of retirement or death."

A mutual aid association law, to provide annuities for employees separated from the service for disability or other reasons, and for their dependents, was passed by the Diet in 1948.

Notes

[1] For a brief comment upon bureaucratism, see above, Chapter 1. For the development and nature of the pre-1947 civil service, see H. S. Quigley, *Japanese Government and Politics* (New York, 1932), Chapter 9. A more recent treatment of the prewar civil service is provided by M. J. Esman, "Japanese Administration — A Comparative Review," *Public Administration Review,* VII (1947), 100–112; and by H. H. MacDonald and M. J. Esman, "The Japanese Civil Service," *Public Personnel Review,* VII (1946), pp. 213–224.

[2] The representative was Ashida Hitoshi, the time 1946. Dr. Justin Williams, Chief of SCAP Legislative Division, Government Section, commented upon the resentment expressed by the House of Peers over the drafting of the Diet Law by a committee of the House of Representatives. The House of Peers regarded this action as an encroachment upon the executive ("The Japanese Diet under the New Constitution," *American Political Science Review,* XLII (October 1948), 928–932).

[3] M. Royama, *Nippon ni Okeru Seiji Ishiki no Shoyoso* (Various Aspects of Political Behavior in Japan) (Tokyo, 1949), p. 102.

[4] *New York Times,* October 3, 1945.

[5] *Nippon Times,* November 16, 1945; July 30, 1946.

[6] T. Iwabuchi, "On Bureaucracy," reprinted in English in *Digest Service,* September 28, 1946, from *Kaizo.*

[7] John M. Maki, "The Role of the Bureaucracy in Japan," *Pacific Affairs*, XX (December 1947), 391–406. This article is a concise and informed treatment of both general and contemporary aspects.

[8] Recalcitrance among the lower ranks was typified by the resignation of 350 members of the Ministry of Commerce in resentment at the minister's attitude toward the lease of a building for a dancehall; they were taking the receipts from rental to supplement their meager salaries (*Nippon Times*, March 11, 1947).

[9] Text of law, as amended in 1948–1952, issued in English, by Ministry of Labor, *Japan Labor Code* (Tokyo, 1953), pp. 643–684. An American specialist in public administration, Blaine Hoover, was adviser in the drafting of the original law.

[10] A more accurate translation is "National Civil Service Board."

[11] A commissioner forfeits office by transferring his membership from one party to another if one of his colleagues is a member of the latter.

[12] Impeachment may be brought for misfeasance, malfeasance, or nonfeasance; also for mental or physical incompetence. On January 4, 1949, a rule of the Authority required Commissioners to take this oath of office: "I do solemnly declare that I will support and protect the constitution of Japan which recognizes that sovereign power resides with the people. I firmly swear that I, as a servant of the community, will be deeply conscious of my responsibility for performing public duties in a manner so consistent with democratic practices as to promote maximum efficiency, will respect the law enacted by the will of the people, and will perform official duties with diligence and justice." (*Official Gazette*, Extra No. 3, January 4, 1949, p. 1.)

[13] *Official Gazette*, Extra No. 132, November 12, 1949, p. 33; this printed list omits two of the sections in the Recruitment Bureau. The subsequent changes are reported in National Personnel Authority, *Annual Report*, 1953, pp. 13–14 and Appendix i.

[14] *Nippon Times*, August 25, 1948.

[15] *Official Gazette*, No. 1018, August 20, 1949, pp. 1–7. During the period from October 1949 through 1954 the Authority received 1,849 appeals. The Authority accepted 836 appeals and either approved, revised, or canceled the original actions, rejecting only 87 appeals (National Personnel Authority, *Annual Report*, 1954, pp. 10–11).

[16] *Official Gazette*, No. 323, October 15, 1948, pp. 1–12; Extra No. 51, December 22, 1948; Extra No. 24, April 3, 1950; No. 1432, January 6, 1951, pp. 2–6.

[17] In 1950 an American dollar was legally exchangeable for 360 yen; on the black market it would bring twice that amount.

[18] Rule of the National Personnel Authority, *Official Gazette*, No. 1432, January 6, 1951, pp. 2–6.

[19] National Personnel Authority, *Annual Report*, 1953, pp. 35–36. This was the sixth salary recommendation made by the Authority up to that date. Because of the several types of supplementary allowances provided for by law, it is extremely difficult to ascertain exactly the income of a civil service employee.

[20] *Official Gazette*, Extra No. 55, May 30, 1949, pp. 1–3.

[21] *Ibid.*, No. 1465, February 15, 1951, pp. 3–6.

[22] *Ibid.*, No. 1480, March 5, 1951.

[23] *Current Notes on International Affairs*, Department of External Affairs (Canberra), XIX (September 1948), 603–604.

[24] MacArthur's letter was dated July 22, 1948. It averred that "trade-unionism in government . . . has but limited application and cannot substitute for or challenge duly constituted . . . agencies exercising the sovereign power."

[25] Article 16 of the supplementary provisions to the National Public Service law states: "The coverage of the Trade Union Law (No. 174 of 1949), the Labor Relations Adjustment Law (No. 25 of 1946), the Labor Standard Law (No. 49 of 1947), and the Mariners Law (No. 100 of 1947), and any orders issued under the provisions of these laws, shall not apply to any personnel of the regular service as defined in Article 2."

[26] *Official Gazette*, No. 1506, April 5, 1951, pp. 9–11.

17

The National Diet

WRITING in 1932, one of the authors commented, "Presumably, however, the process of democratizing the Diet will be gradual and will move in step with similar changes in the other departments of the government." [1] Despite the unanticipated reforms of the period of the Occupation, it is the authors' belief that the comment remains valid today. On the one hand, it is erroneous to regard the pre-Occupation Diet as wholly lacking in power or in respect for its responsibilities as a body representative of the people. On the other hand, it is equally erroneous to take the will for the deed and to assume that new, more liberal laws and rules assure liberal institutions. The latter assumption is especially dubious when one knows that the "will" was prompted, and to some degree determined, by SCAP. Probably the remembrance of defeat suffered under oligarchical rule will, as in the decade of the 1920s after the military debacle in Siberia, operate as a dam against the detractors of parliamentarism. The Diet may enjoy a honeymoon era in which, by wise use of its powers, it may establish itself in popular confidence. But it is faced by many of the old antagonists and is handicapped by inexperience and self-depreciation. It begins a new life amidst an international crisis calling for a strong executive. Gradual progress toward the full implementation of its constitutional position is all that may be reasonably and fairly anticipated.

Diet Building

The Diet building is a fitting symbol of the new status of the national parliament. It was dedicated on November 7, 1936, after a construction period of nineteen years, during which 26,500,000 yen were expended upon it. Claimed to be constructed wholly of Japanese materials, it is massively built of white stone, with a square central tower topped by a cupola, and is situated on high ground west of the imperial palace enclosure. The new capitol of Japan is the finest modern structure in the country. The interior is attractively embellished with marble pillars and wall panels, while the chambers of the Houses are paneled in beautiful wood and silk. Behind curtains of red silk and gold on the highest floor level of the House of Councillors stands the imperial throne. The desks of the presiding officers and secretaries-general are placed several steps above the main floors, below them are the tribunes from which formal speeches are delivered, and below them the desks of the clerical staff. Chairs for cabinet ministers are placed to right and left of the presiding officers' desks, above the main floor level. Balconies run along the side and rear walls of each House. Commodious committee and caucus rooms, a printing plant, and all the facilities of a modern legislative building mark the Diet as one of the world's finest structures of its kind. An excellent library is housed in a separate building.

The Houses

The new national Diet (*kokkai*), like the old imperial body (*gikai*), is bicameral, composed of the House of Representatives (*shugi-in*), and the House of Councillors (*sangi-in*). Both houses are elective, both are representative of all the people. Constitutionally, "no discrimination because of race, creed, sex, social status, family origin, education, property or income" may be enacted against candidature. To be eligible for either House a Japanese national must have resided continuously for three months in one city, town, or village, and must not have been adjudged incompetent (mentally) or be undergoing punishment for crime. Representatives and councillors have the same functions, privileges, immunities, and perquisites; they receive the same salaries. The Houses are not replicas of one another, nor of any other legislative body.

The Diet Law, drafted not by the cabinet but by a committee of the House of Representatives, was enacted on March 19, 1947, and has been amended several times. Approximately one-fourth of its provisions are entirely new, the remainder being drawn from the old

Law of the Houses, many of them more or less modified. Departures from former procedures are noteworthy, including the elimination of sectioning and of committees of the whole. Also dispensed with were the requirement of three readings of bills and restrictions upon petitions.[2] Each House has a body of rules which complement the Diet Law and which are of similar tenor in both Houses. For the conduct of joint committees and meetings there are additional rules mutually adopted by the Houses.[3]

Until recently the House of Representatives maintained the membership of 466 established by law in 1925. Following the return of the Amami Islands to Japan by the United States in 1953, a new election district was created, and the membership of the chamber was increased to 467. Members must be more than twenty-five years of age. They serve for four years and are eligible for re-election for any number of terms. The tendency of prewar voters to re-elect experienced members is observable in the postwar electorate. Businessmen predominate in the House of Representatives; government officials, lawyers, and journalists are well represented. Farmers are notably less numerous than in prewar Diets; in proportion to their percentage of the population they are seriously underrepresented. Labor has increased its representation, but not significantly. Its major support in the House comes from the lawyers, journalists, and educators — who hold fewer seats than formerly — rather than from its own ranks. Most striking as a departure from accustomed ways is the appearance of women members. Unfortunately their numbers declined from thirty-nine to twelve between 1946 and 1949 and to eight in 1955. High educational qualifications continue to mark Representatives, though the percentage of those graduated from universities or colleges has dropped from what it was in prewar days. The average age of members since 1945 has been about fifty years and is slowly rising.

The House of Councillors, of 250 members, is a third smaller than its predecessor, the House of Peers. Terms of members are six years; half are elected every three years. Members must be over thirty years of age. Since all other required qualifications are identical with those for Representatives, it is not surprising that the two Houses closely resemble one another. The tradition of a House "above the battle" of politics was extinguished when popular election of Councillors replaced imperial appointment of Peers. That this was unpalatable to officialdom is suggested by a poster circulated by the Election Administration Commission during the 1950 campaign. The House of Councillors was described by it as established "to restrain the lower House when the latter becomes an arena of political struggle or when a majority party in it becomes oppressive." [4] Proposals were seriously considered, while the new Diet was being planned, for representation of economic and vocational elements. These proposals were deemed impracticable but it is apparent that in providing for elections by national and prefectural constituencies the Japanese hoped to attract, and to aid in being elected, persons of considerable distinction and correspondingly wide reputation.

As in the House of Representatives, businessmen hold a disproportionately large number of seats, and ex-officials are the next largest group. Educators are more numerous, proportionately, than in the House of Representatives, lawyers and journalists less numerous. Farmers and laborers are relatively poorly represented. A small but distinguished group of former Peers linked the old exclusive House with the new body. Eleven women were elected in 1947, five in 1950; the resulting total of women members was twelve. This number dropped to ten following the 1953 election. With few exceptions the Councillors have attended institutions of higher education. Their average age in 1947 was fifty-five years and is rising.[5] Although the first (1947) House, with a large plurality of nonparty members, carried forward the Peers' tradition of separatism, subsequent elections established the parties as controlling forces.

Sessions

Diet sessions are of three types, ordinary (*tsujo*), extraordinary (*rinji*), and special (*tokubetsu*). They are numbered consecutively, without distinction as to type. Ordinary sessions are convoked annually, at the instance of the cabinet, by imperial rescript, to begin within the first ten days of December.[6] The rescript must be issued at least twenty days before the date of convocation. Normally, sessions continue for 150 days, from the date of convocation, but they may be extended, either by agreement between the Houses or by the House of Representatives alone if it cannot obtain agreement from the House of Councillors. It is customary for the Houses to adjourn late in December for a lengthy New Year vacation, but the consequent loss of time is less crippling than that suffered by the Diets under the Meiji constitution, limited as they were to ninety-day sessions. The cabinet may request, but has no power to order, the prolongation of a session.[7] Against the legal superiority of the Diet must, however, be reckoned the political influence of the cabinet, particularly when one party has a majority in the House of Representatives. This consideration applies to the exercise of all the functions of the Diet.

Extraordinary sessions may be called between ordinary sessions; special sessions may be called after elections, before an ordinary session has been held. The former are frequent and for varying periods.[8] Constitutionally, after the House of Representatives has been dissolved, an election must be held within forty days, and the Diet must be convoked within thirty days after the election. Extraordinary sessions are, like ordinary and special sessions, convoked by imperial rescript. As with ordinary sessions, control over length and extension of extraordinary and special sessions is exercised by the Diet, the decision of the House of Representatives taking precedence if the Houses disagree. An extraordinary session may be demanded by one-fourth of the members of either House. The Houses must agree upon a recess longer than ten days but either House may recess for shorter periods.

An unusual provision of the constitution enables the cabinet, "in time of national emergency, to convoke the House of Councillors in emergency (*kinkyu*) session." Since that House is not subject to dissolution and is continuously possessed of a quorum it is always available for action. It may legislate in emergency sessions, except upon fiscal and financial measures, but its acts "become null and void unless agreed to by the House of Representatives within ten days of the opening of the next session of the Diet."

Organization of the Houses

Members assemble in their respective Houses in the forenoon of the date of convocation of a session. Newly elected members present their election certificates to the secretariat to be verified from the lists submitted by the proper national election authorities. When one-third of the members, constituting a quorum, have been seated, the president (*gicho*) of the House of Councillors and the speaker (also entitled *gicho)* of the House of Representatives take their places. Should either House lack a presiding officer at the beginning of a session, the first order of business is the election of a new one. Until the election is held, the vice-president or vice-speaker presides, or, in the absence of these officers, the secretary-general. Presiding officers are elected by secret ballot in the House of Councillors, and by secret or signed ballot — as decided by the House — in the House of Representatives. Their tenure coincides with their terms as members. The other officers of each House are the vice-president (vice-speaker), president *pro tempore*, chairmen of standing committees, and the secretary-general.

Following certification of members and, if necessary, election of presiding officers comes the election of chairmen of the standing committees — necessary only if vacancies have occurred, since the chairmen are elected for the duration of their terms as members, subject to the authority of each House to remove a chairman. The Houses may, and customarily do, leave the selection of chairmen of committees to their presiding officers. Secretaries-general also are elected by each House or may be appointed, upon vote of the relevant House, by its presiding officer. Members of standing committees are named by the presiding officers. The election of a prime minister, if the premiership is vacant, completes the selection of officials essential to the conduct of parliamentary business.

Seats are assigned to members by the president or by the speaker at the beginning of each session, each desk having a number and a small corner post inscribed with a member's name. Customarily, members are seated by parties, the principal government party in the center of the semicircular arrangement, flanked by supporting parties. The opposing parties and independents sit on the sides — the Communists farthest to the left.

During these preliminary activities, the two presiding officers have come to an agreement upon a date for the opening ceremony. Upon that date the emperor reads a brief rescript to the members of both Houses in the chamber of the House of Councillors after an introductory statement by the speaker of the House of Representatives.[9] The speaker presides unless unable to be present, in which event the president of the House of Councillors takes his place. The opening ceremony in ordinary sessions may be held either before or after the

New Year recess.[10] It may be delayed for several weeks in other sessions by political maneuvering and by the cabinet's occupation with the preparation of policy statements and the drafting of bills. Although the opening ceremony may be completed within fifteen minutes, it is impressive. The prime minister and his cabinet colleagues, the president of the Supreme Court, and the president of the Board of Audit attend the ceremony. The emperor enters, reads his rescript standing before the throne above and behind the desk of the president of the House of Councillors, and retires. The meeting is adjourned.

Addresses by the prime minister, the minister of foreign affairs, and the minister of finance, in separate sessions of the Houses, form a bridge between old and new business as the Diet gets under way. These addresses purport to appraise the country's situation at home and abroad, to set forth the principal issues to be dealt with, and to outline the general lines along which the cabinet's policies will run. They tend to be phrased in vague, noncommittal terms which leave the government free to move in whatever direction it finds expedient and practicable. Members utilize fully their right to interpellate at length, following delivery of the addresses on policy. Many days are wasted in blunderbuss denunciations corresponding in emptiness to the ministerial statements. When the shadow-boxing has been completed the Houses are ready to settle into the routine of legislation.

Status of Members

Each House is the judge of the qualifications of its members, except for those prescribed by the election law, which are subject to judicial determination.[11] Procedures in the two Houses are identical in the event that any member questions another's qualifications. The "prosecuting" member presents to the presiding officer a written statement of his objections, which is then transmitted to a special committee. The "defendant" member may engage counsel at public expense, and is entitled to appear with counsel before the committee. When the committee's report is before the House he may argue his case in plenary session. Decisions are taken by more than a two-thirds vote of the House, and no explanation of the decision need be given.

Members of the Diet are protected by the constitution in the exercise of their functions. They may not be held liable outside their respective Houses for statements made or votes cast within them. They may not be arrested during a session without consent of the House concerned unless apprehended while committing a crime. A member under arrest at the opening of a session of any type must be released, upon demand of the House, for the period of the session. The cabinet, in asking consent of a House for arrest of a member, must submit a copy of the judicial request submitted to it prior to issuance of a warrant of arrest.

Salaries of Diet members, while low, are much higher than formerly, being set by law at the rate paid to vice-ministers.[12] Members hold passes for free travel, third class, on government-owned railways, buses, and ships while on official business. They exercise the franking privilege for official documents and correspondence. Each member is entitled to office space and a secretary. Retirement allowances are authorized. Official residences are furnished by the state to the principal officers of the Diet. Chairmen of committees have official cars and chauffeurs. Such provisions as these contribute appropriately to the dignity, freedom, and effectiveness of the people's representatives.

Diet members are eligible for appointment — without loss of membership — not only to the cabinet, but to positions as parliamentary vice-ministers, government delegates, commissioners, and advisers, and in other administrative capacities. However, a member's House must be consulted and give assent to such appointments unless they are specifically authorized by law. In the past, parliamentarians have allowed themselves to be seduced by the executive through their eagerness to enjoy the perquisites and prestige attaching to administrative appointment, thereby contributing to the paralysis of the Diet. The cabinet's utilization of its power to make such appointments in large numbers became a scandal. Its effect was to lower the liaison role played by parliamentary under-secretaries in the United Kingdom to one which facilitated executive domination of the Diet. This practice is continuing despite the Diet's erection of a legal safeguard for its members. Regrettably, the taste for plums does not appear to be diminishing. The Houses acquiesce apparently without compunction in the appointment of hundreds of their members as government delegates. These sinecures have replaced the parliamentary councillorships.

Disciplinary measures may be taken against an unruly member by a presiding officer, even to the extent of arrest. Each House is guarded by a police force subject to the control of the presiding officer. The respective disciplinary committees deal with cases submitted to them by vote of the Houses, which subsequently take action upon their reports. Four degrees of punishment are prescribed by the Diet law: admonition, requirement of apology, suspension, and expulsion. Presiding officers may refer to the committees the cases of members who absent themselves unduly from House sessions. A two-thirds vote is necessary to expulsion, and re-elected members must be received back into the fold.[13]

Committees

Reflecting the heightened authority of the Diet, twenty-two standing committees replaced the former four or five in each House.[14] In 1955 the number of these committees was reduced to sixteen. Though required by law to be identical in title and scope for each House, these committees may and do vary by House in the number of members. By agreement, the Houses may establish new standing committees and may combine or abolish existing committees. As will be seen from the list below, most of the committees are correlated with executive agencies; they are the committees for:

The Cabinet
Local Administration
The Judiciary
Foreign Affairs
Finance
Education
Social-Labor
Agriculture-Forestry-Fisheries
Commerce

Transportation
Postal Services
Construction
The Budget
Audit
House Management (Steering Committee)
Disciplinary Measures

The majority of these committees have from 20 to 30 members; the Budget Committee in the House of Representatives has 51 members, in the House of Councillors 45; before 1955 the smallest committees in both Houses were the Library Committees, of 10 members, which have recently been abolished. Members are appointed by the speaker and the president, respectively, and are entitled to hold their places throughout their terms. Since standing committee memberships are, by law, allotted to the parties and other groups in proportion to the number of seats they hold, the speaker or president is authorized to shift members from one committee to another in order to maintain the ratio of group representation. Each member must serve on at least one committee and may not serve on more than two. "Directors," whose principal function is to relieve and assist the chairmen, are elected for each committee by and from its membership. Each standing committee is entitled to two paid research assistants, persons who are not Diet members and who may not hold other employment concurrently or accept government employment for a year after leaving their posts with the committees. Jurisdictional disputes between committees are decided by the presiding officer of the House in which they arise. The corresponding standing committees of the Houses may hold joint meetings for the examination of bills and other matters of common interest.

Special committees are utilized for *ad hoc* investigations. The Houses elect members of special committees, who, in turn, co-opt one of themselves as chairman. All committees may be authorized to function between sessions. A quorum consists of half the membership, decisions are taken by simple majority, and a chairman may cast his vote to break a tie. Whether or not hearings shall be open to the public is for a committee to say except that there must be opportunity for the citizenry to attend hearings on the budget and on important revenue bills. Passes for the hearings are issued by committee chairmen. A committee must report to the House upon its deliberations, and a minority is entitled also to report. Both reports are made part of the House record of proceedings. Minutes are kept by each committee and printed copies are provided for each member of the House concerned.[15]

The Diet has one standing committee of both Houses — the Legislative Committee of the Houses. It is composed of 18 members, 10 from the Representatives, 8 from the Councillors, elected by their respective Houses. The chairmanship is held alternately, from meeting to meeting, by a member of each House selected by the committeemen from his House. Members hold office throughout their terms. For the conduct of business a majority of the members from each House must be present. A two-thirds vote is required to pass recommendations. Meetings are not open to the public. Minutes are kept and printed copies distributed to all members of the Diet.

This committee may meet during plenary sessions of the Houses and, with Diet approval, between sessions of the Diet. Its purpose is to provide a forum for the discussion of problems related to the

Diet's powers and procedure. Relations between the Houses and between them and the cabinet, new methods for the conduct of legislation, difficult issues of procedure — these and similar matters are within the purview of this general committee. The Legislative Committee does not receive or draft bills. It considers problems and offers recommendations. It is expected to take a broad view of the whole Diet and of its powers and responsibilities, and to make recommendations for its improvement toward the status intended for it by the constitution.

The Legislative Process

The order of the day for each House is fixed in advance by its presiding officer, published in the *Official Gazette,* and distributed to members. The House Management (steering) committees advise upon the arrangement of the calendar, but changes may be made in the printed order only by consent of the House concerned. Full stenographic minutes are kept, which include attendance, the record of matters received and action taken, reports of committees, interpellations and speeches, statements and documents accepted as supplementary to proceedings, votes taken, and other relevant items. After correction by the presiding officer, the minutes, except for matters of a confidential nature, are published in the *Official Gazette,* which is available to the public. Laws passed are published separately in the *Gazette.*

Forms of legislation include motions, resolutions, bills, and statutes (laws). Motions may be offered by one or by several members. If offered by a single member, they are seldom seconded, but are accepted and put by the chairman without seconding. The English word "bill" is used in translation for the Japanese *ho-an* (bill) and also for *ketsugi-an* (resolution). A treaty is introduced into the Diet as a treaty-bill *(joyaku-an).* The three types of bills are dealt with similarly except in the case of resolutions to be confined to one House.

Petitions submitted by citizens receive committee consideration and may be recommended for adoption and forwarded to the cabinet for action. The Houses act independently upon petitions. The many hundreds of petitions received absorb an undue share of the members' time, but indicate the continued faith of the citizenry in an ancient institution.[16]

The lawmaking process may be initiated by the cabinet, by a single member of either House, by a committee, or by "handing over" a bill to the presiding officer. Since 1955 an individual member must receive the prior approval of twenty other members before he is entitled to introduce a bill. Measures necessitating an outlay of funds require the support of fifty members before introduction. Government bills are submitted to one House for action, and to the other — within five days — for preliminary consideration. The latter House awaits the decision of the former before taking action. Private members' bills may be similarly referred if a presiding officer so decides. Ordinarily a presiding officer refers any bill to the standing committee within whose purview its subject matter falls. At this stage a bill receives careful consideration. Public hearings may be held if the president or speaker authorizes them at the request of the committee chairman — which he does as a matter of course. When the committee is ready to report the bill out, the presiding officer, with the advice of the steering committee, places it on the order of the day for action. The chairman of the reporting committee explains the bill, together with committee amendments, in plenary session, and his explanation is followed by the report of the committee minority if there is one. This stage constitutes the only required reading of the bill. Supporters and opponents of the bill then debate the issues or interpellate upon them, or both interpellate and debate. A bill which fails to receive majority support in a committee need not be reported out unless it was transmitted from the other House or a report is demanded by twenty members. Amendments may be proposed by twenty members or by the cabinet upon consent of the House. Votes are then taken upon amendments and the bill. If the bill receives a majority vote, it is declared passed. This very simple and speedy procedure may be shortened still further in the event that the House votes to omit reference to committee. The proposer of the bill then explains its provisions, the House may interpellate and debate upon it, a vote is taken, the bill is passed or rejected. It then is sent to the other House, where it may be explained by the proposer or by the chairman of the standing committee of the House which has passed the bill.

A House may call for an interim report from a committee, and it may limit the time allowed for committee consideration. It may submit a bill to a special committee or resubmit it to a standing committee. With approval of a presiding officer, a committee may meet during a plenary session. It may request testimony by cabinet ministers, who may also initiate appearances at committee hearings. It may call private persons as witnesses, providing them with transportation and living allowances. Members of the Diet may be authorized to travel for purposes of direct observation, a privilege that is highly appreciated.

As in Western parliaments, failure of the two Houses to agree upon all provisions of a bill passed by both may prompt recourse to a joint or conference committee. In this situation the Diet Law favors the House of Representatives, which may refuse a request from the Councillors for a joint committee when the request follows disagreement upon a bill other than a budget bill transmitted from the Representatives. The Councillors may not refuse such a request from the Representatives. In all other circumstances neither House may refuse the other's request for a conference committee. The advantage conceded to the Representatives, which is unlikely to be permanent since it was agreed to only after acrimonious debate in the House of Peers, is a corollary of the power of the Representatives, by a two-thirds vote, to repass a bill rejected by the Councillors. It is of small consequence in view of the difficulty of obtaining a two-thirds vote, and is unlikely to be used except with relation to bills which have received large majorities in the House of Representatives.

Joint committees are composed of twenty members, ten elected by each House. The required quorum is two-thirds of each delegation; the chairmen are selected by their delegations and serve alternately. A two-thirds vote is required to decide upon a definitive draft, which is sent by the committee to the House that requested joint committee consideration. If agreement cannot be reached, each delegation reports the fact to the House it represents. Neither House may amend a definitive draft agreed upon in a joint committee.

As a rule plenary sessions of the Houses are open to the public, but they may be closed to it by a two-thirds vote. The Representatives meet at 1 P.M., the Councillors at 10 A.M. Secretaries count the members present, and if a quorum is lacking, the presiding officer may summon members from outside the chamber. Two forms of discussion are employed: interpellation and debate. Interpellations, when employed, precede debate, and to a considerable degree resemble it, although the expression by an interpellator of his own views is contrary to the rules. They are addressed to cabinet members and are ordinarily submitted in outline to a presiding officer, who may disallow them but may be overruled by the House. The cabinet must reply within seven days either in writing or orally. By permission of the House, a member may present an urgent interpellation orally and may ask supplementary questions orally, thereby giving this procedure the semblance of debate. This means that the minister or ministers to whom questions are addressed must be present in a House when the questions are brought before it. The ordeal by interpellation may be embarrassing. Undoubtedly members enjoy the spectacle and gain intellectual agility from participating in it. Upon motion of a member interpellations may be followed by debate and by a vote. But debate has made little headway; both in committee and in plenary sessions, the time is devoted primarily to interpellations. It may be assumed that the extensive reliance upon interpellations, which was consistent with the subordinate position of the Diet under the Meiji constitution, gradually will diminish as the Diet grows in self-confidence and members more fully realize the nature and uses of debate. It would appear, indeed, that a transformation is taking place of interpellation into debate, as members give less and less emphasis to inquiry, more and more to statement.

Debate is conducted by speeches delivered from the rostrum by members who have notified the presiding officer of their views and been listed, alternately for and against a bill or proposition, for recognition. Committee members receive priority on the list. Brief statements may be made from the floor. Closure of interpellations and of debate may be declared by a presiding officer either at discretion or upon vote of the House upon a motion for closure — not debatable — proposed by twenty members. Voting is done *viva voce*, by standing in response to a presiding officer's request, by signed ballot, or by secret ballot. *Viva voce* voting is highly informal, members merely calling out "no objection" (*igi ga nai*) upon a presiding officer's inquiry, the latter then declaring that he finds no objection. The roll-call yea and nay vote is not employed in the Diet. In the third procedure, members in favor of a measure, as the roll is called, deposit white ballots bearing their signatures in the ballot box at the front of the chamber, members opposing it depositing signed blue ballots. For a recorded vote upon a nominee, a member deposits a white ballot bearing his own and a nominee's in one box, a wooden name plate in the other. For a secret ballot each member casts an unsigned ballot indicating his preference into one box, his name plate into another.

Bills passed by both Houses, or by the House of Representatives alone, are sent to the cabinet. Exceptions are bills which apply only to a single locality. These must be approved by the people of that locality before they may be promulgated. From the cabinet bills are presented for the emperor's signature and seal. They are then countersigned by the prime minister and by ministers especially concerned with the subject matter. The final actions upon them are the imperial statement of promulgation and its publication, together with the laws, in the *Official Gazette*.

Free Discussion

Article 78 of the Diet Law provides: "Each House must, during the term of a session, meet at least once every three weeks for the purpose of conducting free discussion in relation to government by its members. A subject under discussion may be put to a vote of the House upon motion of a member." This unique feature was devised to provide an opportunity for members to gain experience in free-for-all debate in a climate of discussion undominated by members of the cabinet. It exists outside the legislative process but as an aid to its improvement. Originally contemplated as obtainable through greater emphasis upon use of the committee of the whole, the needed independence of attitude subsequently was decided to be more likely to develop in an entirely separate form. Although Diet members made some use, under SCAP prodding, of the opportunity for gaining greatly needed experience, their interest soon flagged. It would seem unlikely that "free discussion" will be maintained for any considerable period.[17]

The difficulty which members find in freeing themselves from bureaucratic direction is revealed in the rules under which "free discussion" is carried on. They provide for questioning cabinet ministers, for prior designation of participants, for allotment of time on a proportionate basis, and for other features of the accustomed legislative process. The less prominent members have benefited most, possibly because the leaders are not interested in a purely educational activity.

Seasoned politicians may well regard it as unnecessary or beneath their dignity.

Legislative Bureaus

To aid members in bill-drafting, each House maintains a legislative bureau, consisting of a director, secretaries, and other personnel. Directors are appointed by the speaker and the president respectively, with approval of the House concerned. Bureau administration is supervised by the presiding officers of each House in accordance with regulations approved by the steering committees.

Control of Proceedings

The president and speaker exercise great authority over their respective Houses. Neither is purely a moderator. Both are subject to party pressures, though keenly observant of their responsibility for faithful application of the Diet Law and the rules of the Houses, and for fair treatment of all members. Members are alert for signs of discrimination and are likely to express themselves caustically when irritated. Yet their consistent waiver of rights of election of committee chairmen, of voting, of debate, etc., in deference to their presiding officers, has aided to establish firm control, and, as a rule, smooth and rapid transaction of business. Exceptions arise when members, under emotional stress, indulge in jibes, catcalls, and other forms of interference with the order of the day. Brawling and minor mayhem have resulted oftener than members may care to recall. While antics of this sort occur in both Houses, they are less frequent in the House of Councillors.

Collaborating closely with the presiding officers, the House Management or steering committees assist in drafting the agenda, supply information upon precedents, suggest chairmen and members for committee appointments, and in other ways function as rules committees. Party whips also aid in keeping the legislative machinery operating. They introduce motions expressive of the decisions of their parties, suggest speakers to take part in interpellation and debate, and keep party members in touch with their leaders and with developments in the Diet.

Notes

[1] H. S. Quigley, *Japanese Government and Politics* (New York, 1932), p. 200.
[2] Justin H. Williams, "The Japanese Diet under the New Constitution," *American Political Science Review*, XLII (October 1948), 928–932.

The New Japan

[3] The description of Diet organization and procedure is based upon these documents published in Japanese and English in the *Official Gazette*.

[4] *Nippon Times*, May 29, 1950.

[5] *The 1947 Japanese House of Councillors Election*, Report No. 4334, Office of Intelligence Research, Department of State, January 15, 1948, Appendix B.

[6] "The date of convocation, however, must be such that the term of office of Diet members will not expire during an ordinary session" (Diet Law, Article 2). In 1952, Liberal Secretary-General Masuda Kanesichi affirmed that the quoted sentence qualified, in effect, the previous sentence of Article 2, permitting a session to be convoked on any date prior to December 10 which might be necessary in order to provide 150 days between such date and the expiration date of a term of the House of Representatives (*Nippon Times*, April 23, 1952).

[7] The cabinet attempted, in June 1947, to exhibit authority to extend a Diet session for three weeks. The Diet repudiated the cabinet's notification and extended the session for fifty-two days by resolution.

[8] Extra sessions were numerous under the Meiji constitution; ordinary and extra sessions totaled ninety-two; to date under the new constitution twenty-four sessions of all types have been convoked.

[9] At the opening ceremony in November 1949 Speaker Shidehara escorted the emperor to his chair but handed him the wrong document — the address of the speaker. The emperor waited good-naturedly while the secretary-general informed Mr. Shidehara of his mistake. An apology at the palace and much criticism by politicians and the press were embarrassing consequences of his slip for the aged statesman (*Nippon Times*, November 2, 1949).

[10] Legislation as well as other business may be carried on prior to the opening ceremony.

[11] See below, Chapter 18.

[12] Members' monthly salaries, because of the inflation of the yen, rose from 3,500 yen on May 3, 1947, to 57,000 yen at the end of 1951; the salaries of presiding officers at the latter date were 80,000 yen, of vice-presiding officers 60,000 yen, of secretaries-general 60,000 yen per month. Ordinary members received an expense allowance of 500 yen per day during sessions or when serving on committees between sessions; those who were cabinet members or parliamentary vice-ministers received similar allowances amounting to 25 per cent of their salaries. The spiral of inflation since 1951 has necessitated additional increases — in some cases amounting to nearly 100 per cent.

[13] A *cause célèbre* in the record of disciplinary action was that of Izumiyama Sanroku, minister of finance in 1948 and a Representative. He became drunk at a dinner given by himself in the Diet building and grossly insulted a woman member, Mrs. Yamashita Harue, who was reputed to be fond of sake herself. Both members were summoned to explain their conduct, but the minister resigned his seat in the House rather than submit to discipline. Mrs. Yamashita appeared and made a vigorous attack on Izumiyama and his party, the Democratic Liberals, which, she asserted, must share his shame for lack of discipline and of respect for the responsibilities of Diet members. She was cleared. (Minutes, House of Representatives, *Official Gazette*, Extra, December 14, 1948, p. 24.)

[14] Originally set at twenty-one, the number of committees was reduced to twenty by the elimination of three and the addition of two committees in revisions of the Diet Law, Article 42. The eliminated committees were those of Culture, of Mining and Industry, and of Electricity; the added committees, those on Administrative Research and Civil Service and on Economic Stabilization. The original number was re-established in October 1948 by a division of functions between the Committee for the Prime Minister's Office and the Committee for the Civil Service, which replaced the single Committee on Administrative Research and Civil Service. In 1949 the Communications Committee was replaced by committees on Postal Services and on Telecommunications (see *Official Gazette*, Extra No. 122, October 26, 1949). The list as

printed here follows some regrouping of functions and modifications of committee titles. For information on recent structural changes in the Diet committee system the authors are indebted to Dr. Hattie K. Colton.

[15] The Legislative Reorganization Act passed by the Congress of the United States in 1946 was the model for many provisions of the Diet Law.

[16] During the second session, 1948, the House of Representatives received 2,883 petitions, of which 1,791 were accepted, 1,276 adopted (Minutes, House of Representatives, *Official Gazette*, Extra, July 6, 1948, p. 43).

[17] In 1949 a member of the House of Representatives complained that interest in "free discussion" had waned because members preferred to express their ideas in committee hearings; few members continued to attend during "free discussion" periods (*ibid.*, November 27, 1949, p. 15).

18

Elections

Postwar Election Laws

THE Japanese initiated the demand for electoral expansion in the closing years of the nineteenth century, and this movement slowly gained momentum in the next two decades, culminating in the enactment of manhood suffrage in 1925.[1] Occupied Japan, under the steadfast prompting of SCAP, accelerated the pace of electoral reform. As major governmental reforms were instituted, election rules and voting qualifications were written into separate House of Representatives, House of Councillors, and local government election laws. In 1950 the basic principles of these distinct statutes were codified into a composite law which outlines the electoral system as it exists today.[2]

In December 1945 the Diet undertook a revision of the 1925 House of Representatives Election Law. The new regulations were a major step toward an expanded electoral base, setting the pattern for postwar voting qualifications and election procedures. The age requirement of voters was reduced to twenty and that of candidates to twenty-five. For the first time in Japanese history voting privileges and rights of candidature were granted to women, increasing the size of the electorate to 37 million. The law divided the country into fifty-three large constituencies, each allocated one representative per 150,-000 people. The elector generally voted for more than one candidate, depending upon the size of the election district. The House of Representatives was elected under this statute in April 1946.

The 1947 constitution cast into fundamental law the newly established principle of universal suffrage, to be applicable henceforth in both national and local elections. Article 15 affirmed the inalienable right of the people to choose and dismiss their public officials, guaranteeing universal adult suffrage and the secrecy of the ballot. Other articles provided that both houses of the Diet were to consist of the elected representatives of the people; that there should be no discrimination in the qualifications for voting or Diet membership on the basis of race, sex, creed, social status, family origin, education, property, or income; that a general election for members of the House of Representatives must be held within forty days from the date of dissolution; and that both executive and legislative officials of the various local governments should be popularly elected. [3]

Anticipating the implementation of the new constitution in May 1947, SCAP encouraged the holding of four elections in April. To be elected were a new House of Representatives, Councillors for the popularly constituted second chamber, and executive and legislative officials for the restructured system of local government. The regulations governing the House of Councillors and local elections closely paralleled those established by the 1945 House of Representatives Election Law. The Jiyuto (Liberal party) and Shimpoto (Progressive party), however, had expressed considerable dissatisfaction with this statute, especially the provision for large electoral districts, and they urged important amendments. The issue became politically significant in March when the Yoshida government introduced a controversial election bill into the House of Representatives, with the four scheduled elections only a few weeks away. After tumultuous debates marked by partisan coloration and occasional fisticuffs, the revision was enacted into law on March 31, following an extension of the Diet session. The new law granted voting privileges to certain categories which had traditionally been denied the ballot: heads of noble families, bankrupts, those receiving public or private charity, and those with no definite domicile. The law of 1947 also established 117 medium-sized districts for House of Representatives elections, with the voter casting his ballot for only one candidate. In addition, local election committees chosen by their respective bodies were to replace the prefectural governors, city and town mayors, and village headmen as election supervisors — an innovation in Japan's electoral history.[4]

The House of Councillors Election Law, which came into force on

August 19, 1948, stipulated the same voting qualifications as the statute governing the House of Representatives, but the age of candidature was set at thirty. The Local Autonomy Law of April 1947 likewise specified identical voting qualifications, but gubernatorial candidates were to have reached the age of thirty and mayoralty and legislative aspirants the age of twenty-five.[5]

Other important innovations in electoral legislation were implemented after the 1947 elections, becoming operative for the first time in the election of 1949. In December 1947 a National Election Administration Commission was created to supervise all Japanese elections, a responsibility formerly assumed by the home minister.[6] In the following year, the Diet, with an eye toward the prevention of corruption in elections, provided for the public management of specified campaign activities in House of Representatives contests, and for the partial financing of such campaigns by funds from the national treasury.[7] The Diet also enacted a statute rigorously controlling political contributions and expenditures.[8] In view of the resulting maze of election laws and regulations, there was a need to bring the election system under the umbrella of a single statute. This the Diet did in April 1950 by the passage of a composite election law covering both national and local contests. The 1950 statute, with subsequent amendments, constitutes the legal framework of the prevailing election system.

Election Districts

In elections to the House of Representatives Japan has experimented with three types of electoral districts. The first election law in 1889 established small single-member constituencies, with a *gun* (county) generally constituting one district. The 1900 statute provided for large constituencies, each returning from two to twelve members; and municipalities with a population over 30,000 were designated as separate districts entitled to one seat. The revised law of 1919 returned to the small single-member system, but in 1925 the plan was abandoned in favor of medium-sized, multimember constituencies. After a brief experiment, under the 1945 statute, with very large districts, each electing from four to fourteen representatives, the Yoshida government in 1947 secured a return to the medium-sized constituency, which has been retained in subsequent electoral legislation. Under this system Japan is now divided into 118 election districts, each sending from one to five members to the House of Representatives.[9]

None of these election district plans has been universally applauded by Japanese political leaders. Those who advocate discarding one system for another are suspected of gerrymandering motives, and they meet strong resistance from those who fear the dilution of their own political strongholds. The prewar Seiyukai, traditionally powerful in rural areas where often a local leader influenced the voting patterns of his bailiwick, long cherished a desire for the small-district plan. The Seiyukai cabinet of Hara Takashi was able to institute this system in 1919, and the scheme had the endorsement of many Jiyuto leaders in postwar years.

The advocates of the single-member district contend that electioneering in small constituencies brings the candidate into closer contact with the individual voter. Campaigns in a smaller area, they argue, ease the financial and physical burden of the office seeker, thus encouraging the filing of competent candidates who could not otherwise afford to run. It is further suggested that the election of only one member from a district intensifies the contests and accelerates the trend toward a two-party system. It should be noted, however, that in prewar years the defenders of the small-district plan often urged its adoption on the ground that minor parties would have more adequate representation. The proponents of the large-district system fear that national political figures, lacking the time to mend local fences, may be eclipsed by less qualified candidates who have become well known within small districts. They maintain that the intensive campaigns promoted by the single-member plan encourage bribery, expand the influence of bosses, and invite government interference in elections. Actually many politicians concentrate on the limited area where their personal influence is greatest, at the same time relying upon the extra votes they pick up in centers which they cultivate less intensively. Since the adoption of manhood suffrage, the medium-sized district has been the only system upon which agreement has been possible.

In the selection of the one hundred members of the House of Councillors who represent the national constituency, the whole nation is considered a single electoral district. This method was designed to secure the election of qualified, well-known leaders from all areas of endeavor. Many of the national constituency candidates concentrate their campaign activities in one or two prefectures, relying upon supplementary support from the rest of the nation to sweep them into office. One hundred fifty Councillors are elected from the forty-six prefectures, each constituting an electoral district and returning from two to eight members.[10]

The cities and counties are election districts for prefectural assembly seats, although in sparsely populated areas several districts may be combined. Cities, towns, and villages are entitled to establish districts for their assembly elections, but apparently this has been done only by the five major cities, which have established wards as electoral units.[11]

Voter Registration

In contrast to the American system, where registration is the responsibility of the individual voter, public officials in Japan take the initiative in preparing lists of qualified electors. By September 15 of each year the election administration committee of each city, town, and village distributes registration cards to every home. By this method they ascertain the name, address, sex, and birth date of each qualified voter who has been continuously domiciled in the area for at least three months. In the case of mariners who are unable to meet the residence requirement, the committee confers with shipowners whose offices are in the electoral territory. A basic register of all qualified electors is prepared by October 31, and it is posted for public inspection for a fifteen-day period, commencing on November 5. During that time a citizen may protest the omission of his name, and if the decision of the local election authorities is adverse, he is entitled to institute legal proceedings to secure his voting rights. Supplementary lists are prepared for those whose names do not appear on the basic register, but who have since qualified for an approaching election. Victims of disaster forced to move to another community where they cannot meet the domiciliary requirement may also have their names placed upon the supplementary list.

Nomination Process

A contest for membership in the House of Representatives is called a general election; Councillors' seats are filled by an ordinary election;

and local assemblymen are chosen in a common election. These three types of elections and those for the positions of governor and mayor are held within thirty days before the expiration of the term of office, and public notice of such contests is given for a specified number of days in advance of the polling date. When dissolution disrupts the normal tenure of the members of the House of Representatives or the local assemblies, an election takes place within forty days from the date of dissolution.

Party conventions and primary elections are not a part of the simplified nominating procedures in Japan.[12] A citizen desiring to become a candidate for public office must notify the district election authorities; the period of notification varies from twenty to five days in advance of the polling date, depending upon the level of the public office involved. An elector whose name appears on the voters' list may name someone else as a candidate with the consent of the person named. At the time of notification either the candidate or his "recommender" must file with the election officials a prescribed form listing the name, birth date, occupation, and political affiliation of the office seeker. In the case of nominations for executive posts in towns and villages, the office-seeker must also accompany his filing application with the signatures of thirty or more electors who support his candidacy.

Except for contestants in elections below the city level, each candidate is required at the time of filing to present proof that he has deposited specified amounts of cash or their equivalent in bonds with appropriate financial officials. The size of the deposit varies with the level of the office sought. Instituted in 1925 to discourage frivolous candidacies, the filing fee is retained by the government if the candidate receives fewer votes than the legally required minimum. In the 1952 election the national treasury netted over four million yen from forty-two Tokyo aspirants for seats in the House of Representatives who forfeited their deposits.[13] This system, however, has not solved Japan's problem of trivial candidacies. For some candidates the loss of the deposit may be offset by gains. An election campaign is one method of self-advertising for business or professional reasons. A nuisance candidate who writes his name with the same *kanji* (characters) as a bona fide aspirant can afford to pay the deposit, demand a larger sum from his namesake whose electoral success is menaced, and then withdraw from the race with a handsome profit. When office seekers were screened under the early purge directives, some candidates filed merely to divine their political status, and then withdrew from the contest. In the 1946 general election some politicians were more interested in obtaining the privileges awarded to candidates (specified sums from frozen bank deposits and the purchase of cheap paper which could be resold at black market prices) than they were in winning Diet seats.

In Japan it is not mandatory that a candidate be a resident of the district in which he is running for election. A nationally prominent politician might successfully compete in a constituency in which he has never lived; however, the election prospects of the ordinary candidate are enhanced if he can claim residence or birth in the district. A candidate may not campaign for two offices simultaneously, nor may a member of one assembly hold concurrent membership in another.

Despite the ease with which a person is entitled to herald his candidacy, the political parties nevertheless speak with a loud voice in the selection of candidates. In prewar elections each political organization commonly left the recognition of "official" candidates to an election committee in the Tokyo headquarters of the party. Thoroughly conversant with the political situation in the local districts, campaign strategists often accepted the candidates proposed by the leaders of the party organization in the constituency. Party members who persisted in filing for an election race against the wishes of the national office were in serious danger of expulsion from the organization and of defeat at the polls. In the 1928 election, 70.6 per cent of the official Seiyukai candidates were elected, while but 15 per cent of the unofficial candidates were successful; the corresponding Minseito percentages were 72.5 and 24.6.

In comparison with prewar elections, there has been since the surrender a marked increase in the number of candidates contesting seats in the House of Representatives, although there has been a steady decline over the 1946 peak with each successive election. In the period from 1928 to 1938, an average of 1.7 candidates competed for each seat in the chamber. In 1946 the ratio had jumped to 5.7, thereafter declining to 3.3 in 1947, 2.9 in 1949, 2.66 in 1952, 2.2 in 1953, and 2.18 in 1955.[14]

Elections

Never an important factor in prewar Japanese politics, unaffiliated candidacies have been prominent since 1945, although there has been a noticeable decline in recent elections. In the 1946 House of Representatives election, approximately half of the candidates ran as independents or as representatives of tiny splinter parties. Many politicians were reluctant to commit themselves to a political organization which might subsequently come under the strictures of SCAP. During this confusion inchoate party structures and unstable political allegiances stimulated the major parties to give reluctant backstage support to unaffiliated politicians. In the 1947 general election, however, the proportion of independent and minor candidates declined to 25 per cent, and the significant diminution continued in each subsequent contest, reaching a postwar low of 12 per cent in 1953. Unaffiliated and splinter party candidates seeking membership in the House of Councillors constituted 58 per cent of the total candidacies in 1947, and in 1953 their strength was still evident at the 39 per cent level. In prefectural and local elections the percentage of candidates competing for executive and legislative posts without benefit of formal major party affiliation was even higher. In 1947 almost 70 per cent of the gubernatorial aspirants, 88.5 per cent of those seeking the mayoralty and the position of village headman, 41 per cent of the prefectural assembly candidates, and nearly 90 per cent of those contesting local assembly seats were in this category. In the 1951 local assembly elections only 40 per cent of the candidates in the five major cities ran as independents, but in other cities the percentage jumped to 73.4, while in the towns and villages it was 95 per cent.[15] In the 1955 prefectural elections, however, there was manifest a greater degree of partisan competition than in previous contests.

A steady decline of independent and splinter party candidacies has taken place in House of Representatives elections. The Japanese experience with this type of election reaching back to 1890, and keen party competition for mass support dating from 1928, may have eased the return to traditional party loyalties and political patterns after initial uncertainties disappeared. Independence in candidature has tended to remain high in second-chamber races where party roots were never deeply embedded, popular election is an innovation, and where a substantial loss of power has probably reduced some of its political attraction.[16] Likewise in elections at the prefectural and local levels, where sweeping electoral and structural reforms of recent enactment have produced an indigestible number of posts to be filled, independent candidates have tended to dominate the ballot. Such a situation, encouraged by the unsettled political scene and confused party loyalties, suggests that opportunism, irresponsibility, and leader-dominated cliques are delaying the development of a responsible party system.

While some of the unaffiliated candidates were nonparty men by conviction, the majority, though not formally committed, were tacitly recognized as semiofficial candidates of the major parties, or intended to join the organization which offered the best "inducements" after the election. Of the 120 members elected to the House of Representatives on independent or minor party tickets in 1946, only 20 had retained their unaffiliated status a year later. Less than two months after the 1947 elections, nearly all the successful independents in both houses of the Diet had either joined a major party or combined to form a bargaining group.[17]

In general, the responsibility for choosing the official candidates has rested with an election committee in the central headquarters of the party. Although frequently dominated by the campaign manager, the committee is composed of chiefs of the local branches and national party leaders. In seeking people to run for office, they are inclined toward candidates with a national or local reputation, political connections, access to campaign funds, or a record free from scandal. The selection committee commonly accepts the candidate suggested by the local organizations, although it reserves the right to overrule the subordinate branches and assign a stronger candidate.[18] Dissension between the central election committees and the local party chapters over the selection of recognized candidates apparently reached its peak in the 1949 campaign. Misunderstandings arose when ambitious candidates in filing their notifications listed their political affiliation without consulting the official organization; consequently candidacies were mushrooming under party labels without the knowledge of the party concerned. The national headquarters of the Minshu-Jiyuto provoked considerable resentment when, to avoid possible vote-splitting, it announced a reduction in the number of its official entries after many candidates had completed the notification procedure. In some cases the central election committees rejected the recommendations of the local branches, and often the substitutions they made were not acceptable to constituency leaders. In that election a total of eighty candidates lost their official status by action of party officials in Tokyo, who exerted some control over the selection by their ability to withhold financial and campaign support. The rejected candidates were notified of the withdrawal of national party recognition, but when some refused to change the political affiliation initially declared at the time of filing, they continued to be officially recorded under that designation.[19]

In the future the hand of the party organization may be somewhat strengthened in the matter of candidate selection. A cabinet order implementing the 1950 election law provides that a would-be candidate listing his political affiliation at the time of filing must also produce a document from the party organization certifying that the entry is correct.[20]

The Campaign

Japanese laws governing the conduct of campaigns have been notoriously stringent, perhaps reflecting a certain distrust of democratic procedures on the part of those who were compelled to grant suffrage concessions. Prewar regulations placed restrictions upon the number and size of posters, frowned upon parades and demonstrations, and prohibited house-to-house canvassing and the transportation of voters to the polls. Supreme authority over the supervision of campaigns and the conduct of elections rested with the home minister. Besides the power to issue limitations upon the use of letters and pictures, he exercised control over the police and the prefectural governors who were charged with the surveillance of the electoral process. It was common practice for an incoming ministry to replace incumbent governors with their own henchmen, and a strategic shifting of prefectural executives often signaled preparation for an election.

In the early days of the Occupation, election regulations were relaxed considerably, and the 1946 House of Representatives race, conducted under the watchful eye of SCAP, was characterized by much unmolested campaigning on street corners, uncensored election bulletins, and vigorous press coverage. However, with the development of gasoline and paper shortages and the inflationary rise of campaign costs, the Diet asserted its power to reimpose strict regulations upon political activities and campaign publicity. To have relied upon the ordinance authority of the home minister in such matters would have tempted the government to take political advantage of the scarcities. The restrictions were designed to curb the increase in campaign costs and election irregularities and to encourage filing by qualified candidates who lacked the financial resources to compete with politicians who were supported by prosperous black-market operators. The rigorous controls in effect during the 1949 campaign — more restrictive than those of prewar days — were severely criticized by voters, politicians, and the press. Rigid limitations were placed upon the speechmaking activities of the office seeker, and his party was prohibited from circulating literature on behalf of his candidacy. During much of the campaign period, one section of the election law was interpreted by officials as forbidding newspaper support of or opposition to a given candidate or party. The paucity of information about candidates resulted in a lack of popular interest in the election. One newspaper poll suggested that a majority of the voters had been exposed to little or no campaigning.[21] Although the election regulations were relaxed somewhat in 1950, subsequent changes made in nearly every session of the Diet have continued to place serious limitations upon certain forms of campaign activity accepted as commonplace in most countries.

In 1947 a nine-member National Election Administration Commission was established to supervise all Japanese elections, replacing the home minister in that role. Selected by and accountable to the prime minister and the Diet, it was charged with the collection of election data and the general management of campaigns and elections, including some phases of party activity. A hierarchy of subordinate committees, reaching from the prefectural level down to the smaller local areas, was set up to implement the electoral policies enunciated by the central commission. Each prefectural assembly elected an election committee of six members to supervise the work of lesser city, town, and village committees within its jurisdiction. In practice the local committees have not, in many instances, played the role originally assigned to them. Because the major portion of the financial burden is borne by the national treasury, the prefectural executive was held responsible for the expenditure of the funds. As a consequence, important policy decisions have often rested with local government officials rather than with the election committees legally charged with making them.[22]

In 1952 the Japanese moved a step closer to the prewar system of election administration. The National Election Administration Commission was dissolved and replaced by the Local Autonomy Agency. Since that time the Election Division of the Autonomy Agency has supervised the election system. This supervision is conducted by the Central Election Administrative Committee, with a membership of five, for the election of Councillors from the national constituency and for referenda upon judges of the Supreme Court. The director-general of the Autonomy Agency supervises all other elections. In both instances, supervision is administered through the election administration committees of the localities.[23] If the power of the local election committees is usurped by local government officials who take their orders from the prefectural governor, and if the latter is made responsible to one national administrator rather than to an independent commission, the prewar system of election management may be on the horizon.

The obstruction of the ordinary channels of candidate-voter communication through press, poster, and speech restrictions has traditionally challenged the ingenuity of the seasoned Japanese politician. Likewise in postwar campaigns there has been no lack of imaginative techniques designed to attract the attention of the voter without violating the letter of the election law. Legislators, intent upon regulating campaign speeches, did not foresee the possibilities in tape recorders. A statute that limited electioneering activities through press media was likely to be silent on the scattering of literature from airplanes, the distribution of matches with election appeals on the boxes, the construction of park benches emblazoned with campaign slogans, or the lending of name-draped umbrellas which shielded the constituent from the rain and the candidate from a technical violation of the law. When paper shortages necessitated fewer campaign posters, armadas of motor vehicles descended upon the electorate, carrying office seekers who broadcast their appeals through loudspeakers. Occasionally fireworks were used to spell out the name of a candidate, or bargain sale advertisements were posted with the photograph of the politically ambitious merchant attractively displayed. The more subtle methods of electioneering, such as flooding the district with

New Year greetings, attending birthday celebrations of constituents, and treating electors to tours of the Diet building and visits to near-by shrines, were also common tools of the politician's trade.[24] Meticulous regulations invite veteran campaigners to employ tactics hardly envisioned by the framers of the statute, and frequent revisions in greater detail become necessary to encompass the most recent wave of electioneering versatility. In these circumstances, the enforcement problems facing the election authorities are many and perplexing.

Illustrative of campaign restrictions in Japan is the 1950 election law and some of the recent alterations. The writers of this statute intended that the campaign period be of short duration, varying from thirty days for elections to the House of Councillors and twenty-five days for those to the House of Representatives to ten days when town and village offices are at stake. Theoretically, electioneering is forbidden until the candidate has filed his nomination papers, which can be done only after the election date has been announced. In actuality, however, the campaign period is generally much longer than the law allows. As the "smell" of an approaching election reaches the sensitive nostrils of incumbent politicians, the Diet chambers are emptied by the scurry of anxious representatives to their constituencies to "lecture" and "explain" before the campaign officially begins. The line between servicing the needs of constituents and actual vote solicitation is very difficult to draw; consequently, the incumbent has an initial advantage over an opponent who might be accused of premature electioneering should he summon a political gathering before he can legally become a candidate.

In order to reduce campaign expenses so that resort to questionable financial practices may be rendered unnecessary, the Japanese are experimenting with quasipublicly managed and financed campaigns. The plan was sponsored chiefly by the Shakaito (Socialist party) and the Minshuto (Democratic party), which were frequently unable to match campaign chests with the well-financed Jiyuto. Under the system the government performs more services for the candidate than is the case in other countries. Prefectural and local election committees have been authorized to sponsor joint speech meetings (*tachiai ensetsu*) in each district when Diet and gubernatorial elections are scheduled. The meetings, at which opposing candidates are invited to present their political views from the same platform, are arranged and conducted by the local election authorities. Before 1952 the candidate was required to deliver his own speeches at most of the competitive speech marathons. This placed a considerable burden upon the individual office seeker, depriving him of campaign assistance from nationally known party leaders. Subsequent amendments in the election law enabled friends of the candidate to appear at joint meetings on his behalf. Voluntary competitive speech meetings for lesser officials may be held at the instance of the subordinate election committees. The joint speaking rallies have become one of the principal means by which a candidate reaches the voter.

To minimize the election costs of the candidate, the government assumes a considerable share of the responsibility for campaign publicity. Under the system a person seeking major public office is allocated gratis specified numbers of such items as franked postcards, posters, and transportation tickets. He is also entitled to limited amounts of newspaper advertising space and radio time without cost. Local election committees are generally instructed to post a list of all candidates and their party affiliation at a limited number of public places in each district. Election authorities in each district are likewise responsible for the publication and distribution of an election gazette which displays the name, photograph, party, and political views of each Diet and gubernatorial candidate. Gasoline for motor vehicles and paper for posters are also made available in limited amounts to candidates, although the cost of these items is not borne by the public treasury.

A candidate may also hold a specified number of private campaign meetings after notifying the election committees concerned. Under the 1950 statute, the local election authorities were required to provide a meeting hall for one such engagement and to publicize the rally. Election officials may issue certificates to permit street-corner speeches, although the restrictions upon this type of campaigning are much more severe than in most Western nations. The quality of campaign oratory has not greatly improved in postwar years. Japanese politicians continue to talk in vague generalities, their exuberance signifying little beyond the usual pleas for peace and prosperity.

Nonpublic campaign publicity — that provided by the candidate or his party — is presently under punctilious regulation. The statute limits the number of campaign offices which a candidate may establish, and it specifies the type of food and drink which may be served at the headquarters. The office seeker and his aids are not allowed to solicit votes by house-to-house visitation; demonstrations and parades are forbidden; and party workers may not electioneer under the guise of seeking signatures for petitions. The latter restriction was aimed at the Communists, who used the ruse to circumvent the doorbell-ringing limitation. It is illegal for candidates and their party organizations to distribute literature beyond stipulated amounts, and their campaign posters must conform to a specified size. In the 1955 campaign, shouting the name of a favorite candidate through the streets was forbidden; additional restrictions were placed upon the use of loudspeakers; and motor vehicles could not be elaborately decorated to attract the attention of the voter. These restrictions deprived the candidate of popular avenues to the electorate. Under a regulation passed in 1952, newspapers and magazines were not allowed to publish the results of public opinion polls or to comment upon the candidates or the election unless they had been in continuous publication for a prescribed period before the polling date or had been approved for third-class mail. Another post-Occupation regulation applicable to elections for the House of Representatives restricted campaign activity on the part of those political organizations which were unable to field more than twenty-five candidates throughout the nation. This placed under serious handicap those candidates representing minor parties or seeking office without benefit of party affiliation.

In a sincere effort to conduct fair and inexpensive elections, Japanese legislators have seriously curtailed the role of the press and restricted the campaign activities of candidates and parties. The present law has been criticized for its prohibition of the less costly methods of electioneering accessible to all candidates, while permitting the more expensive methods. Meticulous regulations tend to favor the incumbent whose name has been before the electorate and whose political experience constantly unfolds new vistas of electioneering technique not anticipated by the framers of the law. On the other hand, the inexperienced newcomer, without access to campaign publicity, tends to remain unknown to the electorate. Under a statute which obstructs the ordinary channels of political communication, it thus becomes more difficult for the "new faces" to defeat the "old hands." Although such important factors as the crystallization of party allegiances, the tightening of party discipline, the diminishing influence of purge directives, and the general stabilization of the political scene are undoubtedly operative, the steady decline in the proportion of political neophytes elected to the House of Representatives may be influenced to some degree by the stringency of the election regulations. The following table illustrates the decline of new members and the persistent success of incumbent and former Representatives, especially noticeable in the last three elections. (In these elections the most recent limitations upon political activity were in operation.) [25]

	Prewar Average	*1946*	*1947*	*1949*	*1952*	*1953*	*1955*
New members	29.4%	81%	48%	41%	23%	14%	11%
Incumbents	59.5	8	51	53	30	73	65
Former service	10.8	11	1	6	46	13	22

(Figures given in round numbers for postwar averages.)

Voting Process

There are some 43,000 polling districts in Japan, each accommodating an average of nearly 850 voters. The polling place is generally an elementary school or other public building previously designated and publicized by local election authorities. Voting "overseers," entrusted with the supervision of polling places, are appointed by the appropriate city, town, or village election committees. To ensure fairness in the conduct of the balloting, each election committee likewise selects from three to five poll watchers or "voting witnesses," no more than three of whom may belong to the same political organization. The witnesses assist the overseer in the identification of registered voters, and they sign the election-day minutes which are prepared by the overseer.

When the voter arrives at the polling place on election day, he displays a polling booth entry card which is checked against the voting register. In exchange for this certificate the voter receives an official ballot, and in a private booth he is entitled to vote secretly by writing in the name of his favorite candidate in either phonetic script or Japanese characters. In elections for the House of Councillors, separate ballots are required for national constituency and prefectural candidates. Physically incapacitated or illiterate persons may vote by proxy, and provisions are made for both braille and absentee balloting.

The tabulation of votes begins after the polls are officially closed or on the day following. The counterparts of the voting overseers and witnesses are the ballot-counting overseers and ten ballot-counting witnesses, no more than three of whom may be of the same political party. The minutes, voting registers, and sealed ballot boxes are taken to a designated "ballot-counting place," where the ballots are examined and counted in the presence of the witnesses. In collaboration with the witnesses, the overseer screens invalid ballots, often a difficult process with a write-in ballot inscribed with Oriental ideographs. Minutes are also kept of the counting process, and when the results of the tabulation are compiled, the relevant documents are forwarded to the "election meeting chairman," an official appointed by the election committee to collate the returns of the several polling places or voting districts within his jurisdiction. When all the reports of the counting overseers are in the hands of the election-meeting chairman, they are examined in the presence of witnesses and a total ballot count determined. Minutes of this "meeting" are also kept, and all election records are preserved during the tenure of the officials concerned. The work of the election chairman is completed when he reports the results to the responsible election committee, which notifies the successful candidate and gives public notice of the final returns.

In all elections the candidates who have received the largest pluralities are declared the winners, provided that each has exceeded a legal minimum. The minimum is determined by taking a specified fraction of a quotient obtained by dividing the total vote of the district by the number of seats to be filled.[26] The election law is very precise in establishing methods for filling vacancies resulting from invalidated contests or from the death of the official-elect without the necessity of new elections. In such cases the vacant post is generally given to the unsuccessful candidate with the next highest plurality. Election committees are authorized to hold by-elections or runoff elections when the number of vacant legislative seats exceeds a specified percentage of the fixed membership from a given constituency.

That voter participation in Japanese elections has been traditionally high is a bit surprising in view of the system of automatic registration. Ninety-one per cent of the registered electors cast their ballots in the 1924 House of Representatives election. The enactment of manhood suffrage a year later precipitated a decline in voter participation, but in the six prewar elections held under the 1925 law an average of 80 per cent of the eligible citizens still went to the polls.

Although steadily increasing, voting interest in postwar House of Representatives elections is still below prewar levels. Popular participation continues to be highest in prefectural and local elections, generally averaging more than 80 per cent of the electorate. There is a higher rate of abstention in elections for the House of Councillors than in contests for seats in the House of Representatives. Rural voters flock to the polls in much greater numbers than do their city cousins, and women lag behind the men. By-elections and runoff contests attract fewer voters than regularly scheduled elections, the abstention rate commonly reaching 50 per cent.[27]

Both the common practice of petty bribery and intense social pressure influence to some degree the heavy voter turnout. Newspaper editorials and radio broadcasts exhort electors to go to the polls. In some communities lotteries have been conducted, with each voter who performs the obligations of citizenship receiving a ticket for the drawing. Some districts have been known to award bonuses to those subdivisions which can register huge turnouts. In the local elections in 1951, one village dropped a number of aged and illiterate voters from the election list so that it could boast a record balloting of 100 per cent.[28]

Election Finance

As noted previously, the Japanese have instituted the public management of important campaign activities in order to curb the financial manipulation connected with the accumulation of huge campaign funds, and to encourage the candidacy of qualified people who lack financial backing. The government, of course, bears the normal cost of publicizing and administering the election. In addition, however, the expense of political rallies, posters, radio broadcasts, election gazettes, newspaper advertisements, and other services must also be borne by the public treasury. These expenditures are regulated by a statute which fixes a standard of expenses that can be charged to the government account. In 1955, the government outlay included 1,470,000,000 yen for the cost of the campaign, 50,000,000 yen for a "fair elections" drive, and 100,000,000 yen for supervising the election. When these amounts are added to the expenditures officially reported by the individual candidates and their parties, the total legal cost is in excess of 2,000,000,000 yen. Since few office seekers stay within the statutory limit, the actual expense of a Japanese election is much larger than the published accounts indicate.[29]

In addition to providing for a minimum level of campaign service by the government, the election law places a ceiling upon the amount that an individual candidate may spend, and it provides for a strict accounting of campaign receipts and expenditures. A quotient obtained by dividing the number of electors in a given district by the number of seats at stake multiplied by a basic amount fixed by cabinet order gives the sum which an individual may legally spend in his race for office. Thus the average amount allowed candidates for the House of Representatives throughout the whole country in 1953 was approximately 4 yen $\times$ $\dfrac{46,760,000}{466}$, or 401,460 yen. In that election the highest amount allowable to a single candidate was almost 820,000 yen in one of the Tokyo districts, and the smallest sum was slightly over 300,000 yen in a Kagoshima constituency. In 1955 the average was raised to 700,000 yen, varying from a minimum of 520,000 yen to a maximum of 1,350,000 yen.[30]

Each party or political association must keep an accurate account of all income, contributions, and disbursements, including the names and occupations of persons from whom income and gifts are received and to whom expenditures are made. The treasurer of the organization is entrusted with the filing of a special report of all financial transactions within a specified period following the polling date. The reports are sent to election authorities, who publicize the data and make them available for public inspection.

Each candidate is likewise required to make his campaign finance an open book. He is empowered to appoint a trustworthy "accountant," who is responsible for recording receipts and expenditures; the election committee is notified of the appointment. Such material items as food and printed matter and the use of campaign facilities gratis are considered under the category of contributions, to be computed at market value. Other persons concerned with the campaign may receive and disburse money, but they are required to report the transactions to the accountant. The accountant keeps financial records and files reports with the election authorities for subsequent publication and inspection. Campaign expenditures in excess of the legal limit invalidate an election victory. Previous statutes were criticized because the candidate was immune from disqualification if he could demonstrate prudence in selecting and supervising his campaign managers, if he had properly cautioned them against violations of the election law, and if one of his aids was willing to assume responsibility for the illegal transactions. It was common practice to arrange a breach of the regulations in such a way that the candidate was technically innocent and so that minor people connected with the campaign would be punished for the offense. Because the sponsors of a candidate were not compelled to register with the authorities, they were not officially known, and their relations with those who handled campaign funds were not always clear. The appointment, registration, and supervision of the accountant, whose irregularities would affect the election of the candidate, were designed to create greater responsibility for the proper conduct of the campaign. Although the current regulations are not free from ambiguity, they attempt to make the candidate and his principal managers jointly responsible for the financial operations of an election. If the latter are involved in questionable activities, the candidate is disqualified even if he is not personally guilty. However, the disqualification is canceled if it can be shown that the managers were bribed or influenced by the rival candidate in "framed" illegality. Conspiracy to disqualify an office seeker is itself a punishable offense.[31]

Japanese campaigns are expensive operations. Some candidates are able to pay all their expenses themselves, while others are dependent upon outside sources for all or least a portion of the necessary funds. The headquarters of each party in Tokyo has a special fund which can be tapped by recognized candidates. Despite the desire of many political leaders to eliminate shady finance from the electoral process, excessive receipts and expenditures are difficult to prove. Moreover, the penalties for discovered violations have not always been clearly stated in the election laws. As a result, the official financial reports returned from many districts do not accurately reflect the actual disbursements of the candidates, who admit privately that they have exceeded the legal ceiling. Reports indicate that the old "eight hit — five fail" principle still obtains in many constituencies: the candidate who spends 8 million yen will certainly win the election, while his unfortunate opponent who can muster only 5 million yen is likely to lose. Inflation has recently inspired the cynical *nito-ichiraku*, which suggests that a 20 million yen campaign chest ensures electoral success, whereas the expenditure of a mere 10 million yen forecasts defeat. The size of the purse necessary to clinch victory will, of course, vary according to local circumstances, but it is not unusual for parties and their candidates to spend huge sums in entertaining and bribing voters. In the 1951 local elections many gubernatorial candidates were reported to have spent more than 10 million yen, with votes being purchased at the rate of 1,000 yen each in some villages. Some candidates spent from 10 to 20 million yen in the House of Representatives race in 1952, although the average national ceiling fixed by law was approximately 400,000 yen. In another election a year later, the chief cabinet secretary was accused of spending 800,000 yen illegally.[32]

Patterns of Voting Behavior

In spite of the forceful impact of the Occupation upon a defeated Japan, the stream of cultural and social change, though not quite so slow-moving as in prewar decades, has perceptibly lagged behind reform currents of a more technological or institutional nature. Japan is still primarily a rural nation, with agriculture her basic industry and with a considerable portion of her population residing in small towns and farming and fishing communities. Recent census reports list 45 per cent of the population as engaged in agricultural enterprise; only 15 per cent in manufacturing, the next largest industry. This rurality is undeniably an important factor in explaining the politics of both prewar and postwar elections.

The Japanese village — the lowest legal unit in the hierarchy of government — consists of *de facto* subdivisions called *buraku* (hamlets), which are social groupings of families living adjacent to their agricultural lands.[33] While the paucity of data cautions against premature generalization, there is some evidence to show that rural communities have tended to remain more outside the stream of Western influence than have urbanized areas. The peasant farmer is more dependent upon constituted authority than is his city cousin, and he is less inclined to challenge the "old" and to modify it with the untried "new." The persistence of traditional patterns and social forms in the tiny village has made it appear that in many instances older wines have been poured into new institutional bottles. The ordinary peasant, bound by deeply ingrained habits of conformity, tends to be indifferent to problems that do not directly affect his locality. The hierarchical structure of Japanese society, reaching far back into ancient times, recognizes the pre-eminence of the head of the household and the elders of the buraku and village. Inclined to regard the baffling questions of government as the responsibility of those who govern, the villager is content to play a relatively passive role. Consequently he tends to defer to the superior status of the government official, the revered elder, or a figure of political or economic prominence whose family has traditionally looked out for the welfare of the community. These local sages, long recognized for their wisdom in matters of governance, frequently exert considerable influence upon the political attitudes of the more submissive peasants.[34]

In the race for seats in the village assembly, the buraku becomes a *de facto* constituency. To ensure the representation of their social unit in that body, the voters of the buraku often cast their ballots for a candidate upon whom there has been agreement before the polls are open. Under these circumstances, candidates do not overtly struggle for the nomination and subsequent election, since such activity would meet with social disapproval and certain defeat. Consequently an aspirant for an assembly post divines the political situation to ascertain his chances of victory before entering the race. There tend, therefore, to be fewer candidates in village assembly elections than at other levels. In 1951 there was an average of 1.2 candidates for each town and village assembly seat, and 13 per cent of the posts were uncontested. Mayoralty elections are more apt to be competitive, although it is possible for influential assemblymen to agree upon a suitable candidate before the polling date, so that other aspirants will be reluctant to challenge the real political power in the village. In the 1951 town and village contests for mayoralty positions, the rate of candidacy was 1.7 per seat, and it was reported that approximately 34 per cent of the posts were uncontested. One-third of the board of education elections in the towns and villages in 1952 were without contests; and in the 1951 agricultural committee races, actual balloting took place in only 20 per cent of the districts, the majority selecting their committeemen by acclamation.[35] These data, however, must not leave the impression that such local elections automatically give the stamp of approval so characteristic of contests in totalitarian countries. Buraku members do not mechanically support their nominee, and village elders, though influential, traditionally grope for the consensus of the social unit. A recent writer suggests that the practice of sponsoring a single mayoralty candidate by prearranged agreement has been offset by more competitive elections as parties penetrated more deeply into the local areas.[36] He also notes a developing reaction against professional politicians, with younger men of no previous experience being elected to village offices in some localities. However, the rate of independent candidature in elections below the prefectural level remains high, suggesting a lack of concern with formal political affiliation and a centering of attention upon local interests. As previously noted, the abstention rate in such elections is lower than in national voting.

The passivity of the peasant, the lack of clearly defined campaign issues, and the tendency of basic social units toward political solidarity invite the control of huge blocks of votes by knowledgeable and influential leaders in the community. Inheriting a legacy of loyalty and respect that may have been accorded to his family for generations, a prominent local figure is in a position to aid and advise subordinate families in the solution of their daily problems, and it is not unusual for the villagers to turn to him for "advice" on political matters. A recent study disclosed that in one remote village the life of the community centered in one family whose ancestor had founded the settlement more than seven centuries ago. To run counter to the suggestions of the local sage is to risk an avalanche of social disapproval which would be intolerable to the conforming peasant. In 1952 when a young girl charged in a local newspaper that some of the village politicians, including the chairman of the election committee, were buying votes, the young lady and her family were ostracized by their neighbors for bringing disgrace to the community.[37]

This social pattern enables the candidate to secure support by approaching influential people in the local area — a common practice in prewar Japanese politics. In many cases traditional loyalty to a candidate or party, nurtured by continuous patronage and social contact, was so strong that electoral support was virtually assured. Frequently local bosses were bribed to deliver the votes they controlled to the office seeker who could pay the price. Middlemen, often called election brokers, purchased votes in bulk and sold them to affluent candidates. Available votes were sometimes advertised publicly, or suitcases of money transported to doubtful constituencies on the eve of an election.[38] The prewar parties and their perennial candidates were strongly entrenched in particular villages and districts, claiming the allegiance of elders and electors through long-established tradition, family connections, or even monetary expenditures. For many years the village of Kamo supported the candidacy of Inukai Tsuyoshi, and after his assassination the villagers transferred their loyalty to his son.[39] The prestige of the veteran liberal Ozaki Yukio ensured his continuous election to the Diet from a conservative constituency in Mie prefecture from the first election in 1890 until his defeat in 1953.

There is evidence to show that many of these social and political patterns have persisted, perhaps with some modification, despite the wholesale reforms of the postwar era. Although there are scattered reports of volatility on the part of younger voters, boss control continues to flourish in many areas. A campaign manager recently noted a mayoralty election in which the victor received only seventeen ballots less than knowledgeable politicians had calculated ahead of time.[40] The conservative parties have displayed a continuity of popular strength in many constituencies which traditionally supported their prewar ancestors. In the village of Nobuta in Nagano prefecture, for example, the inhabitants have customarily responded to the political nod of the chief landowner, who had been affiliated with the Seiyukai and a member of the House of Peers; in the 1947 elections the Jiyuto captured 57 per cent of the votes in the community.[41] That the Jiyuto benefited from the agrarian strength of the Seiyukai is suggested by the fact that its support in postwar elections tended to be more heavily rural than that of any other political party.

Likewise the Minshuto and its predecessors inherited some of the bailiwicks of the prewar Minseito. In Shimane prefecture the village of Yoshida, under the influence of a landowner of Minseito persuasion, cast 60 per cent of its vote for Shimpoto-Minshuto candidates in the 1947 elections. Similarly, the traditionally Minseito community of Nikaido in Nara prefecture continued to give a majority of its votes to the Minshuto even when its conservative counterpart was making nationwide gains. Shimane prefecture, controlled by the Minseito for many years, cast a large portion of its votes for the Minshuto in 1949, despite the weakening of the organization by defection and scandal.

Because its ancestor had important roots in urban constituencies, the Shimpoto-Minshuto in early postwar elections garnered more votes in the cities than the Jiyuto.[42] However, the fusion of Seiyukai and Minseito elements into the Minshuto and, more recently, into the Jiyu-Minshuto suggests a blurring of ancient loyalties.

These traditional ties give an advantage to the older conservative parties which have many ancient contacts and money enough to establish new ones. Their persistent success in local and prefectural elections tends to reflect somewhat the appeal of tradition in the conservative rural areas. It is difficult for the more recently established parties who sponsor new faces to make an impression upon the local electorate. Since each constituency is allowed more than one seat, it is a common practice for the candidates of a conservative party to divide the district among themselves, each concentrating upon that area where his personal prestige and social or political influence are the greatest. These qualities — family connections, reputation as a speaker or bureaucrat, the prestige that accompanies incumbency, ties with local men of influence — remain significant short cuts to electoral success, especially in agrarian sections. A visit of the premier to a rural constituency is second only to an imperial tour, and it is anticipated that the voter will express his gratitude by casting a conservative ballot on election day. The Kyosanto sensed the importance of personality in appealing to the rural elector when in the 1949 campaign it adopted a policy of nominating people who were prominent in local affairs. Its strategy met with some success, as evidenced by the victory of eleven Communists in agrarian districts.[43]

The proletarian parties are forced to rely more upon the urban areas for their electoral support. In the House of Representatives race in 1949, the Shakaito polled an urban vote in excess of its rural strength in thirty-three of the forty-six prefectures. In the same election, when the Kyosanto reached the zenith of its parliamentary strength, its urban vote exceeded its agrarian support in all but seven prefectures, and twenty-four of the thirty-five successful Communist candidates came from urban constituencies. The Socialists and Communists thus compete for the city vote. In Osaka, for example, the Shakaito captured 21 per cent of the votes in 1947, while the Kyosanto polled only 6.3 per cent. However, popular dissatisfaction with the record of the two ministries with which the Shakaito was associated had seriously injured Socialist prestige in Osaka by 1949. In that election the Kyosanto secured 22 per cent of the ballots in that city, while Shakaito strength dropped to 14 per cent.[44] With the subsequent decline in Communist popularity, the fortunes of both wings of the Shakaito began to rise, each registering gains in the 1952, 1953, and 1955 elections.

A recent study of voting behavior in a section of a Tokyo constituency suggests that labor groups may be more attracted by party and less by personality than is the broad mass of the Japanese electorate.[45] There is certainly some evidence to show that the city-dweller behaves somewhat differently in the voting booth than does his agrarian counterpart, and it would indeed be a hopeful sign if the survey reflected a general trend toward the recognition of party responsibility. However, the post-Occupation political success of many persons released from the purge (popularly called "depurgees"), some of whom were high government officials in prewar decades, suggests that the picture is still largely one of personalities rather than parties.[46]

Election Violations

The election law has generally recognized the following categories of election offenses: (1) fraudulent registration and voting; (2) violation of campaign regulations, such as house-to-house canvassing and excessive use of posters or loudspeakers; (3) bribery and illegal contributions or solicitation thereof; (4) publication of false matter; (5) use of violence, intimidation, and methods obstructive of the electoral process; (6) failure or willful neglect of election authorities in the performance of their duties; and (7) negligence or fraud on the part of candidates, their managers, and parties in keeping financial records and in filing the required reports. The content of an election offense and the corresponding penalties are enumerated in great detail. Conviction may result in the invalidation of the election, the loss of voting and candidacy rights, and fines and imprisonment.

A detailed listing of campaign and election circumscriptions in a dualistic society, harnessed by socially accepted political practices, poses difficult problems of enforcement for the authorities. As outlined above, some sections of the election statute, such as the ceiling upon campaign expenditures, are honored as often in the breach as in the observance. Each election brings a rash of violations, some of which are reported to the authorities by the political opponents of the alleged culprit. Very often victorious candidates are embarrassed by suspected irregularities uncovered after their election has been announced. Apparently a record high of election offenses was reached in 1952, the first post-Occupation contest, when approximately 24,000 cases involving 48,000 persons were reported. Violations in the 1955 election were considerably fewer, although more than in 1953.[47] In postwar years the principal irregularities have been bribery, house-to-house canvassing, distribution of banned literature, campaigning before candidacy, and obstruction of the election process.

Disputed Elections

When an elector or candidate questions the validity of a local or prefectural election, an objection may be filed with the appropriate election committee within a specified period from the date of the election. An appeal from an adverse decision may be made to the prefectural election authorities, after which the dispute may ultimately be transferred to a higher court.

An elector or candidate who disputes the validity of a Diet election may institute legal proceedings in a higher court against the chairman of the responsible election committee within thirty days from the election date. A voter or defeated candidate may also challenge a questionable contest by suing the successful office seeker in the same court within the thirty-day period. The election committee or the court is entitled to adjudge the election completely or partially invalid.

Notes

[1] For a treatment of the prewar suffrage movement and election laws see H. S. Quigley, *Japanese Government and Politics* (New York, 1932), Chapter 13.

[2] *Koshoku Senkyoho* (Public Offices Election Law) is translated in the *Official Gazette*, April 15, 1950. The law has been amended each year since the promulgation of the original statute, but the basic outline remains the same. Useful for the study of the system as presently constituted are: Autonomy Board, Election Section, *Koshoku Senkyo Horeishu* (Collection of Public Offices Election Laws), Tokyo, 1954; *Senkyoho no Enkaku* (History of Election Laws), Tokyo, 1954; *Senkyo-Jiho* (Election Review), June 1955; Fair Election League, *Komei Senkyo Undo Suishin no Tebiki* (Manual for Promoting Fair Election Campaigns), January 1955.

[3] See Articles 43, 44, 47, 54, and 93 of the constitution. Such matters as voting and candidacy qualifications, election districts, and methods of voting were to be fixed by law.

[4] See House of Representatives Election Law, SCAP, Government Section, *Political*

Elections

Reorientation of Japan, Vol. II, Appendix H: 1, pp. 822–844. Articles 8–10 made certain categories of public officials, such as election officials, police officers, and revenue officials, ineligible for elective positions when actively serving in their respective posts.

[5] See the House of Councillors Election Law, ibid., Appendix H: 5, pp. 852–863; and the Local Autonomy Law., ibid., Appendix H: 14, Chapter IV, pp. 907–920.

[6] See the National Election Administration Commission Law, ibid., Appendix H: 26, pp. 1054–1056.

[7] Law concerning Provisional Exceptions to Election Campaigns, Official Gazette, July 29, 1948, pp. 16–21.

[8] Law for the Regulation of Political Contributions and Expenditures, ibid., pp. 1–11.

[9] Under the present system nine prefectures constitute single election districts, while the remaining thirty-seven contain from two to seven districts each. Forty districts return three representatives, thirty-nine return four, thirty-eight return five, and one district (Amami Oshima), added after transfer to Japan by the United States, returns one.

[10] See editorial, "Revising Election Rules," Nippon Times, May 26, 1953. In the 1947 House of Councillors election, over half the national constituency candidates were from Tokyo, and in at least eleven prefectures there were no local candidates for national constituency seats (Department of State, The 1947 Japanese House of Councillors Election, OIR Report No. 4334, January 15, 1948, pp. 22–23). Twenty-five of the prefectural constituencies return two councillors, fifteen elect four, four have six members, and two return eight.

[11] National Election Commission, Election in Japan, Tokyo, p. 8.

[12] See Public Offices Election Law, Official Gazette, April 15, 1950, Chapter IX.

[13] Nippon Times, October 4, 1952.

[14] The candidacy ratios are based upon the total number of candidates listed in Department of State, The 1949 Japanese House of Representatives Election, OIR Report No. 5022, September 1, 1949, p. 106; Jiji Nenkan (Jiji Year Book), 1954, p. 137; The Japan Annual, 1954, p. 44; Nippon Times, February 27, 1955. The decline in candidacies since 1946 reflects the crystallization of political loyalties and the growing strength of incumbents following the initial uncertainties of the purge.

[15] The percentages for House of Representatives elections are based upon totals listed in Department of State, Analysis of the 1946 Japanese General Election, OIR Report No. 3492, May 15, 1946, p. 8; 1949 House of Representatives Election, p. 21; Jiji Nenkan, 1954, p. 137; The Japan Annual, 1954, p. 44; Asahi Shimbun, February 27, 1955, March 1, 1955. House of Councillors percentages are based upon totals reported in Department of State, 1947 House of Councillors Election, p. 22; Jiji Nenkan, 1954, p. 141. There are some indications that the nonpartisan coloration of the second chamber is disappearing, but the relative infrequency of elections is not conducive to party competition. The percentages for local elections are based upon totals recorded in Prime Minister's Office, Statistics Bureau, Statistical Abstract of Japan, 1950, p. 149; Nippon Times, April 18, 1951. One must remember that the 1947 contests were the first local elections and party roots had had little time to develop. Local elections, of course, have inspired party activity at the "grass roots" level, and races for prefectural assembly seats and gubernatorial posts have become more "political." Nevertheless, responsible party competition is apt to be slow in developing, especially in the rural areas.

[16] In the 1947 House of Councillors election, the political parties were not, as a general rule, active in the campaign, although they took a greater interest in the prefectural contests than in those involving the national constituency (see Department of State, 1947 House of Councillors Election, pp. 47–48). The 1953 election for second-chamber seats gave some indication that such elections may become an enticing arena for future partisan strife.

[17] Editorial, " 'Independents' and the Elections," Nippon Times, March 8, 1947; SCAP, Government Section, Political Reorientation, I, 359.

[18] A record free from scandal became an important requirement for candidacy in the 1947 campaign to offset the corruption issue (see Department of State, 1947 House

of Representatives Election, pp. 19–20). The Kyosanto (Communist party) established a special election committee for the 1946 campaign, but in 1947 the selection of candidates reverted to the Politburo. In recent elections the Communists have attempted to limit their candidacies to one per constituency, striving to select candidates who were well established in the local areas. In 1953 the party dropped fifteen candidates because they appeared to generate little popular enthusiasm. A centrally organized and rigidly disciplined group such as the Kyosanto is able to keep dissension between the national headquarters and the local branch offices at a minimum (*1947 House of Representatives Election*, pp. 29–30; *1949 House of Representatives Election*, p. 78; *Nippon Times*, March 24, 28, 1953). In the 1947 elections the central executive committee of the Shakaito (Socialist party) tried to discourage the nomination of Johnny-come-latelys who had joined the organization merely for the purpose of becoming candidates. In 1953 the party of the left-wing Socialists decided to give priority as candidates to incumbent representatives and those who had been runners-up in the previous election (Department of State, *1947 House of Representatives Election*, pp. 27–28; *Nippon Times*, March 9, 1953).

[19] *Nippon Times*, December 31, 1948; Department of State, *1949 House of Representatives Election*, pp. 19–20. At a later election the Jiyuto accorded official recognition to some candidates and quasi-recognition to others.

[20] See Cabinet Order No. 89, Article 88, *Official Gazette*, April 20, 1950.

[21] Department of State, *1946 General Election*, pp. 10–12; *1947 House of Representatives Election*, p. 14. Article 21 of the election law operative in 1949 reads: "During the period of election campaign, no person shall, in the name of advertisement for writings or performances, or under whatever pretense calculated to evade the prohibition stipulated . . . distribute or exhibit writings or pictures chiefly indicating names of candidates, names of political parties or other political organizations, or purporting to recommend, support or oppose any candidates" (*Official Gazette*, July 29, 1948, pp. 18–19). Under the strict interpretation of this article, newspapers were still free to report campaign developments as long as they did not take a partisan position. One edition of both the Kyosanto and Shakaito papers was confiscated for publishing materials in support of their candidates. Article 21 was given a more liberal interpretation in mid-January. On this phase of the 1949 campaign, see *Nippon Times*, January 11–15, 19, 1949. The plight of a conscientious voter who starved for information about the candidates in his district during the 1949 "campaign of silence" and "police-enforced purity" is recounted in an editorial, "A Personal Gripe," *ibid.*, January 15, 1949.

[22] See National Election Management Law, SCAP, Government Section, *Political Reorientation*, Vol. II, Appendix H:26, pp. 1054–1056; Local Autonomy Law, *ibid.*, Appendix H:14, Chapter VII, Section 2, pp. 935–936; Department of State, *1949 House of Representatives Election*, p. 98.

[23] *Koshoku Senkyoho*, 1954, Article V.

[24] See *Japan News*, May 6, 1950; February 19, 1951; *Nippon Times*, April 25, 1951; February 13, 1952; March 23, 1953; editorial, "Revising Election Rules," *Nippon Times*, May 26, 1953; N. Ukai, "Japanese Election Results Reconsidered," *Pacific Affairs*, XXVI (June 1953), 144.

[25] The percentages are based upon totals listed in Department of State, *1947 House of Representatives Election*, p. A6; *1949 House of Representatives Election*, p. 92; K. G. Stewart, "The 1953 Japanese Elections," *Far Eastern Survey*, XXII (August 1953), 113; *Jiji Nenkan*, 1954, p. 138; *Asahi Shimbun* (Tokyo), March 1, 1955. The prewar average of 29.4 per cent, including only elections held since the adoption of manhood suffrage, may be corrupted by the low of 17 per cent in 1937 and the high of 43.1 per cent in 1942. Without these two elections the prewar average of new members is 29.1 per cent. The 1952 percentage is lower than that of any prewar election except 1937, and the 1953 and 1955 figures are lower than any of them.

[26] For example, candidates for the House of Representatives must have obtained one-fourth of the quotient resulting from the division of the total vote by the number of

seats to be filled. The fractions applicable to the respective offices are as follows: House of Representatives and assemblymen of local public bodies, one-fourth; House of Councillors (national constituency), one-eighth; House of Councillors (local constituency), one-sixth; chief of local public body, three-eighths; members of boards of education, one-fourth.

[27] Voter participation in House of Representatives elections since the end of the Occupation has been as follows: 1952, 76.4 per cent; 1953, 74.2 per cent; 1955, 75.8 per cent. Elections to the House of Councillors in 1947, 1950, and 1953 brought out 61 per cent, 68 per cent, and 63 per cent of the voters. For popular participation in a local election see *Nippon Times*, April 25, 1951.

[28] Department of State, *1949 House of Representatives Election*, p. 56; *Nippon Times*, April 29, 1951.

[29] Editorial, "The Election Law Once Again," *Nippon Times*, June 2, 1951; March 16, 1953; H. Nomura, "Money for the Elections," *Asahi Evening News*, February 11, 1955. In 1949 the National Administration Commission received 603,374,000 yen from the national treasury with which to conduct the House of Representatives election, and the local units spent an additional 179,188,722 yen, for which they sought reimbursement from Tokyo. Of the amount allocated to the national commission, 48 per cent was spent for the payment of election officials, 10 per cent for the operation of election committees, 14 per cent for the purchase and distribution of fuel, stationery, food, and other items, and 20 per cent for the public management of the campaign. Candidates were in agreement that the publicity was distributed equitably, but they contended that the amount of the publicity was inadequate (Department of State, *1949 House of Representatives Election*, pp. 41–43).

[30] *Nippon Times*, March 16, 1953; H. Nomura, "Money for the Elections," *Asahi Evening News*, February 11, 1955.

[31] *Koshoku Senkyoho*, 1953, Articles 198, 251; *Nippon Times*, December 31, 1952; February 3, 1955.

[32] Editorial, "The Election Law Once Again," *Nippon Times*, June 2, 1951; *ibid.*, June 1, 1953; F. Ikematsu, "Political Parties Today and Tomorrow," *Contemporary Japan*, XXI (1952), 391; see also "How Votes are 'Bought' in Japan," by a campaign manager, *Asahi Evening News*, January 12, 1955.

[33] For the sociopolitical role of the *buraku* in village politics, the writers have relied upon the pioneering studies of Robert E. Ward, "The Socio-Political Role of the Buraku (Hamlet) in Japan," *American Political Science Review*, XLV (December 1951), 1025–1040; "Patterns of Stability and Change in Rural Japanese Politics," *Occasional Papers*, Center for Japanese Studies, No. 1, Ann Arbor, 1951, pp. 1–6; "Some Observations on Local Autonomy at the Village Level in Present-day Japan," *Far Eastern Quarterly*, XII (February 1953), 183–202; and Paul S. Dull, "The Political Structure of a Japanese Village," *Far Eastern Quarterly*, XIII (February 1954), 175–190.

[34] *Asahi Shimbun*, reported in *Nippon Times*, April 13, 1953.

[35] Editorial, "The Home Stretch," *ibid.*, April 22, 1951. In the five largest cities the rate of candidacy for assembly positions was 3.3 per seat and 2.2 in other cities, *ibid.*, April 18, 1951; July 24, 1951; October 5, 1952. It was reported that in the 1955 local elections six candidates for a mayoralty post withdrew from the race when the village elder suggested that the "peace" of the community should be preserved (editorial, "Today's Local Elections," *Asahi Evening News*, April 30, 1955). The decline of candidature in agricultural and education committee contests also reflects a decline in the importance of those bodies from what was originally envisaged.

[36] Paul S. Dull, *op. cit.*, p. 177.

[37] A. F. Raper and others, *The Japanese Village in Transition*, GHQ, SCAP, Report No. 136, Tokyo, 1950, p. 140; *Nippon Times*, June 30, 1952.

[38] See T. Baba, "Sosenkyo Tempo (Election Maneuvering)," *Kaizo*, February 1930, pp. 73–78; H. Hara, "Senkyo Baishu Monogatari (Stories of Election Fraud)," *Chuo Koron*, February 1932, pp. 227–232.

[39] Robert E. Ward, "Patterns of Stability and Change in Rural Japanese Politics," p. 4.

[40] T. Okie, "Election Sidelights," *Asahi Evening News*, February 23, 1955; Campaign Manager, "How Votes are 'Bought' in Japan," *ibid.*, January 12, 1955.

[41] A. F. Raper and others, *op. cit.*, p. 205.

[42] *Ibid.*; Department of State, *1949 House of Representatives Election*, p. 68.

[43] Department of State, *1949 House of Representatives Election*, pp. 74, 76, 78; *Nippon Times*, January 19, 1949. The Communists were employing "popular front" strategy and sought a cloak of respectability which the Socialists had lost.

[44] Department of State, *1949 House of Representatives Election*, pp. 72, 74.

[45] Noted in N. Ukai, *op. cit.*, p. 145.

[46] In the 1952 election, 140 "depurgees" were elected. In the campaign a year later, public leaders were reportedly encouraging voters to look at the "name" before checking the political affiliation — behavior which responsible officials had formerly attempted to discourage (S. Hasegawa, "Japanese Politics behind the Scene," *Nippon Times*, March 29, 1953). However, the "big names" did not fare so well as in the previous contest.

[47] *Nippon Times*, March 28, 1953; *Asahi Evening News*, April 8, 1955.

19

Major Political Parties
I: Postwar Development

In the modern world the vitality of the party system reflects the health of a political society. The party struggle in prewar Japan had been long and uneven, but its age was a hopeful guarantor of parliamentary vigor.[1] If Japan were to achieve the political goals outlined by her Western occupiers, however, she needed parties that would stimulate political consciousness and give voice to forces that long had been neglected in the Diet. To operate the new machinery of government effectively, the parties would have to cut through social and political patterns deeply embedded in Japan's cultural past. Ancient traditions which perpetuated bitter factionalism, blind obedience to leadership, wholesale corruption, and patent disregard for principle constituted a formidable challenge to the political organizations in the new Japan. The persistence or modification of such behavior since 1945 may indicate some of the basic trends in Japanese politics and will certainly define the major problems confronting her democracy. It is necessary, therefore, to observe the lines of continuity between old and new; strong links with the past generally place restraints upon abrupt, substantive change. It is essential, also, to recognize the emergence of new forces which might stimulate significant departures from the prewar system. A brief chronology of major political developments in Japan since 1946 may be a useful prelude to the analysis of the conservative and left-wing parties made in the following chapters.

The New Japan
Effects of the Purge

Baron Shidehara was premier of Japan when the first wave of purge directives (January 1946) deluged the political community. The initial purge and its wider application in 1947 dealt severe blows to the recently revived Jiyuto (Liberal party), Shimpoto (Progressive party), and Shakaito (Socialist party), and the newly-organized Kyodoto (Cooperative party).[2] The Shimpoto, whose diverse elements included many conservatives who had been tools of the military, was the most vulnerable, losing 238 of its 270 Diet members. Twenty-eight of the forty-six Jiyuto members, half of the small Shakaito group, and all but one of the Kyodoto delegation were likewise declared culpable under the provisions of the purge. Only the Kyosanto (Communist party) remained unaffected, since legal restrictions in prewar years had made Communist representation in the "Tojo Diet" and the ultranationalistic societies impossible.

In some respects the purge was injurious to the cause of party government. The directives were less concerned with an individual's record in the Diet or as a party leader than with his association with militarist and nationalist organizations. Failure to give proper weight to the content of individual action rather than to affiliation removed some exponents of parliamentary government who sincerely believed that the task of a political party was to represent the ordinary voter; replacing them were the "machine" politicians to whom the party was merely an instrument for winning elections. On the other hand, some features of the purge strengthened the position of those who sought an improved party system. The pruning operation encouraged the rise of new political leaders to responsible positions, as older men were temporarily discredited and their traditional links with the voter weakened. This was especially true of the conservative parties. The replacement of prewar leaders by less experienced hands as a result of the purge and the period of uncertainty following the issuance of the directives snapped the direct line of continuity between prewar and postwar parties. The resulting improvisations altered the composition and structure of the party machines and prevented the new from being poured into the identical molds of the old.[3]

The first election in postwar Japan was held on April 10, 1946, in the shadow of the purge. Out of 466 seats in the House of Representatives, the Jiyuto emerged with a plurality of 141, and the Shidehara

278

POSTWAR ELECTIONS, HOUSE OF REPRESENTATIVES

Party	1946 *		1947 *		1949 †		1952 ‡		1953 †		1955 **	
	No. of Seats	% of Popular Vote	No. of Seats	% of Popular Vote	No. of Seats	% of Popular Vote	No. of Seats	% of Popular Vote	No. of Seats	% of Popular Vote	No. of Seats	% of Popular Vote
Jiyuto (Minshu-Jiyuto)	141	24.3%	132	26.5%	264	43.8%	240	48.0%	199	38.9%	112	26.6%
Hatoyama Jiyuto	..	..	..	..	..	..	..	..	35	8.9	..	..
Minshuto (Shimpoto-Kaishinto)	93	18.7	126	25.1	68	15.8	85	18.2	76	17.7	185	36.5
Shakaito	93	17.8	143	26.2	49	13.5	..	..	..	..	..	..
Uha Shakaito	..	..	..	..	..	..	57	11.4	66	13.3	67	13.8
Saha Shakaito	..	..	..	..	..	..	54	9.9	72	13.2	89	15.3
Kyosanto	5	3.9	4	3.6	35	9.6	0	2.5	1	1.8	2	1.9
Independent	80	20.4	13	5.9	12	6.6	19	6.5	11	4.4	6	3.3
Others	52	14.9	48	12.5	38	10.7	11	3.5	6	1.4	6	2.3
Total	464††		466		466		466		466		467	

* Department of State, OIR Report No. 4310, *An Analysis of the 1947 House of Representatives Election*, pp. 57, 63.
† Department of State, OIR Report No. 5022, *The 1949 Japanese House of Representatives Election*, p. 62.
‡ K. G. Stewart, "The 1953 Japanese Elections," *Far Eastern Survey*, XXII (August 1953), 113.
** Embassy of Japan, Information Section, *Japan Information* (mimeographed), March 30, 1955, p. 1; *Nippon Times*, March 1, 1955.
†† Two vacancies.

279

cabinet subsequently resigned. Lacking a majority by nearly a hundred seats, the Jiyuto commenced negotiations with other parties for a coalition agreement. Its president, Hatoyama Ichiro, turned first to the Shakaito, only to discover that the price of its cooperation was the premiership and several key portfolios. After prolonged bargaining the Jiyuto reached an understanding with the Shimpoto, which had been reorganized under the presidency of Shidehara with a view toward entering a conservative coalition.[4] However, plans for a Hatoyama cabinet based upon Jiyuto-Shimpoto support were frustrated by a SCAP directive which declared the would-be premier ineligible for public service. Following another period of backstage maneuvering and political confusion, Yoshida Shigeru, a career diplomat without party experience, was prevailed upon by Hatoyama to accept the leadership of the Jiyuto. This was apparently to be a temporary arrangement, it being generally understood that Yoshida was to return the machine to its master on D- (depurge) Day. The sudden ascendance of a nonparty bureaucrat in the Jiyuto hierarchy and his subsequent rise to the premiership excited the suspicion of veteran politicians and parliamentarians who had been identified with the party struggle before the war. Factional wrangling over the control of the party machinery and the uncertainty of Hatoyama's political future postponed the election of Yoshida to the presidency of the organization.[5]

First Yoshida Cabinet

Yoshida Shigeru received the imperial command to form a ministry in May 1946. In exchange for its promised support of the government in the Diet, the Shimpoto received three minor posts in the cabinet. The new regime, however, was dominated by Jiyuto men and nonparty administrators, nearly half of whom were without experience in prewar party struggles. Jiyuto-Shimpoto cooperation suggested the possibility of merging the two conservative parties — a project which has attracted political craftsmen throughout the postwar years but was not realized till late 1955. In 1946, Shidehara Kijuro, president of the Shimpoto, and Ashida Hitoshi, a Jiyuto leader, were outwardly inclined toward unification, but factions in both parties resisted the maneuver. Shidehara's demand for the presidency of the new structure was rejected by the Jiyuto, which enjoyed numerical superiority, and the plans for consolidation were temporarily halted.[6]

Major Political Parties I: Postwar Development

The Yoshida cabinet reluctantly sponsored important SCAP-inspired reforms: the new constitution, the laws of the Diet, redistribution of land, antitrust legislation, the Labor Relations Adjustment Law, the restructuring of local government, and similar measures. The government unsuccessfully sparred with the problems of food distribution and the low level of productivity, and by the end of 1946 the spiral of inflation had thrown the wage structure out of gear. Spearheaded by the Kyosanto and halfheartedly supported by the Shakaito, militant labor organizations launched an offensive for wage increases and the resignation of the cabinet. Trade union disorders reached their peak in January 1947, and the public employees' union, which was agitating for an impossible threefold increase in pay, scheduled a general strike for February 1. SCAP intervention prohibited the strike, thereby stigmatizing militant unionism and weakening the Kyosanto-Shakaito liaison. Nevertheless mounting opposition to the government among the voters and in the Diet chambers visibly jolted the Yoshida ministry. The premier wanted to dissolve the House of Representatives and schedule an election in order to expand the base of his cabinet, but the government parties were unwilling to face a hostile electorate. To broaden his shaky coalition, Yoshida courted the right-wing faction of the Shakaito. Their entrance into the government would have calmed some of the trade union opposition and at the same time would have split the Socialist ranks. Again, however, the price of Shakaito cooperation was prohibitive. When he reshuffled his cabinet on the basis of its existing support, the premier was accused of dictatorially loading his government with "bureaucrats" at the expense of the "party" men.[7] Shortly thereafter SCAP suggested that the mandate of the Yoshida regime was wearing thin and urged that elections be held in April 1947. In an eleventh-hour maneuver the government pushed through a revision of the election law over the violent opposition of the smaller parties.

With an election on the horizon, party strategists entered another period of intricate bargaining, and a rash of amalgamations rearranged the party lineup. In March 1947 the Kyodoto fused with the Kokuminto (People's party), a splinter group of educators and small businessmen without previous political affiliation, to form the Kokumin Kyodoto (People's Cooperative party).[8] Shidehara again pressed for a Jiyuto-Shimpoto merger, but this move was stoutly resisted by

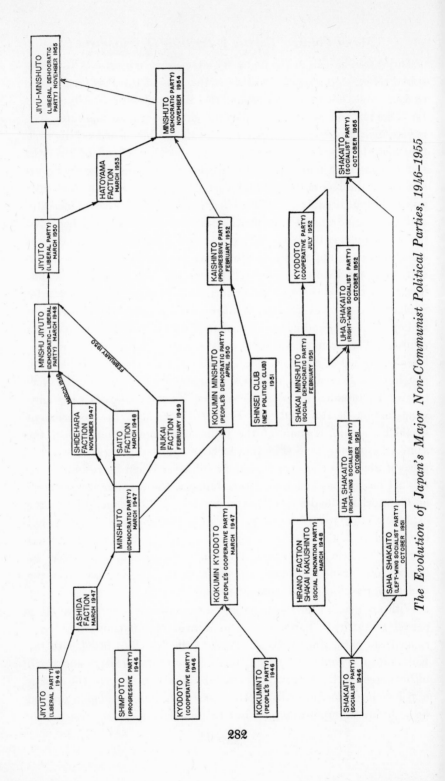

The Evolution of Japan's Major Non-Communist Political Parties, 1946–1955

some of the younger elements of the Shimpoto under the influence of Inukai Ken. As an alternative to absorption and possible domination of their party by the Jiyuto, the Inukai faction urged a reshuffling of the Yoshida cabinet to include either the Kyodoto or the right-wing Socialists, thus enabling the Shimpoto to hold the balance of power in a tripartite coalition. As hopes for such an entente evaporated, Inukai and his followers demanded a reorganization of their party to recover some of its lost prestige and to ensure its existence as an autonomous political unit. Their new conservative program called for "modified capitalism" as a middle way between the position of the Jiyuto and that of left-wing groups. As part of the streamlining process the Ashida wing of the Jiyuto seceded from the parent body and united with the Shimpoto in March 1947 to form the new Minshuto (Democratic party). With the purge of Inukai, however, the balance in the party was tilted slightly toward Shidehara and the "old guard" who, in their distaste for liaison with the Socialists, still looked longingly toward Yoshida and the Jiyuto.[9]

Katayama Cabinet

The House of Representatives election in 1947 produced surprising results, in view of the new election law designed to favor the conservative parties. The Shakaito emerged the strongest party, with 143 seats, compared with 132 and 126 for the Jiyuto and Minshuto. The Socialists were still 91 seats short of a working majority in the lower chamber, and they were hopelessly deficient in the House of Councillors, with only 46 out of a total of 250 seats. Nevertheless the sudden display of Shakaito strength at the polls forecast an important role for the party, whatever the nature of the subsequent government.

On May 23, 1947, Katayama Tetsu, a prominent labor leader in the prewar years, was elected the first Socialist premier of Japan. The minority position of his party made a coalition cabinet inevitable, and Katayama sought to establish a four-party ministry, excluding the Communists. The left-wing elements of the Shakaito, however, favored a tripartite coalition, with both the Jiyuto and the Kyosanto in opposition. Yoshida refused to enter a government headed by Katayama unless the Shakaito purged its left-wing faction — a risky undertaking for the premier, since it would split his party and reduce his plurality in the Diet. As eventually gazetted, the cabinet was made up of the Shakaito, the Minshuto, and the Kokumin Kyodoto, and more than two-thirds of its members had engaged in politics on a national scale before the war. To Yoshida the new ministry was a "mixed family of dogs and monkeys," but he offered support without participation on condition that the left-wingers should be denied portfolios. Katayama and his advisers maintained the right-wing purity of their cabinet, but to forestall schism they distributed vice-ministries and standing committee chairmanships among their doctrinaire brethren.[10]

The Shakaito had detailed a program of basic reform, but it lacked Diet strength and administrative talent to secure the enactment and implementation of a far-reaching program. Thus Katayama and his party were dependent upon the Minshuto, which was in a strong bargaining position to demand key posts in the cabinet and watered-down legislation in parliament. The new ministry was hardly a cohesive union of statesmen bound together by a common set of ideological principles. As is too frequently the case in Japanese politics, it was a marriage of convenience dictated by personal interests, and hence subject to occasional separations, divorces, and reconciliations as those interests changed.

The Katayama government inherited a worsening economic situation, but its diverse composition made intracabinet agreement difficult and expeditious action virtually impossible. It is true that some important legislation — much of it SCAP-inspired — reached the statute books: the abolition of the Home Ministry, the reorganization of the police system, the reform of the public service, and the enactment of measures providing for unemployment insurance, a Labor Ministry, and the decentralization of industry. But the fear of precipitating a political crisis encouraged cabinet leaders to postpone issues and to utilize executive decrees as a means of avoiding Diet struggles. Frequently it was the impatient prompting of SCAP which goaded the cabinet to appropriate action. The question of state control of the coal mines broke the political calm and paved the way to schism. The Shakaito version of the bill had been watered down in cabinet battles before its introduction into the Diet; nevertheless some Minshuto affiliates violated party discipline by voting against the compromise measure. Eventually the Shidehara wing of the Minshuto, which had never been reconciled to participation in a Socialist government, seceded from the party. This faction organized a temporary bargaining group and waited for a favorable opportunity to join with Yoshida's Jiyuto.[11]

In addition to embracing the Minshuto dissidents on the coal-mine issue, the conservatives made enticing overtures to Minister of Agriculture Hirano Rikizo, seeking to stir up suspicion within the Katayama regime and to weaken further its base of support. Hirano, an agricultural organizer and right-wing Socialist, aspired to the leadership of a political group of his own and to cooperation with a Yoshida-Shidehara entente. To counteract such intrigue, the Shakaito dismissed Hirano from the cabinet and set the stage for his subsequent rescreening and purge. With the ousting of their chief, the National Farmers' Union segment of the right-wing Shakaito withdrew from the party in March 1948, establishing the Shakai Kakushinto (Social Renovation party).

The scramble for the vacated cabinet post uncorked the smoldering animosities within the Shakaito, signaling the end of Katayama's tenure. The left-wing faction, which had watched a conservative party control a Socialist cabinet, upbraided the prime minister and his Shakaito colleagues for compromising official party doctrine. Growing restive in their subordinate role, the leftists exhibited their displeasure by nominating for the Hirano seat a candidate who was objectionable to the Minshuto and Kyodoto elements of the ministry. When Katayama selected a minister who was acceptable to all factions, the doctrinaire elements of his party reserved the right to criticize government policy, despite the pressures for harmony within the organization. At the national conference in 1948 the left-wing group fought for greater representation in party councils, and it successfully pushed the policy of the organization far enough to the left so that it was unpopular with the cabinet coalition.

Sensing a ministerial crisis which would overturn the Katayama regime, the Minshuto and Kyodoto began casting about for new allies. In an appeal to the Jiyuto to support him for the premiership, Ashida Hitoshi demanded the expulsion of left-wing influence from the Shakaito. A faction of the Jiyuto sought an immediate union with the Shidehara bargaining group; but this move was blocked by those who saw in the Ashida overture the possibility of inviting all the Minshuto into the Jiyuto — an amalgamation which the Ashida men might veto if they saw Shidehara, a recent renegade, in the Yoshida camp. Ashida, however, envisaged a broader organization which would include the Kokumin Kyodoto. The latter, fearing a subordinate role in the Minshuto scheme, turned instead to the splinter association of Hirano. Minimizing policy differences, the architects of these political alliances were willing to jump to the right or to the left, depending upon the inducements offered. As in-fighting and proselyting continued, the stock of the Katayama cabinet fell to an alarmingly low level. When the left-wing Socialists defied party discipline on the budget estimates, the embarrassed premier submitted his resignation, and his action was applauded in most political circles.[12]

Ashida Cabinet

After a fortnight of interparty negotiations Ashida Hitoshi was elected to the premiership on February 21, 1948, by a narrow margin. His previous defection from the Jiyuto impeded the establishment of a conservative coalition, whereas his cordial relations with Nishio Suehiro, secretary-general of the Shakaito, encouraged an alliance with the left. Ashida, however, was unable to form a cabinet until March 10, and then only by making concessions to the left-wing faction of the Shakaito which he had so recently denounced. The new ministry consisted of six Minshuto men, two from the Kokumin Kyodoto, and eight Shakaito leaders, two of whom were of the leftist variety. Ashida's concessions, ententes, and appointments had provoked rebellion within the more conservative wing of his party, with some groups seceding to bargaining status and others to close association with the Liberals. At last Yoshida and his coterie embraced the Shidehara faction and other dissident elements from the Minshuto camp, merging in March 1948 to form the Minshu-Jiyuto (Democratic Liberal party). Six "orthodox" Liberals, objecting to the fusion, established the Nihon Jiyuto (Japan Liberal party), only to be eclipsed in the 1949 election.[13]

One segment of the Socialist left were reluctant converts to the support of the Ashida government, and their strength was sufficient to rock the boat. Attempts to dissolve the several factions and to strengthen party discipline met with little success. Violent disagreement over important budget matters resulted in the expulsion and suspension of disaffected groups from the Shakaito, reducing its Diet membership and noticeably weakening the hand of the cabinet. The

problem became serious in the summer and autumn months as internecine strife disrupted both of the coalition parties and made Ashida's
support in parliament uncertain. The tottering government was unable to withstand the shock of scandal which brought important cabinet and political leaders under suspicion. Nishio Suehiro, the master
tactician of the Socialist right, was indicted for failing to report campaign contributions from a group of building contractors. The left-
wing elements of the party seized this opportunity to demand his ouster, and his departure tipped the balance within the Shakaito in
their direction. When another crop of scandals implicated several politicians, government leaders, and businessmen on charges of bribery,
Premier Ashida submitted his resignation, and the Minshuto and
Shakaito returned to the opposition benches.[14]

Second Yoshida Cabinet

Yoshida Shigeru, in succeeding to the premiership a few days later,
established a Minshu-Jiyuto "caretaker" government with only minority support in the Diet. More than two-thirds of his ministers were
newcomers to the national political scene since the war, and nearly
half of them were government officials or ex-bureaucrats in occupational background. The new cabinet was entirely Minshu-Jiyuto-
sponsored, except for one Ryokufukai* (Green Breeze Society) member and one minister without formal party affiliation. The first single-
party cabinet since the war, it began a series of conservative, Jiyuto-
led governments which was to continue for six years.

Yoshida wanted an early election so that he might appeal for a
majority in the House of Representatives while the ineptitude of the
Shakaito-Minshuto cabinets was still fresh in the minds of the voters.
The opposition parties, on the other hand, desired a postponement
until the new premier and his inexperienced cabinet had acquired some
of the unpopularity which comes with responsibility. After a skirmish
with the opposition parties over the imperial versus the parliamentary
prerogative in initiating a Diet dissolution,[15] Yoshida was at last successful in bringing the Diet session to an end, and the third postwar
election campaign shifted into high gear.

The election held on January 23, 1949, gave Yoshida and his party

* The Ryokufukai is an organization of conservative members of the House of
Councillors.

an absolute majority of 264 seats. The Shakaito and the Minshuto suffered a decline to 49 and 68 respectively, while the Kyosanto reached its postwar crest of 35 seats. By this time important changes in the distribution of power within the Minshu-Jiyuto were becoming quite evident. Since 1948 Yoshida had been gradually consolidating his control over the organizational machinery by recruiting career bureaucrats and former government officials and appointing them to key posts in the party and the government. In order to inject new blood and loyal talent into his machine, Yoshida admitted bureaucrats to party membership before the election and sponsored them as candidates. The election returns were testimony to the success of this strategy: elected in 1949 were 61 career officials, more than three-fourths of whom were Minshu-Jiyuto members; the comparable figure in the 1947 election was 33 government officials, only half of whom were Jiyuto candidates.[16] The crop of new Diet members harvested from the bureaucracy had stronger ties of allegiance to Yoshida than to the professional politicians in the party. The expanding influence of political neophytes was distasteful to the party veterans who had been associated with the prewar Minseito and Seiyukai.

Third Yoshida Cabinet

Yoshida's hegemony in the Diet and the party entitled him to establish a third ministry in February 1949, and this cabinet, after two or three reshuffles, remained in power until the end of the Occupation. The final decision on major appointments was left to the premier, and more than 60 per cent of the portfolios went to postwar newcomers to the party game, slightly over one-third of them to former government officials. Although Yoshida had absolute majority control of the House of Representatives, he issued cabinet appointments to a member of the Ryokufukai, a nonparty bureaucrat, and two business executives from the Minshuto.

After sustaining a painful setback at the polls, the Minshuto was weakened further by an internal feud over the support of the Yoshida ministry and eventual merger with the government party. President Inukai spearheaded the pro-coalition movement over the opposition of the parliamentary caucus, and the party soon split into two distinct wings. The Inukai group, however, was rejected by certain factions within Yoshida's organization which bitterly opposed the merger

scheme of their leader. The amalgamation question became caught in
the crosscurrents of the factional struggle between the "bureaucratic"
and "party" groups, the latter seeking issues and devices by which to
break Yoshida's tightening control of the Minshu-Jiyuto. After several
months of bitter feuding, the premier and his party in February 1950
absorbed the pro-government Minshuto group, but without Inukai.
The expanded organization agreed to the use of its old name, the
Jiyuto. However, the majority of the Minshuto, displeased with
Inukai's "dictatorial" tactics, were in the anti-coalition camp, looking
toward the independence of their party on a platform of "modified
capitalism." Injured by the depletion of its Diet strength, the organization entered into limited cooperation with other opposition parties,
including the Shakaito and especially the Kokumin Kyodoto. As the
1950 House of Councillors election drew near, there were efforts to
join the Minshuto and Kyodoto into one strong anti-Jiyuto group.
Following a series of bargaining conferences, the two parties, together
with a few splinter associations, united to form the Kokumin Minshuto (People's Democratic party) in April 1950, with 67 seats in the
House of Representatives and 43 in the House of Councillors.[17]

POSTWAR ELECTIONS, HOUSE OF COUNCILLORS

	Number of Seats		
	1947 *	1950 †	1953 ‡
Jiyuto (Minshu-Jiyuto)	39	76	93
Hatoyama Jiyuto	. .	. .	2
Minshuto (Shimpoto-Kaishinto)	32	29	15
Shakaito	46	61	. .
Uha Shakaito	. .	. .	26
Saha Shakaito	. .	. .	40
Kyosanto	4	4	1
Ryokufukai	. .	50	34
Independent	112	22	30
Others	17	8	9
Total	250	250	250

* Department of State, OIR Report No. 4334, *The 1947 House of Councillors Elec-
tion*, p. 53.
† *Japan Year Book, 1949–52*, p. 222.
‡ *Nippon Times*, April 27, 1953.

The reorganization of the Jiyuto, the Korean war, and the results
of the House of Councillors election precipitated a major cabinet reshuffle in June 1950. More than three-fourths of the new appointments

went to men unknown to national politics before the war; one-third of the recipients had been government officials. The selections brought another protest from the "old-timers" in the Jiyuto, who were alienated by Yoshida's seizure of their party machinery.[18] Another reshuffle in July 1951, reportedly instituted by Yoshida without benefit of advice from party leaders, brought four new ministers into the government. Of the four, three were of the postwar political generation and the other had been a member of the old House of Peers; three of them were or had been career bureaucrats.[19] By 1951 Yoshida's appointment of loyal ex-bureaucrats and postwar parliamentarians to key posts in the Jiyuto and its cabinets gave him an iron grip on political machinery which the "party" faction deeply resented. The year 1951, however, marked the peak of Yoshida's dominance. Thereafter the return of "depurgees," the decline of his popularity, and the diminution of his Diet majority made bargaining and concessions necessary and schism and secessions inevitable.

Even before the third Yoshida ministry had settled in office, the policy of the Occupation had clearly shifted from reform to economic reconstruction. The stiffening attitude of SCAP pressed the government into an austerity program aimed at balancing the budget, stabilizing wages and prices, allocating raw materials, stimulating increased production, and streamlining the tax structure. Austerity was greeted with little enthusiasm in many circles, and its basic policies were in conflict with the laissez-faire pronouncements of Jiyuto campaign speeches. But the visible hand of SCAP enabled the premier to evade some of the responsibility for unpopular legislation. Yoshida's disinclination to bow before the shrine of SCAP made him a reputed bulwark of Japanese institutions against the evangelical zeal of the alien reformer. For a time this gave him a high rating among the people and was one factor in his long tenure as premier.

Yoshida opposed with even more vigor the messianic fervor of the Communists whose exploitation of economic and political issues had brought them electoral success. With this "liberalism" SCAP could not quarrel, and it gave its blessing to a program of vigorous suppression. By mid-1949, however, the Kyosanto had entered a period of rapid decline, and for a variety of reasons not directly connected with government policy. Public reaction against Communist-sponsored demonstrations and violence constituted a major setback for the party, and the ouster of Communists from the leadership of important trade unions robbed the Kyosanto of mass organizational support. In early 1950 a Cominform blast at Communist leader Nozaka's moderate policy of "peaceful revolution" within the framework of SCAP directives set off an interlude of factional strife which further weakened the party.[20] For a time the international discipline was resisted, but eventually the Kyosanto accepted Cominform direction, confessed its sins, and began to articulate a more aggressive attitude toward the Occupation. On July 4, 1949, General MacArthur, in a public statement, had cautioned against Communist abuse of the constitutional process for the purpose of seizing power from the legitimate majority by stealth and deceit. Such tactics, he suggested, raised the question whether the movement was entitled to the "validity, sanction, and protection of the law." [21] An attack on Occupation personnel in May 1950, the most flagrant of several exhibitions of hostility toward the United States, occasioned a letter from SCAP to the premier on June 6, ordering the purge of all members of the Kyosanto central committee. The following day a ban was placed upon seventeen editors of *Akahata* (Red Flag), the party organ.[22] Shortly after the outbreak of the Korean war, SCAP ordered the permanent suspension of Kyosanto publications, and at the time of the San Francisco conference of 1951 the government issued warrants for the arrest of eighteen additional Communist leaders for acts inimical to the Occupation. Though the party was not formally outlawed, its important activities were forced underground.[23] Pressure upon the Communist party continued to mount, as teachers suspected of affiliation were handed discharge notices; retrenchment in public services was used to disguise the firing of political undesirables, who were thus removed from the leadership of government unions; and the anti-Red crusade was joined by some private industries which frequently dismissed employees who were Kyosanto members or suspected of being sympathetic to its aims.[24]

The readmission of "depurgees" to political life in 1950–1952 internally disrupted three of the major parties, issuing a challenge to the new forces which had been projected into party leadership by the casualties of the purge. Some depurged veterans of the old Shimpoto, largely politicians of Minseito lineage, formed the Shinsei (New Politics) Club. Working in close liaison with the Minshuto, they looked toward incorporation into a reorganized party. This, however, was a challenge to the Minshuto leaders who had guided the party toward a program of "modified capitalism" since 1948. Another stream of Shimpoto de-purgees entered the Jiyuto, into which their Shidehara- and Inukai-led colleagues had gravitated during the period of exile. Into the Jiyuto also came the veteran parliamentarians who had presided over the founding of the party. Many of them took exception to Yoshida's manipulation of the organizational machinery and his curt treatment of party politicians. With Hatoyama Ichiro as their symbol, this group of depurgees tended to join forces with the professional politicians who had been displaced by the bureaucratic newcomers installed by Yoshida. The release of purged Shakaito leaders strengthened the right-wing faction of the party, intensifying the struggle with their leftist adversaries for the control of the party machinery.[25]

It was during the third Yoshida ministry that the Shakaito split into two separate organizations over the question of the peace treaty. The growing strength of the left (in comparison with the rightist faction) had exacerbated the conflict over pure socialist doctrine, resulting in open schism in January 1950. At that time, however, the Shakaito continued to act as a unit in the Diet, and the local organizations scarcely felt the shock of the simmering disunity in the central headquarters. A patched-up agreement brought the nominal unification of left and right in time for the House of Councillors election in April 1950.[26] The tension raised by the Korean war and the peace treaty issue widened the gulf between the two factions. The doctrinaire Socialists envisaged the party as a proletarian organization which must maintain the purity of its doctrine; the moderates, on the other hand, urged an appeal to middle-class groups as well as workers, and ideological flexibility to meet the challenge of the real world. Premier Yoshida, to whom a separate peace treaty was the best possible alternative for Japan, maneuvered for a supraparty approach to foreign policy.[27] The commitment of the Shakaito to an over-all treaty including China and the Soviet Union provoked the opposition of the right wing after the San Francisco conference, and an extraordinary convention of the party in October produced a division into two warring camps. By this time the schism had disrupted Shakaito unity in the Diet and split the local organizations.[28] The breakup of the Shakaito into two Socialist parties — the Saha Shakaito (Left-wing Socialist party) and the Uha Shakaito (Right-wing Socialist party) — strengthened the hand of the conservatives and even allowed them the luxury of disunity until November 1955.

Opposition to the policies, tactics, and personality of Yoshida crystallized in 1952. The Minshuto, in preparation for a comeback in the expected election, dissolved in February 1952 and re-emerged as the Kaishinto (Progressive party), bringing the Shinsei Club, a few anti-Yoshida Liberals, and scattered splinter groups into its ranks. After considerable dissension, Shigemitsu Mamoru, who had been released from prison, where he had served sentence as a war criminal, was elected to the presidency of the new party, with Ashida serving as special adviser.[29] Yoshida's difficulties were compounded by mounting criticism of his stand on rearmament and by a widening rift in his own organization over the return of Hatoyama. To block the flood of opposition by an appeal to the electorate, the premier dissolved the Diet in August 1952 without waiting for formal legislative censure. He subsequently stirred the fires of rebellion by dismissing two of Hatoyama's henchmen from the Jiyuto.[30] In the ensuing campaign there was little difference between the Kaishinto program and that of the Hatoyama Liberals, a fact suggesting an eventual amalgamation of the two groups.

In the October election for the House of Representatives the Jiyuto won 240 seats, an absolute though somewhat reduced majority — the first time in Japanese history that a regime had been awarded a majority twice in succession. The Kaishinto gained with a total of 85 seats, and both the Uha Shakaito and Saha Shakaito, with 57 and 54 respectively, surpassed the previous strength of the united party. Of the 140 depurgees who were successful in the election, 79 were Jiyuto candidates, 32 were members of the Kaishinto, 13 were from the Uha Shakaito, and 3 from the Saha Shakaito.[31]

Fourth Yoshida Cabinet

The continued political success of Yoshida depended upon his ability to hold both Jiyuto factions under one roof and thus to preserve his majority. Such a precarious balance of political forces added to the bargaining strength of Hatoyama, increasing the possibility of his defection. Yoshida reached a temporary understanding with his rival, thereby securing re-election to the premiership for a fourth term in October 1952. As a concession to his Jiyuto opponents, however, the premier was forced to drop from the cabinet two of his bureaucratic acolytes who were especially distasteful to the "party" faction; he likewise promised the "democratization" of the party machinery, at the same time appointing a few of Hatoyama's lieutenants to posts in the organization.[32] The new cabinet was composed of sixteen Jiyuto men, including one follower of Hatoyama and two representatives of political groups in the House of Councillors, the Ryokufukai, and the Minshu (Democratic) Club. Fifteen of the eighteen ministers were of the postwar political generation and one had been a member of the House of Peers. Six members of the new government could be identified as career bureaucrats or former government officials.

This Yoshida cabinet lasted only six months. The opposition parties in joint effort excoriated the regime for its restrictions upon trade with Communist China and for its plan to scuttle Occupation reforms by centralizing the police and educational systems. The restoration of large financial and industrial concerns and the authority of the government to prohibit strikes were other issues which excited tempers in the Diet. When the Hatoyama clique occasionally withheld necessary support from Yoshida, it embarrassed the premier and weakened his political position. The reinstatement of the two Hatoyama stalwarts who had been expelled and a redistribution of party posts brought only a brief respite. When twenty-two of the Hatoyama rebels and other dissident elements voted for a nonconfidence resolution introduced by the opposition, Yoshida was forced to choose between resignation or the dissolution of the House of Representatives. When he chose the latter, Hatoyama and his followers broke with the Jiyuto and fought the Diet elections as an independent organization.

In the election held on April 19, 1953, the Yoshida faction of the Jiyuto won 199 seats, emerging as the strongest party but relinquishing its majority position. The Hatoyama clique garnered only 35 seats, and the Kaishinto slipped from 89 to 76. Both Shakaito parties made some gains, the rightists capturing 66 seats and the left-wing group 72. In order to survive Yoshida had to restore the unity of his party or turn to Shigemitsu and the Kaishinto.

Fifth Yoshida Cabinet

Although the opposition parties were unable to prevent Yoshida from setting up his fifth ministry, their defeat of Jiyuto candidates for the elective offices of the Diet forecast another period of instability, with considerable opportunity for opportunistic maneuvering. Rarely in Japanese history has the opposition been able to capture the speakership of the House of Representatives, and in those few instances the parliamentary sessions have been marked by more than the usual amount of tumult and fisticuffs. Since the cooperation of the Kaishinto was indispensable to a smooth administration, Yoshida made the necessary overtures for the additional support he desperately needed. Shigemitsu offered qualified cooperation, and Yoshida formed another Jiyuto ministry.[33]

Of the eighteen ministers, four had been prewar members of the House of Representatives, and one had sat in the House of Peers; the remaining thirteen were newcomers to the national political scene. Four members of the cabinet were career civil servants, and two had previously been in that category.

Its minority position left the regime vulnerable in the budget debates, and the opposition lost no opportunity to chide Yoshida for his "slavish" dependence upon the United States. As a concession to the Kaishinto, the Yoshida government modified some of its legislative program, and the Shigemitsu coterie occasionally stilled the parliamentary sea by supporting several measures they had once vigorously opposed. During this uneasy era attempts to unify the Kaishinto and the Hatoyama Liberals ended in failure, and a portion of the latter group returned to the Yoshida fold in November 1953. The government was still short of a majority, however, with the Shigemitsu organization holding the balance of power.

The ministry suffered a major setback which threatened political downfall in early 1954 with the disclosure of a series of scandals involving prominent cabinet and Jiyuto officials. They were accused of accepting gifts and bribes from industrial concerns interested in government subsidies. The refusal of the government to sanction the arrest of two party chiefs drew fire from the opposition.[34] Tempers flared in the Diet, and during the debate on the controversial police centralization bill an outbreak of rioting in the chamber necessitated the intervention of armed guards. Sessions of the Japanese Diet have a reputation for being turbulent on occasion, but these disturbances aroused a popular protest and raised a question concerning the vitality of parliamentary institutions. Recognizing the seriousness of the disorders, the major parties negotiated a nonpartisan agreement to tighten Diet discipline.

To reinforce his shaky regime, Yoshida proposed a merger of the Jiyuto with the Kaishinto — all the Shigemitsu organization if possible, a portion of it if necessary. This strategy aimed at increasing the Yoshida majority and splitting the opposition at the same time. The premier's scheme found favor with the business community, which was disturbed by the political instability, frequent elections, and the possibility of a Shakaito victory. As is usual with projected mergers, the proposal rekindled interfactional strife and opened the gate to wholesale negotiations and bargaining. An obstacle to Jiyuto-Kaishinto union was the demand for Yoshida's resignation as a preliminary step toward reorganization and the reluctance of the premier to step aside. In the meantime the anti-Yoshida faction of the Jiyuto conspired with Hatoyama in the establishment of a new conservative party. This maneuver was reportedly more attractive to the Ashida group than to the main wing of the Kaishinto.[35] The expulsion of two Hatoyama partisans from the Jiyuto for anti-Yoshida activity was the signal for more than thirty of their associates to leave the organization. This paved the way for an amalgamation of the Jiyuto rebels with the Kaishinto, regrouping into the Nihon Minshuto (Japan Democratic party) under the presidency of Hatoyama.[36] The new party accumulated more than 120 seats in the House of Representatives, whittling away the plurality strength of the Jiyuto. Yoshida met this challenge to his power by threatening another dissolution of the Diet, but this strategy met with the opposition of influential officials of his own party, who sensed a Jiyuto defeat at the polls. A few Jiyuto leaders sought to avoid a dissolution by forming a coalition of conservative parties, but they were in a weak bargaining position to execute such a maneuver. On several occasions a proposal to reorganize the Minshuto and Jiyuto into one large organization was rejected by the Hatoyama stalwarts.[37]

In order to unseat the Yoshida regime, Hatoyama and his party entered into an alliance with the Socialist parties, with whom they were in basic ideological disagreement, and the coalition introduced a resolution of nonconfidence into the Diet. Strong pressure from his Jiyuto henchmen restrained Yoshida from his usual practice of dissolving the Diet, and he resigned from the leadership of both the government and his party.[38] His ouster marked the end of an era. Japan had passed from occupation to independence, and now it faced the problem of adjusting its foreign relations to the vicissitudes of the cold war and of diverting the side-channels of alien reform to the main stream of Japanese life. Yoshida had remained continuously in office for more than six years; his five cabinets gave him a total tenure of seven years, nearly equaling the longevity of Ito Hirobumi and Katsura Taro in the early years of the parliamentary system.

Hatoyama as Premier

After another period of backstage negotiation, the two Socialist parties made possible the election of Hatoyama as premier in December 1954. It was generally understood that his government would be an interim regime which would dissolve the Diet and hold a general election.[39] Hatoyama, significantly enough, revived the prewar custom of reporting his accession to the premiership to the Japanese gods at the Grand Shrine of Ise. Except for two ministers who professed no party affiliation, the new cabinet was a Minshuto affair. However, it differed in important respects from some of its Yoshida predecessors. More than half the cabinet members were depurgees, and the same proportion had served in prewar Diets. Slightly less than half the ministers were postwar newcomers, and the regime included only three government officials and one ex-bureaucrat.

The new premier and his party won a plurality victory of 185 seats in the election held on February 27, 1955. The stigma of corruption injured the Jiyuto, which lost more than half its incumbents, including several cabinet ministers. The capture of 112 seats kept it in second place, followed by the Saha Shakaito with 89, and the Uha Shakaito with 67.

Hatoyama was re-elected premier without difficulty on March 18, 1955, and his new cabinet, with only six new faces, was little different from that of his caretaker government. Of the six new ministers, three were of the postwar political generation and two of them were career bureaucrats. With an eye on an election, the Socialists had formed an entente with Hatoyama in order to unhorse Yoshida; now they cooperated with their archrivals, the Jiyuto, in order to isolate the government party. The new alliance secured the election of the Diet officials from the ranks of the opposition.[40]

The New Japan

This parliamentary setback dramatized Hatoyama's minority position in the Diet and forecast stormy weather ahead for the regime. The storm clouds gathered in October 1955, when the Uha Shakaito and the Saha Shakaito, after four years of separation, reunited under one Socialist roof, to become the second largest party in the House of Representatives. The leaders of the two conservative parties had watched with anxiety the growth of Socialist strength in recent elections, and in 1955 there were frequent bargaining conferences aimed at a merger of the Jiyuto and the Minshuto. With the emergence of a reunited, though unsteady, Shakaito, the conservatives intensified their efforts at amalgamation in order to meet the Socialist threat. Their efforts were successful in mid-November, when the two parties united to form the Jiyu-Minshuto (Liberal Democratic party), with 300 seats in the House of Representatives.[41]

Observations on the Party Struggle

Anyone familiar with political developments in presurrender Japan will detect similar patterns and recurring problems in the postwar era. The electorate remains predominantly conservative in its voting habits; in all the lower house elections held under varying political conditions during the period from 1946 to 1955, the conservative parties captured an average of 62 per cent of the seats, while the Shakaito and Kyosanto could win but 26 per cent. In prewar years political professionals such as Hara Takashi and Inukai Tsuyoshi, after serving an apprenticeship in their organizations, were elevated to the presidency of their parties and ultimately selected for the premiership; but well-known career bureaucrats and military heroes also played influential roles both in party and government. Since the war the conservative parties, in their search for officials of eminence and for talent acceptable to SCAP, frequently turned to the political neophytes who had been identified with the government bureaucracy. The prestige of such career diplomats as Yoshida, Ashida, and Shigemitsu beckoned them to presidential roles. Perhaps the function performed by a political party in the opening years of the Occupation demanded leadership by men with the finesse of a diplomat, the experience of a bureaucrat, or the shield of a big name. It was not until after the return of Hatoyama and the prewar parliamentarians to public life that the "party" men regained a strong voice in their political organizations and the government. As in prewar years, the intense rivalry among cliquish factions, more loyal to leader than to party, has resulted in frequent defections and regroupings without regard for party doctrine. With principle shelved, the bonds of union become personal and financial, and the close tieup between voter and boss generally enables the constituency to transfer its party allegiance smoothly and obediently. Continuing a prewar pattern, the new Japan has harvested its crop of scandals and corruption, in which all the major parties have been deeply involved.

Under these conditions single party majorities have quickly disintegrated, and coalition cabinets and parliamentary ententes have been unsteady. The unusual stability of the Yoshida regime was eventually broken by a member of his own party who had twice split the prewar Seiyukai — although Yoshida's lack of political skill was provocative of factional disorder. Interparty jealousy and intraparty feuds have provoked irresponsible and disorderly conduct in the Diet, inviting retaliatory dissolutions so that no parliament has been able to serve out its full term. Amid such acrimonious distractions it becomes difficult to manage the urgent matters of government. Even a party placed in office with a healthy majority will ultimately lose the support of the electorate when the confusion degenerates into chaos. That the Japanese will develop a wholesome party life and develop a corresponding loyalty to parliamentary institutions is at the present time something rather to be hoped for than predicted.

Notes

[1] For a discussion of the prewar political parties in Japan see H. S. Quigley, *Japanese Government and Politics* (New York, 1932), Chapter 12.

[2] On the re-establishment of political parties after the surrender see below, Chapter 7.

[3] K. E. Colton, "Pre-war Political Influences in Post-war Conservative Parties," *American Political Science Review*, XLII (October 1948), 945–948. The author notes the replacement of Kono Ichiro by Ono Bamboku, a machine politician trained by Hara Takashi, as secretary-general of the Jiyuto. For a general discussion of the purge see below, Chapter 8.

[4] SCAP, *Monthly Summation of Non-Military Activities in Japan and Korea*, April 1946, pp. 40–43; *Nippon Times*, April-May 1946.

[5] *Nippon Times*, May 22, 1946; January 4, 1952; June 1, 1952; *New York Times*, May 22, 1946. The presidency was left vacant for a time in case Hatoyama might be promptly depurged by SCAP.

[6] *Nippon Times*, August 9, 1946; SCAP, *Monthly Summation*, October 1946, p. 37.

[7] *Nippon Times*, January 8, 18, 29–30, 1947; February 7, 1947; *Mainichi*, February 1, 1947, translated in SCAP, Allied Translator and Interpreter Service, *Press Translations and Summaries*, February 1, 1947, I:4, pp. 4–6. Apparently Yoshida was not convinced that party men would make capable administrators in a cabinet.

The New Japan

[8] *Nippon Times*, March 10, 1947.

[9] *Ibid.*, October 6, 1946; editorial, "The New Political Ferment," *ibid.*, February 8, 1947; *ibid.*, March 25, 1947; April 1–3, 11, 1947.

[10] *Ibid.*, May 8, 21, 25, 1947; June 24, 1947.

[11] *Ibid.*, June 1, 1947; November 17–30, 1947.

[12] SCAP, *Monthly Summation*, January 1948, pp. 32–37; February 1948, pp. 23–26; editorial, "Disharmony within the Socialist Party," *Nippon Times*, December 8, 1947; editorial, "Rearrangement of the Political Spectrum," *ibid.*, February 7, 1948; *ibid.*, December 14, 25, 1947; January 6, 21, 1948; February 7–8, 1948.

[13] SCAP, *Monthly Summation*, March 1948, pp. 40–44; *Nippon Times*, February 18, 24, 1948; March 14–16, 1948; July 23, 1948; December 4, 1948.

[14] SCAP, *Monthly Summation*, June 1948, pp. 23–25, 36–37; July 1948, pp. 48–49, 52–53; *Nippon Times*, May 8–11, 1948; June 8–12, 1948; July 9, 1948; August 4, 1948.

[15] See above, p. 196.

[16] Department of State, OIR Report No. 5022, *The 1949 Japanese House of Representatives Election*, pp. 93–94. The comparable data for the 1947 election have been compiled from the parliamentary biographies listed in Department of State, OIR Report No. 4310, *An Analysis of the 1947 Japanese House of Representatives Election*, Appendix B. See also editorial, "From Bureaucrats to Politicians," *Nippon Times*, August 2, 1948.

[17] *Nippon Times*, February 9, 1949; March 2, 12, 1949; April 3, 13, 29, 1950.

[18] *Ibid.*, May 7, 1950; June 28, 1950; *The Japan Yearbook, 1949–52*, p. 224.

[19] *Nippon Times*, July 4, 1951.

[20] *Ibid.*, January 8–13, 1950.

[21] *Ibid.*, July 5, 1949.

[22] *Ibid.*, June 6–10, 1950.

[23] *Ibid.*, July 19, 1950; August 1, 1950; September 1, 5, 1950; October 9, 1950; December 11, 1951.

[24] *Ibid.*, June 11, 1950; August 9, 1950; September 2, 1950; November 25, 1950; February 6, 1951.

[25] *Ibid.*, October 17, 1950; editorial, "New Party Lines," *ibid.*, November 30, 1951; S. Hasegawa, "Japanese Politics behind the Scene," *ibid.*, October 27, 1952.

[26] *Nippon Times*, January 16–22, 1950; March 1, 1950; April 6, 1950.

[27] *Ibid.*, June 20, 1950; August 24, 1950; November 15, 1950.

[28] *Ibid.*, January 21–22, 1951; October 25–26, 1951; July 2, 1952; editorial, "The Socialist Feud," *ibid.*, March 11, 1951; editorial, "The Political Pot," *ibid.*, January 14, 1952.

[29] *Nippon Times*, December 18, 1951; February 8, 1952; May 5, 7, 1952; editorial, "Search for a Leader," *ibid.*, January 18, 1952.

[30] *Nippon Times*, September 30, 1952.

[31] Paul S. Dull, "The Japanese General Election of 1952," *American Political Science Review*, XLVII (March 1953), 203.

[32] *Nippon Times*, October 24, 1952.

[33] *Ibid.*, May 17–21, 1953.

[34] *Asahi Evening News*, August 10–11, 1954. The persistent refusal of Yoshida to appear before a parliamentary committee investigating the scandals did not reduce the fury of the opposition.

[35] H. Nomura, "Political Party Troubles," *ibid.*, August 13, 1954; *Asahi Evening News*, August 23, 1954; September 29, 1954. The Ashida faction, which was in a minority position in the party, was composed largely of men with a Seiyukai background, while the Shigemitsu group tended to be Minseito politicians (*ibid.*, September 15, 1954). Shigemitsu, although receptive to Hatoyama's overtures, had kept his lines open to the Yoshida clique. However, his relations with Jiyuto leader Ogata Taketora were not cordial, their enmity stemming in part from a policy disagreement over the necessity of seeking a truce with Chiang Kai-shek (*Nippon Times*, March 20, 1953).

[36] *New York Times*, November 10, 23, 1954; *Asahi Evening News*, November 22–24, 1954; *Japan News*, November 24, 1954; *Nippon Times*, November 24–25, 1954. Shigemitsu became vice-president and Ashida one of the supreme advisers of the new party.

[37] *New York Times*, November 30, 1954; *Asahi Evening News*, November 22, 27, 1954; December 3–4, 7, 1954; January 5, 1955.

[38] *Asahi Evening News*, December 8, 1954.

[39] *Ibid.*, December 10, 1954; *Nippon Times*, December 10, 1954.

[40] *Mainichi*, March 19, 1955.

[41] For details on the party amalgamations in late 1955, the authors are indebted to Dr. George O. Totten.

20

Major Political Parties
II: Composition and Policies

Jiyu-Minshuto (Liberal Democratic Party)

As NOTED above, the closing months of 1955 brought a realignment of political parties in Japan. The business community, alarmed at the display of electoral strength by the two Socialist organizations, had long urged the conservatives to stop their feuding and to merge into one party. The reunification of the Shakaito factions in October forced the hand of Jiyuto and Minshuto leaders, and on November 15 they submerged their personal differences to form the Jiyu-Minshuto. Thus it came about that within ten years of the end of World War II two outwardly united parties, one socialist, the other conservative, faced one another in a struggle for political power.

In the House of Representatives 184 Minshuto members, 115 Jiyuto members, and 1 independent joined the Jiyu-Minshuto caucus, giving it 64 per cent of the seats. Its 118 seats in the House of Councillors constituted 47 per cent of the total membership in that chamber. The conservative amalgamation gave the Hatoyama government the heaviest majority enjoyed by any ministry since the end of the war. The fact, however, that the merger was an entente of expediency, concealing rather than dissolving factional rivalries, imperils the existence of the party as a permanent fixture in Japanese politics. In their bargaining negotiations the competing groups were unable to agree upon a president to head the new organization, and they were forced to entrust the management of party affairs to a committee of four leaders:

Hatoyama Ichiro, Ogata Taketora, Ono Bamboku, and Miki Bukichi. On November 21 Hatoyama resigned the premiership, to be re-elected to that post by the Diet on the following day. This maneuver enabled him to bring representatives of the Jiyuto wing of the new party into his cabinet.

The manifesto of the Jiyu-Minshuto, issued at the inauguration of the party, was an amalgamation of principles and policies enunciated by the two parent organizations. In domestic affairs the party called for a careful study of the new constitution, with a view toward its revision, particularly the "renunciation of war" clause; it also suggested a plan of long-range economic development, but the program was lacking in specifics. In foreign policy the Jiyu-Minshuto platform included the repatriation of Japanese nationals still being held in Soviet territory, the unconditional restoration to Japanese sovereignty of the islands of Habomai and Shikotan and the southern islands of the Kuriles, the summoning of an Allied conference to discuss Japanese claims to the northern islands of the Kurile chain and Karafuto, and the admission of Japan to the United Nations.

It is much too early to attempt an analysis of a party as young and untested as the Jiyu-Minshuto. How the cross-fertilization of Jiyuto and Minshuto personnel and policies within the framework of a single conservative structure will affect traditional party loyalties and voting patterns may be difficult to determine for some time. Unquestionably, however, the Jiyu-Minshuto will be influenced to a considerable degree by the factional rifts, organizational patterns, areas of traditional voting strength, and policy differences of the parties that merged in its formation. For this reason it may be worth while to examine the general composition and policies of the Jiyuto and Minshuto, which, until November 1955, dominated the conservative side of Japan's political continuum.

Jiyuto (Liberal Party)

The Jiyuto, an oblique descendant of the prewar Seiyukai, was till late 1955 Japan's strongest postwar party. In the six general elections held since the war it captured an average of 35 per cent of the popular vote, varying from a low of 26 per cent in 1946 (when many candidates ran as independents) to a peak of 48 per cent in 1952. Even in its 1947 defeat the Jiyuto still ran ahead of its nearest competitor by a narrow margin in the popular balloting. The consistent success of the party entitled it to establish four successive ministries for an uninterrupted tenure of six years. Such a record is without precedent since the clan-led cabinets of Meiji Japan.

Although the Jiyuto made an appeal to the financial, industrial, and commercial interests of certain urban centers, its greatest strength lay in the general conservatism of rural Japan. In these agrarian areas the party attracted the large landowners, some of the smaller agriculturalists, tenant farmers, and ordinary villagers under the sway of influential political leaders. Since the political fortunes of all parties rose and fell in the 1947 and 1949 elections, these contests serve as a crude barometer of traditional support in those cases where an organization displayed persistent strength during both the ebb and the flow of the electoral tide. In these two elections the Jiyuto ran well in Saitama, Iwate, Chiba, and Shizuoka prefectures, two of which are predominantly rural, one moderately rural, and one moderately urban. In the twenty strongest Jiyuto prefectures — the ten best in each election — nine are predominantly rural, five moderately so, five moderately urban, and one strongly urban.[1]

An analysis of the Jiyuto caucus in the 1947 House of Representatives permits a comparison with the Diet membership of other parties in the period from 1947 to 1949. The Jiyuto had the highest proportion of members who had served in prewar Diets, and this was reflected in an older parliamentary delegation:

Party	Percentage of Service in Prewar H. Rep.	Average Age	Percentage below 40	Percentage above 60
Jiyuto	18.1	52.4	7.5	18.1
Minshuto	13.4	50.1	19.0	15.0
Kyodoto	3.2	48.9	12.9	12.9
Shakaito	12.5	48.0	19.5	3.5

In occupational breakdown, approximately 40 per cent of the Jiyuto members of the Diet were business executives. Lawyers, educators, writers, and civil servants were well represented, but less prominently than company directors and corporation presidents. Business leaders were even more conspicuous in the Minshuto, making up more than half the delegation. Kyodoto legislators were predominantly company officials, educators, and agricultural proprietors; the Shakaito was represented by a smaller proportion of businessmen (and of lesser magnitude), labor leaders, lawyers, and journalists and publishers.[2] The leadership of the Jiyuto was divided among businessmen, bureaucrats, and career politicians, the jockeying for position becoming especially bitter after the purge of Hatoyama and the accession of Yoshida. Of the original sponsors who founded the party in 1945, 73 per cent had served in prewar Diets; the average age of the group was sixty-one, with one-third above the age of sixty and none below forty. Journalists and publishers were the most prominent occupational category, followed closely by equal proportions of lawyers, educators, business executives, and government officials. By 1951, after the recruitment of younger bureaucrats by Yoshida, the picture of Jiyuto officialdom had changed markedly. Only 54 per cent were prewar parliamentarians; after six years the average age had risen by only one year to sixty-two, although more than three-fourths of the leaders were now above the age of sixty; and with more than half the party positions occupied by career bureaucrats and former government officials, the proportion of writers and business executives had noticeably declined.

Twenty-eight per cent of all the cabinet members who wore the Jiyuto label between 1946 and 1955 had served in prewar parliaments. This group of ministers were younger than their Minshuto counterparts, their age averaging fifty-four, with 6 per cent above the age of sixty and 4 per cent below forty. Business leaders comprised 40 per cent of the group, bureaucrats and ex-bureaucrats 30 per cent, and writers and lawyers approximately 14 per cent and 12 per cent respectively.

The platforms of Japanese parties have outdone their Western models in platitudes and in their variance from the actual programs pursued in office. A party manifesto, consequently, is little more than a crude index of the basic principles of a political organization. This, of course, is even more true of native parties during a period of occupation by alien powers. Recognizing these conditioning factors, it is nevertheless desirable to trace roughly the changes in the program of a particular party and to compare the attitudes of the several parties on specific issues. In large measure the policies of the Jiyuto reflected the conservative interests of the business leaders, career bureaucrats, and old-line politicians who identified themselves with the party. At the Jiyuto inauguration in 1945, Hatoyama and his associates keynoted the Liberal approach to the political and economic problems of postwar Japan: the maintenance of the throne, the safeguarding of private property, and strong action against communism.[3]

The domestic policy of the Jiyuto rested steadfastly upon the doctrine that imperial centralism is compatible with democracy and essential to national existence. Emphasizing the unity of emperor and people, the party wished to include the teaching of moral precepts and national culture in the educational curriculum. In the clash between parliamentary and executive authority, Yoshida and his colleagues often sought refuge behind the imperial prerogative, treating the Diet with arrogance. Jiyuto cabinets sponsored legislation to bring the police, institutions of local government, and the educational system under the closer purview of the central authorities.

Yoshida and his organization frequently bowed before the shrine of *laissez faire*. They steadfastly opposed the ownership of industrial enterprise by the state; in fact, the Jiyuto premier at one time talked of selling the railways and other state property to replenish the depleted treasury.[4] Hostility toward government direction of business activity led to attacks upon the control of specified foods, industrial materials, wages, and prices.[5] The Jiyuto battled for the legal right of industrial and financial concerns to enter into combines, demanding a modification of the antitrust legislation enacted under the alien tutelage of SCAP. Like many of the Western conservative parties, however, Jiyuto liberalism did not deny government loans and subsidies to business concerns for the rehabilitation, modernization, or even the operation of their plants. Although the Jiyuto was committed to a reduced tax load for the workers, its fiscal program was primarily designed to encourage the acquisition and investment of capital by reducing taxes on corporations and dividends and eliminating levies upon the interest from savings. More prominent in the early years of the Occupation than in the later stages of his tenure in office were Yoshida's appeals to lower-income groups: the construction of low-cost housing, the expansion of the social security system, the encouragement of a yeomanry, and the enactment of a minimum wage and other welfare legislation. It was pressure from SCAP and a belated recognition of the economic facts of life that eventually forced Jiyuto governments to reduce state expenditures and to introduce a program of grudging austerity. Under this policy they became unwilling advocates of the curtailment of subsidies, the revision of the tax structure, and the allocation of raw materials.[6]

From its birth in 1945 the Jiyuto looked on communism as inimical to the Japanese *kokutai* and incompatible with public order. Proclaiming itself the defender of national institutions and a rallying ground of opposition to Kyosanto activities and doctrine, the Yoshida cabinet secured the passage of an antisubversion law. As previously noted, the Jiyuto government restricted the activities of leading Communists and banned their publications. The party was also accused of seeking a firmer control of the educational system to counteract the influence of leftist teachers' organizations. Yoshida and his men frequently exhibited an intense distrust of trade unionism. To them the labor movement was unpatriotically self-interested at best, subversively irresponsible at worst. These anxieties prompted Jiyuto governments to seek the elimination of leftist unions and to urge the legal restriction of strike activities. These restraints included a ban upon strikes in certain categories of employment and the curtailment of political action in which labor organizations might engage.[7]

In foreign policy the Jiyuto was cordial toward the United States, at the same time aiming at a strengthened international position for Japan. In order to secure loans and capital funds for the nation, Yoshida and his associates tried to create a favorable investment climate which would win the confidence of American business. The party supported a separate peace treaty, excluding China and the Soviet Union, when it became clear that this was the only method by which the Japanese could regain their independence. In unison with most of the other parties, it contended that Japan was entitled to have the Kurile, Ryukyu, and Bonin Islands restored to her sovereignty. The Jiyuto was often charged with opportunism on the rearmament question. Immediately after the Korean war, it expressed opposition to rearmament as such, but at the same time the government, under the influence of SCAP, expanded the "police" reserve, contending that it was not an army and hence not in violation of the constitution. Yoshida courted popular favor in the 1952 campaign by his opposition to "immediate" rearmament; he supported instead an "eventual" buildup of military forces when the nation's economy was strong enough to bear the load. After the election his position relaxed somewhat in favor of increasing defensive strength, and in 1955 the party was publicly calling for rearmament within the limits of Japan's economic resources.[8] Many Jiyuto leaders were rather suspicious of normalized trade and diplomatic relations with Communist China and the Soviet Union. They held that these nations were more interested in military items than in consumer goods and that an orientation toward the Soviet bloc would destroy international confidence in Japan. Nevertheless there was some sentiment in the party for a modification of policy toward the mainland of Asia so that the Japanese might speak with a louder voice in Southeast Asia.[9]

Until the defection of Hatoyama, the Jiyuto moved steadily forward under the iron leadership of Yoshida. The well-known leaders of its conservative rival — Shidehara, Saito, and Inukai — were even lured into the Jiyuto camp. Experienced administrative talent at the helm and a program attractive to the basic conservative attitudes of the Japanese voter help to explain the postwar success of Yoshida and his organization.

Minshuto (Democratic Party)

The Minshuto and its predecessors suffered from a serious inability to convince voters that their brand of conservatism was significantly different from that of the Jiyuto. The party ran well in the electoral upheaval of 1947 when it captured one-fourth of the popular vote. But in 1949 it entered a long era of political famine, garnering an average of only 17 per cent of the ballots in three successive elections. However, the return of influential "depurgees" and the subsequent merger with the Hatoyama Liberals reinvigorated the party under the banner of the Minshuto, and in 1955 its stock soared to a high of 36.6 per cent of the electorate. In much of the postwar period the Minshuto organization was the largest single party in opposition, although it was generally ineffective in that role.

The Shimpoto-Minshuto tended to have greater strength in the urban areas than the Jiyuto, and, like its ancient rival, it reached into the rural provinces to capitalize upon its traditional links with the voter. In both the 1947 and 1949 elections the party exhibited strength in strongly urban Kyoto and in moderately urban Ishikawa; moderately rural Fukui, Gumma, and Kumamoto and predominantly rural Shimane likewise displayed their electoral satisfaction with Ashida and his associates. In the party's twenty best prefectures in both elections, three are chiefly urban, three are moderately so, eight are moderately agrarian, and six are strongly rural.[10]

As previously noted, the Democratic delegation in the 1947 House of Representatives was slightly younger than its Jiyuto counterpart, and only 13 per cent had served in prewar Diets. These characteristics can be explained by the heavy casualties of the purge. Business executives, company directors, and corporation presidents were by far the most prominent occupational categories, with lawyers, journalists, publishers, civil servants, agricultural proprietors, and educators clustered together to make up the balance of the caucus.

The Minshuto and its forerunners had a large number of attractive leaders, who were, however, mercurial in their loyalty to the organization, defecting, one after another, from its ranks. Of the men who held *key* posts in the party structure in 1951, 66 per cent had served in prewar Diets; the average age was fifty-nine, with two-thirds of the leaders above the age of sixty and none below forty. That two-thirds of its officials were company directors and presidents reflected again the party's close link with the business world. In the group were also two lawyers and one ex-bureaucrat turned professor and journalist. The influx of the Hatoyama Liberals into the party in 1954 brought some changes in the upper stratum of the organizational hierarchy. Of those who were awarded *key* positions in the ranks of Minshuto officialdom, almost two-thirds had seen Diet service in presurrender days; nearly all were above the age of sixty, the average age being sixty-eight; and a generous sprinkling of journalists, lawyers, and politicians had largely displaced the business-executive group.

The impact of the Hatoyama influx upon the Kaishinto can be seen from an analysis of its leaders who served in various cabinets while wearing the label of the party. The Shimpoto-Minshuto-Kaishinto men who took ministerial posts before the merger were an older group; the average age was sixty-five, more than 80 per cent being above the age of sixty. The party men who served under Hatoyama averaged only fifty-six, and only one-third of them were above sixty. The proportions of leaders who had served in the lower house in prewar days were 58 per cent and 62.5 per cent respectively. Whereas two-thirds of the party members in pre-1954 cabinets were business executives and bankers, only one-third of the Minshuto ministers were in this occupational category. Instead, Hatoyama brought a large group of men associated with journalism and publishing into his government. The proportion of government officials serving in cabinet posts during the Ashida era and the Hatoyama period was less than 20 per cent in both cases. Thus the formation of the Minshuto transformed the leadership of the Democratic group by bringing into the cabinet younger men who were more closely associated with the journalistic world than with the management of commercial and industrial enterprise. Those serving in cabinet positions under Hatoyama were younger than ministers in previous Democratic cabinets and were a younger group than those men currently in charge of the party machinery. As could be readily anticipated, the structural changes wrought by the merger and the subsequent success of the Minshuto at the polls increased factional jealousies within the organization. Although Hatoyama was the focal point of party unity in the ousting of Yoshida, the power of his group was disproportionate to its numerical position, setting the stage for a personal struggle over the leadership of the association.[11]

At its birth the Shimpoto stood upon a platform of sterile conservatism, echoing the hollow pronouncements of its prewar ancestor. After the pruning operations of SCAP, however, the party began to react to changing political conditions, and ultimately it discarded some of its rigid, conservative trappings and came more under the influence of socialism and trade unionism than the Jiyuto. The constant pressure for a union of the conservative parties in opposition to socialism and the frequent defections to the Yoshida ranks imperiled the existence of the organization. To offset the pull of coalition forces on the right and to preserve their independence from the inroads of the Jiyuto, the Shimpoto-Minshuto-Kaishinto leadership was forced to move closer to the center, often forming, especially in the early years of the Occupation, temporary alliances with the Shakaito. These expedient ententes encouraged the modification of Kaishinto doctrine to meet the demands of their left-wing allies. Even when in the same cabinet or in joint opposition, the Kaishinto and the Socialists were to some extent competing for votes in the urban centers, more a stronghold of the Democrats than the rurally based Jiyuto. Hence the Kaishinto was influenced by the organization strategy and ideological appeal of the Socialists, the strategy and appeal that had made the

Shakaito a political force for the Democrats to reckon with in post-surrender Japan.

To carve an independent niche for their party and to disassociate themselves from Jiyuto failures, the sponsors of the Minshuto in 1947 sought a middle way between Jiyuto conservatism and Shakaito socialism. Determined to form a political organization which had "blood relations with the masses," Minshuto propagandists expressed the new liberalism in such idealistic terms as "modified capitalism," "planned economy," "social justice," and "avoidance of class struggle."[12] Again in 1952, at its transformation into the Kaishinto, the same urge to liberal reform permeated the ranks of some of the younger leaders.[13] For most of the postwar period the general objective of the party was to unite those forces of progressive inclination, excluding only the Communists and their fellow travelers. How much the transfusion of Hatoyama's brand of conservatism diluted this program of moderate reform and blurred the doctrinal differences between the Jiyuto and the Minshuto remains a question mark.

In contrast, then, with the frank conservatism of Jiyuto platforms, the Minshuto as well as its predecessors was critical of the untempered conservative approach. The party was in favor of the control of key industries within the system of private ownership, conceding the temporary management of strategic enterprises by the state during periods of crisis.[14] To bolster the ailing middle class the Minshuto supported the levying of heavy taxes upon the excessive profits of inflation and black-market operations and corresponding reductions and inducements for small and medium-sized businesses.[15] Their program generally invited the state to put forward a generous schedule of welfare legislation. The encouragement of cooperatives and the development of an independent yeomanry constituted a bid for agrarian support. For the city worker there were the expansion of public housing, medical services, and social insurance, the creation of profit-sharing schemes, and the healthy development of trade unions. This program, together with public works projects, was designed to relieve the farmer, the small businessman, and the wage earner, who were "panting for breath" in an economic whirlpool.[16] The seeds of conflict over financial policy began to germinate in the opening days of the Hatoyama ministry. Ishibashi Tanzan, an exponent of inflationary measures, was a cabinet colleague of Ichimada Hisato, a financier of the Yoshida school, and an outspoken critic of flabby monetary policies. Although Ichimada as finance minister made pre-election promises of an enlarged housing program, a stronger social security system, and government assistance to the smaller commercial establishments, his program for corporations and the industrial community seemed hardly distinguishable from that of the Jiyuto. Indeed, some Jiyuto leaders claimed the authorship of Hatoyama's economic policies.[17] In its early months in office the Minshuto government showed signs of a moderate approach to labor, in contrast to the restrictive measures sought by Yoshida.[18]

True to its native inheritance, the Shimpoto-Kaishinto-Minshuto occasionally revealed a strain of mystical nationalism not unlike that of other rightist groups. In 1946 when President Shidehara was urging a halfway house in economic policy, he pleaded at the same time for the maintenance of "firm racial unity."[19] Thereafter the platforms of the party frequently included a defense of the imperial institution and made veiled references to the expansion of "national culture." A manifesto in 1950 justified the harmonization of capitalism and socialism on the ground that both right and left extremists were splitting the fatherland.[20] Kaishinto nationalism, not so cleverly disguised as the Jiyuto brand, really blossomed after the outbreak of the Korean war and as the Occupation drew to a close. Depurgees, who had suffered the pain of SCAP directives, returned to the political fold to reclaim responsible positions in the organization. The urge for "independence," "self-reliance," and "freedom from economic dependence upon the United States" was intensified, culminating in a 1955 campaign pledge to re-examine and possibly to revise SCAP-sponsored reforms.[21] The Hatoyama government had been in office only a short time when Minister of Education Ando announced plans to institute courses of instruction on the emperor system in the primary schools.[22]

This resurging spirit of independence likewise breathed through the foreign policy of the Minshuto. Like its conservative rival, the party urged the restoration of certain islands to Japanese sovereignty. Although in initial agreement with the Socialists that the peace treaty should include all former enemies and that the nation should preserve its neutrality in the East-West struggle, the organization shifted position after the outbreak of the Korean war and eventually supported Yoshida's policy at San Francisco. Even before their merger Hatoyama, Ashida, and Shigemitsu attacked Yoshida's program of camouflaged rearmament, hinting that the outright rebuilding of defense forces would be a wiser course.[23] Under the Minshuto banner these leaders advocated the creation of an independent defense force to permit the evacuation of American troops as soon as possible. Although the party was generally more receptive to rearmament than the Jiyuto, in 1955 it backed away from an immediate military build-up, seeking to avoid an arms program that would adversely affect the living standards of the nation.[24]

Wearing the badge of regained national sovereignty, the Minshuto was anxious to fashion a foreign policy independent of external pressures, Hatoyama marshaled conservative support for a policy of *rapprochement* with Communist China and the Soviet Union, looking toward the establishment of trade relations with those nations. Foreign Minister Shigemitsu tended to be more cautious, displaying reluctance on the question of diplomatic recognition and fear of antagonizing the Western democracies with hastily negotiated trade agreements.[25] Despite the lack of consensus in the Hatoyama government over the normalization of relations between Japan and the continent, the general approach of the Minshuto to the problem of China was more cordial than that of the Jiyuto leadership.

It is regrettable that a political party groping for a truly liberal position has been unable to make any substantial progress toward its objective. That there has been no considerable segment of the Japanese population to which it could appeal is a major reason for its general ineffectiveness. Minshuto precepts most nearly approximated those of the major American parties, but among Japanese voters an understanding of and devotion to the principles of representative government appear to be tragically uncommon. The Minshuto and its predecessors suffered somewhat from an overdose of antiquated leadership whose allegiance to the organization was tenuous at best. The middle position of the party left it vulnerable to the entice-ments and machinations of both sides. The failure of its program to win a sympathetic response reinforced a long-established tendency to rely upon personal alliances and tactical maneuvers for political success. As the frequent defections and ententes led to a cross-fertilization of personnel and policies, the doctrinal differences between the two

conservative parties became more obscure, and the Minshuto had
to content itself with lines of action which, in many respects, closely
resembled those of the rival Jiyuto.

Shakaito (Socialist Party)

The Shakaito is a successor to the proletarian parties which blossomed in the 1920s, and it has inherited much of their disunity. In
the view of one scholar,[26] frequent schisms have made "intraparty
cleavage the most important single characteristic of the postwar
Socialist party in Japan." From its birth the party was a heterogeneous coalition of intellectuals, utopians, religious idealists, hard-
headed laborites, Marxian materialists, and a smattering of opportunists. These groups were roughly divided into a moderate right-
wing element, a doctrinaire leftist faction, and for a time a neutral
segment between the two extremes. Under these circumstances it has
been difficult for party chieftains to hold the dissident factions under
one roof and to fashion a unified program of socialism acceptable to
all groups. Despite smoldering personality differences and constant
wrangling over theoretical issues, the Shakaito remained nominally
united until 1951. At that time, however, a second schism shattered the
organization, and it broke into two separate parties, the Uha Shakaito
(Right-wing Socialist party) and the Saha Shakaito (Left-wing Socialist party). Although there were frequent attempts at reunification,
the two organizations went their separate ways for four years. Not till
October 1955 were they able to merge again into one Shakaito camp.
That the feuding factions shelved their ideological differences is doubtful, and it appears likely that the Socialists will fight their political
battles with divided ranks, even though nominally united.[27]

What is remarkable about postwar Japanese politics is that the
fragmented Shakaito, vying with conservative parties in a conservative cultural setting, was able to do as well as it has done. As a united
party it reached its peak in the 1947 election, when it captured slightly
more than 26 per cent of the popular vote. The nadir came in 1949,
when its popularity dropped to 13.8 per cent. In that year the party
actually had more representatives in the conservative House of Councillors than in the lower chamber. The last three contests have been
fought as two separate parties, each averaging 12.8 per cent of the
ballots. Had they been in one camp, the Shakaito vote would have

been 21.3 per cent, 26.5 per cent, and 29.3 per cent, in 1952, 1953, and 1955 respectively. In all the postwar elections the Socialist parties together have captured an average of 22.4 per cent of the total ballots cast. The persistence of Socialist strength and especially the recent electoral success of the left-wing group stimulated the conservative parties to minimize personality differences and to merge into one strong organization.

The Shakaito appeal has been largely confined to the wage earners, intellectual groups, and elements of the lower middle class in the urban areas. All factions of the party depend to a large extent upon the good will of the trade unions, and they seek to represent their organization as the only reliable spokesman of the workingman in the Diet. With less success but with equal assurance the Shakaito groups claim to speak for the small landowners, tenants, and agricultural workers of agrarian Japan. In its 1947 success and the 1949 failure, the party displayed persistent strength in the prefectures of Kanagawa, Tokyo, Fukuoka, and Hiroshima, all of which are predominantly urban; it also commanded consistent support in the moderately rural provinces of Tottori and Kagawa and in strongly rural Shimane. Of the Shakaito's twenty-one strongest prefectures in both elections, ten are predominantly urban and one is moderately so; six are moderately agrarian and four others are strongly rural.[28] The same pattern was evident in the 1955 election. Of the ten prefectures where the Shakaito vote was largest, six are chiefly urban, three moderately so, and one moderately and one strongly rural.[29] In that contest the Uha Shakaito ran well in the urban prefectures of Kanagawa, Hyogo, Fukuoka, Tokyo, Shizuoka, and Miyagi, and in the rural areas of Nagano, Saitama, and Fukushima. Its left-wing counterpart drew its main support from the urban and semiurban provinces of Fukuoka, Aichi, Kyoto, Toyama, Wakayama, and Hokkaido, and in the agrarian prefectures of Gumma, Tottori, and Saga. The electoral fortunes of both Shakaito factions have risen with the corresponding decline of the Communists.

The Shakaito members of the 1947 House of Representatives were younger than their conservative colleagues, with nearly 20 per cent below the age of forty and only 3.5 per cent above sixty. Only 12.5 per cent of the delegation had had prewar Diet experience, although a larger group had engaged in political activity in prewar years. The proportion of business executives was much smaller in the Shakaito than in the right-wing parties, their places being taken by a larger body of journalists and labor leaders. Approximately 12 per cent of the Socialist caucus were lawyers, while in the mere sprinkling of government officials it was lower than the Jiyuto and Minshuto.

Like its political competitors, the Shakaito relied upon its older men with prewar experience for leadership and guidance. Of the officials who held key posts in the party machinery before the split in 1951, none was below the age of forty, 25 per cent were above sixty, and half had served in the House of Representatives before 1945. Lawyers were the predominant occupational category, followed closely by journalists and publishers, labor leaders, and educators, and by a smaller proportion of business executives and bureaucrats.

Roughly the same pattern is revealed by an analysis of the Shakaito leaders who served in postwar cabinets under that label. They were older than the Jiyuto ministers, but younger than the Minshuto appointees. Eighty per cent of them had served in prewar Diets. Labor leaders were foremost in the occupational breakdowns, with lawyers and educators also appearing with great frequency. Journalists and publishers were not so well represented in cabinet circles as they were in the hierarchy of the party itself.

The ideological core of all Shakaito elements is genuinely socialist, and the content of their program is more clearly enunciated than that of the other parties. All factions espouse a planned economic system based upon socialist principles. They endorse unitedly such goals as the nationalization or government control of key industries, the heavy taxation of upper-income groups, and the redistribution of land. Factory legislation and welfare measures, including social insurance, old-age pensions, minimum wage, and loans to small entrepreneurs, likewise find ready acceptance in all Shakaito camps.[30] Although committed to the defense of the monarchy, the members of the party became the disciples of democratic reform, which brought them close to the objectives of SCAP. The Shakaito stood in unison on the abolition of the Privy Council and the vesting of some imperial power in the Diet; they envisioned the democratization of the family system and the reform of legal codes; they called for the healthy development of trade unionism and the defense of political liberty. These basic attitudes, common to the influential leaders of all Shakaito factions, have impelled the party to resist changes in the new constitution and the revision of the labor laws. The party has stoutly opposed, as potential threats to the movement, the outlawing of the Kyosanto and legislation against subversives.[31] It was the Shakaito's stand on the role of labor, fiscal policy, and the question of civil rights that brought the party into sharp contention with Occupation authorities.

The list of goals upon which Shakaito factions are in general agreement is impressive, and when viewed in juxtaposition to the basic ideals of SCAP, the outlook for reform takes on a faint glimmer of promise. But in postwar years it is the area of disagreement in the Shakaito that has been of strategic significance. The basic differences among factions within the organization have limited the effectiveness of the party's role in and out of power, indirectly strengthening the hand of their opponents on either side. The Shakaito has suffered from many of the ills with which European Socialists have been afflicted, but the evil of disunity has been compounded in a Japanese setting with its long tradition of personal leadership and political factionalism. Apart from the conflict of personalities, the differences among the Shakaito membership arise over the interpretation of their common principles, the timing of their socialization, and the tactics of cooperation with other parties. Especially bothersome has been the dispute over the nature of their political organization: a "class" party with education for socialism as the principal aim, or a "national" party appealing to more than the proletariat and willing to modify doctrine in its bid for political power.[32]

Like the old Minshuto, the Japanese Socialists occupy a middle position in the political continuum; the schisms are intensified by the constant lure of the conservatives on the right and the enticements of the Communists on the left. The bitterness engendered by problems of doctrine and strategy when a socialist party seeks to become politically effective was dramatically illustrated by Katayama's ministerial venture in 1947. At that time the Shakaito headed a coalition government, the associated elements of which were so hostile to doctrinaire socialism that they insisted upon the exclusion of left-wing radicals from the cabinet. This left the Socialist ministry without the representation of its militant faction, to whom the program was a religion, and under the handicap of the lukewarm leadership of its moderate wing. In these circumstances the emasculation of the Shakaito pro-

317

gram was not unexpected. Katayama and his Socialist colleagues sought Diet approval for the public control of the coal-mining industry, hoping to use this experience with state ownership as a test case for a broadened program of nationalization.[33] In its final form the statute was a control measure in name only. Their Minshuto partners in the cabinet swelled the Jiyuto opposition, and the Shakaito was forced to accept diluted legislation or vacate its ministerial leadership. The failure of this effort opened the right wing to the charge that in their alliance with conservative parties they were placing ambition for office above socialist principles. In establishing the ministry Katayama and his followers accepted a share in the responsibility for government, at the same time realizing that their minority position would necessitate a compromise of their socialism with Minshuto conservatism in the formation of state policy. If it had refused governmental responsibility until assured of a Diet majority favorable to its ideological principles, the Shakaito would have entered the political wilderness for an indefinite period. In self-imposed exile from governmental power its influence might still be important, but essentially negative in approach. In office, even under the restraint of coalition, the party's strength could be exerted positively, and its leaders, in getting the feel of administering a government, were in less danger of becoming divorced from political reality by doctrinal isolation.

Many of the left-wing dogmatists, however, do not endorse with enthusiasm the philosophy of compromise. Frequently their program has not been tempered by a realistic appraisal of the problems facing the nation. To them the Shakaito is "different" and ought not to contaminate its doctrine by political adventures with conservative heretics. Alliances with the parties of the right endangered the future of the Socialist organization, since the militants, who faithfully supported their party and its doctrine, were repelled by such behavior. They would rather fight a slower educational battle in a truly socialist party in opposition than enjoy the amenities and temptations of office at the sacrifice of sacred principles. The saints in opposition hinted that the alarming drop from 143 Shakaito seats in the House of Representatives in 1947 to 48 in 1949 was due to the failure of the Katayama cabinet to stick to its ideological guns.

While none of the influential members of the Shakaito is inclined to the use of violence, some elements of the left wing have come under syndicalist influence. They contend that organized labor is within its rights in conducting demonstrations and strikes to influence political action, since such efforts may gain economic ends attainable in no other way. Consequently, they have accented trade union activity as an important force outside the Diet to be used for the pursuit of working-class objectives. On the other hand, the rightists, whose strength in the parliament for a time was greater than their influence in trade union circles, emphasized the role of the Diet in social reform and urged restraint upon the activities of labor in the interest of economic stability.

Another source of disturbance within the Shakaito has been the question of its relations with the Communist party. In the opening years of the Occupation the rising cost of living inspired wage demands by the trade unions, the more militant of which had unfortunately come under Communist domination. The Shakaito leadership, right-wing in political complexion, was well aware of the Communist menace, but it could not ignore the legitimate demands of labor and allow the articulation of those demands to go to the Kyosanto by default. The Communist plan for a united front met with the sympathy of a segment of the left-wing faction. In 1947, however, the failure of the labor offensive brought a relaxation of Communist pressure, and co-operation between Communist and non-Communist unions declined thereafter. Such liaison was never officially sanctioned by the Shakaito, and in May 1947 the leftists themselves publicly repudiated suggestions of a united front. Under right-wing control until 1949, the Shakaito continued to resist the overtures of the Kyosanto, and in the electoral campaign the Communists attacked both the right and left wings of the party.[34]

After the fall of the Katayama government — the only Socialist-led cabinet Japan has had thus far — the left-wing influence grew stronger in Shakaito councils, and the size of its delegation in the Diet ultimately expanded. The bitter struggle for the control of the party machinery, brought to a head by issues of doctrine, strained the consensus of such a heterogeneous federation, and in 1951 precipitated the breakup of the organization. Japan's foreign policy in the cold war was the immediate problem which put Socialist principles to the practical test. For more than a year the Shakaito as a party had stood firmly behind its "three principles": a general peace treaty (including

319

China and the Soviet Union), a policy of "neutralism" in the East-West conflict, and hostility to any agreement which would allow a foreign power to build military bases on Japanese soil.[35] The worsening international picture, as revealed by the Korean war and the apparent hopelessness of negotiating an over-all peace treaty, encouraged the right-wing and neutral elements of the Shakaito to review the party platform. On the question of a separate peace and certain aspects of national defense, the moderate Socialists moved closer to the conservative parties. The Shakaito thus reached a difficult fork in the ideological road. The Uha Shakaito turned right and reluctantly took an uncomfortable seat on the outskirts of the Western camp; the Saha Shakaito kept on its leftward path, looking hopefully toward the Indian brand of neutrality and an Asian "third force."

Despite the deep schism, the two Socialist factions continue to look upon some problems through the same spectacles. They, like many of their conservative opponents, support the establishment of trade relations with Communist China and the Soviet Union. The rightists, however, would restrict the export of military items; and the leftists are insistent upon the negotiation of peace treaties with those nations.[36] Both of the factions oppose rearmament and the revision of Article 9 (the renunciation of war clause) of the constitution. The Shakaito of the Right, however, lays claim to "realism" in foreign policy, conceding that rearmament may eventually be necessary, but placing its immediate trust in the United Nations and in limited defense forces without conscription. The Shakaito of the Left is resolute in its opposition to rearmament in all forms and would dissolve the existing defense establishment; neutrality remains its answer to the cold war. The two groups speak of "independence" and "autonomy" in diplomacy, extending their criticism to the security alliance with the United States. Although the right-wing faction supported the peace treaty, the leftists voted against a separate peace and the agreement with America when these matters came up in the Diet.[37]

The left-wing element still firmly resists the enticements of the Communists, although the two are frequently on the same side of a policy question. After leftist leaders won control of the Shakaito in 1949, they rejected the idea of the united front, and they continued to veto such a proposal after the establishment of the Saha Shakaito. The persistent rebuffs to the Kyosanto are an index of the party's attitude, for the independence of the left wing has been frequently imperiled by Communist strategy. In 1955, for example, the Communists withdrew their candidates in selected areas so that the Saha Shakaito might be an indebted beneficiary. It was also to the advantage of the Kyosanto to aid in the election of enough leftists to prevent a constitutional amendment legalizing rearmament. While some individuals who appear to be sympathetic to communism are to be found in the ranks of the left-wing Socialists, it would be unfair to categorize the group itself as a society of fellow travelers. The views of most of the members more nearly approach those of Aneurin Bevan in the British Labour party. Conversely, the leaders of the rightist faction regard themselves as following the lead of Clement Attlee and the majority wing of their British counterpart. However, one important difference is immediately evident: the right-wing Socialists in Britain enjoy the solid support of the trade unions, and this concentration of power has helped to hold the political movement together. In Japan, the ranks of the trade unions have been more disunited than the Shakaito itself, and important segments of union support go to the leftists. Some of the labor organizations, seeking to make the party a vehicle of the proletariat exclusively, have been notoriously rigid in political matters and hostile toward compromise with the right wing. In their struggle for the control of the Shakaito machinery, the leftist politicians have often reflected the doctrinaire attitude of their unions to prevent the alienation of their working-class support. Thus the antagonisms between left and right over the backing of the trade unions and ultimately over the capture of the party have exacerbated ideological differences and placed great obstacles in the way of a merger.[38] The complex of interpersonal relations and trade union dissension, linked with varying intensities of doctrinal commitment, have greatly weakened the Socialist movement and made it an easier target for conservative weapons.

Kyosanto (Communist Party)

The peak of Kyosanto electoral success came in 1949 when widespread discontent with the Katayama and Ashida ministries gave the Communists 9.6 per cent of the popular vote and placed thirty-five of their members in the House of Representatives. Thereafter Communist popularity dwindled to a low of 1 per cent in 1953, rising to

2 per cent in the 1955 election. The popular vote of the Kyosanto has averaged 3.7 per cent in all postwar contests for lower-house seats.

Like the Socialist party, the Kyosanto gathers its principal support from the urban electorate, with some appeal to the tenantry and small proprietors in the rural areas. In the 1947 and 1949 elections for the House of Representatives, the party showed persistent strength in one moderately urban and three predominantly urban prefectures; it also revealed consistent support in one moderately agrarian province and three that are chiefly agrarian. In the two elections the Kyosanto's twenty best prefectures included eight that are mainly urban, two moderately so, three moderately rural, and seven predominantly rural.[39] The pattern was roughly the same in the 1955 contest. At that time the party exhibited its greatest strength in the urban prefectures of Osaka, Kyoto, Tokyo, Kanagawa, and Aichi, and in semi-urban Hokkaido; its rural strongholds were Niigata, Nagano, and Shimane.[40] In 1950 the membership of the Kyosanto was distributed in similar urban-rural proportions; it was highest in one semiurban and four urban prefectures, and in one moderately rural and three chiefly rural provinces.[41]

The analysis of any Communist party presents special difficulties because of the nature of the organization and the understandable reluctance of the comrades to disclose details about its structure and methods. Nevertheless, a glance at the Politburo membership in 1947, noting those characteristics upon which some data are available, may give a general indication of leadership trends in the Japanese Communist party. The members of this strategic body were young men, ranging in age from thirty-six to fifty-six, with the majority in their forties; yet none was a newcomer to the Kyosanto fold, all being tested veterans of the prewar struggle to keep the party alive. Some of these key officials had served a period of tutelage in Moscow. More than half the leaders had been graduated from or studied at college or university, and they classified themselves into such middle-class occupations as journalists, writers, or lawyers. As with the leadership of many left-wing organizations, the members of the Politburo were many years removed from workbench and plow.

The Kyosanto is Marxist-Leninist-Stalinist, interpreting and preaching the gospels of the Communist trinity. Its members regard themselves as the true exponents of "democracy," and their party as the only vehicle for uprooting the feudal and bureaucratic evils which beset the nation. Their aims, policies, and tactics are patterned after those of orthodox Communist parties in other countries. They have demonstrated the same ability to manipulate the flexible doctrine according to the demands of the local situation when possible, or the dictates of the Cominform when necessary. In its frequent disregard of the cultural sentiments and deep emotional attachments of the Japanese people, the Kyosanto has displayed the same lack of political finesse and misplaced sense of timing as its European counterparts.

The Communists took full advantage of the political rights granted in the opening days of the Occupation. Untainted by the purge, the party seized the opportunity to strengthen its hold upon the masses, increasing its power by legal means. The Communists made their appeals attractive by camouflaging their aims in a program of moderate reform by "peaceful" methods. The new social order, to be won in parliament and not on the barricades, called for land reform, the liquidation of monopoly capitalism, and the liberation of small merchants and manufacturers from bureaucratic tyranny. The early programs of the party eschewed full-blown communism, tactfully omitting such items as the abolition of private property.[42] The popularity of the Communist appeal, however, was considerably offset by their disavowal of the emperor system.[43] In the Kyosanto view, the divine institution was merely the anchor of the bureaucracy designed to work the will of irresponsible officials behind the imperial façade. The Communists demanded its replacement by a "people's republic." To keep its train on the "nationalist" track, the Kyosanto proclaimed its desire to be "loved by the people" and de-emphasized its link with international communism. Shortly after his release from prison in 1945, Tokuda Kyuichi intimated that the Nippon Kyosanto should have no relations with the Soviet Union and should reject its offers of monetary assistance. In late 1947, both Tokuda and Nozaka denied that the formation of the Cominform would affect the policies and procedures of the Japanese organization.[44] It soon became apparent that the disavowal of external control was a pronouncement of mythical independence for popular consumption. In 1950, when the Cominform cracked its disciplinary whip, the wayward Kyosanto danced in trembling subordination.

By heralding its "nationalist" appeals in newspaper columns and on streetcorners, the Communists sought to bury their roots in the popular favor. In the initial phase of the Occupation, the Kyosanto profited from the milieu of reform which followed in the wake of military disaster, and its fortunes rose slightly with the tide of social change. As the Occupation lingered, however, the party began to articulate the popular reaction against the extremes of westernization. Sensing the growing frustration of the Japanese, the Communists opposed the imitation of "foreign culture" and called for an early withdrawal of Occupation troops. One of their most successful techniques was the infiltration of labor unions and agricultural associations. As in other countries, the party aimed at the expansion of its political influence through the manipulation of mass organizations. This strategy made possible a degree of control disproportionate to the number of actual Communists in Japan. The success of the Kyosanto endeavor in this early period was measured by the number of trade unions under its domination, the steady increase of party members, and the thirty-five comrades who went to the House of Representatives in 1949.

After 1949, however, the Kyosanto entered a period of rapid decline. The anti-Communist policy of the government, encouraged by SCAP, restricted the propaganda activities of the party and drove its qualified leaders into hiding. In spite of its dedication to "peaceful revolution," the extreme measures of the Kyosanto aroused popular disfavor and provoked opposition elements to challenge the Communist leadership of important unions. The rude behavior of Soviet-indoctrinated repatriates, who had been strategically returned to their homeland, also stimulated a healthy suspicion of Kyosanto policies. The party suffered another setback in January 1950 when the Cominform denounced Nozaka's strategy of peaceful reform as a service to American imperialism. Nozaka reluctantly confessed the error of his ways, and the party admitted its obligation to follow the Cominform line.[45] Factional recrimination, however, continued for several years, and the organization was noticeably weakened. An ex-Communist, Nabeyama Sadachika, recently set forth the dilemma of the non-Russian Communist:

My conversion [from Communism] was the result of my going back to racialism. Unwittingly, I have been endeavoring to find my place in the world of class-consciousness, hoping to find the advance and liberation of humanity therein. Theoretically speaking, the formation of a single-class world ultimately leads to internationalism without any center. Internationalism is a prerequisite in the Communist ideology. However, when Communist internationalism is applied to this world, it cannot exist without a center, but it becomes an internationalism with the Soviet as its center.

It is natural that the class viewpoint should become the Soviet viewpoint. Once I approved such a theory. The Soviet is but the Soviet, and not representative of the world's proletariats. It only represents territory where the proletariat won its first victory . . . To protect and support the Soviet policy constitutes no problem of setting one state against another, but a problem of setting one class against another. Therefore, to obey the instructions from Moscow at the expense of one's own country contributes certainly to the growth of the proletariat class therein, for the benefit of Soviet Russia, but never for the prosperity of that other country.[46]

The clear subjection of the Kyosanto to international discipline brought a reversal of policy and platform. The party claim to autonomy was replaced by an avowedly international orientation within which an alignment with the Soviet bloc was openly sanctioned.[47] On the domestic front, moderation was abandoned for extremism and direct action. Riots and demonstrations, generally with an anti-American coloration, became more frequent and increasingly violent. With an underground organization structured along military lines, the party resorted to arson, sabotage, and killing. In several noteworthy "incidents" the Communists used Molotov cocktails, acid bombs, strong-arm squads, and similar weapons.[48]

The irresponsible militance of Kyosanto groups stirred considerable popular resentment, which was reflected in the Communist failures in the 1952, 1953, and 1955 elections. Perceiving the inadequacy of its methods, the high command of the party modified its tactics to combine underground activity with propaganda appeals by legal means. The subsequent decline in violence was accompanied by a switch to the formula of the united front. Nurturing the tensions developed by the Occupation, the Kyosanto accented its anti-American theme. The Communists pictured Japan as the object of American imperialism, Yoshida as the arm of the conqueror, and Japanese problems as the result of United States policy. Consistent with this motif is the current demand for the withdrawal of United States forces, the elimination of military bases, and the rejection of American aid.[49]

The "peace" offensive has been a parallel theme of the Nippon Kyosanto. The party has consistently opposed rearmament and the revision of the "war clause" of the constitution. The dissolution of the security force is also high on its list of priorities. Capitalizing upon pro-Chinese sentiment in Japan, the Communists agitate for increased trade with the Asian mainland and the normalization of diplomatic relations with China and the Soviet Union.[50] Tailored to fit the grievances of the ordinary citizen, these appeals by an irresponsible party become more effective when legitimate political organizations are identified with scandal and general incompetence. Should the open appeals to anti-American sentiment and the desire for peace prove ineffective, however, the party is preparing for aggressive action at other levels. There is some evidence to indicate the buildup of the Kyosanto structure underground, including the formation of military units. Although a potential danger, the resort of the Communists to armed insurrection on a large scale does not appear to be an immediate threat.[51]

Notes

[1] The Jiyuto strongholds in these elections were as follows: 1947 — Chiba, Kochi, Saitama, Wakayama, Shizuoka, Yamagata, Iwate, Shiga, Okayama, Miyagi; 1949 — Yamaguchi, Kagoshima, Saitama, Iwate, Chiba, Shizuoka, Ehime, Gifu, Ibaraki, Fukushima. A prefecture in which more than 50 per cent of the population lives in cities is considered predominantly urban, 28–50 per cent moderately urban. Predominantly rural areas are those in which fewer than 20 per cent of the inhabitants live in cities, and moderately rural are those in which 20–28 per cent of the people live in urban centers. These election results, and similar breakdowns for the other parties treated in this chapter, have been tabulated from the returns listed in Department of State, *The 1949 Japanese House of Representatives Election*, OIR Report No. 5022, September 1, 1949, Appendix A, Tables 2 and 3.

[2] In this chapter an attempt has been made to examine the leadership of the major parties as evidenced in the following categories: composition of the House of Representatives caucus in 1947, party men who held cabinet portfolios under the label of their organization from 1946 to 1955, and the men who were in key positions in the party structure in 1951. It is not contended that the House of Representatives election in 1947 was typical of postwar contests. A "normal" election may not have been held until 1955, if then. All that is attempted here is a comparison of the membership of respective party caucuses in 1947. Party officials were selected as of 1951, the last year till October 1955 in which the Shakaito was intact. However, the party men in all the postwar cabinets since 1946 have been included in the comparisons. An analysis of this type is complicated by the inadequacies of some of the biographical data, including the generalized nature of many occupational classifications. There is, of course, more information available on cabinet and party leaders than small fry Diet members; however, the pitfalls of an analysis along this line are so numerous that the results can hardly make a claim to infallibility. Nevertheless the available data on major personalities may serve as a useful guide, though a crude one, to changes in party leadership within a given organization (such as the Jiyuto) and to differences in the composition

of such leadership among the several parties. The biographical data have been drawn from the Department of State election analyses, newspapers, standard *Who's Who* references, and the biographical sections of such books as Evelyn S. Colbert, *The Left Wing in Japanese Politics* (New York, 1952). In considering the age factor, the calculations were made as of 1948 when two or more parties were being compared. Roughly the same proportion of business magnates in the Jiyuto caucus in the House of Representatives was reported by Japanese newspapers in the 1953 election (see *Mainichi*, overseas edition, September 15, 1953; *Nippon Times*, April 22, 1953).

[3] SCAP, *Monthly Summation of Non-Military Activities in Japan and Korea*, November 1945, p. 31; January 1946, p. 29.

[4] *Yomiuri Shimbun*, reported in *Nippon Times*, March 17, 1949.

[5] SCAP, *Monthly Summation*, March 1947, p. 28; August 1947, pp. 52–53; March 1948, pp. 43–44; *Nippon Times*, April 25, 1946; March 12, 1947; April 14, 1951; Liberal party platform, *Yomiuri Shimbun*, reprinted in *Digest Service*, June 24, 1947, pp. 20–22.

[6] Liberal party platform, *Yomiuri Shimbun*, reprinted in *Digest Service*, June 24, 1947, pp. 20–22; *Nippon Times*, October 20, 1948; March 25, 1949; *Asahi Evening News*, January 25, 1955.

[7] SCAP, *Monthly Summation*, September–October 1945, p. 31; November 1945, p. 31; March 1948, pp. 43–44; *Nippon Times*, May 23, December 3, 1948; February 17, 1949; May 25, 1951; March 5, August 16, 1952; February 17, 1954.

[8] *Nippon Times*, January 21, 1951; S. Hasegawa, "Japanese Politics behind the Scene," *ibid.*, September 22, 1952; *Nippon Times*, July 18, 1950; September 29, 1952; February 4, October 18, November 4, 1953; editorial, "Election Issues," *ibid.*, March 19, 1953; *Asahi Evening News*, January 25, 1955.

[9] *Asahi Evening News*, August 16, December 23, 1954; January 31, 1955.

[10] The Minshuto strongholds in the two elections were as follows: 1947 — Fukui, Hyogo, Shimane, Kagoshima, Ishikawa, Gumma, Ehime, Kyoto, Tochigi, Kumamoto; 1949 — Kumamoto, Fukui, Gumma, Shimane, Kyoto, Aomori, Saga, Kagawa, Akita, Ishikawa.

[11] *Asahi Evening News*, March 5, 1955.

[12] *Nippon Times*, March 25, 1947; editorial, "A New Party is Born," *ibid.*, April 3, 1947; *Nippon Times*, April 29, 1950.

[13] *Nippon Times*, June 14–15, 1952. Although Shigemitsu does not applaud the efforts of the "Young Turks" in the party, his presidential address attempted to define the philosophy of the new organization.

[14] *Ibid.*, April 1, 1947; March 15, 1947; Democratic party platform, *Yomiuri Shimbun*, reprinted in *Digest Service*, June 24, 1947, pp. 22–23.

[15] Democratic party platform, *Yomiuri Shimbun*, reprinted in *Digest Service*, June 24, 1947, pp. 22–23; SCAP, *Monthly Summation*, February 1948, pp. 37–38.

[16] SCAP, *Monthly Summation*, January 1948, pp. 38–39; Democratic party platform, *Yomiuri Shimbun*, reprinted in *Digest Service*, June 24, 1947, pp. 23–24; *Nippon Times*, March 15, 1947; April 29, 1950.

[17] *Asahi Evening News*, December 11, 1954; January 6, 17, 21, 1955. Shortly after his re-election as premier, Hatoyama defended his plan to reduce direct taxes and to raise indirect levies, if more revenue was needed (*ibid.*, April 28, 1955).

[18] *Ibid.*, March 7, 1955.

[19] *Nippon Times*, July 30, 1946.

[20] *Asahi Nenkan* (Asahi Year Book), 1951, pp. 173–174.

[21] *Nippon Times*, April 29, 1950; January 21, 1951; February 9, 1952; *Asahi Evening News*, November 24, December 13, 1954; February 25, 1955.

[22] *Asahi Evening News*, February 12, 1955.

[23] *Nippon Times*, January 23, 1951; June 1, 14, 1952; September 17, 1952.

[24] *Ibid.*, June 14, 1952; editorial, "Election Issues," *ibid.*, March 19, 1953; *Asahi Evening News*, January 25, 1955.

[25] *Asahi Evening News*, November 24, 1954; December 17–18, 20–21, 1954; January 20, 25, 1955; *Nippon Times*, June 14, 1952.

[26] J. Saffell, "Japan's Post-war Socialist Party," *American Political Science Review*, XLII (October 1948), 959.

[27] *Asahi Evening News*, January 18–19, 1955. Evelyn S. Colbert (*op. cit.* in note 2) gives a reliable, factual, uncolored account which includes the development of the Shakaito up to 1949.

[28] The areas of Shakaito strength in the two elections were as follows: 1947 — Kyoto, Kanagawa, Tokyo, Fukuoka, Shimane, Yamanashi, Tottori, Osaka, Kagawa, Hiroshima; 1949 — Tottori, Shimane, Kanagawa, Fukuoka, Tokyo, Kagawa, Shiga, Gumma, Miyagi, Hiroshima, Akita.

[29] The ten Shakaito prefectures in 1955 were Fukuoka, Shizuoka, Kanagawa, Hokkaido, Tokyo, Kyoto, Osaka, Shiga, Niigata, Miyagi, Hyogo.

[30] *Nippon Times*, April 25, October 1, 1946; March 7, 1947; October 5, 1953.

[31] *Ibid.*, May 2, 1947; January 19, 1949; June 10, October 3, 1950; May 9, July 12, 1952; March 27, 1954; *Asahi Evening News*, February 25, 1955.

[32] *Nippon Times*, January 21, 1950; H. Nomura, "The Proposed Socialist Merger," *Asahi Evening News*, June 17, 1955.

[33] *Nippon Times*, May 2, 1947.

[34] *Ibid.*, May 16, 1947.

[35] *Ibid.*, January 21, 1948; June 10, 1950; January 21, 1951.

[36] *Asahi Evening News*, January 25, 1955.

[37] *Ibid.*; I. Asanuma, "Right-wing Social Democratic Party," *Sekai*, reprinted in *Contemporary Japan*, XXI (1952), 302–304; *Nippon Times*, January 21, August 23, 1951; April 15, 1953; January 23, 1954. For the party votes on the peace treaty and the security pact, see *Nippon Times*, October 27, 1951.

[38] *Nippon Times*, March 12, 1951; H. Nomura, "Why No Socialist Merger?" *Asahi Evening News*, August 20, 1954.

[39] The major sources of Kyosanto support in the two elections were as follows: 1947 — Tokyo, Nagano, Ishikawa, Osaka, Shimane, Kanagawa, Tottori, Okayama, Saitama, Akita; 1949 — Osaka, Tokyo, Tottori, Kanagawa, Nagano, Kyoto, Saitama, Yamaguchi, Ishikawa, Shimane.

[40] *Asahi Evening News*, March 2, 1955.

[41] The membership figures, as compiled by a Special Investigating Bureau of the Attorney General's Office, were as follows: Tokyo, 13,320; Chiba, 4,542; Osaka, 4,390; Niigata, 4,362; Hokkaido, 4,190; Fukuoka, 3,963; Nagano, 3,755; Kanagawa, 3,640; Ibaraki, 3,473 (*Nippon Times*, August 9, 1950).

[42] *Ibid.*, February 13, 1946; June 15, 1947; February 9, 1949. The Kyosanto at one time expressed a willingness to enter a cabinet which included conservative parties (SCAP, *Monthly Summation*, May 1946, p. 25).

[43] *Nippon Times*, January 9, 1946; *Mainichi*, January 7, 1947, translated in SCAP, Allied Translator and Interpreter Service, *Press Translations and Summaries*, January 7, 1947; II: 2, p. 2.

[44] *Tokyo Shimbun*, reprinted in *Japan Review*, January 23, 1948, p. 2. Nozaka's view that it was practicable to develop a socialist state by democratic methods, even during the Occupation, was at that time accepted by the Kyosanto. For other statements of independence see Paul Langer and Rodger Swearingen, "The Japanese Communist Party, the Soviet Union, and Korea," *Pacific Affairs*, XXIII (1950), 345–350.

[45] *Ibid.*; see also S. Nabeyama, "Problems for Socialists and Communists," *Contemporary Japan*, XIX (1950), 35–40. Some documents on the incident may be found in *Nippon Times*, January 10, 1950.

[46] Quoted in review of Nabeyama's autobiography, *Watakushi-wa Kyosanto-o Suteta*, in *Contemporary Japan*, XIX (1950), 124–125.

[47] On the change in Kyosanto policy and the implications of the shift, see Rodger Swearingen, "The Communist Line in Japan," *Far Eastern Survey*, XXIII (April 1954), 56–61.

[48] The most thorough treatment of the Kyosanto available in English is Rodger Swearingen and Paul Langer, *Red Flag in Japan* (Cambridge 1952). For an analysis of Communist methods see *Nippon Times*, December 11, 1951.

[49] Rodger Swearingen, "The Communist Line in Japan," pp. 58–59; *Nippon Times*, April 15, 1953, December 12, 1954; H. Nomura, "Watch the Communists," *Asahi Evening News*, February 4, 1955.

[50] K. Hosokawa, "Japanese Communist Party," *Sekai*, reprinted in *Contemporary Japan*, XXI (1952), 306–307; *Nippon Times*, April 15, 1953; *Asahi Evening News*, January 25, 1955.

[51] Rodger Swearingen, "The Communist Line in Japan," p. 61.

21

Major Political Parties
III: Organization

In WESTERN society the visible structure of political parties is modified by an intricate network of personal relations and informal organization. The oligarchical and dualistic tendencies of most party
organization are, of course, intensified in the Japanese cultural setting.
This is to be expected in a culture where dualism characterizes so
much of the social behavior and where hierarchical control has not
been tempered by broad experience with democratic institutions. In
Japan each political party has an elaborate display of committees and
agencies, frequently overlapping in function. But effective political
power often is wielded behind the scenes by experienced and dominant
leaders whose prestige commands greater allegiance than do party
regulations and formal structures. The persistence of long-established
cultural traditions is illustrated by the tendency of the parties in postwar Japan to follow the organizational patterns established by their
prewar ancestors.[1]

Party Convention

At the apex of the formal party structure is the annual convention,
or general meeting.[2] This body, which is the constituent and legislative authority of each political organization, generally meets during
the December-January recess of the Diet before the parliament settles
down to its serious work. In a conservative party the conference is
convened by the president, who is also empowered to call it into
extraordinary session. Although Jiyuto rules were silent on the matter,

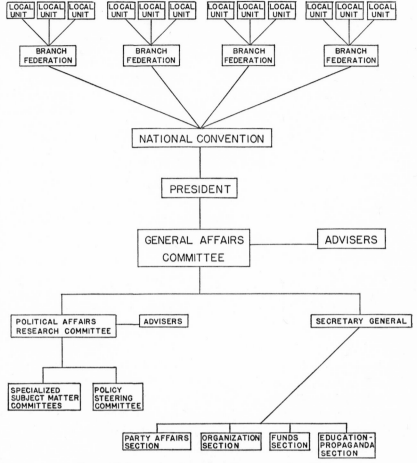

General Organization of a Conservative Party

the Minshuto leader was required to summon the convention into special session upon the petition of one-third of the members or a majority of the party caucus in the Diet. In the Shakaito organization, the general meeting is called by the Central Executive Committee, which may also convene extraordinary sessions and is required to do so when more than half of the provincial federations demand it. Kyosanto rules provide for an annual mass meeting, with provision for special sessions upon the call of the Central Committee or the request of one-third of the membership of the previous convention. In line with developments in other Communist parties, however, the

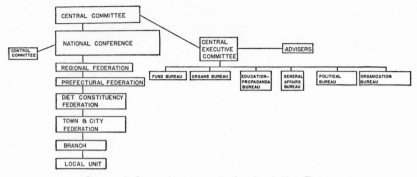

General Organization of the Socialist Party

annual meeting has not been convened with legal regularity, and it is common practice for several years to elapse between sessions.

The party conferences are usually made up of Diet members, former Diet members, headquarters officials, and representatives of the branch units. The latter are frequently the local officials of the organization. In each party the prefecture is the unit of rank-and-file representation. The Central Committee of the Kyosanto is responsible for the apportionment of Communist delegates and the election procedure, and it is thus in a position to wield considerable influence upon the makeup and composition of the annual meeting. The Socialists determine the size of their prefectural delegations on the basis of paid-up membership. In 1950 the convention was attended by 512 regional delegates, including approximately 50 party members who were serving in the Diet.[3] The Jiyuto invited three representatives from each prefectural federation. Using the three-delegate ratio as a base, the Minshuto gave bonus representation to those prefectures that had won election victories, and it authorized the president, with the consent of the General Affairs Committee, to appoint convention delegates from those areas where local organization was embryonic. Appointment rather than election of prefectural delegates has been the common practice, especially in the conservative parties.

In actual operation the conventions of the Jiyuto and Minshuto were not of so great importance as a reading of the party rules would suggest. The conservative parties generally meet for a shorter period, and they select fewer of their officials at the annual meeting than the Shakaito. That only the president was chosen by the Jiyuto conference reflected the strong tradition of personal leadership in that organiza-

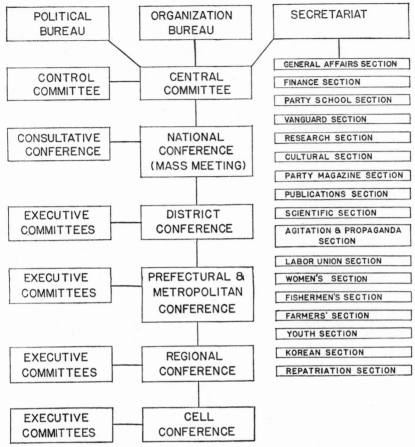

POLITICAL BUREAU	ORGANIZATION BUREAU	SECRETARIAT
		GENERAL AFFAIRS SECTION
CONTROL COMMITTEE	CENTRAL COMMITTEE	FINANCE SECTION
		PARTY SCHOOL SECTION
		VANGUARD SECTION
CONSULTATIVE CONFERENCE	NATIONAL CONFERENCE (MASS MEETING)	RESEARCH SECTION
		CULTURAL SECTION
		PARTY MAGAZINE SECTION
		PUBLICATIONS SECTION
EXECUTIVE COMMITTEES	DISTRICT CONFERENCE	SCIENTIFIC SECTION
		AGITATION & PROPAGANDA SECTION
		LABOR UNION SECTION
EXECUTIVE COMMITTEES	PREFECTURAL & METROPOLITAN CONFERENCE	WOMEN'S SECTION
		FISHERMEN'S SECTION
		FARMERS' SECTION
		YOUTH SECTION
EXECUTIVE COMMITTEES	REGIONAL CONFERENCE	KOREAN SECTION
		REPATRIATION SECTION
EXECUTIVE COMMITTEES	CELL CONFERENCE	

General Organization of the Communist Party

tion. The Minshuto theoretically filled its major offices at the annual meeting, including the president, vice-president, Supreme Committee, and the auditors. However, the conferences of both right-wing parties frequently diluted their formal power by giving perfunctory approval to leaders who had already been agreed upon in factional bargaining. The successful officials had a wider power of appointment in filling subordinate posts than their Socialist counterparts. A right-wing conference also receives brief reports from its officers and passes resolutions which outline the party stand on major issues. The proceedings, however, have been notoriously sterile, often dominated by the Diet members at the expense of the local delegates. Rarely are controversial issues brought to the convention rostrum so that a teller vote becomes necessary. For example, at the Jiyuto conference in 1951 the rearmament question and the proposed security pact with the United States — the two burning issues of the day — were neither debated nor voted upon by the delegates. An open discussion in party conference exposes schism to public gaze and is apt to result in a face-losing vote. For that reason controversial issues are generally ironed out in Diet caucuses or in meetings of the party executive.

The convention proceedings of the Shakaito are less stereotyped, and the delegates have a greater voice in decision-making. Proposals formulated by the Central Executive Committee are first sent to the federation branches for preliminary discussion, and then submitted to the convention for final approval. Reports on party affairs, finance, and Diet matters are received by the delegates, and there is some opportunity for questioning by rank-and-file members. In addition, the Shakaito conference actually chooses more of its officials and major committees than the conventions of other parties. The right and left wings bitterly contested for the control of the party machinery until the final rupture into two separate organizations in 1951. Just as the competition of Socialist parties in Europe has influenced the development and structure of the conservative organizations, the Jiyuto and, more particularly, the Minshuto in Japan tended to imitate the Shakaito in the conduct of their annual conventions.

The legal functions of the Kyosanto conference include the hearing of reports from executive organs, the formulation of policy, the amendment of party rules, and the election of members to the two major committees. As is universally true of Communist parties in other countries, however, the fact that effective political power resides in the Central Committee and its Politburo limits the authority of the mass meeting. The annual conference, which chooses the party executive, is in effect constituted by that executive. Furthermore, Kyosanto regulations prohibit the convention from removing more than one-fifth of the Central Committee membership, and they make conference resolutions subject to the confirmation of the Central Committee.

Each political organization has provided for a decision-making organ to deliberate upon matters of urgency between sessions of the annual conference. In the Jiyuto such crises were handled by the Diet Members' Assembly, a joint caucus of all Jiyuto representatives in both chambers. The decisions of the Assembly had to be approved by a subsequent party convention. Both the Jiyuto conference and its Diet caucus could delegate deliberative responsibility to the General Affairs Board, which was the executive council of the party. In the Minshuto the organ second in the hierarchy of policy-making agencies was the General Affairs Committee, composed of some thirty important party leaders. In the Shakaito interconference decisions are the responsibility of the Central Committee. The Committee, with a membership of approximately two hundred including the headquarters staff,[4] is called into session by a smaller body, the Central Executive Committee. The latter is required to call a meeting within a month if one-third of the members demand it. Liaison between the Central Committee and the Central Executive Committee is achieved by having the same person serve as chairman of both bodies. In the Kyosanto the legally responsible agency between annual meetings is likewise a Central Committee, a small body of approximately twenty members but including all the top leaders of the party. This Communist organ may summon a special national conference, which is a microcosm of the mass meeting and which possesses the same theoretical powers.

Party Directorate

The most powerful organ in each of the major parties is an executive committee, performing essentially the same function in each organization but operating in each case under a different name. This directorate, embracing the principal leaders of the party, is the *de facto* policy-making body as well as the center of party administration. The political importance of the executive agency places a premium upon membership, necessitating the representation of geographical and factional interests in rough proportion to their political strength. The size of the committee is periodically expanded to give representation to splinter groups which may be enticed into formal affiliation with the party.

In the Jiyuto the executive committee, known as the General Affairs Board, was made up of thirty directors. The majority of the directors were co-opted from Jiyuto members of the Diet who were grouped for the purpose into nine geographical regions and the directors chosen in proportion to the party strength in each area. In addition, the president was empowered to select no more than ten directors, not necessarily Diet members. In 1952 the Board consisted of twelve members elected by Jiyuto parliamentarians in the House of Representatives, eight from the House of Councillors, and the ten presidential appointees.[5] The General Affairs Committee of the Minshuto was likewise chosen by regional caucuses of Diet members at the ratio of one to seven. Provision was also made for the representation of former Diet members and for the nomination of a specified number of committee members by the president. The executive council of the Shakaito organization is the Central Executive Committee, generally composed of thirty members. Some members are chosen by the national conference, others are selected by the Central Committee, and some are members automatically because of the party offices they hold. The Central Committee of the Kyosanto, with a maximum membership of thirty-five, is theoretically elected by the mass meeting; however, effective control of the party machinery has generally rested with a group smaller than the regulations allow. When the Committee became a victim of the anti-Communist drive, it was replaced by a smaller Temporary Central Guidance Committee, made up of second-rate leaders. It should be readily apparent that the executive councils of the non-Communist parties have been heavily loaded with Diet members or those closely associated with the legislative process.

In political organizations the world over, effective control of policy and management tends to shift from large, unwieldy bodies to smaller, more efficient organs. In Japan, by this process, the legally superior convention abdicates in favor of the executive committee, and the latter frequently gives way to an inner clique responsible for the day-to-day operations of the party. The General Affairs Board of the Jiyuto elected a smaller group of standing directors to handle matters referred to it by the parent body. The Minshuto made no such provision for an inner executive; however, the seven-member Supreme Committee was entitled to exercise executive authority in the absence of a president. On the question of dissolving the Diet in 1948, the strategy of the Shakaito was apparently decided by a conference of Socialist cabinet ministers and high party officials. The large, unwieldy Central Committee functions according to the letter of party regulations only when the smaller executive body is badly split. Political organizations in Japan have been known to elevate their discredited leaders to a high-sounding but politically impotent group and to transfer *de facto* authority to a new management committee. The

Central Committee of the Kyosanto breaks down into an eight-man Politburo, comprising the leading strategists of the party. This agency deliberates upon major policy matters, and its decision is submitted to the Central Committee for final approval. Since Politburo members are also leading spokesmen in the Central Committee, the latter rarely withholds its stamp of approval from the consensus achieved by the party leaders.[6]

The executive committee of each major party has important *de facto* responsibilities involving policy, personnel, finance, and general party management. The special committees and subcommittees are under the direct supervision of this executive council, and it has much control over the planning and direction of the annual conference, including the drawing up of the agenda. The regulations of the Minshuto charged the General Affairs Committee with the consideration and deciding of "important party affairs," and during an emergency the Central Executive Committee of the Shakaito has the power of decision in "important matters," with the qualification that convention or Central Committee approval be obtained within twenty days.

Party Officials

The chief spokesman and key executive official of each political organization is the president in a conservative party and the chairman of the Central Executive Committee in the Socialist party. The Communists technically do not invest executive authority in a single individual, relying instead upon the "collective executive" of their Central Committee. The president of the Jiyuto was elected by the annual convention for a four-year term. The president of the Minshuto was elected by the party conference for a term of one year, as the chairman of the Shakaito executive is also. As noted previously, the chairmanship has been the object of bitter contention at the national meetings of the Socialists. Conference election of the president of a conservative party, however, has been little more than confirmation of a leader who has already been agreed upon following a behind-the-scenes struggle among factional interests. Occasionally the deadlock has been broken and superficial unity restored by the nod of a trusted party elder or political sage. In 1947 Ashida Hitoshi, then secretary-general of the Minshuto, was nominated for the presidency of his organization by a special nine-man committee and elected unanimously at the subsequent party convention. At that time two party elders, Shidehara Kijuro and Saito Takao, were chosen as honorary president and supreme adviser respectively, and the important negotiations for the premiership were left in the hands of the three leaders. In 1952, when the Minshuto was being transformed into the Kaishinto, a selection committee of twenty party lieutenants was authorized to weigh the respective claims of the various factions and to decide upon a suitable leader for the presidency.[7]

While Jiyuto rules made no provision for the temporary replacement of the president when the office became vacant, the secretary-general as second in command of the Shakaito hierarchy succeeds to the chairmanship of the Central Executive Committee when his chief is unable to assume the responsibility. Throughout a large portion of Shimpoto-Minshuto history the party was forced to function without a president — some of the time because the jockeying of strong and jealous factions made agreement upon a single leader difficult. Under these circumstances the party rules provided for the transmission of executive authority to the Supreme Committee when the presidential office became vacant. Such a collective executive is not unusual in Japan when new parties are brought into being. At that time the political situation may render a coalition of splinter groups necessary for bargaining purposes, but the uncertain power balance among the various elements may dictate an executive committee representing all groups as the only possible compromise.* After one faction consolidates its control, the party generally returns to the presidential system, even if the leader is a mere figurehead or represents a "neutral" clique.

The chief executive official of each major party wields considerable power, authorized and assumed, over the control and management of the affairs of his organization. His influence, however, is much stronger in a conservative party than it is in the Shakaito. The Jiyuto, which had a long tradition of presidential domination, authorized its leader to nominate the secretary-general, the advisers, and some of the directors. In addition, the president customarily designated such important officials as the chairmen of the General Affairs Board and the Political Affairs Research Committee. Some of these appointments at one time necessitated the subsequent approval of the Board mem-

* When the Jiyu-Minshuto was formed in November 1955, a "collective presidency," composed of four leaders representing the several factions, was established.

bership and the Diet Members' Assembly, although they generally confirmed the presidential action. However, the rules were changed in 1953 so that these bodies lost their voice in the selection of key officers. This was one of Yoshida's methods of tightening his control of the party against the threat of the Hatoyama faction.[8] Nevertheless, political wisdom dictated that a Jiyuto leader consult with his associates in filling important posts in the party. The factional struggle within the Jiyuto was partially centered upon the method of selecting men for executive positions in the organization. Accusing President Yoshida of strong-man methods, the cliques in opposition frequently urged the democratization of the party machinery. Aided by a few of his close advisers, the Jiyuto chief executive virtually dictated the policy and strategy of his organization. On some occasions the party organs left important policy questions for his negotiation and decision.[9] In postwar Japan most of the presidents of the conservative parties have been career civil servants — inexperienced newcomers to the political party game. Promotion of their bureaucratic acolytes to positions of influence in the party hierarchy has provoked the rebellion of those factions who were closely associated with the party movement long before the war. As recounted in previous discussion, the clash of "party" and "bureaucratic" interests is a partial explanation of the power struggle between the Yoshida and Hatoyama cliques of the Jiyuto.

Whereas the president of a conservative party is, in theory, only an ex officio member of the executive council, the leading figure of the Shakaito is specifically elected to the chairmanship of the Central Executive Committee. But the fundamental distrust of leadership which characterizes Socialist parties in most countries has to some extent deprived the Shakaito chief executive of the extensive power wielded by his conservative counterparts. As outlined above, the national conference selects a wider span of party officialdom and demands more specific reporting from its executive branch. The chairman is much more limited by the collective decisions of the Central Executive Committee; Katayama, for example, deferred to that body on the question of joining the Ashida cabinet in 1948.[10] Nevertheless, the key executive post in all major parties has assumed added importance in postwar Japan. The new constitution has invested the premier with a broad array of executive power, and the presidency of a political party has become the main thoroughfare to cabinet leadership.

Perhaps unconsciously patterned after the prewar genro in their relation to the governmental structure are the advisers or counselors who consult with the president and the executive council. This group of consultants, which has no fixed membership, is elected by the national convention upon the recommendation of the chief executive. Chosen for this role are men distinguished by age, political acumen, long service to the organization, or political connections. Occasionally a party elder facing political eclipse may be elevated to an advisory position to prevent the humiliation of appointment to a subordinate post. The Jiyuto honored Shidehara with the title of Supreme Adviser in 1948, and they urged Hatoyama to accept a similar role four years later. In 1954, the elders of the Jiyuto played a strategic role in forcing the resignation of the Yoshida cabinet, in effect vetoing another dissolution of the Diet.[11] The Minshuto generally had a group of five Supreme Counselors and a smaller band of ordinary counselors who deliberated upon the inquiries submitted to them by the president. The Socialists likewise have a group of consultants to advise the Central Executive Committee and other party organs; serving in this capacity have been such respected leaders of the proletarian movement as Abe Isoo and Kagawa Toyohiko.

Included in the hierarchy of important executive officials in a right-wing party is the chairman of the executive committee. Generally he is elected by the committee members, but the wishes of the president are given special consideration. This officer speaks with an authoritative voice in party councils and may be in line for the presidency of the organization.

If the president is a figurehead, actual power may rest in the hands of the secretary-general, the principal administrative official in each party. The Socialists consider the secretaryship to be a post of great importance; they elect the secretary at the national conference and authorize him to take over the work of the chairman in the absence of the chief executive. Responsible to the Central Executive Committee, the secretary commands the broad span of administrative commissions and agencies which do the organizational spadework for the party. The secretary-general of the Kyosanto, like his counterpart in other nations, is a trusted and experienced comrade, elected by the Central Committee from among its own members. The Communist secretary is theoretically responsible to the Committee for the supervision of a vast network of organizational and propagandist activities.

The president of a conservative party has considerable influence in the appointment of the secretary-general. In the Jiyuto the national conference often confirmed the nomination; in the Minshuto the General Affairs Committee was consulted in the selection. In addition the regulations of a right-wing organization generally direct the secretary to administer party affairs and to carry out the mandate of the various party organs under the instructions of the president. On the eve of party amalgamations or joint endeavor, the exploratory negotiations are often left to the secretaries-general of the participating organizations, the presidents conferring in the later stages of the bargaining.[12] The struggle between the Hatoyama and the Yoshida wings of the Jiyuto was reflected in the selection of the secretary-general. Unhappy with the party machine in strange hands, the Hatoyama faction demanded the election of the secretary by a vote of the national conference. In more recent years the post was filled by a pro-Yoshida man, and the rules were eventually changed to make the office an appointive one. In 1954 Premier Yoshida nominated his chief confidant for the secretary-generalship in an effort to keep his grip upon the disintegrating organization.[13]

In addition to the chairman of the executive board and the secretary-general, the list of presidential conferees includes the chairman of the Policy Affairs Research Committee.[14] In the Jiyuto he was formerly chosen by the party members of the Diet in joint session, but a rule change gave the power of selection to the president. In the Minshuto the president appointed a qualified person to the post, upon the recommendation of the General Affairs Committee. As will be evident in subsequent discussion, the position is not so important in the Socialist party.

In the election of its principal officials, the Kyosanto has not observed the black letter of party rules. As in other parts of the world, the "centralist" features of "democratic centralism" have tended to choke out the "democratic." In 1947 the committee members named by Tokuda and announced by Shiga were unanimously approved by the party faithful at their mass meeting.[15]

Administrative Organs

In addition to its deliberative functions, the executive council of a conservative party has supervisory control over a maze of administrative bureaus and specialized subsections. The managerial responsibility, however, is delegated to the secretary-general, who supervises such agencies as the party affairs, organization, information, finance, and international sections of the administrative hierarchy. Assisting the chief secretary is a small group of deputies and a battery of ordinary secretaries. The deputy secretaries-general are frequently appointed to represent the intraparty factions but may be selected on a geographical basis.[16] The majority of the subordinate secretaries in the Jiyuto were co-opted from the Diet membership, and the remainder were appointed by the president. The Minshuto secretaries were nominated by the president after consultation with the General Affairs Committee.

It is extremely difficult to separate the policy-formulation and policy-implementing functions of the Central Executive Committees of the Socialist party, since many of the chiefs of the major organizational subdivisions are simultaneously members of the executive committee. A horizontal breakdown of the Shakaito administrative machine includes the following:

Political Bureau	*Organization Bureau*	*Organs Bureau*
Diet Section	Organization Section	Organs Section
Local Assembly Section	Labor Section	Publications Section
Political Affairs Research Section	Farmers' Section	
Elections Section	Fishermen's Section	
	Youth Section	
	Cooperative Union Section	
	Women's Section	
	Medium and Small Enterprises Section	

Fund Bureau	*General Affairs Bureau*	*Education-Propagation Bureau*
Finance Section	Liaison Section	Education Section
Party Works Section	General Affairs Section	Information Section
		Propaganda Section

In practice the secretary-general exercises considerable supervisory control over the network of operational agencies.

Major Political Parties III: Organization

The Central Committee of the Kyosanto is divided into three major sections: the Politburo, responsible for the general formulation of policy; the Organization Bureau, which gives guidance to those engaged in propaganda and organizational activities; and the Secretariat, which secures the implementation of Central Committee and Politburo policy. Actually the Secretariat plays the dominant role, its members occupying seats in other bureaus. The secretary-general, prominent in the activities of all three sections, is in a strategic position to influence policy and to control the operational activities of the organization. The administrative machine is broken down into smaller units covering a wide scope of organizational enterprise — labor unions, farmers, women, Koreans, research, finance, culture, publications, schools, agitation and propaganda, scientific techniques, and many others.

Of considerable importance as an operational agency, especially in a conservative party, is the Political Affairs Research Committee. We have already noted that the chairman of this body was a prominent member of the inner circle in both the Jiyuto and the Minshuto. The major function of the Committee is to analyze and report on the legislative and political issues of the day, operating through a system of special subcommittees and assisted by advisers and consultants. This research and policy-drafting agency is guided by the executive committee, which must approve the findings before they become party commitments. The Socialists have a less important Research Section, which is a subdivision of the Political Bureau. The Kyosanto Research Section was headed by Nozaka Sanzo in 1947, and its functions were not so clearly delineated and its operations not so significant as those of the comparable agency in the conservative parties.

Parliamentary Party

The Diet members affiliated with the major parties hold their separate caucuses in the House of Representatives and the House of Councillors and a joint meeting of the party members in both chambers. The parliamentary delegation exerts great power and influence over the policy and administration of a conservative party. As already suggested in the discussion above, members of the Diet are present in full strength at the annual conventions and tend to dominate the proceedings. The Jiyuto caucus became the constituent body when it was

impossible to summon the conference, and the Diet men of the Minshuto could initiate the calling of a special session of the convention.
In both of the conservative organizations the executive council was
largely constituted by the sanction of their respective caucuses. In
later years the important organizational changes in Yoshida's party
were approved by the affiliated Diet members acting in place of the
national convention.

Shakaito legislators do not have the legal authority of their conservative colleagues. Key officials are selected by the conference rather
than by the parliamentary caucus, and the legislative power of the
convention is transferred to the Central Executive Committee when
the parent body is not in session. Socialist rules provide for the control of their Diet members by the national headquarters, although the
chairman of the caucus may attend meetings of the executive to express the attitude of the legislators he represents.

The parliamentary parties manipulate the Diet machinery; every
action, from motions and speeches to interpellations and heckling, is
executed under party label.[17] The individual legislator is bound by
the decision of his political organization, with little opportunity to act
on his own initiative. Each chamber of the Diet has a standing committee, known as the House Management Committee (*giin unei
iinka*), which serves as a steering committee for the legislative machine. The political parties are represented on the steering committee
of each House, with the chairmanship generally being awarded to the
organization which has the greatest political strength. The committee
serves as a clearing house for the resolution of party interests and
makes possible the management of the Diet business by the several
political groups. It is concerned with such matters as the selection of
Diet officials, expenditures from the contingent fund, and session time-
tables, in its chamber. In the early days of the Occupation, especially
when coalition cabinets were the rule, an Interparty Negotiating Conference, comprising the speaker and representatives of the various
parties, was the important steering group. Unanimous agreement of
the Conference was required before an item could be placed upon the
daily agenda of the House, and the parties were theoretically bound
by its decisions. Each party has a Diet committee which is concerned
chiefly with the day-to-day activities of the organization in parliament.

Major Political Parties III: Organization

The tradition of party control is not so well developed in the House of Councillors as in the House of Representatives, although both the conservative and Socialist organizations show signs of increased political activity and influence in the second chamber. Less frequent elections and a higher proportion of independent and neutral members have made it somewhat difficult for the dominant party in the House of Representatives to transform its power into effective control of the Councillors.

Party Discipline

Party members who have violated the rules or discipline of their organization, impaired its honor, or conducted themselves in a manner detrimental to party dignity invite special censure. In a conservative party the expulsion of an ordinary member generally follows the decision of the executive committee; for the expulsion of a Diet member, the consent of the parliamentary caucus has customarily been required.[18]

The Socialist and Communist parties differ from the right-wing organizations in their use of control committees. In the Shakaito framework, this ten-member body is elected by the national conference and responsible to it. The Control Committee, upon request or upon its own initiative, is empowered to inspect the operation of a party organ and its officialdom at any level. It is an independent agency for the hearing of complaints, and, according to party regulations, its decisions must be "regarded highly." After the report of the Control Committee has been heard, an errant Shakaito member may be expelled by the Central Committee or the Central Executive Committee. Individuals who have violated the discipline of the local branches are reported to the national executive; however, in cases of emergency the provincial federation may issue a writ of expulsion which remains valid if subsequently confirmed by the Central Executive Committee.

The Control Committee of the Kyosanto, theoretically elected by and responsible to the national meeting, is composed of no more than ten experienced and trusted party members.[19] Exercising more authority and power than its Socialist counterpart, the agency guards against the infiltration of subversive elements, imposes security measures, and ensures compliance with party decisions by rank-and-file members, officials, and organs. These responsibilities involve joint meetings with the Politburo, constant investigation of party activities at all organizational levels, and examination of disciplinary cases. Once a policy has been accepted, the Communists insist upon immediate implementation. Laxity in attitude and violation of discipline on the part of an individual member may be punished by a variety of sanctions, depending upon the gravity of the offense: warning and admonition, temporary retirement from the post, restricted activity, and outright expulsion. Extreme punitive action may stem from a decision of the cell under the guidance of a higher agency. The expulsion is subsequently confirmed by the regional, prefectural, central, and control committees. A member of the executive council at any level of the hierarchical structure may be read out of the party by a two-thirds vote of the full committee.

Party Finance

The excessive cost of an election campaign in Japan places a heavy financial burden upon the political parties. Since many financial transactions are concealed even from their own members, published accounts of party revenue and expenditures give an incomplete picture of their fiscal activities. Each party levies a nominal membership fee upon those who join (1 per cent of a member's fixed income in the case of the Communists), and it assesses the Diet members on its rolls an additional amount for the "maintenance" of the organization. The Kyosanto also replenishes its treasury with profits from some of its enterprises, especially the sale of publications. The Communist party has reportedly engaged in profitable smuggling and narcotics operations, and many observers suspect that it has had access to hidden Soviet funds.[20]

To fill the enormous gap between party expenses and the trickle of revenue from membership fees and miscellaneous sources, the major parties are forced to rely upon voluntary contributions. As a result candidates and their sponsoring organizations are driven into the arms of those who possess wealth, and party officials are frequently chosen for their ability to tap lucrative sources of campaign funds. In prewar years the Minseito and Seiyukai depended upon the financial support of great business firms, some of whom purchased political insurance by contributing to both parties. Lacking the necessary business connections, the proletarian parties were often handicapped by small budgets.

The restraints upon the zaibatsu during the reform phase of the Occupation shook the pillars of party finance, and the major political organizations turned to the *nouveaux riches*, including building contractors, drug manufacturers, and promoters engaged in black-market operations. High-ranking party officials have been charged with fraud involving contributions from business interests for election purposes.[21] As political uncertainty disappeared and the zaibatsu regained their economic breath, relations between the business community and the right-wing parties approached their prewar status. Early Kyosanto gains and the recent success of the Socialist left have disturbed financial and industrial leaders whose aim is political stability under conservative cabinets. The internecine strife among Jiyuto and Minshuto factions, which frequently upset the political balance and threatened the hegemony of conservatism, often irritated the business community. Businessmen had contributed generously to the campaign purses of their ideological spokesmen, but finally they began to stipulate that the several cliques put their bickering houses in order. For the 1952 campaign, financial and industrial interests donated large sums to the Jiyuto on condition that the party, split by the Yoshida-Hatoyama imbroglio, remain united. With the schism formalized, heavy contributors to the Jiyuto treasury used their influence to effect a *rapprochement* between the two factions. The business world was especially displeased with Yoshida's sudden dissolution of the Diet in 1953. In that campaign some industrialists did not specify the Jiyuto as the principal beneficiary of their contributions, extending financial support to other conservative candidates and in some cases to those carrying the banner of the Uha Shakaito.[22]

The bonds which unite the conservative parties with employers' associations and business establishments generally enabled the Jiyuto and the Minshuto to accumulate larger funds than their left-wing opponents, and the conservatives usually sponsored more candidates. In the 1949 campaign the Jiyuto reported an income of 10,426,735 yen, and the Kyosanto listed receipts totaling 5,155,543 yen. In contrast, the Shakaito and the Minshuto, whose popularity had been lowered by their poor record in office, received a meager 1,433,521 yen and 1,168,384 yen respectively. In the 1952 and 1953 elections the Jiyuto received in contributions twice as much as the Kaishinto, five times as much as the Shakaito groups, and one hundred times as much as the Kyosanto. To avoid the pitfalls of scandal, the business community established in 1955 an Economic Rehabilitation Council whose major function was the pooling of campaign funds and their allocation to the various political parties. With a maximum goal of 200,-000,000 yen, the Council was to distribute the major share of the contributions to the Jiyuto and the Minshuto on an equal basis, the balance going to the Shakaito organizations and the minor parties.[23]

Although the Socialists and Communists get some support from capitalist groups, they are forced to depend largely upon the generosity of other interests. The leftists have apparently cornered a large part of the labor support, but until very recently the unions did not give enormous amounts of financial aid to the candidates they sponsored or to the parties they supported. Labor groups reported expenditures of less than 1,000,000 yen in the 1949 election for the House of Representatives. However, the threat of antiunion legislation in recent years has stirred labor leaders to more carefully organized political action. In spite of the expense of a double campaign in 1953, Sohyo (General Council of Japanese Trade Unions), the largest labor organization in Japan, backed 115 candidates for the House of Representatives and 29 for the second chamber — chiefly left-wing Socialists and Labor-Farmer party nominees. Handicapped by a depleted treasury as a result of its 1952 strike activities, the federation attempted to capture the votes of unionist families and to raise funds by assessing union members. In March 1953 the Socialist left had reportedly received contributions of more than 30,000,000 yen from four unions. In the 1955 election trade unions entered into political combat on an unprecedented scale, setting up elaborate machinery for the collection of campaign funds. Collecting from 80 to 100 yen from each member, the labor organizations more than doubled the financial resources that had been available in the previous election and put more candidates into the field.[24] The Kyosanto, whose financial drives in 1949 aided in its greatest electoral success, receives some trade union support. The Communists also maneuver contributions from some capitalist groups who wish to avoid labor trouble or who catch visions of profitable trade with Communist China.[25]

Major Political Parties III: Organization
Local Organization

Party organization at the grass roots has commanded more attention in postwar Japan than in prewar years, especially among the conservative parties. Before 1945 left-wing politicians concerned themselves with local organization, but Seiyukai and Minseito strategists neglected their provincial vineyards. As a result, many branch offices of the conservative parties were little more than social clubs or loosely delineated spheres of influence under the control of a local political leader. The marked success of the Shakaito and the Kyosanto after the war, combined with local government reforms, inspired the conservative opposition to marshal its strength in the local areas, especially after the establishment of a Socialist-led coalition in 1947. By 1947 the right-wing parties had rebuilt their national machinery, and local allegiances, which had been blurred by the uncertainties of the purge, were more clearly crystallized. The two conservative organizations, which had at first declared a truce on local organization in the hope of fostering union, ceased their collaboration and began to compete at the local level.

To join any Japanese party an individual generally must be sponsored by one or more of the members in good standing. In addition to underwriting the objectives of the organization, the neophyte pays a small membership fee and furnishes such personal data as his age, birth, and occupation, and related information to the party authorities. In the Kyosanto final confirmation rests with the Central Committee, and the sponsor is held responsible for the candidate whom he introduces to the organization. On the whole, Japanese voters do not consider themselves to be members of a specific party, and the requirements for membership, including endorsement and fee, discourage formal affiliation. The comparative extent of grass roots organization in the various parties is revealed by the registration figures supplied to the Attorney General's Office in early 1950:[26]

Party	Number of Organizations
Kyosanto	5,149
Shakaito	1,270
Minshu-Jiyuto	728
Minshuto	288

Because of the nature of its organization and methods, the Kyosanto places the greatest emphasis upon work in the local branches.

Beginning with 1,200 on its membership rolls in December 1945, the party jumped to 6,547 a year later. It reached its peak of 108,692 registered members in early 1950, thereafter declining rapidly until it listed only 45,000 in 1952.[27] The monolithic structure of the Kyosanto resembles that of Communist parties in other countries. The basic unit of organization is the cell, which is formed by three or more party members in a factory, school, residence, or on a farm and approved by the executive committee in the next highest echelon. The cell serves as an agency for the collection of party dues, the distribution of publications, and agitation for Communist objectives among nonparty members. In theory, the governing body of the basic unit is the cell conference, which, if large enough, elects a small executive committee of experienced leaders to conduct the daily work of the organization. In actual practice, the executive dominates the perfunctory activities of the cell conference. This organizational pattern is repeated at each level of the hierarchical scale: a region is composed of cells, a prefectural structure is made up of regions, and a district is formed by combining several prefectures. All the threads are drawn together at the top by the Central Committee. The conference at each level establishes an executive committee which is charged with the management of party affairs in its area. The executive body usually elects a smaller standing committee and a "special division" to plan and direct Communist activities among the units under its jurisdiction. Kyosanto regulations include the principle of democratic centralism, under which the lower agencies must conform to the decisions of the higher body, solidifying a descending chain of command. In 1947 a large number of local committeemen were named by Tokuda and dispatched to the provinces from the central headquarters.[28] Every Communist is obligated to join mass organizations of laborers, farmers, and similar groups to advertise the aims of the party. Three or more comrades in a mass organization — a labor union, for example — form a *party member group*. The function of the *group* is to strengthen Communist influence within the organization itself, and for this purpose it chooses a directorate to plan day-to-day strategy. The *party member groups* form a hierarchical structure corresponding to that of the party organization, and the two are geared together at each geographical level. A joint conference of party agencies and the directorates of the mass organizations coordinates the activities of both structures and links them with the policy of the Kyosanto. These organizational methods enable the Communists to exert control and influence in trade unions and agricultural associations greater than their numerical strength would warrant.

The simplest form of Shakaito organization is the unit, formed by five or more members in the same area or place of work. Units in the same factory, ward, village, or city are united into a branch; branches, in turn, may be organized into a prefectural federation. Branches in a House of Representatives constituency may establish a conference, and federations in a given area may hold regional conferences in order to maintain liaison with one another. The formation of units, branches, and federations is approved by the Central Executive Committee. Labor unions and, to a lesser extent, agricultural associations are loosely linked with the Socialist parties as "supporting organizations." Such affiliation may secure Shakaito approval if certain requirements are met: the policy of the supporting organization must be consistent with the Socialist platform, at least half of the executive staff must be party members, and the policy-forming body of the trade union or agricultural association must have urged the support of the party and its candidates. A mass organization with one thousand or more Shakaito members in its ranks is recognized by the Central Executive Committee. Such recognition brings financial responsibility and membership on the executive council if the national conference approves. Smaller supporting organizations are geared to the local federations. Shakaito rules also recognize a category of "party friends" — nonmembers who support the Socialist cause and are recommended by the local branch.

Despite their efforts to invade the conservative countryside, the left-wing parties rely upon the urban areas for the bulk of their electoral support. The following chart outlines the comparative returns from urban and rural prefectures in the 1947 House of Representatives election, in which the Shakaito made gains, and in the 1949 contest, when the Kyosanto reached the peak of its electoral strength:[29]

	1947			1949		
	Conservative	*Shakaito*	*Kyosanto*	*Conservative*	*Shakaito*	*Kyosanto*
Rural	52.4%	22.4%	3.2%	60.8%	12.2%	8.2%
Urban	47.1%	32.6%	4.7%	55.6%	16.2%	13.4%

Because of the close tieup of labor federations with the Socialists or the Kyosanto, the friction between the left-wing parties and among the various factions within each organization has been reflected in the labor movement. The uncompromising militancy of some unions contributed to the Shakaito split in 1951, and thwarted the reunion of the two factions till 1955. Because of the feuding in labor's ranks, the Socialists are unable to depend upon the solid backing of the trade unions as do their British brethren. In 1948 the Sodomei (Japan Federation of Labor) refused its customary blanket approval of the Shakaito, declaring its freedom to support candidates of its own choice. In the election a year later, the leaders of the federation agreed to back only selected candidates of the Socialist party.[30]

The basic unit of the Minshuto was the team, four of which could be organized into a branch in a particular area. Three or more branches located in the same House of Representatives constituency formed a unit chapter, with the approval of the executive authorities one rung higher up the ladder. After the approval of rules, inspection of membership rolls, and general confirmation by the national headquarters, a federation of two or more unit chapters could be organized in each prefecture. The national executive was kept informed of the party activities in all the subordinate jurisdictions.

Jiyuto regulations made little provision for local organization. Subbranches, formed in towns and cities, were united into joint chapters at the prefectural level. The rules of each chapter were subject to the approval of the national executive board. Following a blueprint drawn up by the Jiyuto Club in early 1947, the party developed liaison organizations among farming, labor, fishing, and business groups.

In theory, each major party is highly centralized, the national headquarters keeping a watchful eye upon the provincial organizations. The supervision of local party activities is usually the responsibility of the chief of the Party Affairs Bureau, who works in close harness with the secretary-general. The central executive confirms the establishment of branch units, approves the rules, and examines the membership lists and the roster of elected officials. General policy is formulated by the leaders in the national office, but the suggestions and criticisms advanced by local representatives on the executive are generally taken into account. The frequent shifting of political allegiances develops friction between Tokyo headquarters and the branch units, resulting in occasional demands by the lower echelons for the democratization of the party machinery. Often national-local tensions arise over the selection of candidates. The chiefs of the branch offices are usually members of the election committee, and the national office, in the interest of harmony, is inclined to accept their recommendations whenever possible. The election committee, however, may be under the domination of the secretary-general or a campaign manager representing the top leadership of the party. Should the national decision meet with the resistance of local organizations, the headquarters may use its control of the purse strings as a disciplinary measure to push recalcitrant units into compliance.

Personalized Politics

Political parties in Japan have been, to some extent at least, the prisoners of the cultural past. Parties in the Western sense are a relatively recent importation whose roots run shallow in Japanese political soil. Their organization and operational effectiveness were initially conditioned by the types of people who joined — samurai, government officials, and business leaders — and by political traditions and group values which were confirmed by long centuries of social acceptance. Competing with older and more reverenced institutions, such as the military and the bureaucracy, the parties were unable to make a sharp break with an ancient culture and its feudal ethics. Their political inheritance has placed some limits even today upon the parties as agencies of the popular will.

Although outwardly cleansed of its feudal forms, the intricate social system of Japan still contains remnants of feudal organization and ideology. In the Tokugawa period of Japanese history, the lord-vassal relation served as a model for the weaker elements of the community who looked to strong leaders for their security and welfare. In accordance with a strict ethical code, the *oyabun* (boss) provided food, clothing, and protection for his underlings; in return the *kobun* (follower) owed absolute obedience and loyalty to his leader. Seniority among the *kobun* ranked the *anibun* (elder brother) above the *ototo-bun* (younger brother), reinforcing the discipline and the hierarchical relation. Although initially altruistic in tone (and occasionally performing welfare functions even today) the *oyabun-kobun* organizations later tended to degenerate into fraternities of labor gangs, ruffians, and brokers of hidden influence. The *oyabun* was a paternal despot in his own bailiwick, willing to guard his preserve by the use of force. In the confusion which followed the surrender in 1945, powerful *oyabun* and their henchmen operated in the construction industry, coal mines, and market places. Frequently they became involved in the black market, gambling operations, and political hooliganism. In the rural areas the *oyabun-kobun* relation has traditionally been reflected in the deference of the tenant to the landlord.[31]

The leader-follower tradition, probably an outgrowth of the family system and reinforced in the schools, has left a deep imprint upon the Japanese social structure. It has found expression at all levels and in all sorts of relations: employer to employee, government to civil servant, military officer to foot soldier, and political leader to political follower. In the basically hierarchical social system, the individual who seeks advancement is expected to enter into a personal relation with men of influence. The leader under whom he serves and to whom he must give allegiance thus becomes a guarantor of security and status. At the same time the individual must enter into a similar relation with protégés of his own who will enable him to overcome the power of his rivals. In both situations the reciprocal obligations are those of paternalism and obedience which exist between master and servant.[32]

Steeped in the old samurai tradition and organized around *oyabun-kobun* loyalties were the prewar ultranationalist societies. Such organizations — the Gen'yosha (Society of the Black Ocean), the Kokuryukai (Black Dragon Society), the Rosokai (Society of Mature Men), the Kokuhonsha (State Foundation Society), the Kokusuikai (National Essence Society), and many others — proclaimed the virtues of their native culture, striking out against the invasion of Western ideas. At home they bitterly opposed the "radical" tendencies of socialism, labor unions, and liberal thought. Their foreign policy was a chauvinistic demand for expansion on the continent by the force of Japan's national power. The members of many patriotic societies included thugs and ruffians who terrorized those suspected of "un-Japanese" thought and activity. Supported by powerful upper-class groups who regarded them as patriotic, gangs of hooligans frequently resorted to assassination and other forms of violence to attain their jingoistic goals. Bands of *soshi* (bullies) often broke up political meetings, smashed speakers' platforms, intimidated public officials, and attacked Diet members in the tribune of the House of Representatives. The leaders of the patriotic societies had close personal connections with the business world, military factions, and the political parties.

Clusters of small rightist societies mushroomed in Japan after the surrender, and in early 1946 there was an attempt to weld some of the organizations into an "Imperial Subjects' Front" to combat communism. The aim of these superpatriots was the preservation of the national culture, and their slogans were redolent of the totalitarian attack upon parliamentary institutions in the 1930s.[33] However, the rebirth of nationalism was delayed by SCAP decrees which formally dissolved the patriotic societies and purged their leadership.[34]

Studies of ultranationalist groups in postwar Japan have been scant and the findings inconclusive, largely because the data are extremely difficult to obtain. As a result, generalizations at this time are impossible, and observations can be no more than tentative. Because of the underground nature of the patriotic societies and their long history of social acceptance, it was unrealistic to assume that the mere issuance of decrees would completely root them out. There is evidence to suggest that during the early years of the Occupation the rightists kept skeletonized organizations alive by informal contact.[35] The conditions and circumstances which had nurtured the growth of ultranationalism in the past were extant in a more objectionable form as a result of Japan's defeat and the consequent reforms wrought by alien hands. The attempted renovation of Japanese institutions to fit Western models, changes in the legal status of the emperor, the growth of the Socialist party and trade unions, the emergence of the Communists from the shadows of the underground, and the recurring waves of political scandal — all these developments re-inspired the secret organization and the cult of terror of prewar years. Nationalist diehards, nursing the trauma of humiliating defeat, deeply resented the liberal reforms of the conqueror which threatened their cultural inheritance.

The Korean war and the pressure for rearmament brought some militarist groups and their patriotic appendages into the open. Less than two years after the Occupation had ended, Japanese officials were reporting the existence of between 750 and 800 rightist organizations, embracing a membership of 300,000. By 1953 several groups of patriotic societies sought integration into joint fronts and "national salvation" movements whose aim was the rebuilding of the fatherland, the glorification of the Japanese race, and opposition to communism. Prominent in the negotiating conferences were "depurged" rightists, including some who had led prewar organizations and who had been involved in the military coups of the 1930s. Although sharing common nationalistic tenets, the societies which have blossomed in recent years represent a diversity of interests: some are made up of ex-*kempeitai* members interested in the release of war criminals; some are dedicated to the veneration of the emperor; others are devoted to the welfare of army and navy veterans; others appeal to dissatisfied farmers; and a few have adopted antimilitarism as their creed.[36]

Many ultranationalist groups continue to eschew political activity and frown upon those rightists who present themselves as candidates for Diet seats. As in prewar years, their strategy is to exert pressure outside the framework of the parliamentary system. On the other hand, some societies have become "political" since Japan regained her independence, and their leaders have sought public office. Some "big name" nationalists were elected to the Diet in 1952; however, they did not congregate in any one political party, and they do not appear to have formed a cohesive group in their parliamentary activities. The "patriots" did not fare quite so well in the 1953 and 1955 elections.

The renewed activity of the ultranationalist societies is, of course, a potential threat to liberal reform and the democratic forces in Japan. However, there is no present evidence to suggest that these groups approach their prewar strength or influence. Moreover, the existence of strong personalities in each organization seems to make the coordination of their activities as difficult today as in the past. In 1955 extreme rightist candidates secured less than 1 per cent of the popular vote, and the Communists captured only 2 per cent.[37] It appears that the Japanese people have thus far successfully resisted the conspiratorial appeals of both right and left extremists.

The leader-follower tradition remains influential in the polling booths and in the political parties of Japan. *Oyabun-kobun* social groupings are convenient units to draw into a political machine, and politicians have traditionally cultivated them.[38] In recent years gang leaders have been receptive to the establishment of direct and indirect liaison with national and local organizations. When an *oyabun* announces his candidacy for local office, the citizens of the area frequently assume that he is the person to represent them, and opposing candidates do not appear. Huge blocks of votes under the control of one boss are attractive to the leaders of all parties, leading to a mechanical type of competition in which knowledgeable politicians wield unseen power on a vast scale.

An important political leader generally has his private group of satellites who are intensely loyal to him and who look to him for personal advancement. Often the loyalty to the leader takes priority over allegiance to the wider party organization. Thus the members of a political faction might obediently follow their chief out of the party into a bargaining group or even into the camp of the opposition. The veneration of men of prestige and status explains to some degree the *de facto* power of the purgees who frequently governed their political domains by "consultation" and "advice" after their nominal removal from positions of influence.

The ancient patterns of loyalty have, of course, been modified by the complexities of modern life. To regard the *oyabun-kobun* relation as the sole basis of loyalty to a political chief would indeed be an oversimplification. In modern Japan the pressure of other claims and demands frequently cuts across the more traditional types of obligations. Loyalty in Japanese politics has been complicated by the lure of government office, the cash nexus, and the informal contact and association which develop in club and office. Personal loyalties, financial favors, the promise of a government post, and similar appeals are utilized by political leaders to build, hold, and expand their "following." But, regardless of the competing claims which a politician must weigh on the eve of an important decision, the allegiances tend to be personal rather than party in nature.

With an important political leader managing an obedient clientele or offering inducements to those who join his ranks, it is not surprising that the parties have become faction-ridden in the mad scramble for power and advantage. As pointed out elsewhere, all the Japanese parties have been weakened by internecine strife, stemming from personal dislikes, proselyting, and factional rivalries. These party disturbances frequently have their roots in prewar developments. Attracting a following by his personality, status, prestige, or money, the leader of a faction may be content to act a "bit" part in the party drama; but eventually his seniority or the size of his group may encourage him to ask for a "supporting" role. If his expanding influence is not recognized by the director, the factional chieftain may signal his flock to withdraw from the cast because of the promising roles in a new production. In a fractionalized party system, one group moving at a strategic time may be in a position to upset the delicate political balance and wield an influence greater than its numerical strength would suggest. As previous discussion has indicated, each major party in postwar Japan has suffered from rifts and defection. Even the normally well-disciplined Communists have not been spared the pain of schism. That the Kyosanto has not completely escaped feudal influence is indicated by the selection of its leaders largely on the basis of seniority and the attachment of younger members to a powerful older figure, to whom they look for political preferment.[39]

Under these circumstances, a political party is little more than a loose association of factional interests. These divergent units must be conciliated and held in proper balance if the organization is to become or remain an important political entity. Controlling an independent source of strength, a factional chieftain is frequently able to stir the political pot by moving his followers into a bargaining group or a competing party when the lure of office or financial reward makes the transfer of loyalty worth while. The evanescent quality of such political attachments stimulates constant jockeying for position, with allegiances shifting at every change of the political barometer. Both the leader of a faction and the president of a factious party are called upon to perform brokerage functions which are largely geared to their personal ambitions and those of their followers; political issues and principles are frequently relegated to a subordinate role. The president must skillfully appease and purchase if he is to maintain the fragile equilibrium among the divergent cliques which make up his political strength. But the unsteady coalition of elements in the party and the constant threat of backstage maneuvering invite suspicion and mistrust in the upper stratum of leadership. A party president may be reluctant to discuss confidential matters of strategy in the presence of a lieutenant who is friendly today but who might be in political competition a month later.

Thus the personal rivalries and schismatic tendencies of Japanese parties obstruct effective discipline and make strong, positive action by the united party extremely difficult. Too often personal loyalties, political ambition, and party expediency have had a superior claim over the basic needs of the nation. As a result, neither the programs nor the strategy of the major parties has really won the trust and confidence of the ordinary citizen. The leader-follower relation, embracing the dominant role of the boss and the financial purchase of loyalty, has slowed the development of popularly based parties. Social pressures frown upon political nonconformity, and there has been little understanding of party responsibility. As long as the common citizen accepts submissively as his normal lot the dictation and irresponsibility implicit in factional politics, the Japanese parties seem ordained to remain crude instruments of popular control.

Notes

[1] On prewar party organization see H. S. Quigley, *Japanese Government and Politics* (New York, 1932), pp. 247–251.

[2] For general material on party organization the writers have relied upon the 1950 regulations of the respective political organizations. Translations of the party rules were provided through the courtesy of Dr. Justin Williams, chief of the Legislative Section of SCAP. For factual and interpretative data the authors are especially indebted to Kenneth E. Colton, formerly an analyst in the Civil Intelligence Section of SCAP.

[3] *Nippon Times*, January 17, 1950.

[4] A Central Committee meeting in 1951 was attended by 159 members. Seventy-two were regional representatives, 35 were from each House of the Diet, and 17 were party executives (*ibid.*, June 19, 1951).

[5] *Ibid.*, November 12, 1952.

[6] *Ibid.*, September 9–10, 1948; Rodger Swearingen and Paul Langer, *Red Flag in Japan* (Cambridge, 1952), pp. 93–94; "Character and Strategies of the Communist Party Analyzed by Able Journalists," *Jiyu Kokumin*, reprinted in *Japan Review*, June 13, 1947, p. 11.

[7] *Nippon Times*, May 19, 1947; March 7, 1952.

[8] *Ibid.*, April 14, 1950; July 1, 31, 1952; September 19, 26, 1953.

[9] *Ibid.*, November 3, 1949; April 14, May 7, 1950; May 26, July 4, 1951; January 10, 1952; July 1, 1952; January 26, 1953; *Mainichi*, January 15, 1947, translated in SCAP, Allied Translator and Interpreter Service, *Press Translations and Summaries*, January 23, 1947; III: 7, pp. 7–8.

[10] *Nippon Times*, May 6, 1948.

[11] *Ibid.*, March 18, 1952; K. Fukuma, "Yoshida's Resignation: The Inside Story," *Asahi Evening News*, December 29, 1954.

[12] For example, see the negotiations in 1954 between Hatoyama and the two Socialist parties (*Asahi Evening News*, December 9, 1954).

[13] H. Nomura, "Political Party Troubles," *ibid.*, August 13, 1954; *Nippon Times*, July 1–2, 1952; January 26, 1953.

[14] *Asahi Evening News*, December 10, 1954.

[15] "Japan Communist Party's Underground Strategy," *Sempu*, reprinted in *Japan Review*, June 10, 1948, pp. 20–22.

[16] *Asahi Evening News*, December 13, 1954.

[17] See Justin Williams, "Party Politics in the New Japanese Diet," *American Political Science Review*, XLII (December 1948), 1163–1165.

[18] Under the change in Jiyuto rules in 1953 the expulsion of a party Diet member could be decided by the General Affairs Board alone, without the approval of the parliamentary caucus (*Nippon Times*, September 26, 1953).

[19] See "Japan Communist Party's Underground Strategy," *Sempu*, reprinted in *Japan Review*, June 10, 1948, pp. 20–22.

[20] Rodger Swearingen and Paul Langer, *op. cit.*, pp. 102–103.

[21] " 'New Yen' Society and Politics," *Sekai Hyoron*, reprinted in *Japan Review*, August 1, 1947, p. 25; T. Nagata, "Political Funds and Political Parties," *Digest Service*, May 1948, pp. 11–14.

[22] F. Ikematsu, "Political Parties Today and Tomorrow," *Contemporary Japan*, XXI (1952), 403; S. Hasegawa, "Japan Politics behind the Scene," *Nippon Times*, October 27, 1952, April 4, 1953; *Nippon Times*, March 23, 25, May 20, 1953; *Mainichi*, overseas edition, September 15, 1953; *Asahi Evening News*, March 20, 1954.

[23] See Robert A. Scalapino, "Japan and the General Elections," *Far Eastern Survey*, XXI (October 29, 1952), 151; Department of State, OIR Report No. 5022, *The 1949 House of Representatives Election*, p. 39. One National Election Administration Commission report for 1949–1950 listed party receipts roughly as follows: Kyosanto, 122,-876,000 yen; Jiyuto, 42,897,000 yen; Shakaito, 11,254,000 yen; Minshuto, 4,966,000 yen (*Nippon Times*, March 2, 1950). For the registered contributions in 1953, see N. Ukai, "Japanese Election Results Reconsidered," *Pacific Affairs*, XXVI (June 1953), 143; *Nippon Times*, May 30, 1953; April 3, 1954. See also II. Nomura, "Money for the Elections," *Asahi Evening News*, February 11, 1955. In the 1955 campaign the Economic Rehabilitation Council collected 115,000,000 yen and distributed money to the major parties as follows: Minshuto, 45,000,000 yen; Jiyuto, 45,000,000 yen; Uha Shakaito, 3,300,000 yen; Saha Shakaito, 1,700,000 yen (*Nippon Times*, March 25, 1955; see also issue of March 29, 1955).

[24] *Nippon Times*, March 29, 1955; Department of State, *The 1949 House of Representatives Election*, p. 85; *Nippon Times*, March 31, April 27, 1953; *Asahi Evening News*, January 27, 1955. There has been some dissension between the trade unions which supply the funds and want to call the tune, and the Socialist political leaders who desire to retain their autonomy over candidates and policies.

[25] Rodger Swearingen and Paul Langer, *op. cit.*, p. 102.

[26] Editorial, "Party Roots and Funds," *Nippon Times*, March 2, 1950.

[27] *Nippon Times*, March 2, 1946; January 4, 1951; July 23, 1952. A report of the Public Safety Investigating Agency in 1955 listed Kyosanto membership at approximately 60,000. The breakdown of members was reported as follows: students, 30 per cent; laborers, 22.8 per cent; office workers and government employees, 21.9 per cent; and merchants and entrepreneurs, 14.5 per cent. The number of cells was listed at 5,783 (*Asahi Evening News*, June 4, 1955).

[28] "Japan Communist Party's Underground Strategy," *Sempu*, reprinted in *Japan Review*, June 10, 1948, pp. 19–20.

[29] This table has been compiled from the election returns reported in Department of State, *1949 House of Representatives Election*, pp. 107–108.

[30] *Ibid.*, pp. 87–88.

[31] See Harry E. Wildes, "Underground Politics in Post-war Japan," *American Political Science Review*, XLII (December 1948), 1149–1162. See also the series of three articles on "Japan's Boss System," *Nippon Times*, April 16–18, 1948. For the feudal origin of these relations see James Murdoch, *A History of Japan* (London, 1925–1926), III, 40–43; George B. Sansom, *Japan, A Short Cultural History* (London, 1931), pp. 291–293, 364–367, 431–433, 463–465, 499–504. Robert A. Scalapino, *Democracy and the Party Movement in Prewar Japan* (Berkeley, 1953), pp. 118–134, presents some interesting hypotheses concerning the feudal impact on modern social and political life.

[32] T. Kawashima, "Japan's Social Setup," *Nippon Times*, October 27, 1951.

[33] SCAP, *Monthly Summation of Non-Military Activities in Japan and Korea*, January 1946, pp. 29–30; March 1946, p. 38; *Nippon Times*, January 27, 1946.

[34] See above, pp. 100–101.

[35] See R. Guillain, "The Resurgence of Military Elements in Japan," *Pacific Affairs*, XXV (September 1952), 211–225.

[36] *Ibid.*, pp. 211–212; *Yomiuri Shimbun*, reported in *Nippon Times*, March 29, 1953; *ibid.*, May 23, 1951; October 3, 1952; June 11–12, 14, July 29, September 22, December 9, 1953; *Mainichi*, overseas edition, July 15, 1953.

[37] H. Tiltman, "What Lies Ahead for Hatoyama," *Asahi Evening News*, April 1, 1955; K. Murata, "The Rejected Rightists," *Nippon Times*, March 14, 1955.

[38] Harry E. Wildes, *op. cit.*, pp. 1155, 1158–1159.

[39] "The Man Ashida," *Mainichi*, reprinted in *Digest Service*, April 1, 1948, p. 1; *Asahi Evening News*, March 5, 1955; Rodger Swearingen and Paul Langer, *op. cit.*, p. 217.

22

The Courts

JAPAN'S judicial system is an arm of the central government. Its structure resembles that of its predecessor, while differing from it in certain respects.[1] No provision for local courts or police courts was included in the postwar reform of local government, although consideration was given to the rounding out of local autonomy by a division of the judicial power between the national and the local authorities. Thus the traditional centralized system of courts and procurators (state's attorneys) ensures for the constitution, laws, and administrative instruments uniformity of interpretation, and for the central government a judicial attitude favorable to its interests.

"The whole judicial power is vested in a Supreme Court and in such inferior courts as are established by law," states the constitution, Article 76. Under the old constitution all power, judicial included, was vested in the emperor. Although the courts were entitled to exercise the judicial power on behalf of the emperor independently of the executive, the control of appointments, salaries, etc., by the executive and the close liaison of judges and procurators with administrative officials operated to minimize the independence of judges when faced with an expression of executive preference in a case before them. Actually, the traditional principle, under which judicial administration was conducted as a branch of the executive function, was still influential in the thinking of Meiji and Showa judges. The new constitution clarifies the status of the judiciary, contributing thereby to the implementation of the principle of independence.

Perhaps it was to be anticipated that a challenge to the independence of the courts should come from the Diet, newly panoplied with power. Such a challenge did come on May 6, 1948, when the Judicial Affairs Committee of the House of Councillors passed a resolution calling for an inquiry into unjust judicial decisions. Subsequently it voted to extend the survey to cover relations between the procurators and the judges. The Committee was aroused by a district court decision releasing a woman who had killed her three children. The challenge was met promptly and vigorously by the Chief Judge of the Supreme Court. He contended that the Committee's resolutions were unconstitutional since the Diet had no general power to supervise the courts but was limited by Article 62 of the constitution to inquiries related to legislation in process.[2]

Professor Takayanagi Kenzo, one of Japan's foremost authorities in the field of Anglo-American law, stated in 1951 that "the adoption of the American concept of judicial power . . . and the consequent sweeping reform of the judicial system are perhaps the most far-reaching of the changes effected along these lines." He was referring to the modification of Japanese law along "common law lines." He pointed out that "the Anglo-American idea of legal primacy — not to say judicial supremacy — is diametrically opposed to the Confucian moral and political traditions" which have underlain Japanese law for a thousand years. Like other innovations hurried into Japanese law during the Occupation, this idea is part of a new musical score. "Artists of the law must play the music. Here indeed the genius of a nation necessarily will reveal itself."[3] The sweeping character of the changes is not evidenced, however, by the structure of the present system.

The Judicial Hierarchy

A Supreme Court (*saiko saibansho*) and four categories of inferior courts — high courts, district courts, family courts, and summary courts — compose the judicial hierarchy.[4] The first three replace the former Supreme Court (*daishinin*), courts of appeal, and district courts.[5] The family and the summary courts are new. The old local courts and the police courts have no counterparts in the new system.

The Supreme Court, seated in a beautiful new building in Tokyo, is composed of fifteen judges, one of them legally recognized as Chief Judge and President of the Court. It may sit as a grand bench, with all members present, or, for less important matters, in petty benches

of three or more judges. The high courts, of which there were eight
distributed throughout the country in 1952, vary in membership and
may have branches if the Supreme Court deems them necessary.
These courts also sit as full benches or in groups of three or five judges.
There were forty-nine district courts in 1952. Normally a single judge
sits on a district bench, but the statutes define categories of actions
to be tried by three-member benches. The Supreme Court may establish branches of district courts, designating the judges who shall serve
thereon. Family courts also are normally but not in all instances presided over by a single judge. Laymen are associated with these courts
as counselors and conciliators. Summary courts are uniformly presided
over by a single judge.[6]

All judges in each court of the hierarchy constitute a "judicial assembly" for that court. These assemblies are entrusted with deliberation upon judicial administration for their respective courts. The Supreme Court has supervision, in matters of administration, over the
inferior courts; each high court, district court, family court, and summary court supervises courts inferior to it within its jurisdictional
area. But the supervisory power does not apply to the judicial function. Each court is provided with a secretariat to administer miscellaneous affairs and with bailiffs for the delivery of documents. Within
the Supreme Court two Institutes are established, one for judicial research and the training of judges and other court officials, the other
for research in relation to clerical functions and for the training of
court clerks.[7] In addition to the faculties of these Institutes, "judicial
research officials" are attached to the Supreme Court and the high
courts. Their function is to conduct research related to litigation in
process, upon the orders of judges. The Institute faculties and the
research officials are members of the national civil service. Those of
the first class are appointed by the cabinet upon recommendation of
the Supreme Court; second-class officials are appointed by the Supreme Court; third-class by the Supreme Court, a high court, or a
district court in accordance with rules made by the Supreme Court.
Disciplinary penalties, including dismissal, are applied to court officials other than judges by the courts, except that in the case of
officials of the first class the cabinet exercises the power of dismissal
if requested to do so by the Supreme Court supported by the court
officials' higher disciplinary committee.

The Courts

The student body of the Judicial Institute is composed of young persons who have passed the judicial category of the higher civil service examinations which are conducted under the auspices of the Ministry of Justice. These students are termed "judicial apprentices." They are paid a small salary and their normal period of Institute study is two years. Success in the examination which follows the study period qualifies the apprentice for appointment to a variety of positions, experience in which, in turn, qualifies for judicial appointment.

Appointments and Tenure

All judges are appointed. The Chief Judge (President) of the Supreme Court is appointed by the emperor after designation by the cabinet.[8] The fourteen associate judges are appointed by the cabinet and their appointment is attested by the emperor.[9] A provision of the Court Organization Law of 1947 (Article 39, Section 4), required that the cabinet appoint a consultative committee to advise it upon the above appointments. This provision was repealed after one trial of the procedure, which operated to transfer the appointing power to the committee.[10] Supreme Court judges must be at least forty years old when appointed and must be "persons of broad vision and extensive knowledge of the law." Lawyers and professors of law as well as judges, procurators, and others of comparable experience are eligible for appointment. Quite interestingly, only ten of the Supreme Court judges are required to have had a career of ten years' duration in the legal field. Required qualifications for the inferior courts also are high but do not include an age minimum. Judges of all inferior courts are appointed by the cabinet, but they must be selected from lists of eligibles submitted by the Supreme Court.[11] It is apparent that the Court Organization Law favors the selection of the same type of career judges that dominated the pre-reform courts. Lawyers and professors of law were eligible for appointment under the old law, but very few of them were appointed. Judicial *esprit de corps* on the one hand and low salaries for judges on the other kept them out. Without freer participation by noncareer judges the courts will tend to function as a branch of the national administration. The fact that many of the sitting judges were retained when the new courts were inaugurated tended to retard the evolution of an independent judiciary.

The increased self-assertiveness of practicing lawyers and wider recognition of the value and dignity of their profession are factors working toward the reduction of judicial bureaucratism. Japan's bar associations, organized in a national federation, determine, through registration or refusal to register, whether or not an applicant shall be admitted to the practice of law. Applicants must satisfy both the local bar association in which they seek membership, and the federation, that they possess the required knowledge of the law. The bar associations continue to be regulated by law but by strenuous effort they obtained a large degree of autonomy through passage of amendments to the Lawyers' Law in 1949. By maintenance of high standards of admission, ethics, and learning the bar associations are rising in the respect of the people. Their members are thereby opening the way to greater participation in the judicial function and to a more practical and humane interpretation of the law.

Appointments to the Supreme Court are permanent, with retirement at the age of seventy years. All other judges are appointed for ten-year terms and may be reappointed. High and district court judges must retire at sixty-five, summary court judges at seventy. Although the elective procedure has been eschewed, the citizenry is afforded opportunities to review appointments to the Supreme Court. A majority of the voters at the first general election following the appointment of a Supreme Court judge may recall the judge. Similarly at ten-year intervals the right of recall may be exercised.[12] This right may not, however, be applied to the Chief Judge. Thus legal provisions on the one hand confer a most unusual right upon the people in relation to Supreme Court judges appointed by the cabinet and on the other withhold the right in relation to the Chief Judge, who is titularly an appointee of the emperor, though actually named by the cabinet. As Dr. Alfred C. Oppler remarks, "such a referendum, for all practical purposes, will usually not constitute an effective check . . . the rejection of an individual judge by the majority of the voters could materialize only in the rare case when militant agitation stirs up wide-spread resentment over an unpopular judgment which affects a large segment of the population. Such mobilization of public emotions in the judicial province can sometimes prove of doubtful value as it may strike a lonely dissenter whose non-conformity of today might become the truth of tomorrow."[13] In the test of the review provisions which was made in connection with the general election of

January 1949 all fourteen associate judges were very heartily endorsed.[14]

Judicial tenure is protected by constitutional and statutory law. A judge is not subject to disciplinary action by executive officers. He may be removed by the appointing authority only if the judge himself petitions for dismissal or if a proper court adjudges him to be mentally or physically incompetent. His salary must be "adequate" and may not be reduced during his term of office.[15] He may be impeached by the House of Representatives and tried by a court composed of members of that body and of the House of Councillors. The courts themselves are judges of judicial offenses against the standards of the judicial service and of the mental and physical competence of judges. For offenses charged against Supreme Court and high court judges jurisdiction rests in the Supreme Court; for others it lies in the high courts. That the courts are not likely to take this responsibility lightly was suggested as early as 1950, when four judges of the Supreme Court were first requested by their colleagues to resign and subsequently — since they refused to resign — fined 10,000 yen each because they had overlooked a newly issued rule of criminal procedure.[16] Judges are prohibited from holding other salaried positions and from engaging in politics or business.

Jurisdiction

Except for minor claims and for offenses liable to a fine or a lighter penalty, which are handled in the summary courts, civil and criminal actions are heard originally in district courts. However, the high courts have original jurisdiction over cases to which specified articles (77–79) of the criminal code apply.[17] The family courts also share in the exercise of original jurisdiction, dealing primarily with matters amenable to arbitration and conciliation, but also exercising a limited power of judgment in controversies within families.[18] These courts also function as juvenile courts, applying the Juvenile Law.[19]

The Supreme Court's jurisdiction is exclusively appellate; the high courts and district courts also hear appeals and complaints arising out of actions in courts below them. While the high and district courts hear appeals on questions of fact (*koso*) as well as of law (*jokoku*), the Supreme Court hears only *jokoku* appeals and complaints (*kokoku*). The former exclusive jurisdiction of the Supreme Court over cases of treason and serious offenses against the imperial family no longer exists. Moreover, that Court has been relieved of part of its former load by transfer of final *jokoku* (legal) appeals to the high courts. The Supreme Court, of course, may hear any appeal if it so desires.

Judicial Review

A wholly unprecedented arrow in the judicial quiver is the power to declare unconstitutional "any law, order, regulation or official act." [20] This power, obviously an expression of deference to American practice, ranks the courts on a level with the Diet, but places them in a delicate position between that body and the cabinet. Should they antagonize the Diet in exercising the power, their judgment would fall to the ground unless upheld by the executive and brought into operation by it. Since the independence of the judiciary of Japan depends upon its support by the Diet against the executive, a power which threatens that support is a double-edged sword. That the courts fully appreciate this fact is suggested by the gingerly approach they have made toward implementation of this new power. [21]

Final authority rests with the Supreme Court, sitting as a grand, i.e., full, bench. However, the inferior courts also may exercise the power of review and they have done so in a number of cases. In one instance a branch of a district court applied to a patricide a general provision of the criminal code applicable to homicide rather than the more severe penalty required by the code in cases of patricide. The judges did so on the theory that the latter provision was a remnant of feudalism and that it violated the principle of the new constitution which recognized the equality of all Japanese. [22] In two other cases a local assembly bylaw which required that permission of the local public safety commission be obtained before a mass demonstration or parade could legally be held was declared unconstitutional by the Kyoto district court but a similar bylaw was upheld by the Fukuoka high court. Freedom of assembly was the issue raised in both cases. [23]

Presumably the power of judicial review, if it is maintained, will be exercised in issues under litigation, not as the basis of advisory opinions to the Diet or other public bodies. For the comparatively weak judiciary of Japan to lend substance to expressed fears that the courts may seek a position of supremacy by challenging a statute or executive order independently of a case before them would be injudicious. On the other hand the able jurists in the system can contribute effectively to the evolution of constitutional government through the restrained application of the power of judicial review.

The Rule-Making Power

The constitution invests the Supreme Court with the power to determine "the rules of procedure and of practice, and of matters relating to attorneys, the internal discipline of the courts and the administration of judicial affairs." [24] The power covers the procurators and may be delegated, for inferior courts, to such courts. The Supreme Court, thus admitted into a realm hitherto tenanted only by administrative officials, has not attempted to write the basic procedural codes but has supplemented the codes with lengthy bodies of rules.[25] To those it has added a large number of rules affecting court organization and procedure, the procuratorate, and the legal profession. The exercise of this power has involved the Court in a heavy burden of legislation at a time when its attention to the application of a vast complex of new laws and orders was of crucial importance.

Court Procedure

Constitutionally, trials are conducted and judgments declared publicly unless a court unanimously decides that a public hearing would be harmful to public order or morals. However, certain types of issues must always be adjudicated in the public hearing — those relating to political offenses and to civil rights.[26] Before spectators are ordered to leave a courtroom the presiding judge is required to state the reason for closing the hearing to the public, which is entitled to return to hear the verdict in any case. While the judges have long had authority to keep spectators in order and to expel disturbers from the courtroom, not until 1952 was the offense of contempt of court legally recognized and made punishable by fine or imprisonment.[27] This law was badly needed not only to enable the judges to restrain outbursts of irrelevant oratory by counsel and to prevent violence against themselves both in and out of courtrooms but also to cut down the waste of time for which legal procedure is notorious.[28] Following the completion of arguments the judges deliberate in private. Decisions normally are rendered by majority, and any judge may write a dissenting opinion, a new practice which has been effectively utilized in Japan.

No considerable changes in the Code of Civil Procedure were made during the postwar era, the third of the great reform periods through which Japan has passed.[29] Criminal procedure was altered to bring it into closer conformity with the common law principles of the occupying powers. The accusatory approach replaced the inquisitorial. The preliminary examination by a procurator was abolished. A limit of twenty days' detention of an arrested person to permit preparation of charges by a procurator was enacted. Indictment has continued to rest with the procurators, but inquest committees may investigate complaints that they have failed to bring indictments and may make public the results of such investigations.[30] An accused person is entitled to an attorney and to knowledge of the charges against him. He is presumed to be innocent; his accusers must prove guilt, whereas formerly he was required to prove innocence. He prepares his defense on the basis of the indictment and need not inform the procurator in advance of trial as to the nature of his defense. His counsel is no longer seated below the procurator.

Habeas corpus procedure was enacted by the Diet in 1948 during the premiership of Ashida Hitoshi.[31] Under this law "a person whose freedom of action is restrained *without the proper legal procedure* may apply for its recovery . . . " (Article 2). The court may dismiss the application for lack of evidence or it may issue a writ demanding the reason for the restraint and conduct an investigation. Its subsequent action upon the application depends upon its judgment of the evidence submitted in justification of the restraint. The underlying principle of this procedure differs fundamentally from that upon which habeas corpus is applied in the courts of Anglo-Saxon peoples. In Japan the law is designed to prevent a person without legal authority, whether a jailer or a brothelkeeper, from holding another person against his will. The court, therefore, in considering an application for habeas corpus, is not concerned with the evidence of probable guilt, but solely with whether or not the restraint is the act of an authority legally competent to perform it. Thus it is only as the courts' interpretation of "the proper legal procedure" broadens to limit the arbitrariness of procurators and police that this pseudo habeas corpus will operate as anything more than a reaffirmation of the prerogatives of duly constituted authorities.[32]

No provision for trial by jury was included in the reformed judicial system. A jury law, enacted in 1923, was in force from 1928 to 1947.[33]

Comparatively slight use was made of juries, litigants preferring to rely upon the knowledge and integrity of judges rather than upon their inexperienced and timid peers in a jury box.

In view of the fullness with which police records are kept it appears anomalous that verbatim court reporting and the publication of reports are not practiced in Japan. Judges and lawyers must depend upon their notes as a case proceeds. Summaries are published by legal journals, and a quasiofficial volume of Supreme Court reports is published monthly by the *Hosakai* (Jurists' Society).

Administrative Litigation

Japan, the bureaucracy par excellence, dispensed with its Court of Administrative Litigation while under the influence of SCAP advisers. Its new code of civil procedure and the administrative litigation law established the principle that any allegedly illegal act of an administrative officer or agency could be challenged in the ordinary courts. The latter statute also permits the courts to issue injunctions against intended damaging acts of officials unless the injunction would be contrary to the public interest or is opposed by the prime minister. The old administrative court had enjoyed a large area of jurisdiction over such cases, and it will be of special interest to observe Japanese officials brought to book in the same courts which try the man from the shop and from the farm. It is true that the administrative court was severely criticized for the slowness of its procedure, but the remedy suggested had not been to abolish the court but to establish additional benches — original and appellate — to replace the greatly overburdened court, which sat either en bloc or in sections.[34]

The Procurators

Although the prosecuting attorneys at the several levels of judicial action no longer are attached to the courts, they function in relation to them as in the past.[35] Constitutionally they are subject to the rule-making power of the Supreme Court. They are officials of the ministry of justice, prosecuting and defending actions on behalf of the state. For each rank of courts there is a corresponding procuratorial office; the Public Procurator General heads the entire system and it is only through him that the minister of justice may control a procurator engaged in litigation.

371

The higher procurators — the procurator general, assistant procurator-general, and superintending procurators (i.e., the chief procurators in the high procurators' offices corresponding to the high courts) — are officials of the first class appointed by the cabinet, and their appointments are attested by the emperor. Other procurators are first- or second-class officials; if first-class, they are appointed by the cabinet, if second-, by the prime minister. Assignments to offices are made by the minister of justice. The retirement age is sixty-five years for a procurator general, sixty-three for other procurators. Salaries are fixed by statute. Required qualifications are high, appointments being made from among judges, judicial apprentices, research officials, lawyers, staff members of the ministry of justice, persons who have passed a higher officials' examination, professors of law, and other comparable categories. While it remains possible to staff the procuratorate with bureaucrats, the spirit of the law calls strongly for a more varied and versatile body of prosecutors.

Tenure is protected by the legal requirement that a specially qualified examining committee composed of procurators, judges, and lawyers shall certify mental or physical or other disability before a public procurator may be dismissed. However, he may be placed on half-salary as a supernumerary official by the minister of justice, and he is subject to a variety of disciplinary penalties in company with other members of the national public service.[36]

Procuratorial business is principally the investigation of allegedly criminal offenses. Indictment after investigation, prosecution of the case, and supervision of the execution of judgments are procuratorial functions. Procurators also defend the state in actions brought against it. In civil matters they may represent the public interest by requesting or providing information and by performing other legally authorized functions. Like the judges, they are overburdened and find themselves unable to carry out investigations thoroughly.[37] However, their inclination to assure themselves a favorable verdict in court makes them prolong investigations unnecessarily. This attitude, a holdover from the old regime, is anything but helpful to the attainment by the courts of their legal status. The procurators no longer sit on a dais alongside the judges trying a case. But they quite naturally find difficulty in modifying their older attitude regarding the nature and importance of their functions.

The Courts

A Field for Improvement

In addition to a new constitution, the revision and replacement of Japanese laws brought into operation new or partially new codes of civil law, criminal law, civil procedure, criminal procedure, and commercial law, and a multitude of new statutes, administrative orders, and judicial rules. Although SCAP draftsmen sought honestly to avoid dictating changes, and while a generally friendly relation was maintained between them and their Japanese collaborators, the basic changes in the constitution, some of which were deeply resented by Japanese statesmen and scholars, called for correspondingly profound changes in the codes and other laws. The resulting burden upon judges and procurators was heavy and contributed to the slowing of the already slow tempo of court procedure. Unfortunately also the "flood of post-war legislation left virtually untouched the greatest weakness of the Japanese legal system, namely, a cumbersome code of civil procedure which necessarily makes litigation both time-consuming and costly and in many cases leads to a virtual negation of justice." [38] This criticism may be unduly severe, since the new code of civil procedure simplifies the treatment of appeals, but Japanese legal scholars are the first to admit that the courts function at glacial speed. Delays are due to the leniency of judges in granting continuances, the trial of cases piecemeal, the lack of verbatim reporting, the unwillingness of procurators to initiate prosecution without an airtight case, and similar retarders.[39]

For the courts it must be noted that the increase in litigation outran that of judicial personnel some 25 per cent between 1941 and 1951. Also that 60 per cent of civil cases and 85 per cent of criminal cases are disposed of within six months.[40] Moreover, in the absence of a system of probation the judges become probation officers, involved in lengthy inquiry into the social factors affecting the actions of accused persons. And of some consequence is the failure of the Diet to provide adequate offices, telephone service, and supplies for the courts and procurators. Remedial legislation was enacted in 1950, but it was not adequate, particularly in relation to the overburdened Supreme Court. In November 1953, 4,000 cases were pending before the Supreme Court, and the Bar Association was demanding action to relieve the situation.[41] In October 1954, a House of Representatives subcommittee recommended that the number of Supreme Court judges be increased from fifteen to thirty and that there be a grand bench of nine judges and six petty benches of five each. It further recommended that current restrictions on the appeal of criminal cases to the Supreme Court be relaxed.[42]

Notes

[1] For the pre-reform judicial system see H. S. Quigley, *Japanese Government and Politics* (New York, 1932), Chapter 14. For the new courts and legal reforms, the authors acknowledge a special obligation to Alfred C. Oppler's articles cited hereafter. Dr. Oppler's position as Chief of the Legislation and Justice Division, Legal Section, GHQ, SCAP, involved his participation in the drafting of the new laws. Fortunately his previous experience and his disposition toward this difficult and delicate enterprise assured its greatest possible success. Recommended also are T. L. Blakemore, "Postwar Development in Japanese Law," *Wisconsin Law Review*, July 1947, Part 1, and R. B. Appleton, "Reforms in Japanese Criminal Procedure under Allied Occupation," *Washington Law Review*, XXIV (1949), 401–430.

[2] Article 62 of the Constitution, relied upon by the Committee, provides: "Each House may conduct investigations in relation to government, and may demand the presence and testimony of witnesses, and the production of records." The issue is covered in the *Nippon Times*, May 21, 1949.

[3] From an address before the International Academy of Comparative Law in London; published in *Nippon Times*, January 21, 1951.

[4] Court Organization Law, *Official Gazette*, No. 311, April 16, 1947, pp. 1–7; also amendments to that law, *ibid.*, October 29, 1947, p. 1; July 15, 1948, (The Juvenile Law), pp. 4–11; December 21, 1948, pp. 2–6; April 14, 1950, pp. 1–3.

[5] Even the more liberal jurists opposed dropping the old name, which means "great deliberative hall," and substituting the new, meaning "the highest court." They were apparently influenced by attachment to a title which antedates the Meiji constitution.

[6] In 1952 there were in operation 8 high courts, 6 high court branches, 49 district courts, 232 district court branches, 49 family courts, 232 family court branches, and 568 summary courts (Alfred C. Oppler, "Japan's Courts and Law in Transition," reprint from *Contemporary Japan*, XXI, June 1952, p. 18).

[7] Court Organization Law, Article 14; Partial Amendment Law, *Official Gazette*, No. 1213, April 14, 1950, pp. 1–3.

[8] Constitution, Article 6, Section 2; this provision was a Diet-proposed amendment designed to assure the Chief Judge a status second only to that of the prime minister.

[9] Determination of the numbers of members any court shall have is left to legislative action by the Diet.

[10] The eminence of committee members rendered their advice mandatory by Japanese standards; in effect the cabinet was thus deprived of its constitutional power of appointment.

[11] Constitution, Article 80, Section 1.

[12] Constitution, Article 79, Sections 2 and 3; also implementing law in *Official Gazette*, November 20, 1947, and enforcement ordinance, *ibid.*, Extra, May 25, 1948.

[13] Alfred C. Oppler, "Japan's Courts and Law in Transition," p. 9. Dr. Oppler notes, however, that the right of recall might be used to check abusive employment of the cabinet's power of appointment, e.g., an attempt to "pack" the Supreme Court.

[14] Printed ballots bearing the names of persons to be voted upon were used for the first time in Japan in the 1949 review of Supreme Court appointees.

[15] For the purposes of the salary scale, the Chief Judge ranks with the prime minister, associate judges with ministers, high court presidents between ministers and vice-ministers, high court judges with officials of the first rank, district court judges with officials of the first or second ranks, assistant judges and summary judges with officials

of the second rank. Safeguarding the judicial salaries the Court Organization Law provides that court expenditures shall be provided for by an independent budget item which shall include a reserve fund (Article 83).

[16] *Nippon Times*, October 20, 1949; May 31, June 15, 25, 1950. Dr. Oppler dryly comments: ". . . judicial independence includes the right of a judge to make an occasional mistake without being publicly castigated." See "Japan's Courts and Law in Transition," pp. 17–18.

[17] Court Organization Law, Article 16, Section 4; Articles 77–79 of the criminal code relate to offenses occurring in riots or civil war.

[18] The family courts have "taken over many functions formerly exercised by the family council, which was connected with the old semi-feudal house system" (Alfred C. Oppler, "The Reform of Japan's Legal and Judicial System under Allied Occupation," *Washington Law Review*, XXIV, August 1949, p. 307).

[19] *Official Gazette*, Extra, July 15, 1948, pp. 4–11.

[20] Constitution, Article 81.

[21] No law or administrative act had been held unconstitutional by the Supreme Court up to the middle of 1952 (Alfred C. Oppler, "Japan's Courts and Law in Transition," p. 20).

[22] *Ibid.*, pp. 21–22. The Supreme Court reversed the decision, 13 to 2.

[23] *Ibid.*, pp. 23–25. Ironically, from the point of view of local self-government, the national government, in consequence of these cases, was reported to be planning to strip the localities of power to regulate mass demonstrations.

[24] Constitution, Article 77.

[25] As an example one may cite Supreme Court Rule No. 32 on criminal procedure, issued December 1, 1948. It is published as *Official Gazette*, Extra No. 37, December 1, 1948 and requires 24 pages for its 302 articles. Dr. Oppler states that "the Supreme Court issued 19 rules in 1947, 44 in 1948, 29 in 1949, 36 in 1950, and 17 in 1951" ("Japan's Courts and Law in Transition," p. 19).

[26] Constitution, Article 82.

[27] A "Law for Maintenance of Order in Courts" was passed on July 7, 1952 (*Nippon Times*, July 8, 1952). Power to punish for contempt of court was withheld out of suspicion that it would encourage judicial arrogance.

[28] Japanese editors condemned defendants' lawyers in trials of Communists for turning the courtrooms into zoos by their tirades and interruptions (*Nippon Times*, November 19, 1949). Five hundred policemen were assigned to guard the courtroom in Tokyo during hearings of the May Day riot cases in 1952 (*ibid.*, June 4, 1952). A gang of Japanese and Korean Communists forcibly removed four defendants from the prisoners' dock during a trial at Hiroshima on May 13, 1952 (*ibid.*).

[29] The first era was that of the seventh and eighth centuries, when the Chinese T'ang Dynasty's laws were voluntarily copied; the second era was that of the latter nineteenth century, when European law was introduced.

[30] See the Law for Inquest of Prosecution, *Official Gazette*, Extra, July 12, 1948, pp. 15–22; also Howard Meyers, "The Japanese Inquest of Prosecution," *Harvard Law Review*, December 1950, pp. 279–286.

[31] *Official Gazette*, No. 699, July 30, 1948, pp. 1–2.

[32] Yet one may agree with Dr. Oppler that "in a country where involuntary servitude of women and children had been almost customary . . . the remedy, in making the courts the guardians of the personal freedom of the people, should have tremendous ideological value" ("The Reform of Japan's Legal and Judicial System," p. 320). In 1952 a writ of habeas corpus was presented before the Supreme Court on behalf of twenty-nine Koreans and one Formosan who were serving prison sentences after conviction as war criminals. The writ was argued for on the ground that after April 26, 1952, when the peace treaty took effect, legal authority for the imprisonment lapsed (*Nippon Times*, June 27, 1952).

[33] H. S. Quigley, *op. cit.*, pp. 285–286.

[34] *Ibid.*, pp. 287–289.

[35] The Public Procurator's Office Law, *Official Gazette*, No. 311, April 16, 1947, pp. 8–12.

[36] Article 25 of the basic law provides: "Except in those cases mentioned in the three preceding articles [and in the text of this chapter] a public procurator shall not, against his will, lose his office, be suspended from the conduct of his duties, or suffer a reduction of salary unless by disciplinary action." Whether or not this article inhibits a minister of justice from transferring an assistant procurator-general to a lesser post without his consent was an issue between the procurator-general and the attorney-general in March 1951. Before it had been settled the assistant procurator-general resigned (*Nippon Times*, March 5, 1951).

[37] *Nippon Times*, July 16, 1949, a letter from an overburdened procurator.

[38] Comment of a reputable foreign lawyer practicing in Japan, Mr. E. V. A. de-Becker, in *Nippon Times*, August 20, 1951.

[39] Article by T. Kurashige, *Nippon Times*, June 22, 1950. One postwar case, that of the Showa Denko scandals, dragged along for two and a half years, from May 1949 to December 1951.

[40] Statement by the secretary-general of the Supreme Court, *Nippon Times*, February 19, 1952; apparently it does not take account of appeals.

[41] *Nippon Times*, November 24, 1953.

[42] *Ibid.*, October 11, 1954.

23

Local Government

THE new system of local government is based upon the principle of local autonomy. "Regulations concerning organization and operations of local public entities," states the constitution (Article 92), "shall be fixed by law in accordance with the principle of local autonomy." However, in view of the fact that this principle was regarded as embodied in the local government code of Meiji, basically drafted by a scholarly German adviser, Albert Mosse, it is apparent that, as interpreted in Japan, local autonomy may exist within a highly centralized and bureaucratic system.[1] Lacking a tradition of self-government at any level, the Japanese people, except in a few large cities, have been even slower to rally to the standard of home rule than to that of parliamentarism. The political parties have until recently, neglected the interests of prefectures and localities, often fighting local elections upon national, not local, issues. The local assemblies, like the Diet, have had too little power to serve confidently as training grounds of democracy. New weapons were placed in the hands of the people by the Local Autonomy Law of 1947.[2] But the vitalizing of the principle of local autonomy can progress only as the citizenry accepts it and fights for it.

Local Public Bodies

The "ordinary" local public bodies, all of which are juristic persons, are the metropolis (Tokyo-to); Hokkaido; the two *fu* (urban prefectures — Kyoto and Osaka); the forty-two *ken* (rural prefectures); the *shi* (cities), except those designated as "special" cities; the *machi* or *cho* (towns); and the *mura* or *son* (villages). These units embrace all the rural and island, as well as the urban, area of Japan. Okinawa prefecture (the Ryukyu Islands) was lost to American forces during World War II, but Japan was not required to renounce title to the area in the peace treaty. It may be anticipated that if and when the government of the United States considers that the necessity of control for strategic reasons has ceased, the Ryukyu and Bonin Islands will be relinquished to Japan. A number of local administrative areas — notably the *gun* (subprefectures or counties) — are not ranked as legal persons. Wards of Tokyo are "special" wards which have the status of cities. The five major cities — Osaka, Kyoto, Nagoya, Kobe, and Yokohama — are divided into administrative wards. All other cities have electoral divisions known as precincts (*cho* or *chonai*), as do the wards. Cities, towns and villages all exist within one or other of the larger units, including the metropolis and the urban prefectures.

Postwar Japan did away with the regional grouping of prefectures established during the war but retained the metropolitan area combining the former prefecture and the former city of Tokyo, also a feature of wartime centralization. In general, the map of local areas remained unaltered. Only the Diet may alter metropolitan or prefectural boundaries or names, but such changes may be made for the municipalities by the governor of the relevant prefecture if they are proposed by resolution of the prefectural assembly. Unless the Diet takes it upon itself to settle issues relating to the disposition of property arising out of boundary changes, they are left to be decided by agreement among the localities involved.

To become a city, a town or village must have at least 30,000 inhabitants, 60 per cent of whom are engaged in urban occupations. It must also look like a city, having appropriate commercial buildings, and 60 per cent of its buildings must stand within the urban core of the city. Metropolitan or prefectural bylaws determine the circumstances in which a village may ascend to the rank of a town. There are some 10,000 municipalities in Japan, of which approximately 270 are cities.

Structure of Local Government

All ordinary local public bodies have the same general governmental organization. Thus it is possible for the Local Autonomy Law to deal with them all under the same titles and subtitles. They vary in powers, and in size, designations, and numbers of component organs. But in all are to be found a "chief" and his auxiliaries and an assembly. All chiefs and assemblies are elected, all have four-year terms. All assemblies are one-chamber bodies. Uniformity, not variety, is more obvious today than it was under the former code.

Tokyo-to, Hokkaido, and the prefectures compose a higher category of local public bodies having supervisory powers over component bodies. They are all essentially prefectural and are grouped together in sections of laws and cabinet orders which distinguish between their functions and those of the municipalities. While national legislation does not mark their distinction by specifically recognizing a superior or higher and an inferior or lower class of localities, the distinction is obvious to one who analyzes the laws and orders on local government. It will be convenient, in considering this subject, to employ the two terms "prefectural" and "municipal," the former being understood to comprehend Tokyo-to, Hokkaido, and the prefectures, the latter the cities, towns, and villages.

The Local Executive

The chief of a prefecture is the governor; of a municipality, the mayor. To be eligible for the governorship a person must be a Japanese national aged thirty or over; for the mayoralty he must be twenty-five or over.[3] A candidate may be of either sex and is not required to reside in the locality in which he is seeking office. A chief may not be concurrently a member of the Diet or of a local assembly. His post is salaried, as are those of his subordinates.

A governor may be removed by the prime minister for failure to administer national affairs according to laws or directives. A mayor who fails similarly may be removed by the relevant governor. However, a chief is entitled to appeal to the courts and to recover his qualification for office if the appeal is sustained. He does not thereby regain the office from which he was ousted. A chief may be requested to resign by the passage of a nonconfidence resolution in the relevant prefectural or municipal assembly. The resolution requires a two-thirds quorum to pass. If the chief exercises his option of dissolving the assembly and calling for an election, the newly elected assembly may unseat him by a second nonconfidence vote, which requires only

379

a simple majority of a two-thirds quorum. The citizenry possess a third procedure for removing a governor or mayor, that of recall, inaugurated by petition of one-third of the electorate and completed by vote of a majority in a recall election. It may hardly be contended that legal means are lacking to check arbitrariness in a local executive, but efforts of assemblies and voters to unseat governors have been fruitless.

From one to three assistant-governors and one or more assistant-mayors are appointed by the relevant chiefs and are removed by them without recourse. The chiefs determine what duties these officers shall perform. In part their functions are political, in part administrative. Where there is more than one assistant chief it is probable that one will be chosen from a political party other than that of which the chief is a member. In the absence of the chief an assistant chief has authority to act for him. These officers are in a true sense political aids, not mere secretaries.[4] In the unlikely event that a locality finds itself without an official legally competent to deputize for the chief, the prime minister may appoint a temporary governor; similarly, a governor may appoint a temporary mayor.

Within the localities the official staff includes an accountant or treasurer and such other officers as may be provided for in bylaws. These regularly include an auditor. Standing or special committees of experts for the conduct of investigations may be established similarly. Branch offices or wards are commonly utilized by the prefectures and larger municipalities; these are directed by the chiefs and are without autonomous status. Branch offices are set up also to aid in local administration of national functions and are financed out of the national treasury. While national establishments normally require Diet approval, the laws authorize a considerable number of exceptions. Thus the appropriate national ministries are still free to establish local branches in the listed categories.

Tokyo, the metropolis, is required by statute to maintain bureaus of general affairs, finance, welfare, economic affairs, construction, health, and labor. It may, if necessary, establish a separate bureau of buildings by bylaw. Hokkaido and the prefectures are required to maintain divisions of general affairs, welfare, economic affairs, public works, health, and agricultural land. They may add, by bylaw, a division of agriculture and forestry or one of commerce and industry, and divisions of fisheries, labor, and buildings. Hokkaido is authorized, in addition, to establish a division of development. All public bodies of the prefectural category may also set up by bylaw agencies for the management of public utilities. Municipalities may decide for themselves what departments of administration shall be maintained.

Executive Powers

The governors and mayors coordinate administration and represent their respective localities. A chief must serve two masters, since he functions as an agent of the national government in national matters and as an officer of the prefecture or municipality in local matters. He appoints, removes, and supervises the principal officials of the locality. He may set up sections within bureaus or divisions of administration. He is responsible for preparation of the local budget, for the collection of taxes and fees, for the payment and audit of appropriations, and for the management of property. He is the custodian of official instruments and documents. He may, in an emergency, use private property for a public purpose, with due compensation. He may go so far as to order the inhabitants to defend themselves in situations of danger or calamity. His legislative instrument is the regulation, which he issues without reference to the assembly. He may prescribe fines up to 2,000 yen for violation of regulations.

A chief is empowered also to exercise the powers of an assembly in emergencies which call for prompt action. He may do so, furthermore, if an assembly fails to convene or to take action within its powers which the chief believes to be necessary. He may expend money for duly authorized purposes or in emergencies, despite an assembly decision to strike out or reduce budgetary items for such expenditures. If the assembly persists in its opposition to these items, the chief may construe its attitude as equivalent to a nonconfidence vote and dissolve the assembly. Although, as above noted, the newly elected assembly may compel the chief to resign, the likelihood that the voters will sustain the chief in the election makes the power of dissolution a stronger weapon than the nonconfidence vote.

Governors exercise a considerable authority over the chiefs of municipalities within their respective prefectures. While subject to the competent national ministers in their operations as organs of the national government, they share with them the directive power over municipal heads operating as national organs. A governor has no power to remove a mayor, but may seek a writ of mandamus to compel performance of legal responsibilities. He may delegate prefectural functions to a municipal chief or require the chief to aid him in the exercise of prefectural functions. His powers of coordination are extensive, permitting him to "direct and supervise" municipalities, call for their records and accounts, and annul the dispositions of their chiefs. In the event that several prefectures have common problems relating to the municipalities, their governors may designate one of themselves to deal with them.

In addition to their routine activities the chiefs, particularly the governors and the mayors of the cities, have important political and social responsibilities. They are drawn increasingly into service for the political parties. They must meet the press, listen to complaints of citizens, and address public gatherings. Trips to Tokyo for interviews with national officials and to intercede for grants-in-aid occupy much of their time. Twice a year the governors meet in conference (*chiho-kankaigi*) at the capital. This conference affords an opportunity to present common prefectural needs unitedly and to discuss them with national officials. Each category of chiefs also maintains an association for the consideration of mutual interests and the promotion of cordial relations. These associations have become highly important centers of cooperative effort. They maintain offices in Tokyo in which research and publication upon local administrative problems are carried on. Since all municipalities are included in the associations, the annual and special conferences of the town and village chiefs are likely to be attended by several thousand mayors.

Election Administration Committees

Contributory to the realization of local self-government is the provision for election administration committees in each local public body. Their function, as indicated by the title, is to manage the national and local elections. They are autonomous within each locality, but the municipal committees are supervised by those of the prefectures. Their members are elected for three-year terms by the local assemblies.[5] Six qualified voters are chosen for prefectural committees, four for the municipalities. A maximum of two members of the former, of one member of the latter, may belong to the same political party.

Committees elect their chairmen from their membership. Members may not participate in proceedings in which the interests of close relatives are involved. They receive a small honorarium.

Inspection Commissioners

For the maintenance of efficient and honest administration each prefecture is required to set up an inspection commission. Each municipality is authorized to do so by bylaw. Four members, appointed by the chief with the assembly's approval, compose a commission. Two members must be assemblymen; two must be private citizens of "special knowledge and experience." Their term of office is two years, and they are remunerated from public funds.

The commissions conduct regular and *ad hoc* inspections of administrative offices and public enterprises. They may act upon their own initiative at any time or upon the request of the assembly or of local administrators. Recipients of grants-in-aid, loans, or other assistance are subject to inspection. The commissions report to the respective chiefs and assemblies. They also report to boards of education, public safety commissions, and other agencies.

The Local Legislatures

Each local public body has an assembly elected by Japanese nationals aged twenty or above whose residence has been, for three consecutive months immediately before an election, within the municipality in which they seek to vote. Candidates for election must be twenty-five years old or over. In the municipalities they must be residents; in the prefectures residence is not required. For the prefectural assemblies election districts are the same as those of the cities and subprefectures (*gun*). Cities, towns, and villages may be electoral districts, while in the larger cities wards or especially established districts may be utilized.

Assemblies vary in size with the population of the locality. For the metropolis and other prefectures they run from 40 to 120 members; for the municipalities the minimum number is 12, the maximum 48. Members may not be, concurrently, members of the Diet or of a local administration. Their term is four years and they may be re-elected without limitation. Towns and villages may substitute general meetings of their electorates for assemblies.

Regular sessions are held six times a year, extraordinary sessions when necessary. Normally both regular and extraordinary sessions are called by the chief of the local public body, but he is obliged to call an extraordinary session if it is demanded by at least one-fourth of the assembly. Decisions upon the length of sessions, recess, and adjournment are made by the assembly. Chairmen of assemblies are elected by the assemblies. Standing and special committees are employed. Members may introduce bills for bylaws on any subject except finance. Action upon bills is taken by resolutions passed by a simple majority, and the enactments are termed bylaws. Discussion is conducted with galleries open to the public unless secrecy is voted by two-thirds of the members present. Rules of procedure are made by the assemblies. Minutes are kept. Petitions of citizens may be received and forwarded with recommendation for action to executive officers. Members receive salaries, but they do not enjoy the immunities of Diet members from legal liability for statements made in assembly sessions.

Powers of Assemblies

The assemblies possess the power to enact bylaws within the sphere of authority of the localities concerned. They may prescribe prison terms up to two years, fines up to 100,000 yen, and lesser penalties, for violations of bylaws. They determine the annual budgets and receive the annual reports of the auditors. They exercise the power to tax and to set fees for public services. They enter into contracts and regulate the management of public property and funds, respond to legal action against the locality, and decide upon compensation to be paid for damages caused by its officers. They may conduct investigations related to local affairs and may demand that officers and other persons appear before them and give testimony. The public documents of the locality are open to them. They are required to maintain a library and to provide it with official gazettes and other materials for the use of assemblymen and the citizenry.

In operation, assemblies are comparatively weak. The low salaries of their members, which are insufficient for maintenance, reflect their inferiority. Members often are persons of small ability and slight education. (Their mediocrity has not prevented them from seeking to establish pension systems for themselves, applicable upon completion of a single term!) Although they meet, in practice, about once a month, their members seldom introduce bills, but defer to the chief. During the February session, however, in which the budget is decided, committee discussions are likely to be spirited. Like the chiefs, the chairmen of the assemblies have associations — separate for cities, towns, and villages — for discussion and promotion of common interests. These associations also maintain national offices and research staffs in Tokyo. Since they have certain interests in common with the administrative heads, a Local Self-Government Institute is supported by and serves both groups of associations. The Institute of Municipal Research, of Tokyo, is a seventh member of the Institute.

Chief-Assembly Relations

The legally prescribed relation between a governor or mayor on the one hand and an assembly on the other resembles that of the executive to the legislature in a parliamentary system. A chief submits bills to the assembly and has a limited veto power. The assembly sends its bylaws to the chief for signature and promulgation. The assembly's power to compel the resignation of a chief already has been noted; also the power of a chief to dissolve an assembly and to call for the election of a new assembly. Clearly, the assembly has the final word whether or not the chief shall continue in office. A chief may, however, exert control over an assembly in the following ways:

1. By returning to it any resolution to which he objects, with a request for reconsideration. If the assembly passes the resolution a second time, with a two-thirds majority, the resolution becomes final.

2. By returning to it a resolution or notification of an election which the chief alleges to be illegal. If the assembly maintains its position the chief may bring a court action against it.

3. By threatening to use his power to issue bylaws if the assembly fails to meet.

4. By threatening to use his power to expend funds for administrative services.

In practice these controls, added to the powers and the greater prestige of the executive office, would seem likely to prevail over the assembly's legal superiority. However, elective chiefs have not been inclined to assert their powers and prestige. Rather there has been noted a tendency on both sides to resign office when differences appear to be irreconcilable.

"Special" Local Public Bodies

Special cities, special wards, associations of local public bodies, and property wards fall within the legal category of special local public bodies. Special cities, which are administered similarly to the five major cities, are designated as such by statute. Such designation is made occasionally in order to recognize exceptional circumstances. Hiroshima and Nagasaki, which were the first cities to undergo atomic bombing, were designated, respectively, as "international peace" and "international culture" cities. The citizens of these cities exercised their constitutional right to approve the designation. Special cities exist legally outside any prefecture and are, therefore, exempt from prefectural control and taxation. Moreover, they receive special national subsidies. Quite naturally the prefectural bodies are strongly opposed to the efforts of the five major cities to obtain this status, since the prefectures depend upon their wealth as a major source of tax revenue.[6]

As noted previously, special wards exist only in the metropolis and are administered as cities. Associations of local public bodies may be set up with the permission of the prime minister or the governor by a group of ordinary and/or special localities. All ordinary units, from the metropolis to the village, may enter into such associations "for the purpose of managing jointly a portion of their affairs." Towns and villages may go further and enter into "whole affairs" associations, doing away with their separate executive officers and assemblies, but retaining their identities as separate localities. "Partial affairs" associations of municipalities may be decreed by cabinet order and organized by a governor if the public interest warrants such action. These associations, like their members, are legal persons. They may be dissolved in the same manner as they are created.

A property ward may be established by a portion of a city, town, village, or special ward for the purpose of maintaining a piece of property or an establishment belonging to that portion of the locality. Such a ward may be authorized by the governor and assembly of the prefecture within which it is situated, or by the mayor and assembly of a special city, to have its own assembly or general meeting to deal with the property or establishment which led to its creation. It is entitled to a proper share of the revenue for the conduct of its special functions.

Local Government

Auxiliary Local Bodies

A number of historical territorial divisions are recognized in Japan for administrative purposes but not as legal entities. The largest island, Honshu, is composed of the five ancient regions geographically described as Tohoku, Kanto, Chubu (Tokai), Kinki, and Chugoku. Kinki often is referred to as Kansai, though the latter area is but part of Kinki. Other historically named regions on Honshu are Hanshin, Keihin, Chukyo, Kannon, and Shinechi. None of these are important administrative centers today, but they continue to have significance as self-conscious political areas.

The most important of the older units to administrators are the *gun*, which are employed in all prefectures as electoral districts and for census-taking and other purposes. Through the *gun* chief, the governor sends information and directives to towns and villages. Cities, however, are not included within the operations of a *gun*. They retain social significance, and many private associations are organized on a *gun* basis.

While uniformity of structure is lacking in the localities, it may be stated that in a majority of the towns and villages there are nuclei, sometimes without inhabitants, known as *oaza*, *aza*, or *koaza* (sections), and *buraku* (hamlets). *Oaza* formerly were villages and continue to be regarded as centers for management of the irrigation system and for religious and ceremonial purposes. *Aza* and *koaza* are utilized for the registry of land titles and boundaries. Hamlets are essentially social-economic units "consisting of the families living and cultivating land within an area smaller than a village and usually smaller than an *oaza*." [7] Of ancient origin, the *buraku* were officially reorganized and given new responsibilities during World War II, aiding the war effort by conducting the local rationing administration, gathering information, stimulating patriotic efforts, and executing national control orders. They were declared illegal, at SCAP's demand, in 1947, but continued to exist, to elect their *burakukai* — assemblies — under new titles, and to perform numerous functions. Their heads are appointed by the mayor from among their leading citizens. Professor Robert Ward estimates that between 40 and 50 per cent of the present population resides in the hamlets. He suggests that "research at this level will shed new and important light on the political, economic and social attitudes and behavior of the Japanese people." He presents interesting evidence to support his tentative conclusions, related to a limited area, that the *buraku* are preserving the tradition of family control of local affairs, that *buraku* administration is by no means autocratic, that it is indispensable as a means of informing the people regarding action affecting them which has been taken at higher levels, and that party politics and national government are powerfully affected by the standards and procedures of *buraku* society.

Within the cities are historical subdivisions, similar to and probably descended from the *buraku*, known as *chonai* (precincts or blocks) with their assemblies (*chonaikai*), which correspond to the *burakukai* in the towns and villages. Their historical ups and downs follow those of the *buraku*. Within both these residual "block associations" the *tonarigumi* (neighborhood associations), of still older origin, continue to display vitality. These are groups of approximately ten households, with a chief (*kumicho*) selected by themselves and often reluctant to accept an onerous, unsalaried, and thankless job. The heads of households or representatives meet in the home of a member of the association and their discussions culminate in a declaration by the *kumicho*, without taking a vote, of the general sentiment of the meeting. Rarely is this declaration challenged, since the chief's integrity must not be questioned nor his dignity impaired. But silence does not necessarily imply consent nor does it guarantee that the decision will be supported by all members.

The *tonarigumi* are the termini of the nerves connecting the central brain in Tokyo with the local administrative organs. During World War II, they administered the rationing system, civil defense against air attack, public welfare and relief, the collection of grain, and liaison with women's organizations.[8] They were also utilized as intelligence sources against subversion, media for the sale of war bonds, and for various forms of patriotic demonstration. When the war ended they lost importance, but continued as rations-distributors until abolished by order of SCAP on April 1, 1947, on the ground that they were instruments of ultranationalism and obsolete social ideals.[9] This appraisal has been ably criticized by Dr. Ralph Braibanti and others, who hold that the neighborhood, hamlet, and precinct assemblies not only performed essential functions but also offered a prepared field for experiments in self-government. Japanese sentiment was divided upon the value of the associations. In practice, however, they survived the Occupation in the guise of "voluntary" associations. Thus the block and neighborhood bodies are playing a larger role than they played before 1940.[10] In October 1951 a newspaper poll found 65 per cent of the persons polled in favor of re-legalizing the associations, only 18 per cent opposed.[11]

Political Rights of Citizens

In addition to exercising their rights of voting and candidature, Japanese nationals of voting age may participate in local government through various forms of direct action. Two per cent of the voters in any local public body may demand, over their signatures, that a by-law be enacted, amended, or repealed. This right does not extend to bylaws relating to taxes or other sources of revenue. The assembly need not take the action demanded, but it must consider it and report to the initiators through the local chief.[12] Similarly, 2 per cent of the voters may demand action by an inspection commission. The commission, or, in a locality which lacks a commission, the chief, must make the inspection requested and report findings.

One-third of the local electorate may demand, over their signatures, the dissolution of the assembly. This demand is presented to the election administrative committee, which must submit it to the voters. Majority support of the demand compels the assembly to resign. The same procedure is applicable to a single assemblyman and, as previously noted, also to the chief of the local public body. Other administrative officers must be removed by a chief upon demand of one-third of the voters if the local assembly approves the demand.

Local Public Service

The local public service, for which a law drafted in 1949 under the supervision of the cabinet was passed by the Diet in December 1950, was modeled closely upon the national system.[13] The service has two categories, special and regular, like the national service. Within the special service are the political officers whose positions are elective, their confidential secretaries, and persons holding temporary or part-time posts. They are not subject to civil service rules. Within the regular service are the administrative officers and employees of all types of locality, also of the boards of education and local police agencies.

Two types of commissions, one for the prefectures and designated cities, the other for all other local public bodies, are replicas in greater or lesser degree, of the Personnel Authority in the national system.[14] Each prefecture and each of the five major cities has a personnel commission, each of the other localities an equity commission. These commissions are established by the local assemblies, subject to general principles laid down in the local public service law. Their members, three in number, are appointed by the governor or mayor, with assembly approval, for terms of four years. National standards of qualification and disqualification apply to these appointments. Commissioners may be removed by the same process, but only for incompetence or illegal or subversive conduct, and charges against them must be presented in a public hearing of the relevant assembly committee. Personnel commissioners may serve on full or on part time; equity commissioners are part-time officers. These positions are salaried, the rate of salary being determined severally by the prefectural and local public bodies.

Personnel commissions perform the normal functions of civil service administration: investigation of all aspects thereof; recommendation of measures of betterment; development of systems of classification, compensation, training, and equitable treatment of employees; and conduct of examinations and the listing of examinees for appointments. Equity commissions are limited to the duties implied by their titles: the hearing of complaints and the adoption or recommendation of measures to assure justice. Thus the great majority of Japan's cities, towns, and villages have agencies to safeguard employees but no agencies to adapt and operate principles worthy of being safeguarded. Decisions upon complaints are reviewable only by the commissions which make the decisions, but judicial action may be sought to settle an issue of legal competence.

Appointments and promotions are made from eligibility lists compiled on the basis of ability determined by competitive examination, records of performance, and other evidence. Competitive examination is required unless the relevant personnel commission authorizes selection upon other criteria only. This rule does not apply in localities lacking a personnel commission. There the local administration has the option of utilizing examinations or dispensing with them. Eligibility lists normally contain five names for each available position, arranged in the order of examination grades. The appointing officer may select any one of the five. Discrimination among eligible persons on the basis of race, creed, sex, social status, family origin, or political views is barred by law. By arrangement with the National Personnel Authority, other national agencies, or other local agencies, a local personnel commission may obtain collaboration in the examination or selection process or may delegate the examination power to another agency. Similarly a local commission may list eligibles from among examinees successful in a national or another local competition.

Local governments having personnel commissions are required to set up a classification of positions in the regular service. This power is vested in the assemblies and is exercisable through the passage of bylaws. Allocations of positions to their proper classes and a periodic review of allocations are functions of the personnel commissions. Both the assemblies and the commissions are called upon to develop and operate their classification systems in consonance with those of the national government and of comparable localities.

Salaries and other conditions of employment also are set by local bylaws, with due consideration of living costs, and of the compensation received in the national service, other local systems, and private enterprise, and of hours and working conditions in the several occupations. While all local public bodies are required to enact pay schedules in which standards for salary increase are stated and provision is made for overtime pay and other supplementary allowances, only in localities having personnel commissions are employees aided by expert coordination of compensation with position and regular investigation of working conditions.

Employees are under the same restrictions as national civil servants with regard to political activities within the locality of their service. They are free, however, outside their respective localities, to engage in political campaigns within the limitations that apply to all the citizenry. They may enter employee organizations — this privilege does not extend to policemen and firemen — but such organizations, as in the national service, are denied the rights of collective bargaining and striking. They are, however, entitled to negotiate with local public bodies regarding compensation, hours, and other conditions of work, including social or welfare activities. Individuals also enjoy the privilege of negotiation.

An employee may present a personal complaint concerned with compensation or other conditions of work to the relevant personnel commission or, in the absence of such a body, to the equity commission of his locality of employment. Investigation must be made and such action taken as lies within a commission's power, which is limited to recommendation of remedial action to the appointing agency. An employee subjected to discipline or removal is entitled to receive a written statement of charges and to appeal to the relevant commission for review of the action taken against him. He is further entitled to a hearing, which must be open to the public if he desires it. At this point a commission's powers extend to revision or cancellation of the action, and to requirement of monetary compensation for loss of salary, if it disapproves the action. It is not, however, empowered to compel an appointing agency to implement its findings.

Excellent principles for maintaining employee morale, providing against loss of income in the event of injury, illness, or retirement, and assuring the welfare of dependents, are embodied in the local public service laws. Their effectuation in the required local bylaws providing for training schools, health and recreation programs, mutual aid systems, and pensions necessarily is conditional upon the availability of funds. A considerable number of prefectures and municipalities maintain training schools or institutes, some of them with excellent up-to-date buildings and equipment. Significantly, although the National Personnel Authority exhibited an interest in assisting the local services to maintain high standards — for example, by offering advice upon training programs — the attitude of the localities has been, in general, suspicious, a rather healthy one in the light of history. In 1952 a Public Service Training Council was established cooperatively by the national, prefectural, and municipal training institutes. Its purpose is to raise in-service training standards by providing information and professional advice.

Education in the Localities

Before 1948 education from kindergarten to university was under the control and direction of the Ministry of Education. Within a prefecture the governor, directed by the Ministry, executed the laws and ordinances of the national government. Postwar legislation provided for a considerable degree of decentralization.[15] The Board of Educa-

tion Law of 1948 implements the liberal principles of the Fundamental
Law of Education of 1947 by requiring the prefectures and the five
major cities to elect boards of education and to bring them into operation by November 1, 1948.[16] The remaining cities, and the towns and
villages, were required by this law to elect and activate boards by
October 1950. Subsequently, because of shortage of funds, the municipalities were allowed to postpone the establishment of boards until
1952.

The boards — seven members in the prefectures, five in the municipalities — are elected for terms of four years. All members of a board
but one, who is elected by and from the relevant local assembly, are
elected by the people. Each board appoints a superintendent to administer the system. The boards are independent of the local governments except as controlled by the necessity of relying upon them for
the major part of their financial support. They are authorized to
establish schools, determine curriculums, select textbooks, certificate
and appoint teachers, and draw up budgets. Municipal boards must
submit annual and occasional reports to prefectural boards. Prefectural boards report to the Ministry of Education. But the Ministry is
not legally entitled to determine policy for, or to exercise administrative control over, the prefectural or municipal boards. The Diet, of
course, may authorize specific national controls, and the localities are
not protected by the constitution from such legislation. Private schools
fall under the regulation of the prefectural governors, but the first
article in the Private School Law of 1949 states that its purpose is
"to promote their sound development by guaranteeing their autonomy
and enhancing their public nature."[17] Universities and other institutions of higher education are not administered under the Board of
Education Law.

Apathy rather than enthusiasm has characterized the attitude of the
people toward local control of education. They doubt that the Ministry of Education, which continued to lay down a multiplicity of directives relating to educational standards and requiring extensive reports, is sympathetic to the new system. They doubt the capacity of
themselves and their neighbors to carry responsibilities which to their
minds require expert knowledge. Witness their inclination to elect
teachers to the boards and the persistent efforts of the teachers' unions
to seat their members: a natural application of the well-understood

393

principle of bureaucratism. Voting in elections for board members has been lighter than in other local elections. Shortage of funds has hurt the prospects for popular support of local educational autonomy. On the other hand the numerous and active parent-teacher associations are seeking earnestly to implement the principle of local control of education.

Local Police

Postwar legislation sought to limit the national authority over prefectural and municipal police, and, as in the field of education, to bring the people into closer association with police administration. To these ends the Police Law of 1947 provided not only for national rural police but for autonomous forces in all municipalities with a population of 5,000 or more.[18] By an amendment, however, towns and villages were permitted to waive the right to set up their own police if their citizenry, by plebiscite, so decided. The local agency in which authority was vested in each area, including the metropolis and Hokkaido, was a public safety commission of three members appointed by and under the jurisdiction of the chief of the local public body. Members might not be police officers or appointive civil servants, and not more than two of them might belong to the same political party. The law indicated that public-spirited citizens such as might be candidates for the local assembly were considered to be the most desirable type of member for a public safety commission.

Prefectural public safety commissions functioned as national agencies, participating in administration of the national rural police. The prefectures did not have their own police forces, and prefectural commissions were specifically barred from exercising either administrative or operational control over the municipal police systems.[19] They lacked the power of appointment of police officers and were subject to national control of administrative matters, i.e., "matters relating to the organization and budget of the police as well as to personnel affairs of its officials." However, operational control, which includes the maintenance of public order, protection of life and property, prevention and suppression of crime, detection of offenses, apprehension of suspects, control of traffic, serving of warrants of arrest, detention of arrested persons, and the execution of other court and procuratorial orders, was exercised by both prefectural and municipal commissions.

Municipal commissions were under the administrative control of the relevant municipal public bodies. Bylaws of the municipalities determined matters of personnel and organization, subject to standards set by statute. The funds for maintenance were provided from the municipal treasury. Indirectly, therefore, the general supervisory authority of the prefectures over the municipalities affected the municipal police administration. National direction of local police might be assumed by the prime minister in the event of a national emergency.

Within a national total of 95,000 men each municipality was authorized in 1947 to fix the number of its police. The villages and small towns found the maintenance of their own systems too expensive for them. By plebiscite a large majority of them voted to surrender the privilege, thereby falling under the national system. This trend was hastened by the difficulty experienced in the apprehension of suspects due to the ease of flight from one jurisdiction to another. The right of a municipal policeman to pursue a fugitive 500 meters into an adjoining locality failed to meet the needs of effective law-enforcement. The smaller localities found that the competition of their larger neighbors and of the national system prevented them from obtaining qualified men. Bossism in the commissions was another crippling factor; favoritism toward black-marketeers and smugglers also was experienced.[20]

Consequently it is not surprising that in June 1954 the Diet passed a new Police Law which went into effect on July 1, 1954. Under it the national and local police were reorganized into forty-six prefectural police forces. The remaining municipal forces were abolished, but something of the Occupation principle of decentralization was salvaged through the continuance of prefectural public safety commissions. These, however, are now under the supervision of a National Public Safety Commission, headed by a minister without portfolio. Both the national and the prefectural commissions are composed of private citizens of learning and experience. Within the national government there is also a Police Agency, which controls operational standards throughout the prefectures. Thus the old system has been re-established but with an element of popular participation.

Financial Administration

The Local Government Law places in the chief of a local public body the authority to draft an annual budget and to submit it to the assembly. The fiscal year is the same as the national — from April 1 to March 31. Supplementary budgets are handled in the same manner. After action by the assembly, a prefectural chief must report the budget to the Local Finance Commission. Similarly the municipal chief reports to the relevant governor. The localities are not, however, subject to budgetary revision by a higher authority so long as they remain within the powers legally allotted to them. They may not borrow money without permission of the Local Finance Commission.

Monthly and semiannual audits of receipts and expenditures are required by law. These are conducted by inspection commissions or, in localities having no commissions, by their mayors. A final accounting, prepared by the treasurer, is submitted annually by the chief to the assembly and subsequently to the higher authorities. It is also made public in summary form. Any citizen has the right to demand an investigation by an inspection commission or chief in the event that he has evidence of the misuse of public funds or property or of entrance into an unlawful contract. If dissatisfied with the results of an investigation, the citizen may sue for legal action against a suspected official.

Prefectural and municipal revenues are obtained from designated local taxes, the operation of public utilities, fees, fines, rentals, lotteries, voluntary contributions, etc., and from national subsidies. Maximum tax rates are set by the national government. The principal direct local taxes are the income tax, the property tax (municipal), which replaced the house and land tax in 1950, and the enterprise tax, the last-named being in part an indirect tax. In 1949–1950 only 37 per cent of the local tax revenue came from direct taxes.[21] Total local expenditures were approximately 376 billion yen in that year, of which 143 billion came from national subsidies and grants and 40 billion from voluntary contributions. Local spending was about two-fifths of the total cost of national and local government (960 billion yen).[22] In response to a recommendation of the Shoup mission (a group of American economists headed by Professor Carl S. Shoup, which made a study of the system of taxation in 1949), the Japanese government provided by law for annual equalization grants to the prefectures and municipalities.[23] Aimed "to strengthen the independence of local bodies. . . . without impairing their right to manage their property, affairs and administration independently," this law replaced the Distribution Tax Law, under which a percentage of receipts from the national income and corporation taxes had been distributed, on a variety of bases, to the local public bodies. It did not, however, eliminate the practice of subsidization. The principle which the law seeks to implement is the equalization of the public services in the poorer localities with those in their more wealthy neighbors. The grants vary, therefore, with the need and with the extent of the services provided by a locality. The requests of the municipalities for grants are channeled through the prefectures and the Local Finance Commission to the cabinet. Extraordinarily detailed data must accompany the requests.[24] No condition or specification as to the use of the grants may be laid down by the national government.

Customarily the rates at which the principal local taxes are assessed have been set by the prefectures. The municipalities have added a percentage — usually 100 per cent — to these rates. Thus the prefectures, including Tokyo-to, have had approximately the same share of local tax revenues as the municipalities within their respective boundaries. Each locality levies and collects its share of the taxes. The prefectural tax office is also agent for the national administration in the collection of taxes. In 1950 the surtax system was modified by the passage of a law authorizing the municipalities to levy taxes upon separate sources of funds at rates to be set by the local assemblies.

An interesting but outdated vestige of feudal tax administration is the part played by trade associations *(kumiai)* in the present system. Tax offices permit the associations to bargain with them upon the amount to be paid by their members. The sum agreed upon is then assessed upon the members either by agreement among them or by the boss *(oyabun)* who dominates the association. Each member then makes his tax return for the amount assessed, filing and paying individually or through the association. The Shoup report condemned this practice as lending itself "to racketeering, boss-domination, favoritism and diversion of funds," and strongly urged that it be abandoned.[25]

Brief mention should be made of other recommendations of this report, one of the genuinely valuable contributions of the Occupation, the more so because highly competent Japanese scholars and administrators collaborated cordially in its preparation. It recommended that the municipalities receive a larger share, the prefectures a smaller share of the tax revenue; that local taxes be increased, national subsidies reduced in number and amount; that the municipalities abandon surtaxes on prefectural taxes, utilizing others restricted to themselves; that there be fewer taxes; and that the rates on the inhabitant's tax be more than doubled, those on real estate more than tripled. All these proposals are conducive to the firm establishment of local self-government. Quite naturally they have been welcomed cordially by the municipalities.

To supervise local financial administration the Diet passed the Local Finance Commission Establishment Law, at the suggestion of the Shoup mission, in May 1950.[26] The law provides for a commission of five members attached to the Prime Minister's Office. Although appointed by the prime minister with consent of the Diet, three of the five members are recommended, respectively, by the national association of prefectural governors and assembly chairmen (jointly), the associations of city mayors and chairmen, and the associations of town and village mayors and chairmen. The commission is under legal mandate to contribute to the realization of the principle of local autonomy — a rather naive admission of the inertia to be overcome. Its responsibilities include the conduct of research upon intergovernmental financial relations, the provision of advice in this field for the localities, and the administration of functions of the national government related to the equalization grants.

The commission also is empowered to decide controversies between localities regarding jurisdiction under the Local Tax Law, to authorize changes in the income-basis of the municipal inhabitant's tax, to determine the multiplication factor for farm-land taxes, to authorize nonlegalized local taxes, to grant permission for the raising of loans, to designate localities which may conduct lotteries, horse races, and bicycle races, and to demand financial data and reports from the local public bodies. It exercises its powers as an adjunct of the cabinet and submits opinions and reports to it and to the Diet.

It is apparent that the dependence of the local public bodies on the national government for more than half their funds is a major impediment to the progress of local autonomy. On the other hand, to deprive the localities of needed subsidies would mean the breakdown of their activities. Only if they successfully assert their constitutional right to adequate and unmortgaged sources of local revenues will they be able to throw off their financial guardianship and to justify home rule through self-support. Only if they are determined to regard such essential functions as the provision of public education and the maintenance of public order as properly local — not merely locally administered on behalf of the national government — will they have a solid foundation upon which they may assert this right.

Local Autonomy, Principle versus Practice

With the abolition of the Ministry of Home Affairs in December 1947 the "governor" on the engine of local administration was removed. While that ministry had not monopolized central powers over the localities, the prefectural governors were appointed and directed by it, and they dominated local affairs. Consequently, in so far as central authority continued to operate in the localities, it became necessary to provide new agencies and procedures to fill the vacuum. A plethora of agencies of national ministries and boards resulted, dealing with price control, land, food, charcoal, labor, trade, industry, economic stabilization, etc.[27] The Diet then prohibited the establishment of local agencies of the central government except by statute. In 1949 it set up a Local Autonomy Agency as an external organ of the Prime Minister's Office, with a minister of state as director.[28] Within the Agency a committee of twelve persons (reduced to eight in 1950), representing the Diet, the localities, and the public, was constituted to aid the director in exercising many of the responsibilities formerly carried by the Home Ministry. The Agency was, however, directed to carry on its work in the spirit of the principle that local self-government was to be realized in accordance with the Local Autonomy Law. In 1950, as already noted, a second national supervisory body, the Local Finance Commission, took over the responsibilities of the Local Autonomy Agency in the field of finance. In practice the Commission is, however, a mere advisory aid to the Agency.

The postwar constitution and legislation narrowed the scope of prefectural powers, widened that of the other localities, restricted prefectural control of the latter, and expanded the electoral system in the localities. The Diet is forbidden by the constitution to enact a special law, applicable only to one public entity, without the consent of the locality. It cannot abolish the assemblies or require that their members or the governors and mayors become appointive officers. It must tolerate a modest appearance of local self-government. The localities remain, however, from the metropolis to the villages, creatures of the national government. Their powers are delegated and enumerated, and are exercisable only if laws or cabinet orders have not been issued within the delegated field.

Localities within a prefecture are further limited by the concurrent legislative powers of the prefecture. To quote the Local Autonomy Law:

The affairs [with which an ordinary local public body may deal] are generally as follows *except in cases where they have been provided for in laws or in cabinet orders duly authorized by law.* [Article 2, paragraph 3; italics added.]

A local public body shall not deal with its affairs *so as to contravene any laws or cabinet orders or ministerial regulations* duly authorized by law, and, furthermore, a city, town or village or a special ward shall not deal with its affairs *so as to contravene any bylaw of the metropolis, district or rural prefecture concerned.* [Article 2, paragraph 6; italics added.]

Although no constitutional or legal delimitation assures any of the local public bodies a specified field of independent authority, the legislative provisions for the new order patently seek to distribute the functions of government in a manner that will combine effective administration with popular participation at all levels. Distribution has been extremely difficult to accomplish to the general satisfaction. Upon first passage, the basic law contained no listing of subjects upon which local authority might be exercised. In 1948 a paragraph containing twenty-one sections enumerating such subjects was added to Article 2 of that law.[29] Embraced within this amendment are maintenance of public safety and welfare; establishment and management of roads, parks, public utilities, schools, hospitals, etc.; ownership of property; collection of taxes and fees; and other "public affairs." However, the amendment failed to indicate boundary lines between the spheres of the several units of local government.

In 1949 the Diet provided for a "Local Administration Investigation Committee" attached to the Office of the Prime Minister.[30] Composed of five members, three of whom were nominated, respectively, by the associations of prefectural governors, city mayors, and mayors of towns and villages, the committee's principal mission was to solve the problem of the proper distribution of functions among the localities. Its recommendations, submitted a year later and supplemented in 1951, reveal difficulties encountered, but do not present a clear-cut or confident response to its directive.[31] While the committee favored centralization, it stated that "affairs which will entail extreme inefficiency and improper operation if placed in charge of the municipalities" should be left to the prefectures. No principle of regional distribution is recognized in this statement; rather it carries an inference that the municipal governments are likely to be less efficient than the prefectural, leaving the way open to the extension of prefectural control over matters by nature municipal. The basic law operates similarly, since it authorizes any local public body "to adjust and coordinate the activities of the public bodies and other similar bodies within the area of an ordinary local public body." Even more specifically, it provides that "the metropolis, district or urban or rural prefecture may enact necessary provisions in its bylaws relating to the administrative affairs of the city, town or village unless otherwise provided for in laws or in ordinances duly authorized by law."

The committee offered detailed recommendations upon the distribution of functions relating to education, welfare, sanitation, labor, agriculture, forestry, fisheries, commerce and industry, transportation, public works, and other matters. In many instances it favored a division of functions among state, prefecture, and municipality in dealing with a single matter, in others cooperative action, and in still others restriction to a single authority. While the municipalities were to be allotted a considerable share of responsibility, they were not to be left free of prefectural supervision or interference. The committee's difficulty in trying to reconcile old and new principles is reflected in its opinion that: "*Fu* [urban prefectures] and prefectures are not local public bodies superior to cities, towns and villages. However, on account of the fact that they contain in their areas cities, towns and villages, they may serve as liaison between the state and the municipalities and adjust extraordinary inequities among the municipalities. The relations of the prefectures to the municipalities are analogous to those of the state to the prefectures."

It is apparent that the problem of distribution can be solved only through a process of trial and error over a period of years. In the meantime the central government, and with its support the prefectural governments, will reserve to themselves functions which ultimately may be turned over to the municipalities.

The ultimate outcome cannot now be predicted. The conservative national government is not sympathetic toward local autonomy. The Local Autonomy Agency is more concerned to establish uniformity than to stimulate a spirit of local self-consciousness. The people are, in general, apathetic. The election of governors and mayors is favored over appointment, but the dearth of able and liberal candidates from political parties compels voters to choose between former bureaucrats and venal *oyabun* (bosses) in many municipalities. Instances occur of local resistance to national interference and to bossism.[32] Municipal chiefs and assemblymen struggle valiantly and with some success to prevail upon the national administration to reduce the number of its agencies in the localities and to surrender tax bases instead of increasing subsidies. Strong and widespread resentment is expressed, particularly by the major cities, against the restraint and financial waste that accompany prefectural supervision over the municipalities.[33] Reduction of the number of prefectures and localities is advocated by students of administration on technical and financial grounds. The extensive substitution of boards for individual administrators is widely criticized as cumbersome and extravagant.

A Local Administration Simplification Headquarters, set up in November 1951 by the Yoshida cabinet, augurs well for local efficiency, ill for local autonomy. Its mandate is to prepare reform measures for submission to the Diet, but it is not obliged to implement the recommendations of the Local Administration Investigation Committee referred to above.[34] A bill to make the ward chiefs of Tokyo-to appointive was introduced by the cabinet early in 1952. This bill expressed the general attitude of prefectural officials, who prefer the prewar system.[35]

Notes

[1] For the Meiji system, see H. S. Quigley, *Japanese Government and Politics* (New York, 1932), Chapter 15. Professor S. Shimizu concluded a valuable chapter on Meiji local government with these words: "It is to be particularly noticed . . . that the *gun* and the prefecture are different in the extent of autonomy in [from] the city, the town and the village" (S. Okuma, *Fifty Years of New Japan*, London, 1909, p. 333). More recently Professor Tsuji Kiyoshi has emphasized the importance of achieving unity as the feudal system was being replaced. He noted that the government issued the new local government codes in 1888 and 1890, exhibiting no realization of the relation between the establishment of local self-government and the inauguration of the Diet. Dr. Tsuji comments, ". . . our local autonomy came into existence prematurely under the coercive will to achieve centralization, and the result was that our local autonomy was deformed and the indispensable foundation of centralization in

Japan as a modern state was greatly weakened" (*Nihon Kanyosei no Kenkyu* [Studies in Japanese Bureaucracy], Tokyo, 1952, pp. 147–154).

[2] Articles 92–95 of the constitution compose a chapter on local self-government. The basic law is the Local Autonomy Law, promulgated on April 17, 1947, and several times amended (basic law published in *Official Gazette*, No. 312, April 17, 1947, pp. 4–41, and in *Japan Year Book*, 1946–1948, pp. 44–81). The law came into force on May 3, 1947, except for the provisions relating to police administration, which were brought into force subsequently by separate laws. Amendments to the basic law were published in the *Official Gazette* as enacted.

[3] Public Offices Election Law, Article 10 (*Official Gazette*, Extra No. 27, April 15, 1950, p. 8). Articles 17–73 of the Local Autonomy Law, relating to elections, were repealed in 1950 (*ibid.*, p. 72).

[4] Ralph J. D. Braibanti, "Executive Power in Japanese Prefectural Government," *Far Eastern Quarterly*, IX (May 1950), 231–244.

[5] If an assembly fails to elect an election committee, a temporary committee may be appointed for a prefecture by the prime minister, for a municipality by the governor.

[6] *Nippon Times*, May 16, 1950; November 13, 1951.

[7] Robert E. Ward, "The Socio-Political Role of the *Buraku* (Hamlet) in Japan," *American Political Science Review*, XLV (December 1951), 1025–1040. See also the same author's "Patterns of Stability and Change in Japanese Rural Politics," in *Occasional Papers* (Center for Japanese Studies. University of Michigan), No. 1, 1951, pp. 1–6; see also A. F. Raper and others, *The Japanese Village in Transition* (Report No. 136, Natural Resources Section, SCAP, 1950), pp. 192–208. John F. Embree's *Suye Mura, A Japanese Village* (Chicago, 1939), is the most thorough study of the village available in English.

[8] Ralph J. D. Braibanti, "Neighborhood Associations in Japan and their Democratic Potentialities," *Far Eastern Quarterly*, VII (February 1948), 136–164.

[9] Undoubtedly a major factor in the abolition of the block and neighborhood associations was the desire to evade the huge task of applying the purge to their many thousands of leaders.

[10] *Nippon Times*, March 25–26, 1947.

[11] *Ibid.*, November 12, 1951.

[12] The citizens of Tokyo utilized this right in December 1951 to obtain repeal of the metropolitan bylaw on public security (*ibid.*, December 20, 1951).

[13] *Official Gazette*, No. 1415, December 13, 1950, pp. 1–16. For the national public service see above, Chapter 16.

[14] The designated cities are the five major cities and the special cities.

[15] The so-called Fundamental Law of Education, a statement of broad and liberal principles, was passed on March 31, 1947, the School Education Law on March 27, 1947. Both became effective on April 1, 1947. These laws are available in the *Japan Year Book*, 1946–1948, Appendix, pp. 220–227.

[16] The Board of Education Law was passed on July 5, 1948; published in *Official Gazette*, Extra, July 15, 1948, pp. 14–22, it is reprinted in SCAP, *Political Reorientation of Japan*, II, Appendix H:44, pp. 1207–1215.

[17] The Private School Law is reprinted in the *Official Gazette*, Extra No. 144, December 15, 1949, pp. 1–13.

[18] *Japan Year Book, 1946–1948*, Appendix, pp. 142–150; in force March 7, 1948.

[19] For a sketch of the postwar police system, and especially the 1954 changes in the law, see the pamphlet *The Japanese Police*, prepared by the Police College in 1954, pp. 1–16.

[20] See article by T. Shuji, *Nippon Times*, March 8, 1949.

[21] SCAP, *Report on Japanese Taxation by the Shoup Mission* (Tokyo, 1949), I, 10. The local income tax replaced an inhabitant's tax based upon value of the residence in 1950.

[22] *Ibid.*, pp. 8, 27. The figure for voluntary contributions is an estimate, not a veri-

fiable amount. These contributions are similar in fact to the taxes for which no legal authorization has been given and which are also a feature of the local system.

[23] By the Local Finance Equalization Grant Law (May 30, 1950); *Official Gazette*, No. 1249, May 30, 1950, pp. 7–16.

[24] See the regulation covering preparation of requests, which covers 108 pages of *Official Gazette*, Extra No. 43, March 31, 1951.

[25] SCAP, *Report on Japanese Taxation by the Shoup Mission*, IV, pp. D59–D62; Goro Hani declared in the House of Councillors that *oyabun* were squeezing 60,000,000 yen annually out of *tekiya* (street-stall) operators in Tokyo and paying but 10 per cent of the take to the tax office (*Nippon Times*, November 30, 1947).

[26] *Official Gazette*, No. 1249, May 30, 1950, pp. 1–7.

[27] R. Hara, *Gyosei Soshiki no Doko* (Trends in Administrative Organization) (Tokyo, 1948), pp. 14–35.

[28] *Official Gazette*, Extra No. 56, May 31, 1949, pp. 19–23.

[29] *Ibid.*, July 20, 1948.

[30] *Ibid.*, Extra No. 147, December 24, 1949, pp. 1–3.

[31] Mimeographed reports issued by the Investigation Committee on December 22, 1950, and September 22, 1951. The chairman of the committee was Dr. Kambe Masao, onetime mayor of Kyoto.

[32] Karuno village successfully resisted the Finance Ministry's attempt to take possession of a building allocated to it for a school (*Nippon Times*, May 22, 1948). In the town of Honjo a liberal group of younger citizens forced gangsters out of the assembly and mayoralty (*ibid.*, October 8, 1948).

[33] The Local Finance Commission published figures in March 1952 which revealed a deficit of 10,400,000,000 yen for the fiscal year 1951–1952 in 44 prefectures (excluding Tokyo and Osaka), and of 5,888,000,000 yen in the five major cities. The report stated that large deficits were general in the cities, towns, and villages, the total another 14,000,000,000 yen. For more recent data see H. Nomura, "Rural Finances Hard Hit," *Asahi Evening News*, June 24, 1955.

[34] *Mainichi*, September 22, 1951; *Nippon Times*, November 27, 1951, March 2, 1952.

[35] For a recent review of local governmental modifications of Occupation reform measures, see Kurt Steiner, "Local Government in Japan: Reform and Reaction," in *Far Eastern Survey*, XXIII (July 1954), 97–102.

APPENDIXES AND INDEX

APPENDIX I

*The New Constitution of Japan**

PREAMBLE

We, the Japanese people, acting through our duly elected representatives in the National Diet, determined that we shall secure for ourselves and our posterity the fruits of peaceful cooperation with all nations and the blessings of liberty throughout this land, and resolved that never again shall we be visited with the horrors of war through the action of government, do proclaim that sovereign power resides with the people and do firmly establish this Constitution. Government is a sacred trust of the people, the authority for which is derived from the people, the powers of which are exercised by the representatives of the people, and the benefits of which are enjoyed by the people. This is a universal principle of mankind upon which this Constitution is founded. We reject and revoke all constitutions, laws, ordinances, and rescripts in conflict herewith.

We, the Japanese people, desire peace for all time and are deeply conscious of the high ideals controlling human relationship, and we have determined to preserve our security and existence, trusting in the justice and faith of the peace-loving peoples of the world. We desire to occupy an honored place in an international society striving for the preservation of peace, and the banishment of tyranny and slavery, oppression and intolerance for all time from the earth. We recognize that all peoples of the world have the right to live in peace, free from fear and want.

We believe that no nation is responsible to itself alone, but that laws of political morality are universal; and that obedience to such laws is incumbent upon all nations who would sustain their own sovereignty and justify their sovereign relationship with other nations.

We, the Japanese people, pledge our national honor to accomplish these high ideals and purposes with all our resources.

CHAPTER I. THE EMPEROR

Article 1. The Emperor shall be the symbol of the State and of the unity of the people, deriving his position from the will of the people with whom resides sovereign power.

Article 2. The Imperial Throne shall be dynastic and succeeded to in accordance with the Imperial House Law passed by the Diet.

* Text as in *The Constitution of Japan*, Cabinet Secretariat, Tokyo, 1947.

Article 3. The advice and approval of the Cabinet shall be required for all acts of the Emperor in matters of state, and the Cabinet shall be responsible therefor.

Article 4. The Emperor shall perform only such acts in matters of state as are provided for in this Constitution and he shall not have powers related to government.

The Emperor may delegate the performance of his acts in matters of state as may be provided by law.

Article 5. When, in accordance with the Imperial House Law, a Regency is established, the Regent shall perform his acts in matters of state in the Emperor's name. In this case, paragraph one of the preceding article will be applicable.

Article 6. The Emperor shall appoint the Prime Minister as designated by the Diet.

The Emperor shall appoint the Chief Judge of the Supreme Court as designated by the Cabinet.

Article 7. The Emperor, with the advice and approval of the Cabinet, shall perform the following acts in matters of state on behalf of the people:

Promulgation of amendments of the constitution, laws, cabinet orders and treaties.

Convocation of the Diet.

Dissolution of the House of Representatives.

Proclamation of general election of members of the Diet.

Attestation of the appointment and dismissal of Ministers of State and other officials as provided for by law, and of full powers and credentials of Ambassadors and Ministers.

Attestation of general and special amnesty, commutation of punishment, reprieve, and restoration of rights.

Awarding of honors.

Attestation of instruments of ratification and other diplomatic documents as provided for by law.

Receiving foreign ambassadors and ministers.

Performance of ceremonial functions.

Article 8. No property can be given to, or received by, the Imperial House, nor can any gifts be made therefrom, without the authorization of the Diet.

CHAPTER II. RENUNCIATION OF WAR

Article 9. Aspiring sincerely to an international peace based on justice and order, the Japanese people forever renounce war as a sovereign right of the nation and the threat or use of force as means of settling international disputes.

In order to accomplish the aim of the preceding paragraph, land, sea, and air forces, as well as other war potential, will never be maintained. The right of belligerency of the state will not be recognized.

CHAPTER III. RIGHTS AND DUTIES OF THE PEOPLE

Article 10. The conditions necessary for being a Japanese national shall be determined by law.

Article 11. The people shall not be prevented from enjoying any of the fundamental human rights. These fundamental human rights guaranteed to the people by this Constitution shall be conferred upon the people of this and future generations as eternal and inviolate rights.

Article 12. The freedoms and rights guaranteed to the people by this Constitution shall be maintained by the constant endeavor of the people, who shall refrain from any abuse of these freedoms and rights and shall always be responsible for utilizing them for the public welfare.

Article 13. All of the people shall be respected as individuals. Their right to life, liberty, and the pursuit of happiness shall, to the extent that it does not interfere with the public welfare, be the supreme consideration in legislation and in other governmental affairs.

Article 14. All of the people are equal under the law and there shall be no discrimination in political, economic or social relations because of race, creed, sex, social status or family origin.

Peers and peerage shall not be recognized.

No privilege shall accompany any award of honor, decoration or any distinction, nor shall any such award be valid beyond the lifetime of the individual who now holds or hereafter may receive it.

Article 15. The people have the inalienable right to choose their public officials and to dismiss them.

All public officials are servants of the whole community and not of any group thereof.

Universal adult suffrage is guaranteed with regard to the election of public officials.

In all elections, secrecy of the ballot shall not be violated. A voter shall not be answerable, publicly or privately, for the choice he has made.

Article 16. Every person shall have the right of peaceful petition for the redress of damage, for the removal of public officials, for the enactment, repeal or amendment of laws, ordinances or regulations and for other matters; nor shall any person be in any way discriminated against for sponsoring such a petition.

Article 17. Every person may sue for redress as provided by law from the State or a public entity, in case he has suffered damage through illegal act of any public official.

Article 18. No person shall be held in bondage of any kind. Involuntary servitude, except as punishment for crime, is prohibited.

Article 19. Freedom of thought and conscience shall not be violated.

Article 20. Freedom of religion is guaranteed to all. No religious organization shall receive any privileges from the State, nor exercise any political authority.

No person shall be compelled to take part in any religious act, celebration, rite or practice.

The State and its organs shall refrain from religious education or any other religious activity.

Article 21. Freedom of assembly and association as well as speech, press and all other forms of expression are guaranteed.

No censorship shall be maintained, nor shall the secrecy of any means of communication be violated.

Article 22. Every person shall have freedom to choose and change his residence and to choose his occupation to the extent that it does not interfere with the public welfare.

Freedom of all persons to move to a foreign country and to divest themselves of their nationality shall be inviolate.

Article 23. Academic freedom is guaranteed.

Article 24. Marriage shall be based only on the mutual consent of both sexes and it shall be maintained through mutual cooperation with the equal rights of husband and wife as a basis.

With regard to choice of spouse, property rights, inheritance, choice of domicile, divorce and other matters pertaining to marriage and the family, laws shall be enacted from the standpoint of individual dignity and the essential equality of the sexes.

Article 25. All people shall have the right to maintain the minimum standards of wholesome and cultured living.

In all spheres of life, the State shall use its endeavors for the promotion and extension of social welfare and security, and of public health.

Article 26. All people shall have the right to receive an equal education correspondent to their ability, as provided by law.

All people shall be obligated to have all boys and girls under their protection receive ordinary education as provided for by law. Such compulsory education shall be free.

Article 27. All people shall have the right and the obligation to work.

Standards for wages, hours, rest and other working conditions shall be fixed by law.

Children shall not be exploited.

Article 28. The right of workers to organize and to bargain and act collectively is guaranteed.

Article 29. The right to own or to hold property is inviolable.

Property rights shall be defined by law, in conformity with the public welfare.

Private property may be taken for public use upon just compensation therefor.

Article 30. The people shall be liable to taxation as provided by law.

Article 31. No person shall be deprived of life or liberty, nor shall any other criminal penalty be imposed, except according to procedure established by law.

Article 32. No person shall be denied the right of access to the courts.

Article 33. No person shall be apprehended except upon warrant issued by a competent judicial officer which specifies the offense with which the person is charged, unless he is apprehended, the offense being committed.

Article 34. No person shall be arrested or detained without being at once informed of the charges against him or without the immediate privilege of counsel; nor shall he be detained without adequate cause; and upon demand of any person such cause must be immediately shown in open court in his presence and the presence of his counsel.

Article 35. The right of all persons to be secure in their homes, papers and effects against entries, searches and seizures shall not be impaired except upon warrant issued for adequate cause and particularly describing the place to be searched and things to be seized, or except as provided by Article 33.

Each search or seizure shall be made upon separate warrant issued by a competent judicial officer.

Article 36. The infliction of torture by any public officer and cruel punishments are absolutely forbidden.

Article 37. In all criminal cases the accused shall enjoy the right to a speedy and public trial by an impartial tribunal.

He shall be permitted full opportunity to examine all witnesses, and he shall have the right of compulsory process for obtaining witnesses on his behalf at public expense.

At all times the accused shall have the assistance of competent counsel who shall, if the accused is unable to secure the same by his own efforts, be assigned to his use by the State.

Article 38. No person shall be compelled to testify against himself.

Confession made under compulsion, torture or threat, or after prolonged arrest or detention shall not be admitted in evidence.

No person shall be convicted or punished in cases where the only proof against him is his own confession.

Article 39. No person shall be held criminally liable for an act which was lawful at the time it was committed, or of which he has been acquitted, nor shall he be placed in double jeopardy.

Article 40. Any person, in case he is acquitted after he has been arrested or detained, may sue the State for redress as provided by law.

CHAPTER IV. THE DIET

Article 41. The Diet shall be the highest organ of state power, and shall be the sole law-making organ of the State.

Article 42. The Diet shall consist of two Houses, namely the House of Representatives and the House of Councillors.

Article 43. Both Houses shall consist of elected members, representative of all the people.

The number of the members of each House shall be fixed by law.

Article 44. The qualifications of members of both Houses and their electors shall be fixed by law. However, there shall be no discrimination because of race, creed, sex, social status, family origin, education, property or income.

Article 45. The term of office of members of the House of Representatives shall be four years. However, the term shall be terminated before the full term is up in case the House of Representatives is dissolved.

The New Constitution of Japan

Article 46. The term of office of members of the House of Councillors shall be six years, and election for half the members shall take place every three years.

Article 47. Electoral districts, method of voting and other matters pertaining to the method of election of members of both Houses shall be fixed by law.

Article 48. No person shall be permitted to be a member of both Houses simultaneously.

Article 49. Members of both Houses shall receive appropriate annual payment from the national treasury in accordance with law.

Article 50. Except in cases provided by law, members of both Houses shall be exempt from apprehension while the Diet is in session, and any members apprehended before the opening of the session shall be freed during the term of the session upon demand of the House.

Article 51. Members of both Houses shall not be held liable outside the House for speeches, debates or votes cast inside the House.

Article 52. An ordinary session of the Diet shall be convoked once per year.

Article 53. The Cabinet may determine to convoke extraordinary sessions of the Diet. When a quarter or more of the total members of either House makes the demand, the Cabinet must determine on such convocation.

Article 54. When the House of Representatives is dissolved, there must be a general election of members of the House of Representatives within forty (40) days from the date of dissolution, and the Diet must be convoked within thirty (30) days from the date of the election.

When the House of Representatives is dissolved, the House of Councillors is closed at the same time. However, the Cabinet may in time of national emergency convoke the House of Councillors in emergency session.

Measures taken at such session as mentioned in the proviso of the preceding paragraph shall be provisional and shall become null and void unless agreed to by the House of Representatives within a period of ten (10) days after the opening of the next session of the Diet.

Article 55. Each House shall judge disputes related to qualifications of its members. However, in order to deny a seat to any member, it is necessary to pass a resolution by a majority of two-thirds or more of the members present.

Article 56. Business cannot be transacted in either House unless one-third or more of total membership is present.

All matters shall be decided, in each House, by a majority of those present, except as elsewhere provided in the Constitution, and in case of a tie, the presiding officer shall decide the issue.

Article 57. Deliberation in each House shall be public. However, a secret meeting may be held where a majority of two-thirds or more of those members present passes a resolution therefor.

Each House shall keep a record of proceedings. This record shall be published and given general circulation, excepting such parts of proceedings of secret session as may be deemed to require secrecy.

Upon demand of one-fifth or more of the members present, votes of the members on any matter shall be recorded in the minutes.

Article 58. Each House shall select its own president and other officials.

Each House shall establish its rules pertaining to meetings, proceedings and internal discipline, and may punish members for disorderly conduct. However, in order to expel a member, a majority of two-thirds or more of those members present must pass a resolution thereon.

Article 59. A bill becomes a law on passage by both Houses, except as otherwise provided by the Constitution.

A bill which is passed by the House of Representatives, and upon which the House of Councillors makes a decision different from that of the House of Representatives, becomes a law when passed a second time by the House of Representatives by a majority of two-thirds or more of the members present.

The provision of the preceding paragraph does not preclude the House of Representatives from calling for the meeting of a joint committee of both Houses, provided for by law.

Failure by the House of Councillors to take final action within sixty (60) days after receipt of a bill passed by the House of Representatives, time in recess excepted, may be determined by the House of Representatives to constitute a rejection of the said bill by the House of Councillors.

Article 60. The budget must first be submitted to the House of Representatives.

Upon consideration of the budget, when the House of Councillors makes a decision different from that of the House of Representatives, and when no agreement can be reached even through a joint committee of both Houses, provided for by law, or in the case of failure by the House of Councillors to take final action within thirty (30) days, the period of recess excluded, after the receipt of the budget passed by the House of Representatives, the decision of the House of Representatives shall be the decision of the Diet.

Article 61. The second paragraph of the preceding article applies also to the Diet approval required for the conclusion of treaties.

Article 62. Each House may conduct investigations in relation to government, and may demand the presence and testimony of witnesses, and the production of records.

Article 63. The Prime Minister and other Ministers of State may, at any time, appear in either House for the purpose of speaking on bills, regardless of whether they are members of the House or not. They must appear when their presence is required in order to give answers or explanations.

Article 64. The Diet shall set up an impeachment court from among the members of both Houses for the purpose of trying those judges against whom removal proceedings have been instituted.

Matters relating to impeachment shall be provided by law.

CHAPTER V. THE CABINET

Article 65. Executive power shall be vested in the Cabinet.

Article 66. The Cabinet shall consist of the Prime Minister, who shall be its head, and other Ministers of State, as provided for by law.

The Prime Minister and other Ministers of State must be civilians.

The Cabinet, in the exercise of executive power, shall be collectively responsible to the Diet.

Article 67. The Prime Minister shall be designated from among the members of the Diet by a resolution of the Diet. This designation shall precede all other business.

If the House of Representatives and the House of Councillors disagree and if no agreement can be reached even through a joint committee of both Houses, provided for by law, or the House of Councillors fails to make designation within ten (10) days, exclusive of the period of recess, after the House of Representatives has made designation, the decision of the House of Representatives shall be the decision of the Diet.

Article 68. The Prime Minister shall appoint the Ministers of State. However, a majority of their number must be chosen from among the members of the Diet.

The Prime Minister may remove the Ministers of State as he chooses.

Article 69. If the House of Representatives passes a non-confidence resolution, or rejects a confidence resolution, the Cabinet shall resign en masse, unless the House of Representatives is dissolved within ten (10) days.

Article 70. When there is a vacancy in the post of Prime Minister, or upon the first convocation of the Diet after a general election of members of the House of Representatives, the Cabinet shall resign en masse.

Article 71. In the cases mentioned in the two preceding articles, the Cabinet shall continue its functions until the time when a new Prime Minister is appointed.

Article 72. The Prime Minister, representing the Cabinet, submits bills, reports on general national affairs and foreign relations to the Diet and exercises control and supervision over various administrative branches.

Article 73. The Cabinet, in addition to other general administrative functions, shall perform the following functions:

Administer the law faithfully; conduct affairs of state.

Manage foreign affairs.

Conclude treaties. However, it shall obtain prior or, depending on circumstances, subsequent approval of the Diet.

Administer the civil service, in accordance with standards established by law.

Prepare the budget, and present it to the Diet.

Enact Cabinet orders in order to execute the provisions of this Constitution and of the law. However, it cannot include penal provisions in such Cabinet orders unless authorized by such law.

Decide on general amnesty, special amnesty, commutation of punishment, reprieve, and restoration of rights.

Article 74. All laws and Cabinet orders shall be signed by the competent Minister of State and countersigned by the Prime Minister.

Article 75. The Ministers of State, during their tenure of office, shall not be subject to legal action without the consent of the Prime Minister. However, the right to take that action is not impaired hereby.

CHAPTER VI. JUDICIARY

Article 76. The whole judicial power is vested in a Supreme Court and in such inferior courts as are established by law.

No extraordinary tribunal shall be established, nor shall any organ or agency of the Executive be given final judicial power.

All judges shall be independent in the exercise of their conscience and shall be bound only by this Constitution and the laws.

Article 77. The Supreme Court is vested with the rule-making power under which it determines the rules of procedure and of practice, and of matters relating to attorneys, the internal discipline of the courts and the administration of judicial affairs.

Public procurators shall be subject to the rule-making power of the Supreme Court.

The Supreme Court may delegate the power to make rules for inferior courts to such courts.

Article 78. Judges shall not be removed except by public impeachment unless judicially declared mentally or physically incompetent to perform official duties. No disciplinary action against judges shall be administered by any executive organ or agency.

Article 79. The Supreme Court shall consist of a Chief Judge and such number of judges as may be determined by law; all such judges excepting the Chief Judge shall be appointed by the Cabinet.

The appointment of the judges of the Supreme Court shall be reviewed by the people at the first general election of members of the House of Representatives following their appointment, and shall be reviewed again at the first general election of members of the House of Representatives after a lapse of ten (10) years, and in the same manner thereafter.

In cases mentioned in the foregoing paragraph, when the majority of the voters favors the dismissal of a judge, he shall be dismissed.

Matters pertaining to review shall be prescribed by law.

The judges of the Supreme Court shall be retired upon the attainment of the age as fixed by law.

All such judges shall receive, at regular stated intervals, adequate compensation which shall not be decreased during their terms of office.

Article 80. The judges of the inferior courts shall be appointed by the Cabinet from a list of persons nominated by the Supreme Court. All such judges shall hold office for a term of ten (10) years with privilege of reappointment, provided that they shall be retired upon the attainment of the age as fixed by law.

The judges of the inferior courts shall receive, at regular stated intervals, adequate compensation which shall not be decreased during their terms of office.

Article 81. The Supreme Court is the court of last resort with power to determine the constitutionality of any law, order, regulation or official act.

Article 82. Trials shall be conducted and judgment declared publicly.

Where a court unanimously determines publicity to be dangerous to public order or morals, a trial may be conducted privately, but trials of political offenses, offenses involving the press or cases wherein the rights of people as guaranteed in Chapter III of this Constitution are in question shall always be conducted publicly.

CHAPTER VII. FINANCE

Article 83. The power to administer national finances shall be exercised as the Diet shall determine.

Article 84. No new taxes shall be imposed or existing ones modified except by law or under such conditions as law may prescribe.

Article 85. No money shall be expended, nor shall the State obligate itself, except as authorized by the Diet.

Article 86. The Cabinet shall prepare and submit to the Diet for its consideration and decision a budget for each fiscal year.

Article 87. In order to provide for unforeseen deficiencies in the budget, a reserve fund may be authorized by the Diet to be expended upon the responsibility of the Cabinet.

The Cabinet must get subsequent approval of the Diet for all payments from the reserve fund.

Article 88. All property of the Imperial Household shall belong to the State. All expenses of the Imperial Household shall be appropriated by the Diet in the budget.

Article 89. No public money or other property shall be expended or appropriated for the use, benefit or maintenance of any religious institution or association, or for any charitable, educational or benevolent enterprises not under the control of public authority.

Article 90. Final accounts of the expenditures and revenues of the State shall be audited annually by a Board of Audit and submitted by the Cabinet to the Diet, together with the statement of audit, during the fiscal year immediately following the period covered.

The organization and competency of the Board of Audit shall be determined by law.

Article 91. At regular intervals and at least annually the Cabinet shall report to the Diet and the people on the state of national finances.

CHAPTER VIII. LOCAL SELF-GOVERNMENT

Article 92. Regulations concerning organization and operations of local public entities shall be fixed by law in accordance with the principle of local autonomy.

Article 93. The local public entities shall establish assemblies as their deliberative organs, in accordance with law.

The chief executive officers of all local public entities, the members of their assemblies, and such other local officials as may be determined by law shall be elected by direct popular vote within their several communities.

Article 94. Local public entities shall have the right to manage their property, affairs and administration and to enact their own regulations within law.

Article 95. A special law, applicable only to one local public entity, cannot be enacted by the Diet without the consent of the majority of the voters of the local public entity concerned, obtained in accordance with law.

The New Constitution of Japan

CHAPTER IX. AMENDMENTS

Article 96. Amendments to this Constitution shall be initiated by the Diet, through a concurring vote of two-thirds or more of all the members of each House and shall thereupon be submitted to the people for ratification, which shall require the affirmative vote of a majority of all votes cast thereon, at a special referendum or at such election as the Diet shall specify.

Amendments when so ratified shall immediately be promulgated by the Emperor in the name of the people, as an integral part of this Constitution.

CHAPTER X. SUPREME LAW

Article 97. The fundamental human rights by this Constitution guaranteed to the people of Japan are fruits of the age-old struggle of man to be free; they have survived the many exacting tests for durability and are conferred upon this and future generations in trust, to be held for all time inviolate.

Article 98. This Constitution shall be the supreme law of the nation and no law, ordinance, imperial rescript or other act of government, or part thereof, contrary to the provisions hereof, shall have legal force or validity.

The treaties concluded by Japan and established laws of nations shall be faithfully observed.

Article 99. The Emperor or the Regent as well as Ministers of State, members of the Diet, judges, and all other public officials have the obligation to respect and uphold this Constitution.

CHAPTER XI. SUPPLEMENTARY PROVISIONS

Article 100. This Constitution shall be enforced as from the day when the period of six months will have elapsed counting from the day of its promulgation.

The enactment of laws necessary for the enforcement of this Constitution, the election of members of the House of Councillors and the procedure for the convocation of the Diet and other preparatory procedures necessary for the enforcement of this Constitution may be executed before the day prescribed in the preceding paragraph.

Article 101. If the House of Councillors is not constituted before the effective date of this Constitution, the House of Representatives shall function as the Diet until such time as the House of Councillors shall be constituted.

Article 102. The term of office for half the members of the House of Councillors serving in the first term under this Constitution shall be three years. Members falling under this category shall be determined in accordance with law.

Article 103. The Ministers of State, members of the House of Representatives and judges in office on the effective date of this Constitution, and all other public officials who occupy positions corresponding to such positions as are recognized by this Constitution shall not forfeit their positions automatically on account of the enforcement of this Constitution unless otherwise specified by law. When, however, successors are elected or appointed under the provisions of this Constitution, they shall forfeit their positions as a matter of course.

APPENDIX II

*The Old Constitution of the Empire of Japan**

PREAMBLE

Having, by virtue of the glories of our Ancestors, ascended the Throne of a lineal succession unbroken for ages eternal; desiring to promote the welfare of, and to give development to the moral and intellectual faculties of Our beloved subjects, the very same that have been favoured with the benevolent care and affectionate vigilance of Our Ancestors; and hoping to maintain the prosperity of the State, in concert with Our people and with their support, We hereby promulgate, in pursuance of Our Imperial Rescript of the 12th day of the 10th month of the 14th year of Meiji, a fundamental law of State, to exhibit the principles, by which We are to be guided in Our conduct, and to point out to what Our descendants and Our subjects and their descendants are forever to conform.

The rights of sovereignty of the State. We have inherited from Our Ancestors, and We shall bequeath them to Our descendants. Neither We nor they shall in future fail to wield them, in accordance with the provisions of the Constitution hereby granted.

We now declare to respect and protect the security of the rights and of the property of Our people, and to secure to them the complete enjoyment of the same, within the extent of the provisions of the present Constitution and of the law.

The Imperial Diet shall first be convoked for the 23rd year of Meiji and the time of its opening shall be the date when the present Constitution comes into force.

When in the future it may become necessary to amend any of the provisions of the present Constitution, We or Our successors shall assume the initiative right, and submit a project for the same to the Imperial Diet. The Imperial Diet shall pass its vote upon it, according to the conditions imposed by the present Constitution, and in no otherwise shall Our descendants or Our subjects be permitted to attempt any alteration thereof.

Our Ministers of State, on Our behalf, shall be held responsible for the carrying out of the present Constitution, and Our present and future subjects shall forever assume the duty of allegiance to the present Constitution.

CHAPTER I. THE EMPEROR

Article I. The Empire of Japan shall be reigned over and governed by a line of Emperors unbroken for ages eternal.

* Text as in H. Ito, *Commentaries on the Constitution of the Empire of Japan* (Tokyo, 1889, 1906).

The Old Constitution of the Empire of Japan

Article II. The Imperial Throne shall be succeeded to by Imperial male descendants, according to the provisions of the Imperial House Law.

Article III. The Emperor is sacred and inviolable.

Article IV. The Emperor is the head of the Empire, combining in Himself the rights of sovereignty, and exercises them, according to the provisions of the present Constitution.

Article V. The Emperor exercises the legislative power with the consent of the Imperial Diet.

Article VI. The Emperor gives sanction to laws and orders them to be promulgated and executed.

Article VII. The Emperor convokes the Imperial Diet, opens, closes and prorogues it, and dissolves the House of Representatives.

Article VIII. The Emperor, in consequence of an urgent necessity to maintain public safety or to avert public calamities, issues, when the Imperial Diet is not sitting, Imperial Ordinances in the place of law.

Such Imperial Ordinances are to be laid before the Imperial Diet at its next session, and when the Diet does not approve the said Ordinances, the Government shall declare them to be invalid for the future.

Article IX. The Emperor issues or causes to be issued, the Ordinances necessary for the carrying out of the laws, or for the maintenance of the public peace and order, and for the promotion of the welfare of the subjects. But no Ordinance shall in any way alter any of the existing laws.

Article X. The Emperor determines the organization of the different branches of the administration, and salaries of all civil and military officers, and appoints and dismisses the same. Exceptions especially provided for in the present Constitution or in other laws, shall be in accordance with the respective provisions (bearing thereon).

Article XI. The Emperor has the supreme command of the Army and Navy.

Article XII. The Emperor determines the organization and peace standing of the Army and Navy.

Article XIII. The Emperor declares war, makes peace, and concludes treaties.

Article XIV. The Emperor declares a state of seige.

The conditions and effects of a state of siege shall be determined by law.

Article XV. The Emperor confers titles of nobility, rank, orders and other marks of honor.

Article XVI. The Emperor orders amnesty, pardon, commutation of punishments and rehabilitation.

Article XVII. A Regency shall be instituted in conformity with the provisions of the Imperial House Law.

The Regent shall exercise the powers appertaining to the Emperor in His name.

CHAPTER II. RIGHTS AND DUTIES OF SUBJECTS

Article XVIII. The conditions necessary for being a Japanese subject shall be determined by law.

Article XIX. Japanese subjects may, according to qualifications determined in laws or ordinances, be appointed to civil or military or any other public offices equally.

Article XX. Japanese subjects are amenable to service in the Army or Navy, according to the provisions of law.

Article XXI. Japanese subjects are amenable to the duty of paying taxes, according to the provisions of law.

Article XXII. Japanese subjects shall have the liberty of abode and of changing the same within the limits of law.

Article XXIII. No Japanese subject shall be arrested, detained, tried or punished, unless according to law.

Article XXIV. No Japanese subject shall be deprived of his right of being tried by the judges determined by law.

Article XXV. Except in the cases provided for in the law, the house of no Japanese subject shall be entered or searched without his consent.

Article XXVI. Except in the cases mentioned in the law, the secrecy of the letters of every Japanese subject shall remain inviolate.

Article XXVII. The right of property of every Japanese subject shall remain inviolate.

Measures necessary to be taken for the public benefit shall be provided for by law.

Article XXVIII. Japanese subjects shall, within limits not prejudicial to peace and order, and not antagonistic to their duties as subjects, enjoy freedom of religious belief.

Article XXIX. Japanese subjects shall, within the limits of law, enjoy the liberty of speech, writing, publication, public meetings and associations.

Article XXX. Japanese subjects may present petitions, by observing the proper forms of respect, and by complying with the rules specially provided for the same.

Article XXXI. The provisions contained in the present Chapter shall not affect the exercise of the powers appertaining to the Emperor, in times of war or in cases of a national emergency.

Article XXXII. Each and every one of the provisions contained in the preceding Articles of the present Chapter, that are not in conflict with the laws or the rules and discipline of the Army and Navy, shall apply to the officers and men of the Army and of the Navy.

CHAPTER III. THE IMPERIAL DIET

Article XXXIII. The Imperial Diet shall consist of two Houses, a House of Peers and a House of Representatives.

Article XXXIV. The House of Peers shall, in accordance with the Ordinance concerning the House of Peers, be composed of the members of the Imperial Family, of the orders of nobility, and of those persons who have been nominated thereto by the Emperor.

Article XXXV. The House of Representatives shall be composed of Members elected by the people, according to the provisions of the Law of Election.

Article XXXVI. No one can at one and the same time be a Member of both Houses.

Article XXXVII. Every law requires the consent of the Imperial Diet.

Article XXXVIII. Both Houses shall vote upon projects of law submitted to it by the Government, and may respectively initiate projects of law.

Article XXXIX. A Bill, which has been rejected by either the one or the other of the two Houses, shall not be again brought in during the same session.

Article XL. Both Houses can make representations to the Government, as to laws or upon any other subject. When, however, such representations are not accepted, they cannot be made a second time during the same session.

Article XLI. The Imperial Diet shall be convoked every year.

Article XLII. A session of the Imperial Diet shall last during three months. In case of necessity, the duration of a session may be prolonged by Imperial Order.

Article XLIII. When urgent necessity arises, an extraordinary session may be convoked, in addition to the ordinary one.

The duration of an extraordinary session shall be determined by Imperial Order.

Article XLIV. The opening, closing, prolongation of session and prorogation of the Imperial Diet, shall be effected simultaneously for both Houses.

In case the House of Representatives has been ordered to dissolve, the House of Peers shall at the same time be prorogued.

Article XLV. When the House of Representatives has been ordered to dissolve, Members shall be caused by Imperial Order to be newly elected, and the new House shall be convoked within five months from the day of dissolution.

Article XLVI. No debate can be opened and no vote can be taken in either House of the Imperial Diet, unless not less than one third of the whole number of the Members thereof is present.

Article XLVII. Votes shall be taken in both Houses by absolute majority. In the case of a tie vote, the President shall have the casting vote.

Article XLVIII. The deliberations of both Houses shall be held in public. The deliberations may, however, upon demand of the Government or by resolution of the House, be held in secret sitting.

Article XLIX. Both Houses of the Imperial Diet may respectively present addresses to the Emperor.

Article L. Both Houses may receive petitions presented by subjects.

Article LI. Both Houses may enact, besides what is provided for in the present Constitution and in the Law of the Houses, rules necessary for the management of their internal affairs.

Article LII. No Member of either House shall be held responsible outside the respective Houses, for any opinion uttered or for any vote given in the House. When, however, a Member himself has given publicity to his opinions by public speech, by documents in print or in writing, or by any other similar means, he shall, in the matter, be amenable to the general law.

Article LIII. The Members of both Houses shall, during the session, be free from arrest, unless with the consent of the House, except in cases of flagrant delicts, or of offenses connected with a state of internal commotion or with a foreign trouble.

Article LIV. The Ministers of State and the Delegates of the Government may, at any time, take seats and speak in either House.

CHAPTER IV. THE MINISTERS OF STATE
AND THE PRIVY COUNCIL

Article LV. The respective Ministers of State shall give their advice to the Emperor, and be responsible for it.

All Laws, Imperial Ordinances and Imperial Rescripts of whatever kind, that relate to the affairs of the State, require the counter-signature of a Minister of State.

Article LVI. The Privy Councillors shall, in accordance with the provisions for the organization of the Privy Council, deliberate upon important matters of State, when they have been consulted by the Emperor.

CHAPTER V. THE JUDICATURE

Article LVII. The Judicature shall be exercised by the Courts of Law according to law, in the name of the Emperor.

The organization of the Courts of Law shall be determined by law.

Article LVIII. The judges shall be appointed from among those who possess proper qualifications according to law.

No judge shall be deprived of his position, unless by way of criminal sentence or disciplinary punishment.

Rules for disciplinary punishment shall be determined by law.

Article LIX. Trials and judgments of a Court shall be conducted publicly. When, however, there exists any fear that such publicity may be prejudicial to peace and order, or to the maintenance of public morality, the public trial may be suspended by provision of law or by the decision of the Court of Law.

Article LX. All matters that fall within the competency of a special Court shall be specially provided for by law.

Article LXI. No suit at law, which relates to rights alleged to have been infringed by the illegal measures of the administrative authorities, and which shall come within the competency of the Court of Administrative Litigation specially established by law, shall be taken cognizance of by a Court of Law.

The New Japan

CHAPTER VI. FINANCE

Article LXII. The imposition of a new tax or the modification of the rates (of an existing one) shall be determined by law.

However, all such administrative fees or other revenue having the nature of compensation shall not fall within the category of the above clause.

The raising of national loans and the contracting of other liabilities to the charge of the National Treasury, except those that are provided in the Budget, shall require the consent of the Imperial Diet.

Article LXIII. The taxes levied at present shall, in so far as they are not remodelled by a new law, be collected according to the old system.

Article LXIV. The expenditure and revenue of the State require the consent of the Imperial Diet by means of an annual Budget.

Any and all expenditures overpassing the appropriations set forth in the Titles and Paragraphs of the Budget, or that are not provided for in the Budget, shall subsequently require the approbation of the Imperial Diet.

Article LXV. The Budget shall be first laid before the House of Representatives.

Article LXVI. The expenditures of the Imperial House shall be defrayed every year out of the National Treasury, according to the present fixed amount for the same, and shall not require the consent thereto of the Imperial Diet, except in case an increase thereof is found necessary.

Article LXVII. Those already fixed expenditures based by the Constitution upon the powers appertaining to the Emperor, and such expenditures as may have arisen by the effect of law, or that appertain to the legal obligations of the Government, shall be neither rejected nor reduced by the Imperial Diet, without the concurrence of the Government.

Article LXVIII. In order to meet special requirements, the Government may ask the consent of the Imperial Diet to a certain amount as a Continuing Expenditure Fund, for a previously fixed number of years.

Article LXIX. In order to supply deficiencies, which are unavoidable, in the Budget, and to meet requirements unprovided for in the same, a Reserve Fund shall be provided in the Budget.

Article LXX. When the Imperial Diet cannot be convoked, owing to the external or internal condition of the country, in case of urgent need for the maintenance of public safety, the Government may take all necessary financial measures, by means of an Imperial Ordinance.

In the case mentioned in the preceding clause, the matter shall be submitted to the Imperial Diet at its next session, and its approbation shall be obtained thereto.

Article LXXI. When the Imperial Diet has not voted on the Budget, or when the Budget has not been brought into actual existence, the Government shall carry out the Budget of the preceding year.

Article LXXII. The final account of the expenditures and revenue of the State shall be verified and confirmed by the Board of Audit, and it shall be submitted by the Government to the Imperial Diet, together with the report of verification of the said Board.

The organization and competency of the Board of Audit shall be determined by law separately.

CHAPTER VII. SUPPLEMENTARY RULES

Article LXXIII. When it has become necessary in future to amend the provisions of the present Constitution, a project to the effect shall be submitted to the Imperial Diet by Imperial Order.

In the above case, neither House can open the debate, unless not less than two-thirds of the whole number of Members are present, and no amendment can be passed, unless a majority of not less than two-thirds of the Members present is obtained.

Article LXXIV. No modification of the Imperial House Law shall be required to be submitted to the deliberation of the Imperial Diet.

No provision of the present Constitution can be modified by the Imperial House Law.

Article LXXV. No modification can be introduced into the Constitution, or into the Imperial House Law, during the time of a Regency.

Article LXXVI. Existing legal enactments, such as laws, regulations, Ordinances, or by whatever names they may be called, shall, so far as they do not conflict with the present Constitution, continue in force.

All existing contracts or orders, that entail obligations upon the Government, and that are connected with expenditure, shall come within the scope of Art. LXVII.

APPENDIX III

Imperial Rescript, January 1, 1946:
Repudiation of "False Conceptions"

In greeting the New Year, We recall to mind that the Emperor Meiji proclaimed, as the basis of our national policy, the Five Clauses of the Charter Oath at the beginning of the Meiji Era. The Charter Oath signified: —

1. Deliberative assemblies shall be established and all measures of government decided in accordance with public opinion.

2. All classes, high and low, shall unite in vigorously carrying on the affairs of State.

3. All common people, no less than the civil and military officials, shall be allowed to fulfil their just desires, so that there may not be any discontent among them.

4. All the absurd usages of old shall be broken through, and equity and justice to be found in the workings of nature shall serve as the basis of action.

5. Wisdom and knowledge shall be sought throughout the world for the purpose of promoting the welfare of the Empire.

The proclamation is evident in significance and high in its ideals. We wish to make this oath anew and restore the country to stand on its own feet again. We have to reaffirm the principles embodied in the Charter, and proceed unflinchingly towards elimination of misguided practices of the past, and, keeping in close touch with the the desires of the people, we will construct a new Japan through being thoroughly pacific, the officials and the people alike, attaining rich culture, and advancing the standard of living of the people.

The devastation of war inflicted upon our cities, the miseries of the destitute, the stagnation of trade, the shortage of food, and the great and growing number of the unemployed are indeed heart-rending. But if the nation is firmly united in its resolve to face the present ordeal and to seek civilization consistently in peace, a bright future will undoubtedly be ours, not only for our country, but for the whole of humanity.

Love of the family and love of country are especially strong in this country. With more of this devotion should we now work towards love of mankind.

We feel deeply concerned to note that consequent upon the protracted war ending in our defeat, our people are likely to grow restless and to fall into the Slough of Despond. Radical tendencies in excess are gradually spreading and the sense of morality tends to lose its hold on the people, with the result that there are signs of confusion of thought.

* This translation is by D. C. Holtom; another translation is printed in SCAP, Government Section, *Political Reorientation of Japan*, II, Appendix B: 3b, p. 470.

Imperial Rescript, January 1, 1946

We stand by the people and We wish always to share with them in their moments of joy and sorrow. The ties between Us and Our people have always stood upon mutual trust and affection. They do not depend upon mere legends and myths. They are not predicated on the false conception that the Emperor is divine, and that the Japanese people are superior to other races and fated to rule the world.

Our Government should make every effort to alleviate their trials and tribulations. At the same time, We trust that the people will rise to the occasion, and will strive courageously for the solution of their outstanding difficulties, and for the development of industry and culture. Acting upon a consciousness of solidarity and of mutual aid and broad tolerance in their civic life, they will prove themselves worthy of their best tradition. By their supreme endeavours in that direction, they will be able to render their substantial contribution to the welfare and advancement of mankind.

The resolution for the year should be made at the beginning of the year. We expect Our people to join Us in all exertions looking to accomplishment of this great undertaking with an indomitable spirit.

APPENDIX IV

*The Imperial House Law**

* Law No. 3, *Official Gazette*, No. 237, January 16, 1947, pp. 1–3. The writers have made slight alterations in the text for the sake of clarity.

CHAPTER I. SUCCESSION TO THE IMPERIAL THRONE

Article 1. The Imperial Throne shall be succeeded to by a male offspring in the male line belonging to the Imperial Lineage.

Article 2. The Imperial Throne shall be passed to the members of the Imperial Family according to the following order:

1) The eldest son of the Emperor.
2) The eldest son of the Emperor's eldest son.
3) Other descendants of the eldest son of the Emperor.
4) The second son of the Emperor, and his descendants.
5) Other descendants of the Emperor.
6) Brothers of the Emperor and their descendants.
7) Uncles of the Emperor and their descendants.

In case there is no member of the Imperial Family as under the numbers of the preceding paragraph, the Throne shall be passed to the member of the Imperial Family next nearest in lineage.

In the cases of the two preceding paragraphs, precedence shall be given to the senior line, and in the same degree, to the senior member.

Article 3. In case the Imperial Heir is affected with an incurable and serious disease, mentally or physically, or there is a serious hindrance, the order of succession may be changed by decision of the Imperial House Council and in accordance with the order stipulated in the preceding Article.

Article 4. Upon the demise of the Emperor the Imperial Heir shall immediately accede to the Throne.

CHAPTER II. THE IMPERIAL FAMILY

Article 5. The Empress, the Grand Empress Dowager, the Empress Dowager, Shinno, the consorts of Shinno, Naishinno, O, the consorts of O, and Jo-o shall be the members of the Imperial Family.

Article 6. The legitimate children of an Emperor, and the legitimate grandchildren of an Emperor in the legitimate male line shall be Shinno in the case of a male, and Naishinno in the case of a female. The legitimate descendants of an Emperor in the third and later generations in the legitimate male line shall be O in the case of a male and Jo-o in the case of a female.

Article 7. In case an O succeeds to the Throne, his brothers and sisters who are O and Jo-o shall specially become Shinno and Naishinno.

Article 8. The son of the Emperor who is the Imperial Heir is called "Kotaishi" and in case there is no Kotaishi, the grandson of the Emperor, who is the Imperial Heir, is called "Kotaison."

Article 9. The Emperor and the members of the Imperial Family may not adopt children.

Article 10. The institution of Empress, and the marriage of any male member of the Imperial Family shall be passed upon by the Imperial House Council.

Article 11. A Naishinno, O, or Jo-o, of 15 years of age or more, shall leave the status of Imperial Family member according to her or his own desire and by decision of the Imperial House Council.

Besides the case as mentioned in the preceding paragraph, a Shinno (excepting the Kotaishi and the Kotaison), Naishinno, O, or Jo-o, shall, in case of special and unavoidable circumstances, leave the status of Imperial Family member by decision of the Imperial House Council.

Article 12. In case a female of the Imperial Family marries a person other than the Emperor or a member of the Imperial Family, she shall lose the status of Imperial Family member.

Article 13. The consort of a Shinno or O who leaves the status of Imperial Family member, and his direct descendants and their consorts, excepting those females who are married to other members of the Imperial Family and their direct descendants, shall lose simultaneously the status of Imperial Family member. However, as regards his direct descendants and their consorts, it may be so decided by the Imperial House Council that they do not lose the status of Imperial Family member.

Article 14. A female, not of the Imperial Family, who is married to a Shinno or O, may, upon the loss of her husband, leave the status of Imperial Family member according to her own desire.

When a female mentioned in the preceding paragraph has lost her husband, she shall, in case of special and unavoidable circumstances besides the case as under the same paragraph, leave the status of Imperial Family member by decision of the Imperial House Council.

In case a female mentioned in the first paragraph is divorced, she shall lose the status of the Imperial Family.

The provisions of the first paragraph and the preceding paragraph shall apply to the females married to other members of the Imperial Family mentioned in the preceding Article.

Article 15. Any person outside the Imperial Family and his or her descendants shall not become a member thereof except in the cases where a female becomes Empress or marries a member of the Imperial Family.

CHAPTER III. REGENCY

Article 16. In case the Emperor has not come of age, a Regency shall be established.

In case the Emperor is affected with a serious disease, mentally or physically, or there is a serious hindrance and is unable to perform his acts in matters of state, a Regency shall be instituted by decision of the Imperial House Council.

Article 17. The Regency shall be assumed by a member of the Imperial Family of age according to the following order:

1) The Kotaishi, or Kotaison.	4) The Empress Dowager.
2) A Shinno and an O.	5) The Grand Empress Dowager.
3) The Empress.	6) A Naishinno and a Jo-o.

In the case of No. 2 in the preceding paragraph the order of succession to the Throne shall apply; and in the case of No. 6 in the same paragraph, the order of succession to the Throne shall apply *mutatis mutandis*.

Article 18. In case the Regent, or a person falling in the order of assumption of Regency, is affected with a serious disease, mentally or physically, or there is a serious hindrance, the Imperial House Council may decide to change the Regent or the order of assumption of Regency, according to the order stipulated in the preceding Article.

Article 19. When, because of minority of the person falling in the order of assumption of Regency or because of the obstacles mentioned in the preceding paragraph, another member of the Imperial Family has become Regent, he shall not yield his post of Regent to the said member of the Imperial Family who has the precedence on the ground of his attainment to majority or the removal of those obstacles, except in the case such person happens to be the Kotaishi or Kotaison.

Article 20. In case the obstacles mentioned in Article 16, paragraph 2 have been removed, the Regency shall be abolished by decision of the Imperial House Council.

Article 21. The Regent, while in office, shall not be subject to legal action. However, the right to take that action is not impaired hereby.

CHAPTER IV. MAJORITY; HONORIFIC TITLES; CEREMONY OF ACCESSION; IMPERIAL FUNERAL; RECORD OF IMPERIAL LINEAGE; AND IMPERIAL MAUSOLEUMS

Article 22. The majority age for the Emperor, the Kotaishi and the Kotaison shall be eighteen.

Article 23. The honorific title for the Emperor, the Empress, the Grand Empress Dowager and the Empress Dowager shall be "Heika."

The honorific title for the members of the Imperial Family other than those mentioned in the preceding paragraph shall be "Denka."

Article 24. When the Throne is succeeded to, the Ceremony of Accession shall be held.

Article 25. When the Emperor dies, the Rites of Imperial Funeral shall be held.

Article 26. The matters relating to the family status of the Emperor and the members of the Imperial Family shall be registered in the Record of Imperial Lineage.

Article 27. The graves of the Emperor, the Empress, the Grand Empress Dowager and the Empress Dowager, shall be called "Ryo," and those of all other members of the Imperial Family shall be called "Bo"; the matters relating to Ryo and Bo shall be entered respectively in the Ryo Register and the Bo Register.

CHAPTER V. THE IMPERIAL HOUSE COUNCIL

Article 28. The Imperial House Council shall be composed of ten members.

These members shall consist of two Imperial Family members, the Presidents and Vice-Presidents of the House of Representatives and the House of Councillors, the Prime Minister, the head of the Imperial House Office, the Chief Judge and one other judge of the Supreme Court.

The members of the Imperial Family and the judge other than the Chief Judge of the Supreme Court, who are to become members of the Council, shall be chosen by mutual election respectively from among the members of the Imperial Family of age and from among the judges other than the Chief Judge of the Supreme Court.

Article 29. The member of the Imperial House Council, who is the Prime Minister, shall preside over its meeting.

Article 30. There shall be appointed ten reserve members in the Imperial House Council.

As regards the reserve members for the Imperial Family members and the judge of the Supreme Court in the Council, the provision of Article 28, paragraph 3, shall apply *mutatis mutandis*. The reserve members for the Presidents and Vice-Presidents of the House of Representatives and the House of Councillors in the Council shall be selected by mutual election from among the members of the House of Representatives and of the House of Councillors.*

The numbers of the reserve members mentioned in the two preceding paragraphs shall be the same as the numbers of the members in the Council, and the order of assuming their functions shall be determined at the time of the mutual election.

The reserve member for the Prime Minister in the Council shall be the Minister of State who has been designated as the one to perform temporarily the functions of Prime Minister under the provisions of the Cabinet Law.

The reserve member for the head of the Imperial House Office in the Council shall be designated by the Prime Minister from among the officials of the Imperial House Office.

In case there is a hindrance with regard to a member of the Council, or he is missing, the reserve member for him shall perform his functions.

Article 31. As regards the President, the Vice-President and members of the House of Representatives mentioned in Article 28 and the preceding paragraph, they shall be, in case the House has been dissolved and pending the selection of the successors, those persons who were respectively the President, the Vice-President and members of the House at the time of its dissolution.

Article 32. The term of office for the members of the Council, who are members of the Imperial Family and of a judge other than the Chief Judge of the Supreme Court, and for their reserve members, shall be four years.

Article 33. The Imperial House Council shall be convened by the President of the Council.

The Imperial House Council must be convoked, if demanded by four members or more, in the cases as under Article 3, Article 16, paragraph 2, Article 18 and Article 20.

Article 34. The Imperial House Council, unless attended by six members or more, may not open deliberations and make decisions.

Article 35. The deliberations of the Imperial House Council shall be decided by a majority vote of two-thirds or more of the members present, in the cases of Article 3, Article 16, paragraph 2, Article 18 and Article 20; and by a majority vote in all other cases.

In case of a tie in the case of the latter clause of the preceding paragraph, the President shall make the decision.

Article 36. A member may not participate in the deliberation of any matter in which he has a special interest.

Article 37. The Imperial House Council shall exercise only those powers which are provided for by this and other laws.

SUPPLEMENTARY PROVISIONS

The present law shall come into force as from the day of the enforcement of the Constitution of Japan.

The present members of the Imperial Family shall be considered as the members of the Imperial Family under this law; and with regard to the application of the provisions of Article 6, they shall be considered the legitimate offspring in the legitimate male line.

The present Ryo and Bo shall be considered as the Ryo and Bo as under Article 27.

* The following paragraph indicates that this paragraph should be regarded as two paragraphs.

APPENDIX V

*The Imperial House Economy Law**

Article 1. State property which is assigned, or which has been determined to be assigned, to the official use of the Imperial House (called the Imperial House Use Property hereafter) shall be treated as government use property under the State Property Law, and matters pertaining to it will be handled by the Imperial House Office.

In case an item of state property is assigned, or is to be determined to be assigned to the official use of the Imperial House, the matter must be passed by the Imperial House Economy Council. So shall it be also in case the use of any Imperial House Use Property is discontinued or altered.

The Imperial House Use Property shall not be property intended for revenue.

The Imperial House Economy Council shall make the necessary survey concerning the Imperial House Use Property at an interval of not more than five years and make a report to the Cabinet.

When the report of the preceding paragraph has been made, the Cabinet shall report to the Diet the content thereof.

Article 2. In the cases of sale or purchase for reasonable price and of other ordinary private economic transactions, and in any of the cases specified below, a property may be alienated to, or received by, the Imperial House, or a gift can be made therefrom without authorization by the Diet each time:

    1) Giving or receiving of properties not exceeding a certain amount in value as fixed by law separately.

    2) Giving or receiving of properties exceeding the amount of the preceding sub-paragraph, but not exceeding a certain amount in value as fixed by law separately, which has been passed upon by the Imperial House Economy Council.

When the giving and receiving of property takes place more than once during one year between the same parties, the provisions of the sub-paragraphs of the preceding paragraph shall apply to the aggregate amount of such transactions.

In case the amount in value of the properties given by or to a member belonging to the Imperial House under the provisions of 1 or 2 of paragraph 1 in a period less than one year has reached the amount as fixed separately by law, the above provisions do not apply to the giving or receiving of property by such member during the remainder of the year.

Article 3. The appropriation for the expenditures of the Imperial House to be made

* Law No. 4, *Official Gazette*, No. 237, January 16, 1947, pp. 3–5. The writers have made slight alterations in the text for the sake of clarity.

in the budget shall be divided into the Inner Court Appropriation, the Imperial Court Appropriation and the Imperial Family Appropriations.

Article 4. The Inner Court Appropriation shall apply to the daily expenditures of the Emperor and Empress, the Grand Empress Dowager, the Empress Dowager, the Kotaishi and his consort, the Kotaison and his consort, and other Imperial Family members belonging to the Inner Court, and to other miscellaneous expenditures of the Inner Court; a fixed sum shall be appropriated annually as is determined by law separately.

The sums provided as the Inner Court Appropriation shall constitute the Privy Purse and shall not be treated as public money to be administered by the Imperial House Office.

In case the Imperial House Economy Council deems it necessary to change the fixed sum of paragraph 1, it must submit to the Cabinet its opinion thereon.

When the opinion of the Council has been submitted, as under the preceding paragraph, the Cabinet shall report to the Diet the content thereof at the earliest opportunity.

Article 5. The Imperial Court Appropriation shall apply to all the expenditures of the Imperial Court other than those of the Inner Court and shall be administered by the Imperial House Office.

Article 6. The Imperial Family Appropriations shall apply to the sums which are provided as annuities for the maintenance of the dignity of the members of the Imperial Family and those which are provided to the persons who leave the status of Imperial Family member for the maintenance of dignity as persons who have been members of the Imperial Family, in one time payment to be made at the time when they leave their status. The sums of such annuities or one time payments shall be calculated on the basis of a fixed sum as will be determined by law separately.

The annuities shall be calculated according to the stipulations set forth under the following numbers and in paragraphs 3 to 5; and they shall be paid annually to the members of the Imperial Family other than those specified in Article 4.

1) Shinno shall receive:

Married. . . . . The whole of the fixed sum.

Of age and unmarried. . . . . One half of the fixed sum.

Under age and unmarried. . . . . One quarter of the fixed sum.

2) The consort of a Shinno shall receive one half of the fixed sum.

3) Naishinno shall receive:

Of age. . . . . One half of the fixed sum.

Under age. . . . . One quarter of the fixed sum.

4) O, the consort of an O, and Jo-o shall receive sums corresponding to 70 per cent of the amount of the annuities calculated respectively on the basis of Shinno, the consort of a Shinno, and Naishinno.

A married Shinno or O, even after the cessation of marital relationship, shall receive the same amount as before.

A member of the Imperial Family who is the Regent, shall receive 5 times the fixed sum during the term of his office.

A person, possessing more than one status, shall be paid according to the status commanding the highest annuity.

A person who leaves the status of member of the Imperial Family according to the provisions of the Imperial House Law shall receive a sum in one time payment, as determined by the Imperial House Economy Council, and within the limit of not exceeding the amount corresponding to 15 times the amount of the annuity due to the said person to be calculated according to the provisions of paragraphs 2 and 3 and the preceding paragraph.

In calculating the sum for one time payment as under the preceding paragraph, an unmarried or under-age Shinno or O shall be considered as a married Shinno or O; and Naishinno or Jo-o under age as a Naishinno, or Jo-o, of age.

The New Japan

The provision of Article 4, paragraph 2 shall apply to the sums provided as the Imperial Family Appropriations.

The provisions of Article 4, paragraphs 3 and 4 shall apply to the fixed sum of paragraph 1.

Article 7. The Imperial Heir upon his accession to the Throne shall receive such traditional properties as are to be handed down with the Throne.

Article 8. The Imperial House Economy Council shall be composed of 8 members.

The members shall be the Presidents and Vice-Presidents of the House of Representatives and the House of Councillors, the Prime Minister, the Minister of Finance, the head of the Imperial House Office and the head of the Board of Audit.

Article 9. There shall be appointed 8 reserve members in the Imperial House Economy Council.

Article 10. The Imperial House Economy Council, unless there are present 5 members or more, may not open deliberations and make decisions.

The deliberations shall be decided by a majority vote. In case of a tie, the chairman shall make the decision.

Article 11. The provisions of Article 29; Article 30, paragraphs 3–7; Article 31; Article 33, paragraph 1; Article 36 and Article 37 of the Imperial House Law shall apply to the Imperial House Economy Council *mutatis mutandis*.

The post of the reserve member for the Minister of Finance in the Council shall be filled by the Vice Minister of Finance; and that of the reserve member for the head of the Board of Audit by an official of the Board of Audit, who shall be designated by the Prime Minister.

SUPPLEMENTARY PROVISIONS

The present Law shall come into force as from the day of the enforcement of the Constitution of Japan.

Those items of the former Imperial Household Property which are in the use of the Imperial House at the time of the enforcement of the present Law and which have become state property under the State Property Law shall be considered, without a decision of the Imperial House Economy Council, as the Imperial House Use Property, regardless of the provision of Article 1, paragraph 2.

The necessary matters relating to the transitional disposition of the rights and obligations which belong to the former Imperial House Account at the time of the enforcement of the present Law, and which are to be carried over by the State, shall be provided for by Cabinet order.

The Inner Court Appropriation and the sum of annuities under the Imperial Family Appropriations for the fiscal year in which the present Law takes effect shall be provided for on the basis of monthly quotas.

APPENDIX VI

*The Imperial House Office Law**

Article 1. The Imperial House Office shall take charge of state affairs relating to the Imperial House and the Emperor's acts in matters of state provided for by Government Ordinance and shall have the custody of the Imperial Seal and the Seal of State.

Article 2. The Imperial House Office shall have the following personnel:

Grand Steward	First Class
Vice-Grand Steward, one person	First Class
Private Secretary to the Grand Steward, full time one person	Second Class
Grand Chamberlain	First Class
Chamberlains	First or Second Class
Masters of Ceremonies	First or Second Class
Secretaries of the Imperial House Office	First, Second or Third Class
Technical Officials of the Imperial House Office . .	First, Second or Third Class

The respective full numbers of Chamberlains, Masters of Ceremonies, Secretaries and Technical Officials shall be prescribed by Government Ordinance.

In addition to the personnel mentioned in paragraph 1, such personnel as may be required may be assigned as provided by Government Ordinance.

Article 3. The attestation by the Emperor shall be required for the appointment and dismissal of the Grand Steward and the Grand Chamberlain.

Article 4. The Grand Steward shall take charge of the general management of the affairs of the Office, and shall direct and supervise its personnel in connection with their performance of duties.

Article 5. The Vice-Grand Steward shall, assisting the Grand Steward, adjust the affairs of the Office and supervise the work of each bureau, division or agency.

Article 6. The Private Secretary shall, under the orders of the Grand Steward, deal with confidential matters.

Article 7. The Grand Chamberlain shall be in waiting on the Emperor.

Article 8. The Chamberlains shall assist the Grand Chamberlain in performing his function.

Article 9. The Masters of Ceremonies shall, under the orders of their superiors, take charge of matters concerning ceremonial functions and reception.

Article 10. The Secretaries shall, under the orders of their superiors, take charge of the affairs of the office.

* Law No. 70, *Official Gazette*, No. 313, April 18, 1947, pp. 2–3.

Article 11. The Technical Officials shall, under the orders of their superiors, take charge of technical affairs.

Article 12. Such bureaux, divisions or agencies as may be required may be established in the Imperial House Office, as provided by Government Ordinance.

Article 13. The Imperial House Office shall be under the jurisdiction of the Prime Minister.

SUPPLEMENTARY PROVISION

The present Law shall come into force as from the day of the enforcement of the Constitution of Japan.

APPENDIX VII

The Cabinet Law *

Article 1. The Cabinet shall perform functions provided for in Article 73 and other Articles of the Constitution of Japan.

Article 2. The Cabinet shall be composed of the Prime Minister, who shall be its head, and Ministers of State not more than sixteen in number.

The Cabinet, in the exercise of executive power, shall be collectively responsible to the Diet.

Article 3. The Ministers shall divide among themselves administrative affairs and be in charge of their respective shares thereof, each as a competent Minister, as provided for by law separately.

The provision of the preceding paragraph does not, however, preclude the existence of Ministers who have no specific share of administrative affairs to manage.

Article 4. The Cabinet shall perform its functions through Cabinet meetings.

The Prime Minister shall preside over Cabinet meetings.

Each Minister may submit to the Prime Minister any question or matter and ask for a Cabinet meeting thereon.

Article 5. The Prime Minister, representing the Cabinet, shall submit Cabinet bills, budgets and other proposals to the Diet, and shall report on general national affairs and foreign relations to the Diet.

Article 6. The Prime Minister shall exercise control and supervision over various administrative branches in accordance with the policies to be decided upon after consultation at Cabinet meetings.

Article 7. The Prime Minister shall, following consultation at Cabinet meetings, decide on any point of doubt relating to jurisdiction as between the competent Ministers.

Article 8. The Prime Minister may suspend the official act or order of any administration office, pending action by the Cabinet.

Article 9. In case the Prime Minister is prevented from discharging his functions or the post of Prime Minister is vacant, the Minister of State designated by him in advance shall perform temporarily the functions of Prime Minister.

Article 10. In case a competent Minister is prevented from discharging his functions or the post of such Minister is vacant, the Prime Minister, or a Minister of State designated by him shall perform temporarily the functions of the said competent Minister of State.

* Law No. 5, *Official Gazette*, No. 237, January 16, 1945, pp. 5–6. The writers have made slight alterations in the text for the sake of clarity.

Article 11. No provision imposing obligations or restricting rights can be made in Cabinet orders unless authorized by law.

Article 12. There shall be set up under the Cabinet a Secretariat and a Legislative Bureau.

The Cabinet Secretariat shall be in charge of preparing the agenda of Cabinet meetings and other miscellaneous affairs of the Cabinet.

The Legislative Bureau shall be in charge of examining and drafting Cabinet bills and Cabinet orders, as well as examining drafts of treaties, and other legal matters.

Besides the matters mentioned in the preceding two paragraphs, the Cabinet Secretariat and the Legislative Bureau shall assist the work of the Cabinet as provided for by Cabinet order.

The organization of the Cabinet Secretariat and the Legislative Bureau shall be fixed by law separately.

Besides the Secretariat and the Legislative Bureau there shall be set up in the Cabinet necessary offices which shall assist the work of the Cabinet, as provided for by law.

SUPPLEMENTARY PROVISION

The present Law shall come into force as from the day of the enforcement of the Constitution of Japan.

APPENDIX VIII

*National Police Reserve Order**

OBJECT

Article 1. The object of this Cabinet Order is to establish the National Police Reserve and to provide for the organization thereof, etc., for the purpose of supplementing the strength of the National Rural Police and the Local Autonomous Police Forces to the extent necessary to maintain peace and order within the country and to guarantee the public welfare.

ESTABLISHMENT

Article 2. The National Police Reserve shall be established as an organ of the Prime Minister's Office.

DUTIES

Article 3. (1) The National Police Reserve shall perform its duties by order of the Prime Minister in case of special necessity to maintain public peace.

(2) The National Police Reserve shall confine its actions within the scope of its duties and shall not abuse its authority by interfering with the freedom and rights guaranteed to individuals under the Constitution of Japan.

(3) The necessary matters concerning the duties to be performed by the policemen of the National Police Reserve shall be determined by Cabinet Order.

PERSONNEL AND STATUTORY STRENGTH

Article 4. The fixed number of personnel of the National Police Reserve shall be seventy-five thousand one hundred (75,100), including policemen of the National Police Reserve of seventy-five thousand (75,000).

ORGANIZATION

Article 5. The National Police Reserve shall have a headquarters, troops and other necessary agencies.

ORGANIZATION OF THE HEADQUARTERS

Article 6. The Headquarters shall have, besides a Secretariat, a Police Affairs Bureau,

* Cabinet Order No. 260, August 10, 1950, *Japan Year Book, 1949–1952*, pp. 205–206. The writers have made slight alterations in the text for the sake of clarity.

Personnel Bureau, Equipment Bureau, Accounting and Supply Bureau, and Medical Bureau.

DIRECTOR-GENERAL AND ASSISTANT DIRECTOR-GENERAL OF HEADQUARTERS

Article 7. (1) The headquarters shall have a Director-General and an Assistant Director-General.

(2) The Director-General shall be appointed by the Prime Minister.

(3) The appointment of the Director-General shall be attested by the Emperor.

(4) The Director-General shall direct the functions of the National Police Reserve as its chief, under the direction and supervision of the Prime Minister.

(5) The Assistant Director-General shall assist the Director-General in the performance of his duties.

PERSONNEL ADMINISTRATION

Article 8. (1) The positions of the personnel of the National Police Reserve shall be of the Special Service.

(2) The provisions of Chapter 3, Section 6 (except Part 3) and Section 7 of the National Public Service Law (Law No. 120 of 1947), and penal provisions concerning these provisions, shall apply *mutatis mutandis* to the personnel mentioned in the preceding paragraph. In this case "the National Personnel Authority" shall read "the Prime Minister" and "the rules of the Authority" shall read "the Prime Minister's Office Ordinance."

(3) Special provision may be established by Cabinet Order with respect to the application of the Pension Law (Law No. 48 of 1923), of the National Public Service Mutual Aid Association Law (Law No. 69 of 1947) and of the Law concerning the Temporary Measures for Separation Allowances for National Public Service Personnel and Others (Law No. 142 of 1950) to the personnel of the National Police Reserve.

(4) Provisions other than those made in the preceding three (3) paragraphs which pertain to the grades, appointment and dismissal, promotion, pay, uniform and other personnel matters shall be prescribed by Cabinet Order.

DELEGATION OF THE AUTHORITY OF THE PRIME MINISTER

Article 9. The Prime Minister may, when he deems it especially necessary, delegate to another Minister of State the performance of functions authorized by this Cabinet Order.

DETAILS CONCERNING STRUCTURE AND ORGANIZATION

Article 10. Provisions other than those made by this Cabinet Order which pertain to the structure and organization of the National Police Reserve and other necessary matters shall be prescribed by orders promulgated by the Prime Minister's Office.

SUPPLEMENTARY PROVISIONS

1. This Cabinet Order shall come into force as from the day of its promulgation.

2. The Cabinet hereby transfers 20,000,000,000 yen only in the fiscal year 1950–1951 from the amount of the National Debt Expenses in the General Account to the expenses necessary ·for the National Police Reserve Corps.

3. The amount of appropriations which, though the obligations have been incurred within the fiscal year, have not been disbursed on account of their nature shall be authorized to be carried over to and used in the following year.

4. The Prime Minister may, for the time being, have agencies of the National Rural Police handle a part of the business of the National Police Reserve.

5. The Prime Minister's Office Establishment Law (Law No. 127 of 1949) shall be partially amended as follows:

Next to Article 16 — (2) the following article shall be added:

NATIONAL POLICE RESERVE

Article 16 — (3) The National Police Reserve shall be established as an organ of the Prime Minister's Office.

2. The National Police Reserve shall be the organ which is established to supplement the strength of the National Rural Police and the Local Autonomous Police Forces to maintain peace and order within the country and to guarantee the public welfare.

3. With regard to the organization and responsibilities of the National Police Reserve, the provisions of the National Police Reserve Order (Cabinet Order No. 260 of 1950) shall be followed.

6. The provisions of the Trade Union Law (Law No. 174 of 1949), Labor Relations Adjustment Law (Law No. 24 of 1946) and Labor Standard Law (Law No. 49 of 1947), and orders issued in accordance with these laws shall not apply to the personnel of the National Police Reserve.

Index

Index

Index

Russo-Japanese War, 47

Ryokufukai (Green Breeze Society), 287, 288, 294

Ryukyu Islands, 11, 53, 307, 378

Saghalien. See Karafuto.

Saha Shakaito (Left-wing Socialist party): selection of candidates, 273n18; formation, 292–293, 314; 1952 election, 293; 1953 election, 294; 1955 election, 297; and Hatoyama, 297; dissolves, 298; geographical support, 315; foreign policy, 320; and Kyosanto, 320–321; finance, 360n23. See also Labor parties; Shakaito; Trade unions; Uha Shakaito.

Saionji Kimmochi: member of genro, 17, 18, 30, 45, 172, 188; nominates premiers, 30, 33, 39, 44; and political parties, 32, 63; escapes death, 38, 45; death, 43–45. See also Genro.

Saito Makoto, 22, 30–33, 35, 38

Saito Takao: expelled from Diet, 62–63; in revival of parties, 84; on war responsibility, 88; attacks Konoye, 114; on constitution, 135, 159; and Jiyuto, 308; and Minshuto, 338

Sakai Toshio, 135–136

Samurai (warriors), 11, 353–354

San Francisco conference. See Peace treaty.

Sansom, George B., 10

Sasaki Soichi: on constitutional committee, 114, 126n5, 161; in constitutional debate, 150–151, 154–159 passim, 167

Satsuma clan, 15, 17

Sawada Ushimaro, 147–149 passim, 157, 159

SCAP. See Supreme Command for the Allied Powers.

Secret societies. See Patriotic societies.

Security pact, 137, 207–208: party policies on, 313, 319–320, 325, 334

Seinenkai (Young Men's Association), 66

Seisen Kantetsu Giin Renmei (League of Diet Members for the Holy War), 66

Seiyukai (Party of Friends of Constitutional Government): bases of strength, 21, 269, 346; leaders, 22, 29, 32, 38, 79; 1932 election, 29; and prewar cabinets, 29, 30, 31, 33, 59, 73; criticism of Takahashi, 31, 34; and Minseito, 32–33; resistance to militarists, 34, 39, 59; 1936 election, 39; 1937 election, 41; factionalism, 60–61, 299; and postwar parties, 84, 269, 270, 288, 300n35, 303; and election districts, 249; selection of candidates, 252; local organization, 349. See also Minseito.

Self-defense. See Rearmament.

Sengoku Kotaro, 79, 85

Senior Statesmen, 17–18, 45, 214–215

Shakai Kakushinto (Social Renovation party), 225, 285

Shakai Minshuto (Social Democratic party), 36

Shakai Taishuto (Social Mass party), 36, 39–40, 41, 61–62, 65–66, 85

Shakaito (Socialist party): formation, 84–85, 89n9; program, 85–86, 96–97, 181, 225, 258, 284–285, 312, 316–321; and trade unions, 95–96, 281, 348, 352, 360n24; in postwar elections, 96, 283, 296, 298, 314–315, 347; factionalism, 96, 283, 286, 288, 292–293, 314, 317–321, 334, 337, 352, 360n24; in constitutional debates, 113, 130, 134, 137–138, 140–144 passim, 146, 156; geographic support, 270–271, 315, 328n28, n29, 351; selection of candidates, 273n18; and campaign restrictions, 274n21; effect of purge, 278; and other parties, 280, 281, 283, 296, 310–311; in postwar cabinets, 286; reunification of, 298, 302, 314; leadership, 304–305, 315–316; and prewar parties, 314; central organization, 331–344 passim, 351, 359n4; local organization, 334, 345, 349; discipline, 345; finance, 347–348, 360n23; and patriotic societies, 354–355. See also Labor parties; Saha Shakaito; Trade unions; Uha Shakaito.

Shanghai, 30

Shantung, 24

Shaw, Patrick, 224–225

Shi (city). See Cities.

Shibusawa Keizo, 83

Shidehara Kijuro, 24, 26: premier, 83–84, 87–88, 121, 244n9, 278; and Minshuto, 96, 284–285, 338; and constitutional revision, 112, 114–115, 118, 119, 121, 130; in constitutional debate, 149, 150; Shimpoto president, 280, 312; on conservative merger, 280, 281, 283, 285–286; joins Jiyuto, 286, 292, 308, 340

Shiga Yoshio, 85, 341

Shigemitsu Mamoru, 50, 78, 80: president of Kaishinto, 293, 327n13; party leader, 294, 295, 298, 300n35; in Minshuto, 300n36; attacks Yoshida, 313; on foreign policy, 313

Shikotan Islands, 303

Shimada Toshio, 84

Shimizu, S., 402n1

Shimomura Tei, 83, 88

Index

Suzuki Yoshio, 134–140 *passim*
Swope, Guy J., 201n*19*
Tachibana Kozaburo, 42n*2*
Taikwa (Great Reform), 8
Takagi Yasaka, 6–7, 111
Takahashi Korekiyo, 30–31, 33, 34, 39, 172
Takayanagi Kenzo, 147, 156–157, 178, 363
Takano Iwasaburo, 113
Tanaka Giichi, 12, 17, 22, 24–25, 60
Tanaka Kunishige, 32
Tanaka Takeo, 83
T'ang dynasty, 375n*29*
Taxation: constitutional debate on, 142; Minshuto policy, 311, 327n*17*; Shakaito policy, 316; and local finance, 395–399. *See also* Budget; Finance, public.
Teachers. *See* Educators.
Teiyu Doshikai, 36
Tenno. See Emperor.
Terauchi Hisaichi, 39–40
To (special prefecture). *See* Prefectures.
Tohokai, 61–62, 66, 68
Tojo Diet, 73, 84
Tojo Hideki, 12, 50–56 *passim*, 59, 70, 73, 74, 80, 106, 114
Tokonami Takejiro, 40
Tokuda Kyuichi, 85, 323, 340, 350
Tokugawa clan, 9, 10–11, 15, 17, 56, 130–131, 353
Tokugawa Iyemasa, 161, 162
Tokyo, 36, 54–55, 377–380 *passim*, 385, 402
Tonarigumi. See Neighborhood associations.
Tosa clan, 15
Trade associations, 397
Trade union leaders, 304–305, 315, 316
Trade unions: pre-1945 struggle of, 36, 62–63, 66, 76, 354; and Kyosanto, 87, 98, 290–291, 319, 324, 348, 351, 360n*27*; Occupation policy, 93–96; postwar strategy, 95–96, 184, 281, 294, 319; and purge, 104, 108; and new constitution, 180; Jiyuto policy, 183, 291, 307; and civil service, 224–226, 391; in Diet, 230–231; voting patterns, 271; and Minshuto, 310–312; and Shakaito, 315–319, 321, 348, 351, 360n*24*; factionalism, 321, 352; political funds, 348; and rightist societies, 354–355. *See also* Labor parties; Shakaito.
Treason, 367–368
Treaties: legal status, 142, 207; negotiation and ratification, 204, 206, 210; in Diet, 238. *See also* Foreign relations; Peace treaty; Security pact.
Treaty of peace. *See* Peace treaty.
Tribalism. *See* Clans.

Truman, Harry S., 93, 152
Tsuji Kiyoshi, 402n*1*
Tsushima Juichi, 79

Ugaki Kazushige, 37, 40, 44, 47, 57n*2*
Uha Shakaito (Right-wing Socialist party): formed, 292–293, 314; *1952* election, 293; *1953* election, 294; *1955* election, 297; and Hatoyama, 297; dissolves, 298; geographical support, 315; foreign policy, 320; finance, 347, 360n*23*. *See also* Labor parties; Saha Shakaito; Shakaito.
Ultranationalist societies. *See* Patriotic societies.
Unemployment insurance, 284. *See also* Social welfare.
Union of Newspaper and Radio Workers, 183
Union of Soviet Socialist Republics (USSR), 62, 90, 121–122, 174: denounced by MacArthur, 97; and peace treaty, 292, 307, 319–320; policy toward, of Jiyuto, 307–308, of Minshuto, 313, of Shakaito, 319–320; and Kyosanto, 323–326, 346
United Nations, 137, 141, 174, 303, 320
United Nations Charter, 170, 208
United States, 49, 79–81, 90, 121–122, 188: and prewar Japan, 27, 34–35, 61; war with Japan, 44, 59; attitude toward Occupation, 93–94; compared with Japan, 115, 207; influence on new constitution, 130, 156, 166, 170, 178, 181, 204–295; security pact with Japan, 207–208, 209; influence on civil service, 220; influence on Diet Law, 245n*15*; influence on judicial review, 268; Communist hostility toward, 291, 325–326; policy toward, of Jiyuto, 295, 307, of Minshuto, 312. *See also* Department of State, U.S.; MacArthur, Douglas; Supreme Command for the Allied Powers.
Urban areas: representation in prewar Diet, 20; and Shakai Minshuto, 36; electoral participation, 263; under Western influence, 266; and postwar parties, 270–271, 304, 308–309, 310–311, 315, 322, 351. *See also* Business groups; Capitalism.
Ushio Keinosuke, 128
Uyehara Etsujiro, 159, 209

Veto power, lacking in executive, 211
Vice-ministers, 51, 199
Victoria, Queen, 152
Villages, 377–379, 387–389
Violence: and ultranationalism, 26, 35–37,

455

MAR